LORD GOODMAN

By the same author

Hugh Gaitskell
The Group: An Oral History, 1952–1960 (with Michael Summerskill)

As editor

Aneurin Bevan, by Michael Foot, single-volume centenary edition
New Labour in Power: Precedents and Prospects (with Tim Bale)
The Contemporary History Handbook (with Anthony Seldon and Julia Buxton)
Anatomy of Decline: The Political Journalism of Peter Jenkins (with Richard Cockett)
What Difference Did the War Make? (with Harriet Jones)
From Reconstruction to Integration: Britain and Europe since 1945 (with Harriet Jones)

LORD GOODMAN

Brian Brivati

RICHARD COHEN BOOKS · London

For Mridul
and
to the memory of
Mrs Iris Freeman

First published in hardback in Great Britain in 1999

by Richard Cohen Books,
an imprint of Metro Publishing Limited,
19 Gerrard Street, London W1V 7LA

© 1999 Brian Brivati

Brian Brivati is hereby identified as the author of this work
in accordance with Section 77 of the
Copyright, Designs and Patents Act 1988.

British Library Cataloguing in Publication Data.
A CIP record of this book is available on request from the British Library.

ISBN 1 86066 156 4

10 9 8 7 6 5 4 3 2 1

Typeset in Bembo by MATS, Southend-on-Sea, Essex
Printed in Great Britain by CPD Group, Wales

Contents

To understand all is to pardon all
(Goodman's heraldic motto)

Which is the right path that a man should choose?
One that is honourable in itself and that wins him
honour from his fellow men and women.

Ethics of the Fathers
(From Goodman's memorial service)

Acknowledgements

The research for a book about Lord Goodman was originally started by the late Mrs Iris Freeman. She left an archive of extraordinary quality, thoroughness and clarity. When I was asked to complete her work I found that she had almost finished researching and was about to start writing. She had conducted 100 or so interviews and worked on a wide range of sources. The care and neatness of her papers were astonishing and the perception and intelligence of her notes and questions continually enlightening: I had walked into one of the best archives I have ever worked on. I am immensely grateful to her husband, Mr David Freeman, for allowing me to make use of his late wife's work and for his own unwavering support. His patience with my ignorance of the law and his constant advice and wisdom have been invaluable in the writing of this book, and on many subjects beyond the world of Arnold Goodman.

Many other people have been helpful in writing this book. I would particularly like to thank Peter Hennessy, Michael Foot, Gerard Alexander, Ian Gilmour, Joe Bailey, Francis Wheen, Graham C. Greene, John Baker and Paul Foot, for reading and commenting on parts or the whole of the draft manuscript. Also the participants in the witness seminar on the *Spectator* libel case held at the Institute of Historical Research on 25 November 1998: John Baker, Alan Watkins, Peter Carter Ruck, Auberon Waugh, Anthony Howard, and Colin Joseph for taking the chair. A full list of those interviewed by Mrs Freeman follows and I would like to thank everyone who gave their time and memories. Those marked ★ have also been interviewed by or corresponded with the author. Those marked † were interviewed by or corresponded with the author alone. When I came to compile this list I found that a number of the people that Mrs Freeman or myself had spoken to or who had helped in other ways had died. I have left their names in place and record my gratitude to their memory.

Lady Aitken; Professor Wyndham John Albery★; Professor

Lord Goodman

Geoffrey Alderman; Clare Allen; Alex Anderson; Lord Annan*;
Lord Armstrong; David Astor†; Naim Attallah; John Baker*; John
Balcombe; Professor Eric Barendt; Isaiah Berlin; Elliott Bernerd;
Geoffrey Bindman*; Alma and Ellis Birk; Dr David Blackadder;
Christopher Booker*; Barbara Castle; Ian Chapman*; Philip Chody;
Charles Corman; Frank Coven*; Edwina Coven*; Michael Crick*;
Evelyn de Rothschild; Sybil Derrick; Rev. William Dowling*; Lina
Emery; Ralph Emery; Leonard Eppel; Edward Erdman; Anthony
Field*; Paul Foot†; Rt. Hon. Michael Foot†; Lord Gibson; Lord
Gilmour*; Rabbi David Goldberg; Shirley and Raoul Goldman; Sir
James Goldsmith; Professor Jim Gower; Graham C. Greene†; Sue
Hammerson*; Joe Hardstaff; Lord Harewood; Sir Edward Heath;
John Henderson; Professor Peter Hennessy†; Ronald Hill*; Lord
Hoffmann; Ben Hooberman; Anthony Howard*; Peter Hudson;
Richard Ingrams*; Ruth Ives; Amelie Jacobovitz; Sally Ann
Jacobson; Lord Jenkins*; Rhidian Jones; Colin Joseph; Professor
Jeffrey Jowell; David Kessler; Aline Kisch; Martin Kisch; Abe
Kramer; Lena Lalandi; Geoffrey Lawson; Alan Leighton Davis; Judy
Lever; Harold Lightman; Gavin Lightman*; Mark Littman; Anthony
Mallinson; Oliver Marriott; Peter Marshall; Jeffrey Maunsell*;
Christopher Moran; Richard and Sally Mordant; Fionn Morgan*;
Norman Morris; James Morton; Lord Nathan; Sir Brian Neill*; Lord
Neill; Charles Osborne; Joe Penny; Lord Perry; Carol Pittman;
Diana Rawstron*; Margaret Reiss; Manny Rice; John Roberts*;
David Roe; Anthony Rowe; Sir Frank Rogers; Tom Rosenthal;
Desmond Roth; Peter Carter Ruck†; Michael Sayers; Dr Gordon
Screaton*; Richard and Josephine Seifert; David Selbourne;
Dominic Shorthouse; Peter Sigler; Aubrey Singer; Richard Smith*;
Sigmund Sternberg; Jonathan Stone*; Anne Stranders; Sam
Sylvester; Patrick Swaffer†; Jeremy Thorpe; Marion Thorpe; Donald
Trelford; Margaret Usher; Edward Walker-Arnott; Alan Watkins†;
Auberon Waugh*; Gerry Weiss; Arnold Wesker; Francis Wheen†;
Basil Wigoder; Yolande Wigoder; Hugh Willatt; Richard Youard;
Michael Yudkin.

Archival Sources
Modern Records Centre, Warwick; Dr G. R. Screaton at University
College, Oxford; Dr P. M. R. Howell and Dr Richard M. Smith at
Downing College, Cambridge; Joanna Shacklock, Records Office,
University College London; The Clove Club, Hackney Downs

Acknowledgements

School; House of Lords Record Office; Trinity College, Dublin; *Jewish Chronicle*; Ronald Edwards, Willesden United Synagogue Cemetery; Alix Bowyer-Tagg, The Liberal Jewish Synagogue; Librarian, Athenaeum Club; Francesca Franchi, Royal Opera House; The Arts Council of Great Britain; London Borough of Hackney, Archives Department; Dr John T. Green, Royal Society of Medicine; Charles Tucker, Research Unit, London Beth Din; Judith Goldstein, The Israel Museum, Jerusalem; Pat Cunningham, Professional Ethics Division, The Law Society; Matthew Judge, Central Registry, King's College, London.

In addition to the above, Lewis Baston provided much stimulus for this book while we worked together on a history of modernization in Labour's election campaigns, a project supported by the Leverhulme Trust. My colleagues at Kingston University and the Faculty of Human Sciences' History Research budget have fully supported this project and it could not have been completed without their commitment to research. Virginia Preston expertly transcribed the tapes of Mrs Freeman's interviews. I would also like to thank the staff at Metro Publishing, particularly Peter Day for much enjoyable gossip; and Richard Dawes. This book began life at Richard Cohen Books, which sadly ceased trading as an independent small publisher last year. Richard's great adventure might be over but he remains the best publisher and editor in London and New York.

My son Max was born during the final stages of this book and put up with such an intrusion with remarkable resilience, as did my wife Mridul, who has challenged and improved much of what follows.

Given the circumstances in which I came to write this book, it is particularly important to stress that all the arguments, opinions and mistakes in it are my own. Mrs Freeman was a trained solicitor and a first-class biographer, and she would have written a different book from the material she had assembled. Mr Freeman has been extraordinarily helpful and generous with his advice, but he does not endorse nor, I think, necessarily agree with all that follows. If you would like to respond to the book with a reflection or a correction, my email address is B. Brivati@Kingston.ac.uk.

Brian Brivati
Stoke Newington
June 1999

List of Illustrations

The author and publishers are grateful for permission to reproduce the following photographs and cartoons:

Photographs
1   Goodman's mother (The Estate of Lord Goodman)
2   Goodman with his brother Theo (The Estate of Lord Goodman)
3   Goodman with Jim Gower on his right (The Estate of Lord Goodman)
4   Henry 'Mac' Derrick, his wife Sybil and daughter Patricia (Mrs Sybil Derrick)
5   Richard Crossman, Nye Bevan, John Baker and Morgan during the *Spectator* libel action, 1957 (John Baker)
6   Harry Hyams (Hulton Getty)
7   Sir Max Rayne, his wife and Rudolf Nureyev (Hulton Getty)
8   Lord Drogheda, Ann Fleming, Dr Paterno and Goodman, 1971 (Hulton Getty)
9   Lady Avon, 1977 (Hulton Getty)
10 Princess Alexandra with Goodman, 1986 (Catherine Ashmore)
11 William Vassall, 1962 (Hulton Getty)
12 John Profumo, 1963 (Hulton Getty)
13 Mandy Rice-Davies, Christine Keeler, Penny Marshall and Stephen Ward, 1963 (Hulton Getty)
14 George Wigg, 1976 (Hulton Getty)
15 Edward Heath, Jeremy Thorpe and Harold Wilson, 1968 (Keystone)
16 Goodman with Harold Wilson, *c.* 1970 (Sidney Harris)
17 Goodman with Jennie Lee and Lord Snowdon, 1970 (PA News)
18 Goodman, Constance Cummings and Ben Levy, 1969 (Hulton Getty)
19 Edward Heath, Jennie Lee, Goodman and Lord Eccles, 1972 (PA News)
20 Lord Goodman in the 1960s (Keystone)

Every effort has been made to contact the copyright holder in each instance.

Preface

There is not a jot, tittle, scintilla or vestige of truth in any of this farrago of falsehoods.

        (A *Private Eye* pastiche of a Goodman libel letter)

For as long as there has been politics there have been fixers: the people behind the people with power. The phrase which sums them up, *éminence grise*, was coined for 'Père Joseph' (1577–1638), the Capuchin monk who was the adviser and agent of Cardinal Richelieu. Richelieu and Père Joseph plotted at the heart of European politics in an era when power and influence, though exercised through the institutions of church and monarchy, were rooted in mystery, reputation and lineage. In the 350 years since Père Joseph's death the roots of power have gradually shifted from God and the Crown to the people: democracy has replaced absolutism. In theory the age of public accountability banished the grey eminences to the dustbin of history. In practice Richelieu would have been perfectly at home as a democratic politician, and he would soon have found his twentieth-century Père Joseph. The political system might have changed but the need for those who trade on and in power is constant.

In Britain, in the years between the Profumo scandal of 1963 and the election of Margaret Thatcher in 1979, Arnold Goodman was the pre-eminent grey eminence. He was the fixer of Britain's Establishment. His public life was a heady brew of politics, newspapers, law, television, the arts, academe, high society, libel, scandal and secret diplomacy. His power to affect the fate of individual lives and careers was, at times, immense. He was almost always unaccountable to any constituency aside from his clients and, until 1976, his political master, Harold Wilson. Yet Goodman was, if never exactly on the side of the angels, at least mostly harmless. Frequently he helped people: lending money, finding jobs, saving marriages and companies, giving his time to good causes and pressuring his wealthy friends to donate to the charities that he chaired. Most of all he was a friend to a host of private people and a benefactor whose office was often full, like a character from Dickens, with petitioners needing help. Indeed, if all his acts of private generosity were recounted they would fill a dozen volumes. He did these things with humour and good grace, and hundreds swore by the wisdom of his advice and his ability to find a solution to the seemingly insoluble. Before we consider the motivations for the kindness, before we explore the other compartments of his character and career, this aspect of Arnold Goodman needs to be boldly and confidently stated.

Goodman appeared to be a complicated man. In fact, he was very simple. He loved opera, particularly the grand drama of the Verdi variety. He treasured his corner table at the Savoy Grill, with its English school-dinner menu and large jugs of lemonade. He loved to be praised and honoured as exceptional and unique. He enjoyed relationships with a series of trophy widows who, in the main, stood up to and teased him, or else looked after and spoilt him. He loved being cleverer than other people, in his early years waiting until the end of a discussion to introduce a brilliant solution to a problem, in later years arriving late for a meeting, dealing with the most controversial items on the agenda and then disappearing for another meeting. By defining himself almost exclusively in terms of his public role he left very little for himself. Typical of men who forge their identities through work, he died a lonely figure who had almost become a caricature of himself, and in his final years defending his public reputation became a means of defending the life he had chosen. He would therefore have hated the idea of a biography that was not entirely under his control.

His memoirs are frequently entertaining but reveal little about his inner world. They are not really the story of his life but more a collection of his tales, polished at the Sunday evening dining club he ran in the 1970s and 1980s. His conversations with the writer David Selbourne, which were published in the same year as his own book, though more revealing than his memoirs, are so disorganized that one cannot gain a picture of the man from them and Selbourne is, in the end, too fond of his subject.

During Goodman's lifetime the lawyer and writer James Morton was commissioned by Hodder & Stoughton to write a biography of him. Goodman threatened the chairman of Hodder that he would sue for libel on the basis of an early catalogue entry for the book. The impact of the threat made the resulting manuscript so bland as to be unpublishable. The reluctance of Goodman to be written about extends to his friends. Many of his immediate circle, for example the property developer Lord Rayne and Goodman's final companion Clarissa Avon, were reluctant to cooperate with this book. Hints were dropped that an official life would be commissioned, putting Goodman in a proper historical perspective as the story of the public man was told. Four years on there is no sign of any such book. As to the present study, some of his surviving friends may mutter the arguments that Goodman made on a number of occasions for a law of libel that could apply to the dead. He would also, no doubt, have employed some of his choicest insults for certain passages in this book, perhaps describing them, in a favourite adjective, as 'demented'. Such attitudes deterred other biographers while he was alive. As a result we have yet to see Goodman in the round.

For his friends he will always be the White Knight. They will stubbornly insist that he was more Robin Hood than Don Quixote. For his enemies, particularly the *Private Eye* boys and those whom Goodman bested in life, he will remain a bully and a crook. I believe there are substantial criticisms to be made but the allegation that he was dishonest is not true. Nor was he the entirely innocent Blessed Arnold, the great man whose motivation was pure. He was some-thing in between. He was a public figure who did not want to be accountable for his public actions. He was a private man who barely had a life that was not in some way fashioned by his professional and public contacts. By the time of his death he was lauded as the most distinguished British citizen outside Parliament. The purpose of his friends is to maintain that reputation: to keep him posthumously at the pinnacle of his profession and at the heart of the Establishment. The purpose of this book is to bring his historical reputation into proper proportion. I have no wish to rubbish the oracle of the Savoy Grill. There was much good in him.

In the process of writing this book I have developed a considerable admiration for civil servants who try to find lasting solutions to problems and for politicians who put their desire to serve the public to the test of an electorate. Goodman did neither. In the end he was only a lawyer with a genius for negotiation and compromise. The problem with a fixer is that he does not resolve arguments; he merely ends them. In many legal cases a fix is all that is needed to settle an argument. In libel cases the bluffing and chess-playing, the friendliness and humour that were Goodman's forte, usually worked. But in real politics – in running the arts, in building houses, in fighting apartheid - the quick fix can be much worse than the messy business of finding long-term answers. It is on this substantive area of Goodman's life that an evaluation of his public career should focus.

Goodman was a product of his time, one in which negotiation, deal-making and compromise were the grammar of political discourse. The age in which Goodman flourished was the Wilson Age of corporatism, of tripartism and the settlement of disputes through state action. His influence declined in the era of conviction politics under Thatcher, when such compromises were not an option because the state was supposed to be withdrawing from public life. In many ways the Wilson Age was a kinder and gentler time, but we are still living with the legacy of those days of haggling and fixing. Ultimately the role Goodman played was detrimental to the freedoms he professed to love. He was the model for the political creatures that practise their arts of spin-doctoring, deal-making and influence-peddling; neither the first nor the last of his kind. Goodman was part of the solution his times demanded; but there was a price for the quality of the solutions that he found, both generally and for himself. Kissinger said of Nixon's fall that it is was a tragedy of Biblical proportions. Goodman's end wasn't that, but there was something Shakespearian in his flaws and in his compensating qualities. This biography will disappoint his closest friends, who will think it cruel, while his enemies will think it too kind. A Goodmanesque compromise? Perish the thought.

1

Five Miles Across North London

> To anyone who did not have the good fortune to meet her, it
> is impossible to exaggerate my mother's quite remarkable
> qualities.
>
> (Goodman's view of his mother in his *Memoirs*)

Goodman was born on 21 August 1913 at 26 Bodney Road,
Hackney. His birth was registered at the Central Hackney Registry
office on 9 September 1913. He was born at the family's terraced
house below the railway line into Liverpool Street station, to Joseph
Goodman, a master draper, and Bertha Goodman, née Mauerberger.
His first name was listed on his birth certificate as Aby. So he
remained until 1931. In that year his father, now living at 19
Kidderpore Avenue, Hampstead, returned to the registry office with
a statutory declaration that the name entered in 1913 was wrong; it
should have been Abraham. Alfred Wilfred Brown, the super-
intendent registrar, duly made the correction. It is about five miles
across north London from Hackney to Hampstead, but in social
terms the journey is immense. Symbolically, his parents decided that
their new station in life required a proper first name for their son.

Goodman remained Abraham until after the Second World War,
when he became Arnold; he was known as Arnold until 1965, when
he was given a peerage and his first name became Lord. Friends who
had known him before the war sometimes called him Abe: most
people, if they remember him, do so as 'Lord Goodman' – his
peerage defined his public identity. His parents favoured Abraham,
though his mother always called him Abe, and he himself obviously
favoured the more anglicized Arnold – though in later life he
adopted the awkward habit of calling himself Arnold Abraham. He
will be Arnold Goodman in this book.

The part of the East End or, as Goodman described it in his
Memoirs, the lower-middle-class area of north London into which he
was born, was the northern boundary of the East End proper. Such
subtlety in identifying his origins led *Private Eye* to begin one spoof

profile of him: 'The Blessed Arnold was born of poor but wealthy parents.'[1] Later, in real profiles, Goodman talked of a comfortable or prosperous family background. And indeed, having started out in Stepney, his parents soon moved to the slightly wider and more pleasant Amhurst Road, Hackney, before arriving in Bodney Road – which, despite its proximity to the railway line, is still a pleasant enough street. These residential streets of Hackney were on the other side of Victoria Park from the real East End, the ghetto and the point of arrival. Joseph Goodman travelled back into the 'ghetto' to work as a businessman in the drapery trade.

Many of the Jewish immigrants from eastern and central Europe who reached London in the 1860s and 1870s were economic migrants, though political unrest came increasingly to play a part in forcing their emigration. The volume of mass emigration from eastern Europe gathered pace after 1881. Between then and 1900, when Goodman's parents' families were establishing themselves, the Jewish population in London was approximately 135,000, of whom roughly 120,000 lived in Stepney. The Borough of Stepney stretched from Whitechapel in the west to Mile End in the east. By 1901 nearly 80 per cent of London's Jews lived in this area, though the more prosperous were spreading into Hackney, Shoreditch, Limehouse and Bow and in many cases commuting to Stepney for work.[2]

In the 1950s, in the early part of his career, Goodman would present himself as a poor East End Jew who had made good[3] and who liked to give other poor East Enders work in his practice. Later, in different company, he presented a changed image of his past, but he never lost a sense of the place and the values of the environment in which he grew up, not least the emphasis on hard work. He remained something of an outsider in the Establishment which he came to dominate.

There were three separate but overlapping elements in Goodman's 'difference'. The first was his Jewishness, which was most important to him during the early part of his career and towards the end of his life. He was always comfortable with his Jewish identity but also conscious that this made him different from the white Anglo-Saxon Protestants who dominated British life. The second element was that he was born and brought up in trade rather than a profession. His background was therefore not one of generations of lawyers or public servants but of enterprise and struggle. On a simple level what always marked Goodman out from other lawyers of his generation was how hard and continuously he worked. The third element was that he was born into the East End and went to the best school available but not to one of the old public schools. None of these elements was unique to Goodman, but each contributed to his sense of individualism.

In 1873, at the age of 15, Joseph Mauerberger opened a bank account at Standard Bank, London, and began trading. In 1886 the company Joseph Mauerberger and Son was established at 207 Commercial Road, in the heart of Stepney. Goodman's maternal grandfather, the patriarch of the Mauerbergers, had, according to his grandson's *Memoirs*:

> an unsullied reputation and was regarded as a saintly figure. He became the local savant and adviser. Everyone in need of guidance would seek him out. There is an engaging story about a man who came to see him to ask him to explain a document which he did not understand. My grandfather said to him, 'This is an invitation for you to attend a meeting of creditors.' 'Oh,' said the man, 'but I never go to meetings!'[4]

The Mauerbergers came from Lazdijai, a small village near Suwalkig. In the 1880s both were in what was then the Lithuanian region of the Russian empire. Today Suwalkig is in Poland and Lazdijai in the Republic of Lithuania. Life was extremely hard, and growing state-inspired anti-Semitism made it even harder. The family ran the risk of losing their men through their being press-ganged into the Tsar's armies and their property in a pogrom. Joseph had a growing family – Bertha, Arnold's mother, was born in 1887, Israel was born in 1889 and Morris, who was to be a major figure in Goodman's life, in 1890. Joseph's wife died giving birth to Morris, and Goodman's mother and her brothers were brought up by grandparents. When they were old enough to work and take care of themselves, Joseph brought the children to London.

In 1886 Joseph expanded his trading activities by setting up a shipping company on the Cape of Good Hope route: the Mauerberger fortune was founded on the South African end of the business. Goodman was not yet three when Joseph died suddenly in London on 16 June 1916, but he later recounted a vivid memory of his grandfather putting him into a packing case:

> I recollect him only very vaguely . . . as a kindly old man with a grey beard. But I do remember being taken to see him in his little shop in the

Commercial Road, where he lived with his family above the shop, and being popped by him inside a packing case to my mixed delight and terror. I sometimes reflect on the size of the packing case that would be required now to incarcerate me in similar fashion. But I recollect what a lovable old man he was and how he endeared himself to a child who would retain this memory firmly and indelibly.[5]

According to Mendel Kaplan, who wrote a history of the economic impact of Jewish immigrants in South Africa, Israel was a devout Jew who dedicated himself to Hebrew education in South Africa. In 1905 Morris, then aged 15, went to South Africa for the first time. Kaplan's researches into the South African business affairs of the Mauerbergers led him to the following judgement of Morris:

> He was always something of a loner, possibly caused through spending most of the first 11 years of his life largely in the company only of his grandmother and elder sister. He lost an eye in Russia when another child threw a stone at him – suggestive that he was bullied – and this would be another reason for his growing up a loner. His ability was much respected, but in the course of starting a number of businesses, some highly successful and others not, he was apt to make himself disliked. Rational argument was not his strongest suit and the result is that many today recall the rows he had rather than his undoubted business courage and ability.[6]

Morris built the large and profitable Ackerman chain of retail shops in South Africa. When Joseph died it was Morris, rather than his elder brother Israel, who returned to England to settle the estate.

Everything to do with the business was based around the family or other Lithuanian or eastern European Jews. The South African and London businesses grew and prospered through these connections. Joseph's daughter Bertha learned to be a cog in this community in London, and was to become the engine of her family. Joseph Goodman, Bertha's husband, was not to be a success in business. Compared with his brothers-in-law, he was a failure as an entrepreneur, but the family gradually improved their circumstances and *in extremis* uncle Morris was there to help out, if somewhat begrudgingly. Work and family provided the nomenclature and defined the parameters of this world. It was closed in the sense that access was only possible by birth, so that its barriers to the outside world, both protective and restrictive, were complete. This is a culture shared by first- or second-generation immigrant groups, whose motto would be 'we are we and all others are the local people, the English people' and in the case of Jewish families, 'the gentiles'. Such a world is a fertile ground from which identities can grow, but finding one's own place in it can be difficult. Having a parent who does not quite fit in, like Goodman's scholarly father in an extended family dominated by trade, can be disturbing. Immigrant families are frequently the subject of hostility because they are different and because they find solidarity in closed networks of their own. Within their world, difference and failure can also be harshly treated. Another common feature of such families, which are often built on careers in trade, is the pressure on children to escape through education to the professions.

In 1910 Goodman's father was 30 and living at 76 Downs Park Road, Lower Clapton, with his father Hyman Goodman, a corn chandler. He married Bertha, then aged 23, in a double wedding at Kings Hall, College Grove, Mile End, with Bertha's elder brother, Israel Mauerberger, who married Rachel Schufferblatt.

According to Goodman's *Memoirs*, his father was 'an austere, scholarly man who rarely expressed any emotion'. Joseph Goodman did not really fit into the world of the Mauerbergers.[7] He was a distant figure, kindly, bookish – a Talmudic scholar – who lived in a separate world with his books and with music, which he also loved. Naim Attallah, the publisher, wrote a series of interviews and profiles which were published in book form in 1990. One was with Goodman and Attallah asked him whether his father was a shadowy figure. 'He wasn't a shadowy figure,' Goodman replied. 'But he was the less positive figure of the two. He was a very gentle, mild man and I think he was a bit diffident about intruding, but we were as devoted to him as to my mother.'[8] He would take Goodman to concerts at the Royal Albert Hall and then to a large tea at the Trocadero.

Joseph Goodman's great hero was David Lloyd George – he seems to have admired the man as much as the politician. His son inherited his enthusiasm. But what Goodman junior valued most in Lloyd George was neither his social radicalism nor his political skill but his battle with the House of Lords. In his *Memoirs* he uses the battle over the 1911 Parliament Bill to comment that his father could scarcely have dreamed that his own son would one day sit in the House. In later years friends do not remember Goodman speaking of his father, but the image of this retiring, failed businessman, frequently on the point of bankruptcy (to the extent that the leases on all the family homes were in Bertha's name) and all the while trying to keep up with books and music and enjoying the stories of Lloyd George, is a powerful and endearing one. Goodman's *Memoirs* and the recollections of his friends appear to suggest that his father had little or no influence on him. In fact he had a significant role in promoting the importance of politics, books and music.

Goodman's father was not, however, as strong an influence as his elder brother Theo. A sickly child, thoroughly spoilt from an early age, Theo was a passionate lover of the arts and almost devoid of practical ability. He spent his youth writing plays and theatre programmes, reading and educating himself in the things which he cared about. Because of his illnesses, Bertha allowed him considerable freedom, which must in turn have put more pressure on Arnold. Eventually Theo attended university in Ireland during the Second World War, completing a PhD at Trinity College, Dublin. In adulthood he was kept financially by his mother, Arnold and his uncle Morris. In later years he behaved towards his mother more like a husband than a son, taking her to concerts and exhibitions, trying perhaps to smooth the rough edges of trade from the Mauerberger genes.[9]

Theo's role in Goodman's life was crucial: he set the standards that his younger brother adopted for what really mattered in life and taught him that the appreciation of art and music were the only truly valid activities.

Then there was Bertha: the major influence on the development of Goodman's personality. One of his cousins called her the most domineering woman she had ever met.[10] Bertha had been a music teacher and competent pianist, and later taught Hebrew. She was a mother cut from the cliché-soaked cloth of Jewish matriarchy: the life force in the family; the voice urging on Arnold and to a lesser extent his brother, and the dominant presence in their early lives. One receives the distinct impression that Bertha, strong-willed, organized and emphatic, did not let her less materially successful husband forget that she came from the remarkable Mauerberger family. She was also the source of Goodman's considerable bulk.

On the first page of his *Memoirs* he recalls going out to tea in his childhood and consuming 'tea, of course, in ample quantities, delicious egg-and-cress sandwiches, chocolate éclairs, scones and raspberry or strawberry jam', then going home to his mother for 'an ample supper which we consumed with equal appetite'. While Bertha was teaching and the Goodman boys were quite young, they would go from school to the house of Charles Redstone at 51 Upper Clapton Road and have their first tea there and no doubt a second when they got home.[11] A friend of Theo's from the 1930s remembers visiting the Goodman household and Bertha being a good cook who served too much food.[12] Goodman thought his mother not a particularly good cook, not going in for sauces but concentrating on 'meat, sausages, eggs, and [producing] all the basic requirements for survival'.[13] Later he recalls 'substantial lunches' at Manzoni's restaurant in Holborn: 'There, for 1s 6d per day, it was possible to have . . . escalope of veal napolitano, implying a substantial addition of spaghetti. When some sauté potatoes and Brussels sprouts were added to the dish, even my appetite was satisfied. For an additional 4d some kind of suet roll would be supplied, heavily soaked in golden syrup, and if I went wild and added 2d to the bill, a cup of very good coffee lent a proper touch to the feast.'[14]

At home, food was an emotional language. This was an environment — its tone set by Goodman's father — in which emotions were not expressed, so food became a way of showing feeling. Eating was good, a clean plate virtuous and rewarded. Love was shown by providing large helpings, love was returned by cleaning the plate and asking for more. To a post-Freudian ear this may sound a harsh or mocking description, but imagine life in this family if food had not existed as a currency of emotional exchange. In the Goodman household, amid the uncertainties created by Joseph's character and Theo's nature, there was real love between mother and sons, and Bertha had found the vocabulary for its expression: food.

Bertha was not an orthodox Jew and although she kept a kosher household, she was not strict about food. She allowed butter on the table and would have rather seen her sons eat than starve for their religion. The boys were allowed to play sports on Saturdays, and she told Arnold, in later life, that she would not mind if he married a Christian, by which stage, one suspects, she would have settled for any woman who would have provided a grandchild.[15] However, she was a public Jew in the sense that she took an active role in Jewish affairs and supported Zionist causes — indeed there is an old people's home named after her in Israel. Her morality was strict, and Goodman goes out of his way to mention her strong views on sex in his *Memoirs*. The passage is worth quoting at length:

> I do not imagine that she had the faintest idea of those subjects which are the constant conversation in today's atmosphere. I would lay a very large bet that she had never heard of a homosexual. And probably like Queen Victoria, who denied the existence of lesbianism, she would have denied it with equal emphasis. I doubt also that she was concerned with modern ideas of contraception. She would have been astonished at the activities of Mrs Gillick. My father, who was, I think, the least lascivious of men, contrived somehow to have two children. Since I have not the slightest doubt about my mother's virtue, he was undoubtedly the father of them, but I am completely convinced that, having done his duty in that direction, the sexual relationship between my parents ceased completely. However, this did not have the anticipated effect, which today is widely professed, of souring people in their disposition. Both seemed to be perfectly contented and happy without resorting to extramarital comforts. I know also that during the whole of my childhood I never heard the subject of sex remotely discussed.[16]

There are few remarkable passages in Goodman's frequently bland memoirs but this is one of them. He implies that his parental home was a sexless household, and the later frigidity of the relationship between his parents created a more arid atmosphere than even this passage suggests. That he goes out of his way to mention the lack of sexual feeling and his mother's attitude to it underlines the emotionally repressed atmosphere of the Goodmans' home. Speaking of his childhood in later years, he said it had lacked happiness: 'I hadn't found a balanced situation there.' There were 'uncertainties' about relationships with people, 'about the extent to which one promoted one's own activities . . . Anything that isn't positive causes doubt and doubt causes unhappiness.' But he denied that it was an entirely unhappy childhood: 'I loved being a child; I enjoyed being at school.'[17] The strong implication in this and other remarks is that the family home was not the most relaxed of places. The relationship between Goodman's parents was strained. They differed on religion, Joseph being more observant than Bertha, they grew gradually apart and the atmosphere seems to have influenced Goodman in his very negative view of marriage. School was fun, perhaps because it was an escape from the chilly atmosphere at home, where time alone with either parent was fine but tension mounted when the family gathered together.

As Goodman remembered: 'My parents were always hard up for money. My father was not a good businessman.'[18] They avoided suffering real hardship, and by some means Bertha was never short of a pound. She managed the household, searched out bargains and developed a passion for buying British. Goodman recalled being taken on shopping expeditions in Finchley Road and his mother spitting on a foreign kettle which she was offered by one shopkeeper.

Goodman's main schooling was at the Grocers' School at Hackney Downs. In 1872 the Worshipful Company of Grocers, in the City of London, set out to create an establishment on public-school lines, and this was opened in 1876 to cater for the sons of local lower- and middle-class families. Entrance was by examination and at first pupils had to live within three miles of the City.

Goodman's size led to a certain amount of teasing and bullying at the Grocers'. In school photographs he stands a good head and shoulders above the other boys, and this must have influenced his attitude to others and theirs to him.

In his *Memoirs* he recounts the way in which his size had an impact on his school friends and the way he was teased, but he found a way to cope. He set out to get on well with his fellow-pupils. In later life many of his friends commented on his wit and his generosity. The roots of the way in which he learned to use both perhaps lay in these early encounters with school tormentors. A classic defensive mechanism when faced with a bully is to try to charm, to amuse and sometimes to bribe. Goodman seems to have grown adept at all three tactics and, as he remembers it: 'they came to recognize that, although I was probably the largest boy in the school, I was nevertheless an amiable character, and I never had any real problem with them'. One school friend, William Dowling, recalls Goodman as 'the sort of chap who would put his arm around your shoulder and say, "Cheer up, Bill"'; even when they were only 14, he saw Goodman as being 'gifted at handling people'.[19] Sometimes Goodman's mother would be brought into the act. Once, when he showed up with a band of friends for tea, 'my mother did not bat an eyelid. In no time at all a spotless white cloth was spread on our large dining-room table and within five minutes everyone was sitting down to an ample tea.'[20]

Towards the end of his life Goodman was dismissive of the English public-school variety of comradeship and of the English capacity for friendship in general:

> You might find a couple devoted to each other out of homosexual temptation. You can have relationships based on admiration or jealousy; the basis might be 101 different things. But the emotional element of true friendship is at variance with the British temperament. It is an embarrassment.[21]

A cornerstone of Goodman's character was formed as he worked out his relationship to Englishmen while at school and he learnt that in both his size and his Jewishness he was different. To overcome this difference, he made himself useful: but remained the outsider.

As Hackney was more affluent at this time than the East End proper, it was somewhere hard-working immigrant families aspired to live. The Grocers' was part of that appeal. Boys came to the school, an elaborate late-Victorian building facing Clapton Common, from all over London, but those from the immediate area were especially encouraged. It combined a strong emphasis on corporal punishment with games in the classic public-school mode, and aimed to prepare high-flyers for Oxbridge, to get them out of the East End. In 1906-7 the school passed from the control of the Grocers' Company to the London County Council and became the LCC Hackney Downs School, though it was known as the Grocers' for many years afterwards. In 1905 William Jenkins Thomas had become headmaster and he continued many of the traditions that had been started in 1876, particularly in the area of punishment. He liked form beatings – that is, everyone got hit.

During Goodman's time at the Grocers' the Company still had strong links with the school and entry was based on a mix of scholarship and fees. The school was a prestigious and well-equipped establishment with a gym which was converted in the summer into an indoor swimming pool, its own playing fields (at Edmonton) and several fives courts, a fully equipped carpentry workshop, a chemistry lab, front and back playgrounds and a large theatre in which the whole school gathered for morning assembly. It also had a cadet force which was led by its own fife band. There was even the Clove Club, which rowed on the nearby River Lea.

Goodman arrived at the school in 1925, in time to receive some of the memorable cream buns handed out at its fiftieth-anniversary celebrations.[22] He liked English and games. He was also in the cadet force, which was run by Sergeant Major Marley, who also taught gymnastics. School friends remember Goodman as basically lazy, while he recalled a 'love of words' and a pleasure in writing essays but a hatred of science and anything practical. His size should have made him a natural goalkeeper for the football team, but a school friend called Arthur Wood, who later played professionally, was chosen for most of the games. When Goodman did play in goal, he liked it when his own team kept the ball almost indefinitely at the other end of the field. He was also a runner over various distances. But neither football nor running was his game. Cricket was. Indeed it became a passion: 'Every Wednesday afternoon my mother would prepare an immaculately laundered pair of flannel trousers, a white shirt, a pullover, a blazer of a modest character bearing the school emblem of a camel, representing the Company of Grocers which had formed the school, and off I would go.'[23]

In a rare display of bullying on his own part, Goodman acquired a 'small boy' who would bowl to him endlessly in his back garden. He could not hit the 'ball' – usually a piece of cork – very far, because of bad-tempered neighbours, so he became an excellent defensive batsman. He also played tennis, and continued to do so until after the war. Later he added squash; his old friend Jim Gower recalled that he was very effective because he was difficult to get round on the court.[24] He played both tennis and squash better, though with less enjoyment, than he did cricket. He later claimed to have won a colour in tennis at university. His lifelong love of cricket saw him slowly migrate from the wicket to the members' pavilion at Lord's.

The *Memoirs* relate that Goodman matriculated first time, getting 'a distinction in English and a distinction in history, but alas I got the lowest marks the school had ever scored in geography'.[25] His General School Certificate, issued by the University of London, lists him as having been examined at Midsummer 1929 and receiving credits in five subjects: English, history (English and European), French with special credit in the oral examination, elementary mathematics and chemistry. If the distinction he recalls in his *Memoirs* relates to the credit listed on the General School Certificate examination, then Goodman was being modest. What is striking, given his self-confessed aversion to science, is the credits in mathematics and chemistry.

A friend remembers him as neat and tidy in these years, but very much the younger brother. He would tag along behind Theo and his friends on their trips to the Bond Street galleries, where they became a well-known little group. Goodman was drawn to the great Impressionists but mostly he listened. Later, in his twenties, he joined Theo at the Gargoyle Club, still very much the kid brother. In 1927, at 16, Theo enrolled at King's College, London, to study journalism. He stayed on until 1931, when he failed his exams. In 1929, also at 16 and probably through the financial help of Morris Mauerberger, Arnold was allowed to go up to University College London (UCL). In 1929-30 he read Intermediate Arts and then, from 1930 to 1935, Law.[26]

Tuition fees plus board were too much for his family, so Goodman did not attempt to get into Oxford or Cambridge; UCL, on the other hand, allowed him to save money by living at home. There ensued a discussion with his family about his future. As with immigrant families everywhere, medicine or the law topped the list of desirable occupations. Theo's inability or unwillingness to acquire a profession – or, indeed, to make his own way in the world – increased the pressure on his younger brother. While Theo's dilettante lifestyle was tolerated, it did not seem to be an option for Arnold. However, medicine was ruled out by his implacable hatred of science subjects. In a small act of rebellion, he initially registered for history of art, French and Latin before switching after a year to take a course in economics. The lectures were given by Hugh Gaitskell, who had just arrived at UCL and was then rather to the left politically. Though Goodman recalled the lectures as 'cultured and agreeable', they put him off economics. Instead he settled on the law.

Aside from cricket, the only real pleasure he had derived from school was in writing and reading. He loved clear expression – though both his spoken and written style were to become fixed in a pompous version of drawing-room mid-century English, which he took for correct form. Though his first choice of history of art might have sufficed, given these interests law was a natural destination. But it was practicality, as much as desire, which pushed him towards the profession and from the beginning he developed a unique method of practising it. At this stage he did not see law as a means to an end, but even so it was not sufficient to contain his interests completely. Moreover, his initial preference for history of art, French and Latin is revealing. He wanted to be more like Theo, but his role in the family was to carry Bertha's ambitions that at least one of her sons would amount to something. Though there is no record of it, one can detect the gentle but firm hand of his mother in the eventual selection of law as a profession. One son like Theo was enough to worry about and Goodman, not for the last time, found it easier to take the line of least resistance.

As with all of Goodman's early life, the exact sequence of events of his time at UCL is a little unclear. In later accounts of his studies his postgraduate work at Downing College, Cambridge, figures more obviously than the five years it took him to obtain his LL M at UCL – he usually claimed airily to have spent a little time there before Cambridge. In the early 1990s his degrees from UCL disappeared altogether from his entry in *Debrett's*. The highlight in various profiles of his academic career is a Double First from Cambridge. In fact, he seems to have developed slowly academically. Throughout his life the ladder on which he rose tended to be lifted after him and a newer, neater one dropped down for public inspection: few achievements sound neater than a Cambridge Double First. The difference between such invention or confection compared with that of, say, Robert Maxwell, is that in Goodman's case there was nothing terrible in the reality. Grocers' was not a bad school and UCL was a good college, but once the waters are muddied it is difficult to clear them again. In the case of UCL Goodman is generous in his *Memoirs*, noting that: 'the Faculty at University College was a very distinguished one, but more important the collective Faculty in the three major London colleges: University College, King's College and the London School of Economics, I think outshone any other Law Faculty in the country'.[27]

This was the Bloomsbury of the late 1920s and early 1930s, bohemian and highly political. A few blocks from the UCL law faculty, the socialists, the communists and artists of Fitzrovia were living through the tumultuous events of the second Labour government and its aftermath. Goodman, not immune to his time, joined the law students' debating society and met his friends each week for discussions of their studies and the state of the world. These meetings became a pattern which he followed for the rest of his life and formalized in the Goodman dining club formed years later to meet on a Sunday evening for high-quality gossip.

At UCL Goodman made two friends with whom he maintained contact for the rest of his life, Jim Gower and Dennis Lloyd. Gower, to whom Goodman dedicated his *Memoirs*, was, like Goodman, born in 1913 and went up to UCL in 1929. Starting a degree at this relatively young age was not uncommon, but nevertheless it created a bond between them. In addition, they were both living with their parents. They had chosen UCL partly for financial reasons, but Goodman now made the most of his allowance and while Jim took the tube he arrived either in taxis or in his own car. (As soon as Goodman was old enough to drive, his family resources were 'prevailed upon', as he might have put it, to buy a motor car – an asset envied by the other undergraduates.) Money appears to have been no problem. Goodman already stood out. He was a physical presence. His personal maturity was reflected in his being already, in Gower's phrase, 'a bit of a character'.[28] Gower remembers Goodman's confidence in making speeches. The law debating society, which was intercollegiate, had a cup; Goodman won it.

The law library at the London School of Economics (LSE) was much better than those at UCL or King's, so Goodman, Gower and Lloyd would work there rather than at their own college. While visiting the LSE, they took the opportunity to sit in on Harold Laski's lectures. These had a lasting impact on Goodman: 'It was difficult not to be impressed by him. Many unkind things have been said about this remarkable man. He is accused of name-dropping, of unfounded pretensions and of unfounded claims, but to hear him deliver a lecture extemporised, without a single note, in perfectly rounded sentences, without any hesitation or falter was a revelation.'[29] In later years Goodman often tried the same technique for speaking in public with some very good but occasionally disastrous results.

Perhaps influenced by Laski or by direct family experience of the poverty of the East End, the three trainee lawyers worked at a 'Poor Man's' law clinic in Commercial Road. They would arrive at around 6.30 p.m. on a Tuesday evening and see perhaps 20 or 30 people. In an age before the development of the legal-aid system such clinics were not unusual in working-class areas and for the three friends the experience was instructive and interesting. John A. Franks visited the law centre and later recalled the scene: 'At each of the three tables around the room, one of them [Gower, Goodman and Lloyd] sat, to which those seeking advice were directed in turn. The strain and embarrassment this placed on these customers, who leant forward to whisper their problems, could be felt.' On one memorable occasion two rivals were at separate tables without realizing it: 'When one saw the other there was a shouting match, and an undignified scrabble on the floor, and I think both were expelled – I do not recall any conciliation.'[30]

As Goodman remembered it: 'we encountered every kind of oddity and a great number of human tragedies'. Old women who were worried about their security would come in to be reassured that they could continue to live in 'garrets or attics'; often, after being told that so long as they could look after themselves they would be safe, under the provisions of the Rent Restrictions Act, they went away happy and lived in their little rooms until death. There were also frequent cases of dispute between landlords and tenants and a large number of matrimonial cases.

These last tended to feed on themselves. Clients would come in and say, 'I want a divorce.' One of the three friends would then ask them why. 'Well, because I'm tired of him' or 'I'm tired of her'. 'Oughtn't you to go on trying?' they would suggest. To which the client would reply: 'But Mr X was here last week and you advised him that he could get a divorce. Why can't I have one?'[31] Goodman admitted that they often failed to talk clients out of pursuing an action simply because of their persistence. They would then face the cost of the court appearance by a barrister, which could come to £50 or £60 (several thousand pounds in today's money). Gower and Goodman – the former remembers Lloyd as an occasional rather than permanent fixture at the clinics – decided to persuade people to appear in court themselves and save the legal costs. The first such experiment failed miserably when the client was tongue-tied before the judge.

They ran the clinic for three or four years. Roughly speaking, these were the years of the Spanish Civil War, the Labour Party's post-MacDonald surge to the left and slow swing back to the centre and the birth of the Popular Front; the years of the Left Book Club and a great era of political polarization and conflict. The European ideological civil war between totalitarianism and democracy was about to be waged. As a student, Goodman could not play an important role in these great events, but he was touched by the radical spirit of the times and he did his bit. (After which he retreated to a 'small Jewish sandwich bar across the road and ate the most delicious fresh salt-beef sandwiches with pickled cucumber'.) His later judgement on this early philanthropy was characteristically caustic: 'We took a secretary with us and we used to dictate letters by the score and provided a service for nothing that is now costing the nation millions of pounds. But things have changed, since today everyone regards it as their right to have such service, whereas we retained the discretion to turn away any unworthy claimant whom we did not think ought to receive assistance or who we felt quite sure could pay for it.'[32] But the little clinic run by the young Abe Goodman showed a generosity of spirit which was to stay with him throughout his life, even though it was a sideline to his two serious preoccupations of these years: his studies at UCL and his solicitor's experience.

The pressure of his family may have been reflected in Goodman's choice of specialized subjects. Perhaps the plan was that he would work in South Africa after completing his studies, and for this he would need a knowledge of Roman and Dutch Law. In 1993 he told an interviewer that he had thought of practising law in South Africa[33] and a profile in *The Times* in 1983 went so far as to make his 'prosperous' parents South African.[34] Like his friend Jim Gower, he considered an academic career. For the rest of his life he liked to think and talk of himself as 'in background . . . more academic than most solicitors'.[35] Whatever the reason, Goodman studied Roman and Dutch Law in addition to his other subjects. His professor in Roman Law at UCL, and the first academic who seems to have had an influence on him, was Professor Herbert Felix Jolowitz.

Jolowitz had been born in England of German–Jewish parents and studied at Cambridge. Indeed it was probably he who advised Goodman to continue his studies there. In his *Memoirs* Goodman identifies the time he spent studying Roman Law under Jolowitz as the foundation of his flexible attitude to Common Law: 'I owe my critical approach to common law to being acquainted with an alternative system which I rate much higher. Uncritical admiration for the common system of law derives mainly from people who know no other.'[36] There might also be rooted here his more flexible attitude to the reform of the legal profession. At any rate, it was an unusual background and one part of the foundation of his approach to being a lawyer.

The interwar legal and academic worlds had not yet, despite the First World War and the 1920s, thrown off a Victorian formality, and this was to influence Goodman for the rest of his life. His style of phrasing, his sense of personal grandeur, have the air of faded glory holding out against the advance of time. Solicitors' offices in the 1930s were bastions of Dickensian formality in the world of the dive bomber. In his first visit to a law firm he was told by a 'prosperous-looking gentleman who was smoking a large cigar: "There is no money in this profession."'[37] Here Bertha intervened. A friend of hers, a Mrs Lowe, was related to the family who made up the firm of Rubinstein Nash. Goodman joined them as an articled clerk for a premium of £300.

With finals approaching at UCL, he answered a notice in the *New Statesman* for a quiet home in West Sussex which 'offered accommodation to a single person anxious to engage in a sedentary and studious occupation'. The advertisement had been placed by George Milstead, a partner at the publisher Duckworth, and his wife Milly. At their home Goodman was able to prepare for his exams in peace. Occasionally he would take them for a drive in his car.

Goodman was registered for the London bachelor of law degree, the LL B, and in addition to Roman Law studied the conventional subjects of jurisprudence, constitutional law, criminal law, common law, property, conveyancing and equity. At intermediate level he got Seconds in Jurisprudence and Roman and Dutch Law and Thirds in Constitutional Law and Criminal Law and Procedure. He graduated from UCL in 1933 securing an overall second-class degree. Over the next two years, alongside his studies, he prepared and taught courses for the Metropolitan College of Law, a tutorial and correspondence college based in St Albans,[38] and eventually gained his LL M with first-class honours. He tied for second place with three others in the Law Society Finals, sharing the Daniel Reardon Prize.

To continue his study of Roman and Dutch Law, Goodman decided to apply to Cambridge. Trinity Hall turned him down, so on 18 July 1935 he wrote to H. C. Whalley-Tooker, a don at Downing, which was the old college of Goodman's favourite lecturer at UCL, Professor Jolowitz. Whalley-Tooker was an institution at Downing. As Fellow and Emeritus Fellow he was to be at the College for 64 years. He was quiet, kindly and direct; his advice to a student who had received an omega for an essay: 'Why don't you try working up the alphabet?' summed up his style. In 1931 he became Senior Tutor and lectured in the university on the constitutional law of England and Roman Law as a European heritage. In his capacity as the admissions tutor of Downing he received Goodman's letter, which read in part: 'I am endeauavring [sic] to secure admission to a Cambridge College next year, and I am writing to enquire whether there is any possibility of my being admitted to Downing College in the rather unusual circumstances of my application.' The circumstances were his age, 21, his wish to finish his articles that December and therefore come up a term late, as a 'bye-termer', and his desire to study Dutch Law because of 'South African connections' which might mean that he would 'possibly practice in the colony'. Whalley-Tooker requested testimonials from two people, a completed application form and an interview. The testimonial from Professor Jolowitz read:

> I should like to support his application as warmly as I can. I have known Mr Goodman since he first came at a very early age to University College and have found his conduct entirely satisfactory all the time he has been here. He attended my lectures during the first year, and, as he took Roman Law as one of his optional subjects, also came to my LL.B. class. He did well in his final Examination and has also attended my Roman Law class for the LL.M. which he intends to enter for in September. He has worked well and I believe him to have really good abilities. I very much hope that you will be able to accept him, and that he will do well at Cambridge.[39]

The other testimonial, from another UCL lecturer, D. Hughes Parry, was equally good: 'I formed a high opinion of Mr Goodman and of his work. He appears to me to be particularly well qualified by virtue of his academic training and practical experience in a solicitor's office to read for the L.L.B. in Roman and Dutch law at Cambridge.' The references and the application form were due at Cambridge by the beginning of August, but there was a hitch. Goodman was taking a holiday in Surrey and his old headmaster was also on holiday, so he was having difficulty putting the references together. Everything was delayed until October. In the meantime Goodman passed the London master's degree in law, the LL M, and was facing his solicitor's exams. On 24 October 1935, Whalley-Tooker wrote to him to let him know that he had been accepted at Downing but that he would have to pass Part II of the Law Tripos for admission to the Faculty of Law. For this course Goodman had to prove that he had been a full-time member of the University of London for three years and submit his examination certificates. There was a problem with this because of the arrangements Goodman had made for his articles as a solicitor. Eventually the matter was resolved, Downing found lodgings for Goodman and he went up to Cambridge at the beginning of 1936.

Once there, he was promptly sent to the Infectious Diseases Hospital. He sent a note to Whalley-Tooker: 'In an unconscious desire to see every side of Cambridge life, I am in the isolation ward with a mild attack of German measles.' His mother visited him three or four times during the illness and this demonstrated, he later told an interviewer, 'the superiority of Jewish maternity over any other kind'. Goodman spent a quietly studious time in Cambridge. He lived at 8 Glisson Road, one of a terrace of brick-built houses dating from just before the First World War, with a bay window occupying most of the ground floor. The road is a quarter of a mile from the station and ten minutes' walk from Downing College. In the Michaelmas Term of 1936 Downing's magazine, *The Griffen*, reported that members of college could now pay a termly charge of £5 15s.: 'The long and the short of it is that the man who doesn't go to Hall pays more for it, and the man who goes regularly benefits.' Goodman resisted the charm, and his account for that year shows no bill for eating in Hall. The total comes to £27 4s. 3d., including gate fines of 16s., the latter reflecting his already well-established habit of always being late. He spent his time studying and seeing everything at the Cambridge Theatre. Other than his degree, Downing left little impact on him and he little trace on Cambridge.

In a small field of candidates he secured two first-class degrees, in Roman Law and Roman–Dutch Law. He briefly considered an academic career but decided to return to London and find work as a solicitor. The firm in which he had been articled, Rubinstein Nash, offered him a job, but it was mainly to do conveyancing, which did not appeal. One floor above Rubinstein Nash were the offices of Royalton Kisch. Roy Kisch was a fatherly figure, a quiet man who was content with a small practice and a few clients. His real love in life was roses, and he was twice president of the National Rose Society. For Goodman the firm was another good base. Kisch didn't particularly want to build up the practice but he was a solid lawyer. The practice was dominated by a single big property client, Town Investments, and much of the work was conveyancing. Roy Kisch liked to handle the conveyancing himself and wanted Goodman to deal with all the other odds and ends. This suited Goodman and allowed him to learn about the property world, which was to be an important part of his post-war practice and a conduit into the world of the arts and politics – at least at local-government level.

The only significant legal case Goodman was involved in before the Second World War was Read versus Croydon Corporation. The facts of the case concerned a typhoid epidemic caused by contamination in Croydon's municipal water supply in 1937. The well at Addington had been undergoing works that autumn, and one of the construction workers was, unknown to Croydon Corporation or himself, a carrier of typhoid. It seemed probable that sanitary precautions during work on the well had been ignored. Forty-three people died during the epidemic in October and November 1937, but it was brought rapidly under control when the source was detected. Patricia Read, aged 15, fell ill as a result of drinking contaminated water and her father, Alfred Read, sued the Corporation as a ratepayer and as her father.

Goodman acted for Read. The barristers he instructed – H. J. Wallington, Sylvester Gates and his old friend Dennis Lloyd – faced opposition from Croydon's skilled team led by Sir Walter Monckton. The Corporation was found liable; the defence's arguments that no contract existed and that no civil claim could be made were dismissed. Its negligence in failing to chlorinate the water supply while the work was going on in the well was condemned. Most of the special damages (those costs faced by Mr Read as a consequence of his daughter's illness but excluding the £63 11s. cost of the Read family's stay at the Langham Hotel during the illness) were agreed out of court. The judge refused the claim for the hotel costs. The general damages paid to Miss Read as a result of her illness, which had been contested, were set at £100. A precedent had been established. It was a significant case, involving complicated issues (sale of goods, local authority law, two plaintiffs with different sorts of claims: 14 cases were referred to) and it was resolved in favour of Goodman's client.

By the time war broke out Goodman was a qualified solicitor and was developing his style as a 'character'. There was nothing unusual about his life up to 1939 except for a few useful small coincidences. He had studied and done his articles in a central London firm which dealt with much of the publishing and artistic world. He then worked at Kisch's with considerable freedom and began to build up his own clients in the commercial world but also in the arts and publishing. These experiences reinforced the influence of Theo and created for Goodman a hierarchy of aesthetic values which placed a connection with the arts at the top. In turn this connection influenced the way in which Goodman set about shaping his working life.

How deep his knowledge of culture went is a difficult question. The evidence suggests that he acquired culture because he thought it important rather than because it was integral to his personality. For instance, opposite his digs in Cambridge was a cinema, a flea-pit where Goodman went to see everything on offer. Here was an outlet for culture, a break from his studies, and he consumed the daily programme without discrimination, but in later life he rarely alluded to the films he had seen during those years. By then opera had become the art form to which he was most addicted, and it furnished his points of reference. His own accounts of his early life are modest descriptions of his schooling and education and skip to his time in the army fairly quickly. For the personality that absorbs art the first 25 years of life are the most formative. The impact of a picture, poem or piece of music experienced in these years can last a lifetime. From the first 25 years of Goodman's life, there is no poem, no book, no picture, no music that he recalls with any great insight or emotion.

Goodman was about to make his first appearance in the national press. In March 1939 the *New Statesman* ran its weekly competition: A, offering a last-minute excuse, has cancelled his acceptance of an invitation to stay with his friends the Bs at Easter. The Bs discover that he did so in order to stay with friends richer and more socially eminent than them. Readers were invited to compose a suitable letter of not more than 300 words from A to the Bs. In his *Memoirs* Goodman thinks he was about 16 or 17 at the time he entered the competition, but in fact he was 25. Nor could he recollect precisely what he wrote, but called it 'a letter of touching honesty, commenting on the sad state of our society which made it necessary for honourable people to resort to subterfuges to preserve their social and professional positions'. His entry read:

My dear B

I gather from a word Meddle dropped that both you and Barbara are sore about Easter. I wish to be perfectly candid. I did accept your invitation weeks before Easter. I did intend to visit you up to the Thursday before Easter. I did cancel the invitation on the Thursday before the evening by telephone. All this is bad enough, but add to it that my explanation about Aunt Mary was wholly false. The truth, as you know, was that I received an invitation to stay with Splendour at his country house which arrived on the Thursday morning because one of his other guests contracted measles. You ask, therefore, why, instead of being an honoured guest with old and true friends, I should choose to be a stop-gap at a house where demonstrably little store is set by my presence? Your answer is, I'm sure, self-interest; the hope that there might be some pickings from the rich man's table, whereas there was nothing to be expected from you but true friendship and warm kindliness.

How right you are! I know, my dear B, that your generous hospitality will be extended to me time and time again, but, where Splendour is concerned, have I any such hope? I have known Splendour for many long years, and, since his accession to prosperity, he has never recognised my existence, although nobody could have been more useful to him. Was I to reject my only opportunity? Would it not have been foolish, quixotry, and, moreover, would it have been fair to you to thrust upon our friendship the responsibility for having lost this golden chance? If I made a mistake, it was in fabricating an excuse – but is the moment before Easter the right time for a calm analysis of motives and values? It was kinder to leave you to believe that urgent necessity had kept me away, and to leave it to some later occasion – where, alas, I have been, forestalled – to vouchsafe the true explanation.

Yours ever
A

Goodman won first prize for his letter, which was praised for 'a certain eloquence' with which he faced the dilemma.[40]

On 9 May 1939 Goodman's family moved to 5 The Bishop's Avenue, Hampstead.

2

From Widmerpool to Goodman Derrick

As the present situation looks rather grim, I am trying to get into
the Navy, a service where, as one remains stationary, I imagine
I should be more useful than in the army.
(Goodman in letter to his Cambridge tutor, September 1938)

Goodman was trying to join the fight against Hitler as early as 28
September 1938. Many had started earlier by going to Spain in 1936,
but others joined up much later. He was clear in his own mind that
if war came he should fight because he was Jewish; there was also
pressure from his employer. Roy Kisch had seen distinguished
service in the First World War, and now, as Goodman put it:

he conveyed the impression that the outcome of the war largely
depended on my decision to enlist. I was, in fact, not slow to follow his
advice, although I rather doubted whether my own contribution to the
war would prove conclusive. But anyone Jewish had such a burning
resentment towards Hitler and the Nazis, vigorously supported in my
case by a hatred of Fascism, that it would have been poor form indeed
had I lost any time in offering my feeble services.[1]

Goodman wrote to Whalley-Tooker:

I have enquired at the Recruiting Centres and have been told that the
only people they are enlisting are signallers . . . as I have a legal facility
of picking up information rapidly, I might be able to do something more
useful on a ship than wave flags and the purpose of this letter is to enquire
whether you would be good enough to give me an introduction to the
Master who, possibly, might be able to indicate to me some means of
getting on board ship in a different capacity.[2]

He was unsuccessful. Lacking any personal or familial connection with the army, navy or air force, he 'set off to find some suitable organisation which could make use of me'. The young Goodman had few illusions about his possible contribution to the war effort. He saw himself in the role of one of 'the wives of the early settlers in America, who stood by their husbands at the stockades reloading the guns as the Indians attacked'. His friend Jim Gower took the same view. They decided that it would be better to approach the military together. They were joined by Dennis Lloyd. Their early efforts to be recruited into the army having failed, they tried again a year later, in July 1939. Their view, reminiscent of the characters in Spike Milligan's war memoirs, was that 'something needed to be done but perhaps not too much'.

Doing not too much still involved finding a unit that would take them. They tried a number but could not get in anywhere. Gower was working at his office at Smiles & Co. that summer when the telephone rang. 'Goodman here. I think, Gower, we have found the ideal niche for ourselves. Someone, not unknown in academic life, is forming a battery of the territorial army and they're defending a small arms factory. It seems the ideal place.' Gower rushed to Enfield to join Goodman and Lloyd. The academic was Mortimer Wheeler.[3] Wheeler was later made famous by the quiz show *Animal, Vegetable or Mineral*. He was an unlikely warrior but served with some distinction. He had set out to raise an anti-aircraft battery in Enfield, north London, and after organizing local publicity he, plus a few friends he had taken on as staff officers, waited at the recruiting office for volunteers:

> The start was a slow one, and it must have been after nine o'clock when the doorway was filled by an immense figure. For a moment the newcomer surveyed with mild surprise the threadbare scene in front of him and then a quiet voice mounted within him, and he announced his name with a suspicion of hesitation, almost apology. 'A. Goodman, solicitor' went down on the form, and thus a Cambridge graduate headed our list of gunners. Unambitious but out to do his bit.[4]

Goodman, Gower and Lloyd were told to return the next day. After a short interview all three were accepted for the unit, whose role was to defend the Royal Small Arms and the Royal Gunpowder Factories in Enfield.

So the three friends found themselves in the 48th Battery of the

42nd Light Anti-Aircraft Regiment.[5] Goodman's battery was the largest of three components of the regiment – 8 officers and 184 men in November 1939. Numbers rose to 11 officers and 359 men by November 1940. Though actually looking for a quiet spot to do his bit, by the time of the Blitz, Goodman found himself in considerably more danger than many front-line troops.

In the early months the battery began basic training with occasional two-week stints at training camps in Devon and Cornwall. Gower, after dodging a pass on a *chaise longue* from Wheeler's second wife, Mavis, was allowed leave to marry and went home in the evenings.[6] It was almost a year before bombs fell in the Enfield area – the first German raids on the locality took place in the early hours of 10 July 1940 (Hatfield) and 12 July 1940 (Cheshunt). Enfield itself received its first air raid on 26 July, but the plane was seen off after dropping its bombs inaccurately.[7] Goodman himself never felt at all apprehensive and not for one moment did it enter his head that he might be killed.[8]

As Goodman settled into army life he began to write letters to Roy Kisch, who used to read them at the breakfast table at the Spa Hotel in Tunbridge Wells, where he, his wife and daughter-in-law, Anne, were spending the war (he had a little plot in the hotel garden where they let him tend his roses).[9] Goodman regaled the family with tales of being in charge of a unit with a barrage balloon. Wheeler had heard that Goodman did not eat butter, so he took him everywhere with him so that he could have his butter ration. It was a sister battery to Goodman's that had shot down the first aircraft over British skies in the Second World War. Unfortunately it was a British plane, and the whole battalion was put through further aircraft-recognition training.

Recalling his ownership of a car at UCL, there were many Goodmanesque touches which enhanced the comfort of his army life. Bertha, ever conscious of her precious son's needs, had insisted he bring his own camp-bed, mattress and soft blankets. For basic training the recruits took over the Quaker Lane school at Waltham Abbey, where they slept on the floor. Goodman produced his bed. He offered his army blankets to Gower and Lloyd, but they rejected them. The car itself, an ageing Ford Prefect, accompanied Goodman throughout the war. A transport officer forced him to camouflage it so that it looked more like a military vehicle and it would make up the last vehicle in the convoy as the battalion, which became mobile in January 1941, travelled around the country.

In the early days Goodman's size was something of a problem for the army. Boots could not be found that were large enough for his feet and so one day he turned out on parade in carpet slippers.[10] More seriously, the standard-issue uniforms were too small for him, so he had to wear his Jermyn Street suits. While Gower and Lloyd cleaned latrines, Goodman sat at a desk so that he did not get his suit dirty, typing reports with two fingers.[11]

When Goodman woke on his first morning in the army he found that his watch, wallet and cigarette case had been stolen. Suspicion fell on a private nicknamed Gunner Particle. For the next few months Particle stole everything he could. The Commanding Officer, Major McWhatt, decided to try to improve him by giving him responsibilities in the kitchen: with disastrous results. Particle touched Goodman for money to get married and to visit sick and dying relatives. Gradually even Goodman's generosity was exhausted. When he suggested that Particle would earn more money at the gunpowder factory across the street, the private duly deserted. According to Goodman's *Memoirs*, they watched him walking to work at the factory for a couple of months before he was declared a deserter and in November 1940 struck off. The unit's war diary records other deserters being struck off in the following weeks as the battery prepared to leave north London.[12]

In the early months there was little to do but drink. After experiencing his first hangovers, Goodman decided to become teetotal, and remained so for the rest of his life. The trio of friends was broken up for the duration of the war when Lloyd became Wheeler's personal assistant. In November the battery received its first decent guns. These were Vickers weapons that fired a belt of two-pound shells and had a 'predictor' that was used to sight the target plane before the gun was fired. Though Goodman made some effort, it was clear to his superiors that he was not going to make much of a gunner, so he was elevated from gunner to lance-bombardier and put in charge of the battery office. His promotion came about, one suspects, because of the clear evidence of his resourcefulness – the bed, the car, the suits. Almost from the first, therefore, Goodman was in an administrative role. He organized the chaotic office, began learning how the army worked and was quickly promoted to full bombardier.

The battery was being run by a First World War veteran with the rank of battery quartermaster-sergeant (BQMS). He had his own car and was stealing petrol for it. So was everyone else who had his own car, including Goodman; but the BQMS was caught, and his court martial took place in January 1940.[13] Goodman was promoted to replace the unfortunate man. The duty of the BQMS was to provide for the men of the battery and ensure that things ran smoothly, in particular to organize rations and transport. According to Goodman, because Wheeler had filled the battalion with officers whom he knew but who knew next to nothing about the army, they had little to do with day-to-day affairs and left much to the likes of the BQMS. This suited Goodman well. He learned quickly the inner workings of the British military and was immensely efficient. Wheeler later called him the best quartermaster-sergeant in the entire army.[14] Goodman's own view of his role was recorded in his *Memoirs*:

> Anybody who wanted anything material sought my help: from the man who had lost his steel helmet or respirator, to the man who needed an invalid diet or the use of a motor car or the use of some army transport, or indeed almost anything else. A more taxing responsibility was to arrange for the reception of the weapons and their safeguarding. It is impossible to assemble 350 men without having a small number of totally irresponsible ones and one or two irresponsible to a point of lunacy. Thus on one occasion when a Bofors belt was being loaded with two-pounder shells, I discovered the bombardier in charge making use of a small sledge-hammer to hit the shells on their heads so as to force them into the belt. That a disaster did not ensue was a miracle.[15]

Another story from these early days illustrates a typical piece of Goodman thinking. Wheeler was given command of the whole regiment and was replaced by a soldier from the regular army, the aforementioned Major McWhatt. There were tensions between McWhatt and Wheeler which reflected the atmosphere of distrust between regular soldiers and the new volunteers and draftees. The new battery commander had a special talent for drinking a pint of beer while standing on his head. After a successful evening at which the battery had seen a film, the wife of a sergeant tried the same trick and a second lieutenant 'decided, when the lady was most vulnerable, to permit himself a familiarity'. The sergeant hit the officer. The battery captain summoned Wheeler, who 'arrived in a magically short space of time', as though he was waiting for the chance to get the Major. McWhatt was held responsible for the incident and was put under open arrest and taken back in his car to regimental head-quarters, a house called Monkton.

Goodman liked McWhatt, not least because he largely left him alone to run the battery, and he and Gower drove to the headquarters to find 'a forlorn Major McWhatt pacing about in the garden'. When Goodman asked him 'whether as a regular soldier he did not have some powerful friend to whom he could appeal', McWhatt reluctantly told him that he was a friend of the major-general commanding the First Anti-Aircraft Division, to which the 42nd Light Anti-Aircraft Regiment belonged. Goodman and Gower drove straight to Divisional HQ in Knightsbridge, in central London, approached the General and told him what had happened. McWhatt was rescued by his friend, but Goodman never saw him again as the Major was posted to another regiment and eventually promoted to lieutenant-colonel.[16]

On the military side, events became more serious from the spring of 1940. New guns for emplacements around Enfield were provided on 21 August, just in time for a serious air raid on the area. On 30 August the first German planes of the war were brought down over Enfield Highway and Ponders End, though there is no record of whether they were shot down by Goodman's battery. The first death in their regiment on active service came on 15 December 1940.

Wheeler was determined that the battery should become mobile so that, as Gower recalls, 'he could lead the 48th Battery when we re-conquered Western Europe'. He achieved his objective in January 1941 and the battery started to roam England practising the routine for 'moving on' and 'setting up'. As soon as the gunners got used to one site, Wheeler moved them on in convoys, which he led in his ageing Lancer, with Goodman in the rear in his even older Ford Prefect. From February to July they moved all round the country before being transferred to Carlisle for Mobile Training on 29–30 June 1941. It was on this trip that Wheeler decided that the battery should take the mountain paths rather than the road, but the driver of the leading lorry refused to go any farther, telling Wheeler: 'I enlisted to fight Hitler, not to fall off mountains.'[17] On 15 July 1941 the entire 42nd Regiment was mobilized for service overseas and moved to Leeds for final preparation. The 48th Battery, however, became independent of it and continued to roam around until ready to be shipped out.

From 30 August 1941 the battery was based at Ledsham Hall on the Wirral. For much of September 1941 the men moved around between Liverpool and south Manchester, before going on training and exercises in Dorset and Norfolk. Then, at the end of October 1941, they were mobilized at Hale, Cheshire, to be transported overseas. Goodman visited more of Britain in these few short months than he was to do for the rest of his life, which was to be confined to his London and later his Oxford homes.

During the period of mobile training, Goodman and Gower decided that they should try to get themselves a commission. Their first attempts were rebuffed because neither made the medical grade. Then, for once in their long friendship, it was Gower who made the connections and overtook his friend. Somehow he got a letter of introduction to the Deputy Assistant Director of Ordnance Services at Leamington Spa. Along the young sergeant went and had a pleasant conversation about tennis. Then the Deputy Assistant Director said to Gower, 'Of course I'll recommend you for a commission. You don't want to go to OCTU [Officer Cadet Training Unit], do you?' Gower replied, 'I don't want to, but how can I avoid it?' Back came the comment, 'That's all right, we can't have sergeants going to OCTU. I'll recommend you for an immediate commission.' Three days later a letter arrived with a commission and a posting to the Ordnance Depot.

By October 1941, despite Goodman's 'problems with health' – army code for the fact that he was already rather overweight – a commission was 'imminent' (though in fact it did not come through for another four months) and the Regiment was ready for overseas duty. McWhatt had been replaced as Commanding Officer, after the beer-drinking incident, by Captain Steele, who now summoned Goodman. Orders had come through and the 48th Battery was shipping out. Steele told Goodman that he would need a medical examination before he could proceed. The doctor diagnosed asthma and said he could not go. There is a slight question, impossible to answer now, as to why Goodman went to a civilian doctor rather than the army doctor, but he accepted the diagnosis, which, in addition to mentioning asthma, included the observation that he was very fat and would be an 'encumbrance' to his battery if they had to retreat. He watched his comrades set off by train from Manchester, to take a boat to Java, which they reached just before the Japanese invaded the island. Fighting as infantry, many were captured and suffered the harsh regime of the Japanese prisoner-of-war camps for the duration. Only about 70 members of the 48th Battery returned.

Just before Christmas 1941 Goodman was posted to the Officer Cadet Training Unit. In Gower's phrase, 'it was never the same again'. Goodman had now had over a year's experience of the way in which the army worked and he applied it to the OCTU as best he could. In addition, he underwent eight weeks of basic training. A fellow-trainee remembers him as being 'extremely athletic' and riding around on an army bicycle. They also had 'to learn to use motorbikes, which he did very gingerly, surrounded by about four instructors. He was always about half a step out of time when we were marching.'[18] The image of Corporal Jones from *Dad's Army* springs to mind, but in fact, once his army career got going, Goodman was closer to a benevolent version of Widmerpool in Anthony Powell's novel cycle *A Dance to the Music of Time*. He became a military fixer and solver of problems. The discovery that this was his real talent was to change his life.

Goodman was commissioned as a second lieutenant on 4 April 1942 and Gower engineered his posting to the Royal Army Ordnance Corps' (RAOC) Southern Command headquarters, where he was an Ordnance officer for the rest of the war. Within RAOC he was promoted to the rank of acting captain on 3 December 1942 and full captain on 1 July 1943. He was Major Goodman at Southern Command from 18 January 1944, when his name first appears in the main listing for Southern Command rather than for the RAOC Administrative Corps. His title was Deputy Assistant Director of Ordnance Services, alongside Gower (who then went out to Brussels and on to Germany) and one other officer, Major Martin.

Aside from giving his confidence a significant boost – many people described him as being shy and quiet before the war – and helping him to discover his talent for settling disputes and problem-solving in practical situations, the main impact of the war on Goodman was a marked increase in his ambition to succeed. The speed of his promotions once he had been commissioned, and the reports of his general conduct and popularity, together suggest that the initial rebuff, even though it was for health reasons – essentially the first he had encountered since leaving school – had had an impact. And now, of course, he was in a structured world which rewarded effort in a mechanistic way. It was not like performing for his mother's approval or charming or joking to avoid the taunts about his size: there were tangible rewards in status, recognition and power for his ability to do things that other people wanted done. He enjoyed promotion and took pride in his success. In addition he made a series of important contacts. Among these were old friends from the army and from his office at Southern Command, such as Henry 'Mac' Derrick, who arrived at Southern Command in 1942, Frank Usher, who later became the cashier of the Goodman Derrick partnership, George Wigg, who was to provide the vital introduction to Harold Wilson and many others, some of whom became clients, partners or fellow-solicitors.

Another who met Goodman in the war and was a close friend for many years was Frank Coven. Coven and Goodman trained together in OCTU. Later Coven described Goodman as the most interesting man he had met in his life. In time he was to introduce his friend into the new world of commercial television, and Goodman was to be best man when Coven married Edwina, who was also a close friend of Goodman.[19] Over the years Goodman, Frank and Edwina helped one another on slight matters and sometimes important ones. Indeed at Southern Command Goodman rescued Coven from a major embarrassment.

One day they had gone along to the American HQ for a drinks party. Coven had a couple of drinks and went to collect his greatcoat to leave. A 'rather pompous and fussy' little American pushed in front of him and Coven said, 'Are you aware this is a queue?' To which the American replied, 'Arrest the British officer.' Goodman was chatting to an American colonel and they came over. It transpired that Coven had tangled with the Commander of the whole base, a brigadier. Goodman, with the help of the charming America colonel, intervened, calmed everyone down and the matter was settled. On occasions such as this it must have been as much Goodman's physical presence as good sense which was effective.[20]

His role in the Ordnance Corps was not particularly taxing, and the position of the Corps in the army as a whole, while not the most exciting, was one of the safest ways of spending the war. They were not 'the elite of the British army but we were saved from the contempt of the fighting units by the fact that they needed us desperately and were always in quest of our goodwill, since we had control of the multitude of stores, equipment and weapons of every kind'.[21] The Ordnance Corps' HQ was in Government House near Salisbury, and the main command, to where Goodman moved in

1944, was stationed nearby at Wilton House, the home of the Earl of Pembroke.

Goodman summed up his war thus:

> My army adventures might give the impression that I was not conscious of the historic nature of the events that were unfolding around me. When I thought about them, or was reminded of them, I was indeed conscious, but the fact remains that the individual ant has very little notion of the grandeur of the ant heap. I returned to civilian life never having heard a single shot fired in anger except for one adventure in quest of lifebelts that is probably still covered by the Official Secrets Act. My friend Jim Gower had been posted to the 21st Army Group, conducting an invasion some months before the end of the war, but despite the most strenuous efforts Bacon would not release me for overseas service for the simple reason, alas, that I was too useful to him. However, a war uneventful in martial terms was nevertheless replete with fascinating incidents and an opportunity for learning more about the human race than at any time before or later in my life.[22]

When Goodman was demobbed he returned to work for Roy Kisch with an increased salary and a useful set of contacts. Though he might at this point have struck out on his own or tried to gain a partnership in a larger or more demanding practice, he settled back into Kisch's. He seems to have had a genuine affection for Roy Kisch. The partnership was formed in another tiny set of rooms at the old address, 6 Raymond Buildings, Gray's Inn. It was made up of a general office for six staff, a small office for Kisch and a cubicle for Goodman. Opposite the cubicle was a toilet: 'a continuous source of embarrassment as one inevitably emerged as a prominent client was coming through the door'.[23]

One of Goodman's first clients was the Sobranie cigarette firm, for which a childhood friend, Charles Redstone, had gone to work in 1925 at the age of 14. In 1948, having dealt with the naturalization of Charles's father, Isaiah, Goodman handled Sobranie's flotation – his first experience of such a task. Another key early deal was with the men who had, during the war, run the mobile laundries, which were managed from Southern Command. When the war ended they went into the laundry business with Goodman's help and advice. Thereafter he began to build a network of business clients and would propose deals between them for various purchases, takeovers and sales. For example, when one of his laundrymen, Rice Hunt, who owned the Joanna Dearlove laundry, was dying, he arranged for Isaiah Redstone to buy him out. Thus early contacts from pre-war days often overlapped with wartime contacts and together formed an inner circle of Goodman's clients and friends.[24]

A small increase in pay – he received £600 a year but no share in profits – was supplemented by marking of examination papers for the Law Society at four shillings a script, which brought in another £300 a year. By the standards of the time and in the depths of post-war austerity and reconstruction, Goodman was in a comfortable financial position. By the mid-1950s[25] he was also supplementing his income by lecturing in Roman Law at Cambridge twice a week for £7 a week. To minimize the inconvenience to his professional life a typically Goodmanesque arrangement was made whereby he left London by train just before 8 a.m., arriving at Cambridge by 9 a.m. From the station he went by taxi to the Law Schools to begin the lecture at 9.05, while the taxi waited to whisk him back to the station for a train to London that would allow him to be at his office before midday. This elaborate process was repeated each Wednesday and Saturday, initially for ten weeks. He must, in fact, have started out at 7 a.m. for the timings to be plausible. Goodman was modest about his abilities as a teacher, but he was intent on keeping a foot in the academic world and was not able, at this stage in his life, to turn down an opportunity.

Life at Kisch's was undemanding and the atmosphere pleasant. Although Kisch was technically the senior partner, Goodman did much of the work and gradually came to dominate the small practice. The connections with Southern Command provided the nucleus of the small team that was to stay with Goodman. Margaret Smith, who had been his ATS (Auxiliary Territorial Service) secretary at Southern Command, was there, as was his former sergeant, Frank Usher. Cricket was the main link with Usher, who had a trial for Middlesex, and during the war the two played whenever they could.

Supported by these colleagues, Goodman set about making a reputation for himself. His networking skills were, by any standards, formidable and he could turn even unpromising situations to his advantage and to that of his clients. One story illustrates the point. Kisch had encountered two young Jewish refugees, Mendel and Gustav Metzger. The two brothers, aged 16 and 14, had arrived alone and friendless from Hitler's Germany and been looked after by a Jewish lady who provided them each week with a tiny amount of pocket money. They lived in a bombed-out house in the East End and fed off overripe fruit. As Goodman remembered them: 'They were of remarkable and even distinguished appearance: the elder brother had saintly, almost Christ-like, features, with long locks and a beard which was never shaved. The younger was clean-shaven and less handsome. He was in every sense the junior member of the team.'[26] They were aspirant artists and Kisch enrolled them in the John Cass Art School at Whitechapel and started looking for a grant or scholarship to keep them. He was a member of the Education Aid Society Council, which helped Jewish people with access to education, and he applied to it for support. The chairman of the society, Sir Robert Waley-Cohen, was of conservative outlook and insisted that the best place for the boys was the army. An impasse. Kisch asked Goodman for advice and Goodman suggested that they acquire some celebrity endorsements for the boys. Goodman knew Ambrose McEvoy's daughter, whose husband had been in Southern Command, and McEvoy was a great friend of Epstein. The daughter telephoned Jacob Epstein, and later Goodman:

> arrived at Epstein's large house in Hyde Park Gate with a folder of drawings by the two brothers – all, I must confess, in my view absolutely horrible. Epstein was in the kitchen sitting at a vast deal table. I placed the folder before the great man, but as his fingers closed I asked if I might make one observation. 'I would not wish it to influence you,' I said hypocritically, 'but on your decision will rest whether these young men eat or not.' Epstein gave me a fixed look and said nothing. He opened up the folder and thumbed through the various drawings, muttering audibly to himself. 'Not bad. Some talent here I see.' In the end, when I left the room with the folder, I had with me a letter from Epstein testifying to his belief that these young men had some talent which should be encouraged.[27]

Just as Goodman was leaving, Epstein said, 'There is something you might do for me' and produced a bundle of income tax assessments. 'What shall I do with these?' he asked. Goodman stayed on 'for the greater part of an hour writing appeals'.

Each year a new celebrity was recruited for the task and the boys were educated. From such an unhopeful start came contact with Epstein in the first year, the sculptor Frank Dobson in the second and Eric Newton, the *Sunday Times*'s art critic, in the third. Later the brothers became well known in avant-garde art circles.

The Goodman operation was now in full flight. The names and contacts were added to the list and a favourable impression had been made on a small group of individuals. With little else to distract him in these early years, he spun his web wider and wider. A pattern that remained in place for the next 20 years was established: never turn down a job and never fail to turn a job to your advantage.

If he had carried on at Kisch's the scope of his professional life would have grown gradually. His own belief, expressed in his *Memoirs*, that he would have settled for a life there, is somewhat disingenuous. His ambition was to become much more of a major player and the opportunity now presented itself.

In 1947 Ronald Rubinstein died, and the practice in which Goodman had been articled offered him a partnership to replace Rubinstein. First he became the senior partner of Royalton Kisch & Co. and then he merged his practice with Rubinstein Nash. A clerk in the Rubinstein Nash practice remembers Goodman with considerable affection. Ronald Hill returned from the RAF in 1948 as an assistant to one of the young Rubinsteins. Almost as soon as Goodman joined, the young Rubinstein was taken ill with tuberculosis and Hill took on his work. A case was not acted upon quickly enough by Hill, who did not telephone to ask for more time, and a judgement in default of defence was entered against the client. Goodman was not angry and accepted that Hill had been 'put in at the deep end'. He phoned the client and managed to settle the matter within 15 minutes.

Law partnerships in the 1950s were slow-moving and conventional in their business practices. People usually stayed in the same firm for the bulk of their career. Goodman was ambitious and after a relatively short time there were office rumours that he was planning to leave. It had been clear for some time that the structure of a large practice with a number of partners was not in tune with his style. For Goodman work and life were woven intricately together and he wanted to be master of his own destiny. A related problem was that Frank Usher was unhappy. There were already a cashier and an assistant at Rubinstein Nash and there was therefore little work for Usher. The ties going back to Southern Command were too strong for Goodman just to let Usher go, so he was given a desk in Goodman's office and employed mainly to go out and buy cigarettes. At this stage in his life Goodman was a heavy smoker – indeed the habit probably accounted for the asthma that had saved his life during the war. He had a regular order for 1000 cigarettes a month, which he usually got through by the 24th.[28] Usher's reduced circumstances led him one day to say, 'I shall have to give up smoking. I know that you dare not ask for any increase of salary for me, so I must economize and I intend to give up smoking.' Goodman responded, 'Mr Usher, if you give up smoking, I will give up smoking also. It will be good for me and it would be thoroughly unfair that you should have to sit here all day long watching me smoking.' They smoked until the end of the week then gave up – Goodman for ever, Usher until the following Tuesday.

Hill was told by Usher that the break was coming but to bide his time.[29] Towards the end of 1954 Goodman went to see Stanley Rubinstein, the senior partner, and informed him that he was leaving in three months to establish his own firm. He left, taking his staff and a number of clients with him, and founded his own partnership of solicitors with Henry 'Mac' Derrick – Goodman Derrick.

There are many passages in Goodman's *Memoirs* in which he discounts his attachment to money and worldly success, and each such passage signals a major change in his life, usually a major advance. This was particularly the case with his retrospective judgement on the events of the late 1940s and of the early 1950s. Given that, aside from his customary visits to the opera and theatre and regular indulgences in food, he had few interests outside work, it is clear that the pace he was already setting would have stretched him beyond Kisch's. It was equally inevitable that he would either have became the senior partner in that firm or set up his own practice sooner or later. According to Derrick's widow, Goodman told his army colleague in 1946 that if he returned to the law they would set up a partnership together. Such far-sighted careerism is nothing to despise in itself, though perhaps its style was ahead of its time, but it did not fit the image he wished to portray of himself in later years, so once again a more convoluted story was created.

The invention in Goodman's *Memoirs* concerns the explanation of his desire to found his own practice. It should be stressed again, as with so many events in his life, that the true reasons and facts are not that discreditable to Goodman, but still he invents a cover story. In this case he writes that Frank Usher and Margaret Smith (the two later married) came to him and said that they were not happy at Rubinstein Nash and they wanted him to start a new firm. We know that he had already indicated to Derrick that he planned to found his own practice. Everything about him suggested that he was not going to be contained in a practice which he did not dominate. But more than this, the fact that he kept Usher on as his assistant when he joined Rubinstein Nash suggests that he had every intention of setting up on his own sooner rather than later. Goodman was a generous man, but he was not a charity, and he could have released Usher if the possibility of their going alone again was not planned for the short term.

There is another story which supports the view that Goodman intended that his involvement with Rubinstein Nash should be short-lived by legal standards. Goodman reports that the supposed approach by Usher and Smith to set up on his own took place towards the end of 1953.[30] In July or August 1953 Goodman was visited by a 22-year-old man named Philip Chody, who was recovering from an illness. A Goodman client, John Rael, had suggested that Chody visit Goodman to discuss a career in the law. Goodman advised the young man that being a solicitor was a good life but that he should also speak to Jim Gower about being an academic. Chody preferred Goodman. Goodman told Chody that, since he intended to leave Rubinstein Nash, he would become an articled clerk in Goodman's own direct employment. Chody duly joined Goodman but not the Rubinstein Nash practice. If the dating is correct in Goodman's *Memoirs*, then he had firmly decided about a year before the final break took place and three months before Frank and Margaret expressed their wish to leave.

There are two ways of looking at the foundation of Goodman Derrick. On the one hand, in our harsher commercial times, in which competition and business practices are much more competitive, the creation and consolidation of Goodman Derrick reads like a classic business success story; and that is how it should be understood. Goodman was no more and no less effective in his rise than other successful lawyers, no more and no less scrupulous than many have been since. On the other hand, there is no doubt that in the context of the 1950s, and in a number of particulars, his behaviour was fast, almost American. For Goodman it meant that in the space of a decade he went from being the junior partner in the interesting but obscure office of Royalton Kisch & Co. to being the senior partner in his own rapidly expanding practice. Moreover, his portfolio of clients was varied and interesting. There was a base of business and property but more significant were the early forays into publishing, the arts, music and film. In turn the cases, disputes and people he had to deal with allowed him to take on roles outside the law. Rather than the haphazard happenstance of a gentleman-in-law stumbling on good fortune that he liked to portray in his later years, his ascent was the result of the shrewd strategy of an ambitious lawyer. If one ignores his later justifications for his actions in these years, his rapid rise and the growth of his eventual partnership are actually rather impressive.

Goodman Derrick was founded in 1954. Working there in the early days was relaxed and enjoyable. In the first phase of the development of the partnership the hierarchy was clear. Derrick worked quietly on his own, dealing with conveyancing. For complicated cases Goodman was on top, then came John Montgomerie.[31] Frank Usher, who was the cashier, shared Goodman's love of cricket, as did Ron Hill, who joined them from Rubinstein Nash a little later. Before the practice enlarged and became busier and, it should be said, before Goodman developed the self-importance that was to characterize him in later life, lunch-times consisted of cricket matches. The reception area became the wicket, an 18-inch ruler the bat and a squash ball did service for a cricket ball. Goodman, according to his *Memoirs*, bowled 'Test Class' leg breaks. It is difficult to imagine the larger Rubinstein Nash office enjoying such sport.

Though the atmosphere was informal, there was a clear division between officers and privates. Goodman recounts that one of Miss Smith's great virtues was that she would not laugh dutifully at his jokes:

> Her principal value – as I now realise – was her failure to gratify my vanity in any way. I have always regarded myself somewhat complacently as being rather funny and it was healthy to observe the steely indifference with which Miss Smith received my anecdotal humour. It was a constant battle between us. My vain hope was that one day her slightly contemptuous expression and curl of the lip might break into the faintest smile at one of my better jokes. This never happened. It was immensely salutary for me: sycophants laugh immediately the joke is signalled and long before it is delivered. Miss Smith was a magnificent secretary and served me loyally and indeed affectionately.[32]

In contrast Ron Hill remembers her as 'a happy lass . . . full of fun and laughter. She it was who first tagged me "Ronnie" – which stuck with me through the years in a firm in which Christian names was the happy norm.'[33]

At the outset the new firm established itself at 1 Hare Court, with a second office in 2 Dr Johnson's Buildings. This second office was taken over by Derrick. It was his 'fortress or hideaway'.[34] Henry Joseph Mackinnon Derrick was born on 16 December 1916 at Southport. His mother died ten days after his birth and he was brought up by nannies and housekeepers on the Isle of Wight. After prep school Derrick was educated at the King's School, Canterbury, where he was a boarder until 1934, then went on to Exeter College, Oxford from 1935 to 1939. His Finals finished on 13 July 1939 and he married Sybil two weeks later.

They had both grown up on the Isle of Wight, where Derrick's father produced Gilbert and Sullivan and other amateur shows. His father wanted him to enter the law, but his first love was music. He studied law at Oxford, but when his father died he seized his chance and in September 1939 entered the Royal College of Music, in London, to study the organ under Sir Stanley Stubbs. This career was cut short when war broke out and on his twenty-third birthday he was called to cadet training at Warley barracks, and later to Bulford Camp, Amesbury, in Wiltshire. Sybil followed and stayed in the Swan Hotel as Derrick was granted a 'sleeping-out pass'.

Derrick got his commission and was transferred from the Oxford and Buckinghamshire Light Infantry to the Hampshire Regiment, where he remained until they were sent to West Africa's Gold Coast in 1940. He was only five days out from Ireland in a convoy of ships when they were torpedoed. He returned home to the Isle of Wight to get 'kitted out' again, and resailed a month later. He had a year in Sierra Leone as a captain with the Royal West African Frontier Force, then returned home on leave for two months to meet his daughter Patricia, by then five months old. He went back to West Africa, but this posting was short-lived as he contracted malaria and foot-rot. Finally the doctors feared he had blackwater fever, and he was shipped home. He had left England A1 fit, but returned anaemic, with huge bottles of medicine. He then had leave and afterwards transferred to the RAOC and in 1942 was stationed at Harnham, Salisbury, where he met Goodman. They bonded through a shared love of music and knowledge of the law. Derrick was quiet, studious and gifted – qualities that appealed to Goodman.

By the end of the war Derrick, with a growing family, felt it was too late to return to the Royal College of Music. His friend Major Goodman suggested he go back to his law studies and sit his solicitor's finals. The plan, according to Derrick's widow, was that once he was qualified he and Goodman would start their own partnership. He was articled to Goodman at Kisch's, qualifying in August 1948, and then at Rubinstein Nash. He worked at Rubinstein Nash until he and Goodman set up on their own.

Derrick was the organist and choirmaster at St Dunstan-in-the-West in Fleet Street, a post which called for his presence at lunch-time services, as well as at choir practice. He was a quiet, conscientious man. On Saturdays he and his wife would go through their accounts, and one imagines him becoming quietly exasperated by Goodman's lax billing. He was diligent and handled much of the routine work of the practice. In many ways he was an ideal partner for Goodman because he kept the basic work of the firm together while Goodman made business and other contacts. The balance between them was reflected in their respective drawings; for example; in 1957 £10,000 (£150,000 at late-1990s values) was allocated for their salaries: £7500 for Goodman and £2500 for Derrick.[35] Goodman worked with Derrick out of friendship rather than any real commercial considerations, but it was a good working relationship in which each complemented the other.

Goodman built up the practice through relentless networking, and yet the way in which he developed his web of contacts was largely unplanned and often fortuitous. Success obviously breeds its own admirers and in his *Memoirs* are many stories of plaintiffs approaching him after cases and asking him to represent them. Goodman's amiable nature, ruthless acquisition of contacts and undeniable skill usually did the rest. By the time Goodman Derrick was founded, Goodman already knew one future Prime Minister. Edward Heath's father was the builder employed to mend the roof on Kisch's cottage in Broadstairs. One day the young Heath went to see Kisch in his chambers at Gray's Inn, where Heath and Goodman had a brief conversation.[36] But his most important political contact went back to the war. Goodman would not have been the political lawyer he became without Colonel Wigg MP, his old colleague from Southern Command. Wigg was the link to Harold Wilson and Aneurin ('Nye') Bevan and through them to the peerage and the high tide of Goodman's career.

George Wigg was an Arthur Daley for the Labour movement. A fixer and a deal-maker, he was obsessed by security issues and served, with mixed results, as Harold Wilson's eyes and ears. He was tall and lanky and throughout his life betrayed his military background in his manner and style. Wigg became close to Wilson in the mid-1950s and, characteristically, it was over an intrigue and an alleged betrayal. Bevan had resigned from the Shadow Cabinet. Wilson was next on the ballot list and the rule was that the runner-up automatically replaced anyone who resigned. Wigg backed Wilson and encouraged him to take the empty seat. It was a significant moment in Wilson's political rise, the moment when he emerged from Bevan's shadow. Until then Wilson had generally been seen as a junior member of the Bevanites – 'Nye's little Dog'. But now he became more his own man and the newspapers began to see him as an individual rather than as part of the Bevanite group.[37] Wigg was therefore present at the creation of Wilson as the contender for the leadership of the Left.

In the decade that followed, Wigg was heavily rewarded for his loyalty. In return he did whatever Wilson needed doing. This fitted his generous and loyal nature. It also meant that the more insecure of Wilson's enemies had much to fear from this extraordinary man, who enjoyed trying to intimidate people. Wigg was a rather absurd figure given to ringing people up on a Saturday morning and threatening them. How effective any of this was in controlling Wilson's opponents is impossible to say, but the obsession with security affected Wilson himself and reinforced his sense of paranoia about the intelligence world. As it turned out, Wilson had a certain amount to be paranoid about, though little of it came from Wigg's fertile imaginings and none of the activity of rogue elements in British security directed against Wilson was ever prevented by Wigg's interventions. It was the latter's connections with the security services that provided the substance of his sinister reputation.[38]

Wigg then was one of the curious bit-part players of post-war British politics and very much Wilson's creature. Goodman recounted this first meeting with him in the introduction that he contributed to Wigg's memoirs, published in 1972:

I have known George Wigg since we met in the Army. At that stage we were both heroically involved; I was a Major at Southern Command headquarters, conducting an intermittent battle with the War Office, which left me with no time even to remember that there was a more remote though less potent enemy across the Channel. George Wigg was (when I first met him) a Lieutenant-Colonel, but unlike myself was very soon promoted to loftier ranks. He was, as I remember, Army Educational Corps [sic] and conducted an intermittent but wholly friendly campaign against me and the rest of the command in quest of the supplies, finance and other aid he needed to discharge his duties. He demonstrated then what has been his prevailing quality at all times, a wholehearted determination to attain his objective in the most complete and rapid fashion with the least possible regard to intervening obstacles.[39]

These talents were employed by Goodman once the war was over, in unusual ways. While Goodman was still at Rubinstein Nash a routine criminal case came his way and Ronald Hill handled it. Two men were arrested for a burglary from a grocer's shop. One of them, Ronnie Jones, though he had a criminal record, was being employed by the publisher Victor Gollancz. Gollancz was a client of Rubinstein Nash and the brother-in-law of Harold Rubinstein, and Goodman had handled a libel action for him in 1950.[40] Also in 1950 Gollancz had met Jones while visiting Pentonville prison. When Jones was released, Gollancz found him a job as a book packer, 'though he proved a hopeless employee', generally showing up only on pay day. Gollancz was nevertheless 'forgiving and blamed society for his shortcomings'.[41]

When Jones was arrested, Gollancz called in Goodman. In his usual style Goodman was heavily involved at the outset but gradually handed over the case to his juniors. He and Gollancz went to the prison to visit Jones. Both were large men and both were in overcoats. They squeezed into the interview room. Gollancz told Goodman, 'If you have any doubt about his innocence look at him when he smiles. You will see that it is the smile of virtue.' Jones did not smile and Goodman, pretty sure his man was guilty, threw himself into the defence.[42]

The police alleged that at 12.30 a.m. one morning four officers patrolling near Waterloo station had passed an alleyway leading to a bomb-site and seen two figures on the roof of a shop dropping objects down to the street. The police split up, two circling to get behind the suspects, while the other two kept watch. The two men dropped down a fire escape and crossed the bomb-site to the street, where they were arrested. The police maintained that they had been in sight for the whole time. The arresting officers, finding that one of the men was Jones, assumed they had a watertight case, since they knew that he usually admitted his guilt straight off. This time, however, he was going to be defended by a QC. They might have taken a little more care in preparing their case had they known.

Neither of the accused men was wearing gloves, nor were they carrying any goods. The defence established that the goods listed as stolen far exceeded goods recovered from the street. Included in the goods stolen were some sides of bacon. Goodman had forensic evidence produced that showed that Jones's clothes contained no trace of bacon. Moreover, there were no fingerprints on the 'jemmy' which had been used on the skylight, or anywhere else at the crime scene. The police argued that others had been involved and that the men planned to return later to collect what was left on the ground. The men's defence was that they had simply gone on to the bomb-site to urinate. The conclusive hole in the police evidence was provided by Hill, assisted by Wigg.

On a night with similar weather to that of the offence, Hill took Wigg, at the suggestion of Goodman, to the bomb-site and placed him in the position from which the police claimed to have observed everything. Hill retraced the alleged route of the accused. To help, Hill waved a white handkerchief to make himself more conspicuous. Wigg had difficulty keeping track of Hill as a large part of the roof, including the grocer's skylight, was obscured by a flat-roofed bomb shelter. Colonel Wigg no doubt made an excellent witness.

Hill and Wigg presented the defence case as skilfully as they could, but convinced only one member of the jury. However, in the early 1950s this was enough to force a second trial. Goodman attended little of the second trial in person, but went along while the jury was out. The court was empty except for a well-dressed man who turned out to be the husband of one of the jurors. She had been to the bomb-site to see for herself and was convinced that the police evidence was flawed. It was a second hung jury and the men were acquitted.[43] Goodman sent Gollancz a bill for £369 17s. 3d., 'slightly more than a packer's wages for a year', and Gollancz wrote to him: 'I think your charges are extremely moderate, and though of course the total cost is far more than I expected, very largely because of a) the double trial and b) the length each one lasted, I wouldn't have had a penny of it unspent.' Gollancz stuck by Ronnie Jones and eventually, in 1954, got him a job that he liked. Jones married, settled down and kept in touch with his mentor until his death.

With such a close association, it was only natural that Wigg would recommend Goodman to his political colleagues as a lawyer and, because Wigg was on the left of the party, the politicians Goodman encountered were generally left-wing. Goodman himself was not. His politics then and later were liberal, but the association with Bevan and Wilson, both seen as men of the Left, and with Jennie Lee, always seen as the representative woman of the Left, led some to think that Goodman's politics matched theirs. Goodman acquired clients as it suited him and did not question their political beliefs very vigorously, but nor was he particularly influenced by them – he had no strong political beliefs. Indeed his status as an outsider, without political ambitions of his own, was helpful in making these initial political contacts. His big breakthrough was just around the corner, his first major political case: the *Spectator* libel trial of 1957.

3

The Venetian Blind:
the 1957 *Spectator* Libel Trial

Good day to you, Mr Beyfus, we bring to you this afternoon the
case of the Venetian Blind.
    (Goodman to Beyfus at their first meeting on the case)[1]

Mr Carter Ruck, you must grovel further.
    (Goodman's alleged words to Peter Carter Ruck
when discussing apologies)[2]

Goodman Derrick entered the Law List in 1955 with Arnold
Goodman and Henry Derrick as partners. Over the next two years
the practice increased in size and handled a growing number of
commercial clients in property and television. Goodman could have
continued in these fields, with the addition of work in areas like libel
and intellectual property, and become a highly successful lawyer. Part
of the reason that he did not was his friendship with George Wigg.
His break came with the *Spectator* libel case of 1957 and the contrast
between that case and his work for Victor Gollancz a few years earlier
is instructive. Goodman found a stage and found the limelight; he
had an ambiguous relationship with both. He liked being famous but
disliked publicity: it was a balancing act that was to continue for the
rest of his life. His problem was that he wanted to be able to pick up
the telephone and ask anyone to do anything. For this to work he
required fame. But he did not want the scrutiny and accountability
that accompany such a public profile, and he wanted to be able to
withdraw into the quieter world of the law when things became too
intrusive. Thus he was attracted and repelled in about equal measure
by the fame that attached to his name after the events of 1957.

    In February of that year Nye Bevan and Morgan Phillips,
respectively Treasurer and General Secretary of the Labour Party,
were going to Venice for the Annual National Congress of the
Nennite Italian Socialist Party – Nye as a Labour Party observer and
Phillips as a representative of the Socialist International. Bevan's close

parliamentary colleague Richard Crossman, on hearing that Bevan was going, decided to go along too. Bevan left first, travelling alone. Phillips and Crossman, travelling together, followed.[3] Jenny Nicholson, a young British journalist who lived in Italy and was an occasional contributor to the *Spectator*, which was at that time owned and edited by Ian Gilmour, happened to be in Venice at the same time.[4]

Crossman's account of the visit makes clear his distaste for Morgan Phillips. Phillips was a working-class Welshman who had never visited Venice before and was generally known in Labour circles as someone who could not hold his drink. He did not like Italian food, according to Crossman, and 'drank steadily – I think mainly to avoid conversation – with the result that he got tiddly by midday and soaked by dinner'.[5] A story that circulated much later was that Phillips had been drinking throughout the second day of the visit, and at a dinner given by the British Consul had virtually passed out, his head falling into his soup.[6] Crossman does not mention this meeting or these events, though if he had witnessed them they would definitely have appeared in his diary. He does, however, set Phillips's mainly shy, defensive and drunken behaviour against that of Bevan, who was completely at home with the Italians, loved Venice and generally had a good time:

> What a contrast Nye was! Bland, ebullient, impeccably dressed in his beautiful suit, fresh linen, with his handkerchief falling out of his breast pocket, pretentiously discussing the qualities of Italian wine, pretending to knowledge of Venetian architecture, laying down the law about Italian politics with vitality and charm and occasionally with the wildest irresponsibility.[7]

Crossman was essentially freeloading on the trip, and gathering background for an article for the *Daily Mirror*. He attended sessions of the Congress with his interpreters while Bevan had meetings with Pietro Nenni and others as well as talking to journalists. Indeed on the Thursday afternoon of the Congress Bevan gave a press conference to 120 reporters. Meanwhile a leading Italian journalist, Luigi Barzini, told Jenny Nicholson that the British 'delegation' was behaving badly, not taking the Congress seriously enough and not bothering to attend its sessions. Nicholson later claimed that 'the Italians' – though only Barzini is mentioned by name – had complained to her about the amount of time the British delegation had spent in the bars of their hotel and at the Congress and of their boorish habit of swilling down large quantities of whisky with their Italian coffee.

The problem was not that Bevan had done nothing but that he had, as usual on foreign trips, intervened in local political disputes too much and spoken too seriously to the journalists. The criticism, if any was justified, was really about Phillips, who was not having a good trip. As for Crossman, he was not there in an official capacity. It seems that the idea that the Italians in Venice were 'incensed' by the British politicians' behaviour was due either to the disappointment of one journalist (Barzini had failed to get the interview he wanted with the 'delegation') being generalized by Nicholson to make a convincing background to her story, or the conflation of three different people's behaviour into one. However, the impression that Nicholson said that she got was that the three British politicians spent their time in Venice drinking whisky and being boorish. The offending paragraph was submitted to the *Spectator* two weeks after the Congress ended. It stated:

> And there was the occasional appearance of Messrs Bevan, Morgan Phillips and Richard Crossman who puzzled the Italians by their capacity to fill themselves like tanks with whisky and coffee, while they (because of their livers and also because they are abstemious by nature) were keeping going on mineral water and an occasional coffee. Although the Italians were never sure if the British delegation were sober, they always attributed to them an immense political acumen.[8]

Aside from the libel, there are a number of inaccuracies in the paragraph and in the sources given by the *Spectator* subsequently. Only Morgan Phillips, on Crossman's evidence, was likely to have been drinking any great quantity of whisky, given that he rejected Italian food and drink. They were not officially a delegation from the British Labour Party. Crossman, at least, attended some of the Congress and Bevan had spoken about the politics of the occasion at his press conference. It seems likely that what happened in Venice was much as Crossman portrayed it in his diary before he knew of any potential libel. Bevan played high politics, Crossman tried to pick up material for his *Mirror* piece and Phillips felt out of his depth in an alien environment and turned to drink, making something of a fool of himself in front of the British Consul and possibly offending some Italian journalists by his refusal to talk about the Congress. These journalists also saw Bevan drinking his customary quantity of wine, which rarely if ever resulted in his being drunk – but then Bevan's exuberance when stone-cold sober was much like most people's state after taking speed. They conflated the images and moaned about it all to an English journalist who then used it for colour in her piece on the congress.

The offending article appeared on 1 March 1957. Jennie Lee telephoned Goodman to ask him to act for Nye in a libel action against the *Spectator*. She always maintained that Bevan's decision had been taken with some reluctance:

> Throughout his public life Nye put up with a great deal of abuse and misrepresentation without resorting to so much as a threat of legal action . . . but one thing he was not prepared to put up with was any suggestion that when sent abroad, in a representative capacity, instead of doing his job in a responsible manner, he was lurching around in a drunken condition. When the *Spectator* published an account of a Socialist International Conference [sic] in Venice which gave that kind of impression, an apology was all Nye asked for. It was only when this was refused that he began legal proceedings.[9]

From Goodman's account it is also clear that at the outset Bevan was not interested in the money. 'At that early stage there was no question of his wanting damages.'[10] However, Bevan was adamant that he would sue: 'I have been libelled too often, I can get them on this,' he was later reported as saying. Initially, Goodman claims to have tried to deter him from taking action. 'My original advice to Nye was characteristic of the advice that I have given in most libel cases over the years: that the *Spectator* was an unimportant journal and that he was too important a man to bother about it.'[11] This contrasts strongly with Crossman's view that it was Goodman who was most keen, at certain key moments, on prosecuting the case.

Goodman became more averse to prosecuting libel the older he got, and tended to apply his view of his own restraint retrospectively. This is not to say that he did not suggest to Bevan that it was an option to ignore the whole thing: indeed it is likely that this was his initial advice. But if Bevan and his wife were clearly intent on pursuing the action then there was always a chance that they would take their business elsewhere. Goodman wanted Labour Party work, he enjoyed the company of politicians and the world of politics, and a solid win would do him no harm. This was 1957: he was still an obscure solicitor who had made no impact on the national stage. Not acting for Bevan in this case might close a few doors that had just started to open. Further, there was clearly a libel in the article and if the *Spectator* decided not to justify it the chances of winning either a forthright apology or damages were good. Anyway Bevan was very keen to proceed. As quoted above, he had been libelled many times and attacked throughout his career, and here was a chance to hit back. He knew that he had not neglected his duties, though the accuracy of the description of his state of sobriety was less questionable. It is possible that he did not know the extent of Phillips's drinking in Venice, for they had travelled to Italy separately, stayed in different places and been together for only short periods of the trip. He would, however have been aware of Phillips's general propensity for indulgence. If Phillips said he had not been drinking then, maybe somewhat disingenuously, Bevan and Goodman took him at his word – the former with little and the latter with no first-hand knowledge. Whatever the root of Bevan's motivation, it was not money. Both at the start of the affair and in the middle of the case he made it clear that he would settle for an apology.

Bevan told Goodman that both Crossman and Phillips had agreed to take part in the action. They now spoke directly to Goodman. 'Crossman was no less emphatic than Nye Bevan,' was Goodman's memory of the meeting.[12] Once Crossman had decided that the action should proceed he was clearly going to back it, and of the three he had the least to fear in terms of his own behaviour. He had not been drinking heavily and he had attended sessions of the Congress. However, he was well aware of Phillips's drinking during the Congress and therefore knew from the outset that if the case went to court there was the possibility of perjury. However, to Goodman he presented a clear denial of the accusations. So did Phillips. According to Goodman: 'Dick Crossman and Morgan Phillips added that they had seen nothing of the other two which would support the allegations in the piece.'[13]

Phillips was the danger. If his general reputation were well founded, if Crossman's diary record from the February entry were accurate and if the story told by the British Consul – which did not come out until after the case – were true, he had grounds to be extremely nervous about the case. Men with the most to hide often obscure fear behind verbosity. As Goodman remembers that first meeting: 'Morgan Phillips's denials of drunkenness were more forceful even than the other two.' Yet Phillips had most to lose if the *Spectator* tried to justify the piece and produced witnesses against him.

These initial cross-examinations by Goodman of his plaintiffs raise the first and most serious questions about his conduct of the case. We now know that at least two of his clients were being 'economical with the truth' about what happened on the trip. The question is, did Goodman? Two sources suggest that he did. The first is the author and journalist Christopher Booker. Booker was spending the nine months before he went up to Cambridge as an office junior at Goodman Derrick. He accompanied Goodman to meetings. At some stage in the early part of the proceedings, Goodman was attending a meeting near Victoria station. A call came through for him and Booker watched as Goodman made his way downstairs after taking it. Goodman looked puzzled and told Booker and the person they were meeting that he had been talking to Bevan, who had admitted to him that the *Spectator* story was essentially true in terms of their heavy drinking but that it was not the kind of thing that could be said about a future Prime Minister.[14]

The second source is a story which circulated after the case and was put to Goodman as late as 1993, when he vigorously denied it. In this account Goodman convinced Bevan at a party in Chelsea that the action against the *Spectator* could be won whatever the actual truth.[15] One question arises about these early meetings: how much did Goodman press the three plaintiffs? Did he hear and believe what was most convenient for him to hear and believe? His closest colleague on the case, John Baker, is adamant that Goodman had no idea that any of his clients was telling him anything but the truth.

Having received the instructions from their three clients, Goodman, Baker and Ronnie Hill from Goodman Derrick went to see the leading counsel. Their choice was Gilbert Beyfus, a founder of the Inns of Court Conservative Association. Their visit was unusual because often a writ is issued at once where something is obviously defamatory. 'We were anxious about the position of our clients as politicians,' Baker later recalled. 'Gilbert Beyfus had no doubt the article in the *Spectator* was defamatory but he warned us about the defence of justification. It would be hopeless if our clients were not prepared to go into the witness box and stand up to cross-examination because, once such proceedings were started, public men could not withdraw without loss of reputation.'

A letter of complaint was sent to the *Spectator* on 5 March asking for an apology. At this stage in its history, the magazine was enjoying a golden age of quality writing and influence. The staff were surprised to receive the letter and genuinely believed the article had been about the local colour of the Congress in Venice and the differences in political and personal style between British and Italian politicians. Neither the editor nor the deputy editor had considered the piece to contain a libel. Their lawyer, Peter Carter Ruck of Oswald Hickson, Collier & Co., spoke by phone to Goodman after he had received the letter. Goodman told him that his clients would be happy to consider a suitable form of apology and that they certainly 'had no desire to make capital out of the matter which they viewed as one of exceptional gravity'.[16] Following this conversation, the *Spectator* replied to Goodman's original letter of 5 March. The magazine very much regretted that Goodman's clients had considered the article a serious libel and offered to publish in a subsequent edition this apology:

> DEATH IN VENICE
>
> It appears that a reference to the British political observers at the National Congress of the Italian Socialist Party, in our article under this title, has been misunderstood to reflect upon their sobriety whilst in Venice. This was at no time our intention, or that of the writer, Jenny Nicholson. The passage in question was merely intended to illustrate the difference in national approach and the fact that an Englishman would not be so over-earnest as to refuse alcoholic refreshment during intervals of Congress sittings, as opposed to the 'mineral water' attitude of some Continental politicians.
>
> Whilst the article in question was published by us in good faith, we would like to express our regret for any inconvenience to which the paragraph may unwittingly have given rise, and to apologise to the British politicians who were mentioned by name in that article.

The *Spectator*'s immediate offer of a form of apology to the plaintiffs made it less likely that the magazine would try to justify the article. The possibility of a win increased the stakes for Goodman. At the outset Phillips and Crossman, who knew what they had to say was suspect, as well as Bevan himself, would have been happy with an apology. After the *Spectator* offered its wording of the apology the argument focused on this and it became clear that the magazine would settle rather than offer justification. Goodman, even if he might in his heart of hearts have suspected that his clients were lying or indeed knew that Bevan had been drinking, could now push ahead with the case, increasingly confident that they would win in court. It was still a risky strategy because the *Spectator* might have changed the terms of its defence by trying to justify the article right up to the day of the hearing, but the potential win was probably worth the risk – to his clients in terms of damages and the publicity of the retraction, to Goodman in terms of a high-profile victory.

In Goodman's view the problem with the first apology was that it defended the substance of the article and tried to cover the libel with a smokescreen about the difference between Continental and British politicians. Carter Ruck again spoke to Goodman. He expressed surprise that Goodman and his clients had not accepted the first version and asked him – according to Goodman's account of the conversation – 'to take into consideration on compassionate grounds that the *Spectator* was a bravely independent little paper unable to sustain any heavy financial burden'.[17] Goodman replied that he presumed that the *Spectator* had insurance. On 7 March he wrote to Carter Ruck at Oswald Hickson, Collier & Co., telling them that his clients did not consider the draft apology to evince 'a serious and responsible attitude towards a matter of this gravity. The article was a plain assertion of drunkenness and drunkenness of a disgraceful and discreditable character.'[18]

At the same time Ian Gilmour wrote to Crossman expressing his personal regret for what had happened: 'Although this matter is now in the hands of lawyers, I should like to say how sorry I am that you should have found Jenny Nicholson's article offensive . . . It was far from our intention to cast any slur upon any of you.'[19] His solicitors followed this by asking for another try at a draft apology and asking Goodman if his clients would like to draft an apology of their own. Goodman refused this on the grounds that: 'We can't frame an apology without knowing the circumstances in which this untruthful and defamatory statement came to be published.'

Roy Jenkins, who was a friend of Gilmour and a parliamentary colleague of Crossman and Bevan, now played peacemaker. Crossman met Gilmour at a lunch party given by Jenkins and subsequently drafted his own apology for the *Spectator.*

> In an article published by us, describing the 23rd National Congress of the Italian Socialist Party, certain allegations were made about Mr Bevan, Mr Phillips and Mr Crossman, who were present for part of the Congress. These allegations were as absurd as they were offensive and we have since confirmed that there was no truth in them whatsoever. Both our correspondent, Mrs. Nicholson, and ourselves are glad to withdraw them unreservedly, to offer our sincere apologies and to express our regret that they ever appeared in the columns of the *Spectator*.[20]

Gilmour considered this draft and sent Goodman a revised version on 3 April:

> In an article published by us, describing the 23rd National Congress of the Italian Socialist Party, certain allegations which were never intended as such were made about Mr Bevan, Mr Phillips and Mr Crossman, who were present for part of the Congress. These remarks, if taken seriously would be absurd and offensive and we are assured and accept that there was no truth in them whatsoever. Whilst we had no intention of causing offence we and the author, Mrs. Nicholson, now realise that these remarks should not have appeared and we are both glad to withdraw them unreservedly, to offer our sincere apologies and to express our regret that they ever appeared in the columns of the *Spectator*.[21]

Goodman again rejected the form of this apology on the grounds that it contained the repeated assertion that the libel was published in 'good faith' and that this 'could only mean that, your clients are asserting that they had reasonable grounds for believing that the libel was true'. In Goodman's view neither apology was 'serious' enough and 'Neither is an apology for publishing this gross libel, but each purports to express regret that some alleged misconstruction has been put by others on the words. The implication is that the words as construed by reasonable people are perfectly unobjectionable.'[22] Goodman needed to reject the apologies, as he made clear in a letter to Bevan on 15 March, because having offered them in several forms it would be extremely difficult for the *Spectator* to try then to justify the piece. On the same day he wrote to Crossman that they would now be pressing for damages but that he would be 'quite astonished' if the matter were not settled speedily.[23]

The rejection of this second apology forced the issue, and on 6 June Goodman again wrote to his clients, making it clear that the case was likely to come to trial but that he would continue trying to settle the matter.[24] Three weeks later Crossman telephoned Goodman to argue for a settlement. Goodman wrote to Phillips suggesting that they meet to discuss the matter as there was the possibility of a difference of approach between the three clients. On 3 July Crossman wrote to Goodman: 'It has been my personal wish . . . to be satisfied with an abject apology . . . [but if Bevan and Phillips] . . . would desire to get damages, I should, for very obvious reasons, go along with them.' He further wrote, on 11 July, that he would go along with them but would much rather not give evidence himself and 'should regard it as wise if none of us did'.[25]

This exchange of letters raises an obvious question: why was Crossman afraid of having to testify in open court if he was going to tell the truth? Did this letter not at least suggest to Goodman that the politicians had something to hide? Goodman replied to him on 15 July that the consensus was that they would try to settle 'on proper terms' in advance of the trial, but that if it came to it they would have to give evidence. Indeed he thought it would be desirable if they did. However, he retained the hope that the *Spectator* would settle with an abject apology and damages.[26] The court date was set for the second half of November.

On 8 October the *Spectator* paid £1500 guineas into the court – £500 for each plaintiff – in the hope of settlement and published an apology:

> It has been brought to our attention that certain passages in the article 'Death in Venice' published in our issue for the 1st March 1957, have been understood to reflect upon the Right Hon. Aneurin Bevan, Mr. Morgan Phillips, and Mr. Richard Crossman, two of whom were members of the British delegation at the 23rd National Congress of the Italian Socialist Party. The passage in question (written in light-hearted vein) has unfortunately been taken to mean that these leading members of the Socialist Party mentioned in the article consumed such an amount of alcoholic refreshment as to make the Italians (who mainly relied on mineral water) suspect their sobriety.
>
> Although the article was published by us in good faith, we wish to take this opportunity, since these passages have been drawn to our attention, of making it clear that any such imputation was never intended and of course would be quite untrue and insofar as the article could have been construed in this way, or in any adverse sense the passage is unreservedly withdrawn.

We would like to add, in conclusion, our apologies to Messrs. Bevan, Phillips and Crossman, for any inconvenience or annoyance they may have suffered, and to express our regret that the passage was so construed.[27]

At the same time Jenny Nicholson, who was convinced that the politicians had been drinking and was loath to offer any further apology, had been sent back to Venice to see if she could find witnesses prepared to come forward to justify the article. According to one account, she already felt that the decision not to try to prove the article had been taken.[28] The barman at the hotel of Phillips and Crossman and two waiters from the Congress were prepared to give evidence, as was the journalist, Luigi Barzini, though only that Bevan and Phillips had been drinking heavily. No politicians from the Congress were prepared to come forward and though the waiters might be able to indicate the volume of drink it was only Barzini who was prepared to give direct evidence regarding the plaintiffs' conduct, which in effect amounted to the unsuccessful attempt by him to interview them about the politics of the Congress. To defend the article fully, the volume of alcohol and its effect would have to be substantiated. The proof of the article would depend on the word of Barzini and the bar staff against that of the three politicians.

On Wednesday 20 November the Goodman team and their clients met in Beyfus's chambers. Goodman was by this stage, in Crossman's view, determined to fight the action, but there was still a chance that they would accept the *Spectator's* offer of a settlement. In his *Memoirs* Goodman blames the intransigence of the defence for the failure to settle, but in fact he made it extremely difficult for them to do so. Beyfus opened the Wednesday meeting as though the assumption was that the case would be heard. Crossman says he forced Goodman to raise the issue of settling, repeating the assertions of his letters during the summer. Bevan made it clear again, as he had done throughout, that he would be perfectly content with an apology and his share of the money that had already been paid into court. Crossman actually came out harder in this instance than Bevan, demanding that the magazine print his draft of the apology, make it clear in print that he had drafted this apology, and pay the £1500 guineas and all costs. It was agreed that they would wait for the other side to make their offer and then make their counter-offer at 29 minutes past ten. As Crossman recorded in his diary a week or two later: 'I was still determined to settle the case if I could, but I was also aware that Beyfus and Goodman very much wanted to fight it, since they thought they could win and win kudos.'[29]

However, when at 10.15 a.m. the next morning Crossman arrived at Goodman's office, he found Bevan and Phillips. They explained that they had decided to ask for £1000 each. Crossman was again forced to accept the views of his co-plaintiffs, though he felt sure that the *Spectator* would have accepted the terms he had suggested the day before. However, by increasing their demands to £1000 each it meant the *Spectator* would have to double its offer. The attempts to settle having collapsed, the case went ahead.

The *Spectator's* defence was a poorly constructed thing. The magazine had decided – on the offensive advice of its silk, William Fearnley-Whittingstall – that a British jury would never take the word of Italian waiters over a Privy Councillor. No witnesses were called, and therefore the magazine could not justify the piece, throwing away its one advantage before the trial even began. Fearnley-Whittingstall was, according to Crossman, one of the bitterest Conservatives in the country and had been boasting before the trial that he was looking forward to cross-examining Bevan. However, he was already ill – he died in 1959 – and was undermined by the attitude of the trial judge, Lord Goddard. Goddard had been a Judge of the King's Division of the High Court from 1932 to 1938, Lord Justice of Appeal from 1938 to 1944 and from 1944 a Law Lord. From 1946 until his death a year after the trial he was Lord Chief Justice of England. His attitude was crucial to the case.

Fearnley-Whittingstall examined Bevan and Crossman on the morning of the first day, 21 November 1957. Bevan admitted to having had one whisky and some wine, and stated that the article had made him both angry and indignant. Fearnley-Whittingstall got little out of Bevan, who swore on oath that he had not been drinking heavily. Crossman came next and said that in his view they had to sue to get an apology because otherwise 'normal readers would think that we had gone round tiddly at Venice and behaved in an outrageous way where every delegate could see and that we had not done our jobs properly'.[30] Afterwards he admitted to his diary: 'I fancy I was fairly alright, although I was always a danger to my own side, owing to a streak of voluble candour, which works usually but can of course also undo you if the candour lets a cat out of the bag.'[31]

Having managed to get through the morning without telling the whole truth, Crossman realized that the case was won because of the blatantly favourable attitude of the judge. Crossman recorded that 'even after half an hour, it was clear that this astonishing old monster of eighty had made up his mind that we were right and the *Spectator* was wrong'. Goddard behaved in a friendly fashion to the MPs, gently warning Crossman to remember he was not in the House of Commons and should not go on for too long and commenting when Crossman said he had wanted to settle the case, 'Of course, dog does not eat dog' – implying that Crossman as a journalist would not wish to attack a fellow-journalist.

After the trial Fearnley-Whittingstall wrote to Ian Gilmour: 'Goddard was quite shocking and, having ranged himself on Beyfus's side, the latter needed no encouragement to be as offensive as he was irrelevant.' Goodman had initially been worried that they had got Goddard, because he was known as a reactionary; what he did not count on was that Goddard had recently been vehemently attacked in the *Spectator* for his views on hanging, particularly his fondness for the hanging of mentally ill murderers. It seemed as though as soon as he saw the name of the magazine he decided that 'the words were an imputation of insobriety and that the defendants should have apologised fully and freely in the long interval available to them to do so'.[32]

During lunch, with the judge clearly against and with one of the plaintiffs having stated in open court his preference for settling, the *Spectator* increased its offer to £1000 to each plaintiff, plus the apology. Beyfus and Goodman were against settling, both now clear that the case could be won. Crossman argued that once the charges of drunkenness had been made publicly in court they had to be answered in court and they had to win. Bevan and Phillips agreed.

Crossman remembers Goodman discussing, with his clients at lunch, the nature of a good witness. The quality that makes the difference between a good witness and a bad one was self-confidence and quickness of wit. He told them that with Crossman and Bevan Fearnley-Whittingstall had been in trouble because of the confidence and sharpness of the answers; the normal witness, if not defended by the judge, can be hectored and bullied and they had not been. Phillips, who took the stand after lunch, was a different matter. 'He was a sub-normal witness – shifty, fearful, sweating with panic (legitimately, for he'd been drunk for most of the conference) – and within ten minutes Fearnley-Whittingstall was exploiting Phillips's inferiority complex and forcing him to admit things he'd never thought of admitting an hour before.' There were minor factual contradictions; for example, Phillips initially said that he had told his wife when he returned from the trip that the only thing to drink was Vichy water, which he did not like. He later admitted to having had one whisky with a French colleague, paid for by himself.

But most of all it was the manner of his testimony which could have been easily challenged had witnesses been produced that concentrated on his behaviour – even if, as in Fearnley-Whittingstall's view, the jury could not possibly believe Italians over a Privy Councillor, there was the possibility they might have given the nod to Venetians over someone who was so clearly insecure in his account. There were no witnesses to prove the veracity of their article, however. Instead the *Spectator* admitted it had published the article in the 1 March 1957 issue but denied that 'the said words in their natural and ordinary meaning are defamatory'. As soon as it received the complaint it 'expressed their concern' and offered to publish a statement and an apology that was acceptable to the plaintiffs. The magazine's problem was that it was difficult to argue that the article was not defamatory if it had offered an apology. Gilmour was exposed in this respect when Beyfus, against all precedent, revealed full details of the without-prejudice negotiations that had taken place before the case came to court – the judge overruling all objections. Gilmour maintained that they had not been offered a form of apology acceptable to the plaintiffs. Beyfus now revealed the existence of the various drafts of the apology and the meeting between Crossman and Gilmour at Roy Jenkins's house. He went on to call Gilmour a liar, to which Gilmour replied:

> Mr Beyfus, it is not a lie, and I suggest that with your considerable experience of these cases you ought to know full well, this was without prejudice, and the whole basis of 'without prejudice' negotiations is that they should never be published. You have chosen to break those rules, with respect, and I think it very wrong that you should accuse me of lying because I keep them.

The judge took no action to intervene against Beyfus, did not criticize him for exposing the negotiations and indeed, as the cross-examination developed, joined in:

Beyfus: Where were you educated?

Gilmour: At Eton.

Beyfus: Did you go to university afterwards?

Gilmour: Balliol.

Beyfus: And with that education behind you, you say you did not think that to say of three leaders of the Labour Party on an official mission to Venice that they filled themselves like tanks with whisky, obviously in public, casts any sort of slur upon them; is that what you are telling the members of the jury?

Gilmour: Yes.

Beyfus: I will give you an opportunity of withdrawing that. Do you tell them that you thought . . .?

Lord Chief Justice: What do you think it means?

Gilmour: I take it to mean that the plaintiffs enjoyed themselves in the normal way in Venice.

Lord Chief Justice: Is it normal to fill yourself with whisky and coffee like tanks? That is where it comes in. Do not laugh, please, it is not a joke, but I am asking you: is it really the ordinary thing to say that a man is enjoying himself abroad if you say he is filling himself with whisky and coffee like a tank – it means he is drinking to excess, does it not?

Gilmour: Not to excess, my Lord; I think he is steadily drinking.

Lord Chief Justice: What does it mean?

Gilmour: It means he is drinking a good deal.

Lord Chief Justice: Not to excess, but what?

Gilmour: A good deal.

Beyfus: What metaphor would you employ to describe drinking to excess? I suppose you would say drinking like a reservoir, is that it?

Gilmour: I think I would take it to mean – for a number of people, to drink one glass of whisky would be too much for them. Others could drink a good deal, but the fact of the question of the quantity in itself does not seem to me to be pejorative.

Beyfus: The only point of referring to their drinking is to make some sort of point out of it, is it not?

Gilmour: I took it to mean, as my Lord has commented, that this was a background impressionist sketch of the Congress in Venice, and it was not making any particular point except a general one of the failure of Nenni.

Beyfus: I suggest the point of this sentence is to contrast the drunken Englishmen with the sober Italians: that is quite clear, is it not?

Gilmour: No, it contrasts the impression that the writer thought had been given by the English to the Italians.

Lord Chief Justice: She thought that the Italians were considering that these gentlemen were drunk, because of the amount of whisky they had taken. She used in this article which you saw the words 'drunk or sober'.

Gilmour: Yes, my Lord, she used that in the copy.

Lord Chief Justice: You took out 'drunk', though I do not think it makes much difference.

Gilmour: Nor did I. I did not actually take it out.

When Beyfus had finished his cross-examination, Goddard continued to press Gilmour, particularly on his actions after he had met Crossman at the lunch at Jenkins's house; Gilmour said that he immediately set out to contact Jenny Nicholson:

Lord Chief Justice: Why did you do that?

Gilmour: To find out about the reference.

Lord Chief Justice: To see if it was true?

Gilmour: Yes.

Lord Chief Justice: What was wrong with Mr Crossman's draft?

Gilmour: Nothing, my Lord.

Lord Chief Justice: Then why not publish it? You were saying all along you wanted to apologize. Why didn't you?

Gilmour: We took it for granted that an apology acceptable to the other side would be better than one they did not approve. I was under the impression it was universal practice to agree an apology.

Later Crossman judged that Goddard's summing-up was better than Beyfus's final statement. The jury retired for 20 minutes with the judge's summing-up containing only one real crumb of comfort for the defendants: he instructed them not to award excessive damages. They awarded the plaintiffs £2500 each (about £40,000 at late-1990s values).

Goodman was now established as both a leading libel lawyer and the solicitor to Labour's left wing. His motivation in pushing the plaintiffs on to court was probably and not dishonourably mixed. His natural inclination to settle was not to the fore in this instance, but the idea that he condoned perjury to score a win is unconvincing to people who knew and worked with him. The truth probably lies in the middle. Once he was confident of a win he did not press for a compromise as hard as he would have done in other situations because he did have half an eye on his career. Ian Gilmour is sure that the motivation for the clients was financial, but here again the evidence is mixed and for Bevan, at least, the idea of money as a motivation is improbable. Whatever the real agenda here, the result was that Goodman became much more widely known.

The case was front-page news. The trial had also been followed closely in the Labour Party and Goodman featured heavily in the coverage. Bevan was delighted with the win, Crossman relieved. He recorded in his diary: 'Mr Goodman, whom I regard as a pleasant villain, will sleep easier in his bed tonight now that he's got his verdict.'

Few of Goodman's cases had quite as many sequels. A week after the verdict, just before the recording of the Granada television programme *What the Papers Say*, Crossman told the *Spectator*'s assistant editor at the time, Brian Inglis, that they had all been drinking, but that only he had not perjured himself because he had not been drinking whisky. This was not strictly true: the issue was the amount and not the substance. Besides, the other two had admitted to drinking whisky. In 1962 Iain Adamson was preparing a biography of Gilbert Beyfus and he interviewed Crossman:

> Crossman spoke freely to him and said that Bevan and Phillips had been drunk and had committed perjury, but that he had been sober. He also said that Morgan Phillips had not wanted to sue but that Bevan had insisted. 'I've been libelled too often. I can get them on this,' Bevan had told Crossman.

Adamson included the allegations in his book and on 9 July 1963 they were repeated in the *Western Mail* – a paper which hated Bevan throughout his political career – by the 'junior member for Treorchy', Sir David Llewellyn. Bevan's biographer, Michael Foot, offers a spirited defence on the substantial element of the allegation, that they had been drinking whisky in Venice:

> He was landed, much against his will, on an adventure with the press, the one and only libel action he ever took against a newspaper, despite his extensive experience of defamation. It was a libel, as the courts established when the matter came before them later that year, and certainly in Bevan's case a most improbable one, as anybody might discover who inquired about his habits from those who knew him. No one could ever call him abstemious, but hardly anyone ever saw him drink. He rarely drank when he was working, never when he had to make a speech. He had an extremely strong head which seemed unaffected by the quantities of liquor that might upset others. And . . . it

was, among other oddities, highly improbable that he would be drinking whisky when so well-situated to call upon the delights of Soave and Valpolicella.[33]

Foot also defends Bevan over the allegations Adamson makes in his biography of Beyfus. Adamson's book stated that Bevan committed perjury and repeated that he had told a companion that he had been libelled too often and could get them on this. The companion, we know from his diaries, was Crossman. Adamson also said that Beyfus did not know Bevan had been lying. As Adamson had access to Beyfus's papers, Foot asked Beyfus's junior counsel about the case. The latter told Foot that there was nothing in the papers that lent a shred of support to the allegation that Bevan had lied. However, as the source was Crossman and not Beyfus there was no reason for the papers to contain the story.

There the case rested for some 15 years. Then, on 15 April 1978, the *Spectator* ran a profile of Goodman by Auberon Waugh in which he said that, 15 years after the *Spectator* case: 'Dick Crossman was happy to boast to a party of journalists in my hearing that he and Bevan had both been pissed as newts.' The problem with Waugh's version is that the language is wrong. Anthony Howard, having known Crossman for 20 years, later stated: 'I can say with my hand on my heart that it was not the kind of phrase that Dick used.' Alan Watkins, in his study of politicians and libel, *A Slight Case of Libel*, counters that indeed Crossman did not use that phrase but that the implication of what he said at the lunch was clear and made clearer in his diaries: Phillips, at least, had committed perjury and they knew that Phillips was not telling the truth.

The allegations surfaced yet again when Crossman's back-bench diaries were published posthumously in 1981. Goodman was attacked for having clearly known that Crossman, Bevan and Phillips were 'committing perjury'. Anthony Howard wrote in the *Listener* that such a charge was not justified and that it was perfectly clear that two of the plaintiffs had every cause to bring an action but that the third, Phillips, had to be covered up for. Both Crossman and Bevan could hold their drink and neither was anyway likely to have been drinking whisky in Venice: they would both have been drinking wine. 'But Morgan would have said, "another scotch".' Goodman rang up to thank Howard for his support.[34]

There are three explanations for Goodman's role in this celebrated case. First, he was lied to by all three of his clients and in ignorance pursued the case. When, after the case, he heard that the possibility of perjury existed (if Christopher Booker's evidence is put to one side for a moment) he came to believe that Bevan had been telling the truth but was less sure of Crossman and Phillips. In his *Memoirs* he is adamant about Bevan and directly contradicts Booker: 'I never had any reason to doubt his total truthfulness, his honesty and his concern to maintain an immaculate reputation.'[35]

The second explanation is that he knowingly incited the plaintiffs to pursue a case that they could win only through perjury – indeed convincing one of them, in a public place, that the case could be won. Once the story came out he maintained that he had known nothing to contradict the evidence of the plaintiffs and for the rest of his life, in public and in private correspondence, swore that he had not known that at least two of the plaintiffs had lied.

The third possibility is that he did indeed suspect this, especially after Bevan's phone call and Phillips's evidence, but that he convinced himself that they were telling the truth because the case was an important one for his career. As Auberon Waugh put it: 'He was a genial man. He believed what he wanted to believe. He did not open his mind to the possibility that his client was a crook or all the time drunk, so he just carried along as though that were the case and he believed it. He was in his own way an honest man.'[36] At what point he became suspicious, it is impossible to prove now, but having decided to take the case he pushed for its successful conclusion. And then, characteristically, he smoothed the path behind him and denied for the rest of his life and in his *Memoirs* that Bevan ever told him anything to contradict his story. The balance of the evidence and Goodman's character suggests that the third explanation is the most likely. He knew, without knowing, and he did not act on that knowledge, accepting the 'truth' of what his clients told him in order to win the case.

4

The Inside Track

*If I had to give the best pen picture I could contrive of Harold
Wilson, I would describe him as an immensely intelligent man,
rather less – by my standards – than half educated.*
(Goodman on Wilson in his *Memoirs*)

Goodman tried to cultivate the image of a figure who operated above
party politics. But what, if anything, did he believe in? What was his
organizing philosophy? He tended to describe himself as a conventional and unalloyed liberal. To David Selbourne, he even called
himself a Gladstonian liberal, who could not find a 'party manifesto
which expresses those beliefs from my point of view'. He was
consistent, in the public presentation of his political beliefs, in his
speeches in the House of Lords in later years and in his reasonably
frequent newspaper interviews, that he hated cruelty, injustice and
intolerance. Such beliefs hardly form the foundation of a unique
political creed. They suggest a solid libertarian streak in him which
surfaced occasionally in public utterances about there being far too
much legislation. However, he did not adhere to Michael Foot's
favourite description of his own beliefs: that he was a libertarian
socialist. Goodman denied that he was or had ever been a socialist,
telling Selbourne only that he was in sympathy with parts of socialist
belief. His main objection to what he regarded as socialism was the
centrality of the ideal of equality, which he saw as incompatible with
freedom. Moreover, by the time he came to have these conversations
with Selbourne he also felt that the pursuit of equality was both
impractical and damaging to society.

This aversion to legislation and to equality would suggest that
Goodman should have grown, like other socially ambitious left-
leaning members of his generation, into a Thatcherite. He never did.
In part this was because, with the advent of Mrs Thatcher, much of
his hold on the political establishment was removed and, the
networks having moved on, his decline was rapid. It was also partly
because she opposed the kinds of interventions – subsidies for the

arts, for example – that he strongly supported. Also, as he claimed to Selbourne and throughout his *Memoirs*, he had a disdain for material things: 'I am violently opposed to greed, and consider it objectionable that certain people are able to make fortunes without any form of control.'

The way in which he built up Goodman Derrick provides some evidence that this belief was not a pose: any lawyer, or any one else for that matter, who consistently fails to send bills can hardly be described as materialistic. Moreover, he was not concerned with material possessions. His flat was filled with things that had been given as gifts, and, except for the pictures, there was little of beauty or value that he had bought for himself. Indeed no one interested in worldly goods would have purchased the ugly house that Goodman used as his Oxford base. He did not define his sense of self and his sense of success merely in terms of the amount of money he accumulated but in the connections and social status, the access and proximity to events, that the accumulation of clients and the building of networks provided. His personal problems were to pile up when that access and proximity evaporated. Having defined himself through his career rather than through the acquisition of wealth and having formed his emotional relationships as tangents to that career, he was heavily struck when his public life shrivelled and blew away.

However, at the beginning he was happy to sail as close as he could to the wind of power. When Labour won the 1964 general election, his friends and clients were in the ascendant. He turned on many old friends, most importantly Wilson, when he wrote his *Memoirs*, but he never turned on Nye Bevan or Jennie Lee. 'My friendship with Aneurin Bevan gave me a great admiration for him. He was essentially a fair-minded man. But if I had been a Conservative charged with a crime, I would not have wanted him on the jury.' While defending his friends, he also neatly rationalized his distaste for the Tories: 'I couldn't have been a Tory because of the Tories' belief in the sanctity of property. It is a simple belief which binds the Tory Party together.' The argument is neat and circular. Goodman wanted access to power rather than wealth. George Wigg gave him that access, so consequently his 'material' success was assured. He could therefore afford to reject the Conservative Party because of its fondness for wealth. This did not prevent him from working with Edward Heath in the early 1970s, nor would it have prevented him from working for Mrs Thatcher if had she called. What galled him was that she never did. John Major called and he was happy to serve. The one striking feature of his career up to the early 1970s was that he was a vessel which others filled with purpose; he was not driven or governed by an overarching set of ideas. Ideological beliefs, like culture, were not central to his being but acquired as a *post hoc* rationalization of the kind of political associations that he developed.

Later in his conversation with Selbourne, Goodman claimed that he could not join the Labour Party because it had no core ideas and did not implement its manifestos: 'The Labour Party has no comparably simple belief [to the Tories' love of property]; they have been in search of it for generations . . . They are activated by a complex of great ideas.' Equality was not the core idea; or at least it might have been for the leadership but was not for the rank and file. There were things that he supported in Labour's programmes and beliefs: 'Socialists also believe in the abolition of poverty, they believe in social service, they believe in inalienable rights, they believe in a national health service and free education. In these respects Labour is streets ahead of any other party in morality.' However, the problem was with the socialist philosophy of equality: 'Equality could be secured only by divine intervention. Since I do not believe in divine intervention, I do not believe in the possibility of equality either.' More than this, Goodman maintained that the Labour Party's policies would not secure the objectives they were set out on because they were impractical: 'I don't think that socialism will secure the downtrodden to be the uptrodden.' His central objections to the Labour Party were both commonplace and banal: that equality meant levelling everyone down and that Wilson in particular had never implemented an election manifesto.[1]

What is intriguing about these late Goodman observations – and there is little to suggest that these were not long-held views – is how simplistic and unpolitical they are. They show no awareness of Anthony Crosland's 1956 book *The Future of Socialism*,[2] little understanding of either the Attlee government or the 1964–70 government nor of the differences between these and the 1974–9 government both in political position and in their relation to the manifesto on which they were elected. The list could continue. In other words his observations on politics read very much like those of an outsider rather than an insider. Perhaps such naivety was a studied pose that allowed him to position himself above the political fray. This was, after all, one of his favourite self-images:

It is egotistical to believe that one has better powers to see what is going on around one than are shared by one's fellow men. This I do not believe, but I do believe that certain people through chance may find themselves situated at particular vantage points well designed to give a full panoramic view of the social picture which may well be denied to others working industriously in the valleys without the energy or the inclination to ascend occasionally to the hill-tops for a view across the horizon.[3]

On political philosophy, the vision so afforded was at best partial, at worst composed of a saloon-bar triteness mixed with pragmatism and snobbery. Despite his strong political connections there were limits to the extent to which Goodman was a political lawyer in the sense of making political contributions to the development of policy, ideas or winning elections. He was a mechanic of the legal aspects of politics in a number of important cases, but his party political involvement was minimal. Wilson used him in particular against the press because Goodman knew the press well and his threats frequently worked. He used him as a sounding-board about financial and business problems, but he did not talk to him seriously about high politics nor discuss the direction of the party. Goodman was in politics but he was not of it, just as he floated in the world of the Labour Party but never joined it. Perhaps in the long run he would have been happier had he been able to belong a little more to the institutions that he served: they might have given him more comfort in the last years.

The grandest claim for Goodman as an original thinker was made by Selbourne: 'he spoke with great substance, clarity and truth, in perfectly rounded paragraphs. He had a subtle mind – fully capable of judging Isaiah Berlin.' Indeed Selbourne judges Goodman as a greater thinker than Berlin – quite a claim.[4] The question is whether or not he was really a significant thinker in any sense at all or whether Noel Annan was closer to the mark in his judgement that Goodman was 'not an intellectual . . . He does not compete with Sir Isaiah Berlin or Professor Herbert Hart.'[5] A fairer conclusion was that his contribution was considerable, but that it was a practical one.

Goodman met Hugh Gaitskell in the late 1950s, having first encountered him in the 1930s at UCL and through family connections: Gaitskell's wife, Dora, moved in a similar north London Jewish community to Bertha. Goodman was closer to the Bevans, whom Goodman had first met through the millionaire socialist Howard Samuel and got to know well during the *Spectator* case. It was almost impossible, even in the late fifties, to cross over between the Gaitskellite and the Bevanite camps: one had to choose. Goodman chose the Bevanites. As Goodman accurately put it: 'Gaitskell never adopted me in the sense that Harold Wilson did later'; but he was involved with both specific cases, like the Vassall Inquiry, and as one of a number of lawyers who advised the party on legal matters, so his Labour Party years properly start under Gaitskell.

Goodman later wrote:

> Of all politicians, I think, I respected Gaitskell most. He was, when I met him, probably at the height of his powers. He had lost the diffidence and uncertainty that characterized his early leadership of the party. He was confident, high-spirited and plainly impatient to seize the power that was coming so rapidly within his grasp. He was unexpectedly a man of great gaiety and to see him at a dance was an absolute delight. He loved dancing and threw off all the weighty considerations of state and all the pomp associated with political office and became a bright and jolly human being. Working with him – and my own experience with him was brief – was a joy. He didn't argue, he didn't dissent: he agreed or disagreed.[6]

While one might quibble with the picture of a supposedly diffident start to Gaitskell's leadership, it is a neat summary of the man.

The Vassall Inquiry was set up in the autumn of 1962 after an admiralty clerk was convicted of spying for the Russians. William Vassall had been passing secrets to Moscow for seven years. He had been posted to Moscow at the age of 30 as a naval attaché to the embassy. The KGB spotted his homosexuality, something that the British agents who vetted him before he left Britain had missed, and soon entrapped him with compromising photographs from a drunken party. Rather than have his career ruined he agreed to spy for the Russians, who then sweetened the burden with payments. On returning to England he held gradually more significant posts until he was finally exposed four years later, after copying thousands of classified documents for the Russians. His ministerial boss at the time of his arrest, Thomas Galbraith, offered his resignation. Harold Macmillan, the Conservative Prime Minister, accepted it and set up a three-man tribunal under Lord Radcliffe to investigate ministerial responsibility in the case. George Wigg, always interested in security matters, argued in the Commons for a full-scale inquiry into the security services. Gaitskell responded positively and agreed that the Labour Party should seek legal advice. Wigg suggested Goodman. Despite Goodman's later claims not to have acted as an overtly political lawyer, his role in the Vassall Inquiry is significant because he was to ensure that its focus remained firmly on the case and the government, and did not shift to the Labour Party.

The inquiry had been set up under the Tribunals of Inquiry (Evidence) Act 1921. The limits of its powers to call witnesses and the role of lawyers representing those called were not clear. Goodman made an initial application through Gerald Gardiner, later a Lord Chancellor in the Labour government, who represented his party at the Tribunal. Goodman's application argued that when the inquiry opened legal representation should be accorded to Hugh Gaitskell as Leader of the Opposition. Goodman argued that if the inquiry were to enjoy full confidence it should allow representation and that it could do so because it was not governed by the way in which other tribunals had been handled but could decide for itself. In the words of his brief:

> the Tribunal was not a body to which the doctrine of judicial precedence applied. Discretion was given to any particular tribunal appointed under the Act, and no tribunal was bound in law by any decision which any previous tribunal had made as to who appeared or did not appear to them to be interested parties . . . justice will not appear to have been done if, where the conduct of Ministers is in question, the proceedings appear to be conducted by another Member of their own Government.[7]

According to Wigg, Goodman's brief outlined that:

> there had been an Inquiry following the defection of Burgess and Maclean and, soon after that defection, two spies had been found to be at work in one particular Government Department. Thus the present Inquiry should be as thorough and searching as possible but care must be taken to ensure no harm be done to innocent persons.

Goodman argued that Gaitskell's interest was to see that a procedure was adopted that would minimize the risk of injuring innocent people. He therefore wanted the Tribunal to be assisted by

69

independent lawyers who were not members of the government that was being investigated. He established that:

> The Report of every previous Tribunal had been presented to Parliament; in this instance, the Prime Minister had announced he would decide what parts of the Report would be presented to Parliament. It had been usual for the establishment of the Tribunal to be preceded by a brief, factual, non–controversial statement.

'That,' Goodman concluded, 'can hardly be said to have been a distinguishing factor in this particular case.'[8] Lord Radcliffe rejected Goodman's application as presented by Gardiner. The Leader of the Opposition could not have representation. However, legal advice was offered to anyone called as a witness before the Tribunal and some financial support was allowed to witnesses who were not implicated.

Wigg's account of the Radcliffe Tribunal left out one dimension that Goodman recalled vividly in his *Memoirs*: George Brown. Brown, Labour's volatile deputy leader, had been making allegations about Vassall that went well beyond the court case. The young man had developed a close relationship with the young and inexperienced Admiralty Minister, Thomas Galbraith, and kept a large flat in Dolphin Square which had been visited by gay MPs. Brown shared Wigg's liking for intelligence matters but lacked his reserve. At a dinner party Brown had 'very incautiously, said some things that on a literal construction would have implicated the Labour Party in a rather nasty intrigue'.[9] In other words he had alleged that other Tory MPs were implicated in the scandal. Brown's unpredictability would have made him a risk as a witness in any case and if Brown were to be called as a witness at the Tribunal it might deflect attention from the incompetence of the Conservative government on to the conduct of the Opposition.

Goodman maintains that the purpose of the application at the beginning of the Tribunal was to have the Labour Party represented by Gardiner alone and to make it clear that it had no additional witnesses to come other than him; in this way everything that the Labour Party could offer would be given through Gardiner, making it difficult for Radcliffe to call Brown if he had heard about his indiscretions: 'The Labour Party gave its evidence and for practical purposes withdrew from the proceedings. No reference of any kind was made by anyone to George Brown's ill-advised remarks.' Goodman's judgement on Gardiner was scathing. He 'was a strange man: an old Harrovian, an immensely skilful and prosperous silk and a dedicated socialist. There was a Puritan austerity about him that made one doubt whether he ever enjoyed anything at all. I never took a meal with him, but I should be surprised to find that he ate with a good appetite.'

Goodman's role in the Vassall Inquiry was intriguing in a number of respects. First, he was operating as a 'political' lawyer to the extent that his brief for presentation to the Tribunal was designed to secure maximum political advantage. It was meant to keep the pressure on Macmillan and not allow any attention to be diverted on to Brown's indiscretions. Beyond this, it was designed to give Fleet Street some sort of protection in an inquiry that ended up being as much about the freedom of the press – two journalists who refused to reveal their sources were jailed – as it was about spying. The speed with which Goodman had then to change sides and advise Gaitskell on the way in which he could stop leaks to journalists from the Labour Party's National Executive Committee (NEC) and try to force them to disclose their sources was typical of the demands made of a lawyer when acting for clients: whatever his private views or the public stance he was to take later, a new case required a new set of arguments. This underlies one of the many differences between the worlds of politics and the law: consistency in private beliefs does not need to influence the professional conduct of the lawyer; what is required is a standard of ethics and the ability to act in one's client's best interests within the law. In politics the ethical constraints and the needs for consistency place different restrictions on action. In this instance Goodman's switch of sides was a legitimate and necessary part of being a good lawyer. In later instances, for example when he was operating as a lobbyist for interest groups like the Newspaper Publishers' Association, the role of the lawyer in acting for a client on a case-by-case basis would not serve Goodman as well.

In the early 1960s, as at many times before and since, the Labour Party's NEC was leaking information to the press. At times virtually verbatim accounts of its deliberations appeared immediately after they had taken place, especially in the *Guardian*. Gaitskell was annoyed by the leaks, which were almost certainly coming from Richard Crossman on behalf of Harold Wilson, who in 1960 had challenged Gaitskell for the leadership. An NEC report on party organization after the 1959 election had proposed changes in the party structure. One idea put forward by Morgan Phillips and discussed at the NEC was that Labour needed the equivalent of the Tory party chairman. Soon afterwards John Cole, in the *Guardian*, wrote that Labour needed a figure like the current Conservative Party chair, Lord Hailsham. This provided the opening that Goodman needed. In consultation with his old friend Dennis Lloyd he advised Gaitskell that, because of the closeness of the wording between the *Guardian* report and the minutes of the NEC, the Party could sue the paper for breach of copyright. 'We wrote to the *Guardian* on behalf of the Labour Party enquiring the source of this very precise information and – not surprisingly - our request was refused.' Goodman now tried to intimidate the journalists concerned with the power of the law. 'We then issued a writ and proceedings ensued.'

Goodman had charm, he was witty and he could frequently persuade people to do what he or his clients wanted by persuasion. When the charm failed, he would deploy an injured look or simply refuse to understand the grounds for refusal. This time he would deploy the heavy guns first: he would bully, then deploy the charm and humour. On this occasion Goodman Derrick opened with a heavy barrage. The writ had 'a large number of counts, including defamation, breach of copyright, conversion and heaven knows what else'.[10] The allegation was that the *Guardian* had converted to its own use a document which belonged to Morgan Phillips as General Secretary of the Labour Party and had therefore breached copyright; also that Phillips had been libelled because the article suggested that he had been the source of the leak. The writ was a probe to see if the *Guardian* would reveal the source of the leaks. Both the editor, Alastair Hetherington, and the *Guardian*'s Chairman, Lawrence Scott, argued that Cole should remain silent.

Goodman was utterly dismissive of the right of the journalists to protect their source. 'The *Guardian* sought to invoke some sort of privilege, which they could not seriously have believed existed, to protect their publication of the Labour Party's confidential information.'[11] The paper's defence rested on a claim of privilege based on the libel implications of the writ. Goodman took the view 'that no similar privilege was justified so far as copyright was concerned'. In this case, of course, he should not have included the libel charges in the same writ as the copyright charges. However, the *Guardian* lost the attempt to have the case thrown out on these grounds and the litigation reached the stage where the defence would have had to release all its documents to the other side and thereby probably reveal the identity of the leaker, which is what Gaitskell really wanted. In the event the snail's pace of the law saved the paper.

The case dragged on until the Labour Party decided to settle the matter and both sides covered their own costs; the *Guardian* paid a small amount for breach of copyright. Goodman was philosophical about the result. The *Guardian* had suffered what he called a 'continuous reverse' in its attempts to maintain the right to press freedom and to maintain secrecy about its informant; but he

> never knew who the culprit was and was never put into possession of the document or documents which existed and which would certainly have identified that person, since each copy of the minutes had [on Goodman's advice] been numbered. It was a strong probability that the *Guardian* still retained in their archives a numbered copy of the minutes which would have told us immediately to whom that copy had been issued and therefore the name of the informant.

Sixteen years later Cole encountered Goodman at a party and said: 'We never did find out who your source was, did we?' Few people are as precious about their work as journalists and of course it should be clear that issues of the organization of the Labour Party's NEC were not on a par with the national security issues involved in the Vassall case. Even so, the differing role of Goodman is revealing. He was on the side of his clients and his clients' needs: as these changed, so did his position. He was not an ideological or a campaigning lawyer and he did not uncritically exercise the love of freedom of expression which was to motivate his later parliamentary battle with Michael Foot over the closed shop in Fleet Street.

The result of the Vassall Inquiry was that the Labour Party was protected; the Tribunal cleared all government ministers involved and sent the two journalists who refused to reveal their sources to jail. If it had stayed that way Labour might have been judged to have missed an opportunity to score against its rivals. But the Profumo scandal, which broke in the spring of 1963, allowed Labour to press home its advantage. The reason the Labour Party pulled back from its case against the *Guardian* was because of a change of leadership. In January 1963 Hugh Gaitskell died from a rare disease and after a bitter leadership election Harold Wilson was elected.

Goodman was on the fringes of the Gaitskell set and therefore on the fringes of politics. Soon he was to be at the very heart. There is a certain irony in the way in which it was Goodman's expertise in the media that brought him to the attention of Harold Wilson. The irony derives in part from Goodman's own ambiguous relationship with fame and publicity, in part from the fact that one of his key roles for Wilson was to keep Labour affairs out of the media. Despite this it was as a media lawyer that Wilson first made use of Goodman.

The BBC's monopoly over television broadcasting had been removed in March 1954, when the Conservative government introduced a Bill for the creation of independent television. This famous 'licence to print money' opened up a great unknown new market. Goodman's negotiating skill, flexibility and established network in an initially small field made him ideally placed to take advantage of the opportunity. The Independent Television Authority was created after the stormy passage of the Bill and the first chairman was Sir Kenneth Clark. On 25 August 1954 the ITA invited bids from 'those interested in becoming programme contractors' in the first areas to be covered by the new independent network: London, the Midlands and the North.

Associated Newspapers applied for one of the licences in partnership with Rediffusion. Goodman had advised Lord Rothermere and Stuart McClean, the managing director, on a number of matters and now became the legal adviser to Associated Rediffusion. Through this connection he significantly expanded the media side of the practice. In 1956 he advised a consortium headed by Lord Derby in the bid for the franchise for Wales and the West (TWW) and brought the entertainer Jack Hylton into the deal. Goodman attended every board meeting of TWW and 'became their closest adviser'.[12] Sidney Bernstein and Granada had applied for the Commercial Television franchise for the Manchester and Liverpool station and became one of the leading network companies. TWW decided that it wanted Granada to become its parent company – only four of the twelve independent companies actually made programmes on any scale and the others were grouped with these four. Goodman negotiated the deal with Granada and also acquired Granada as a new Goodman Derrick client. His relationship with several television companies continued into the 1960s and he was heavily involved in the 1967 round of television bids, though not all of his clients did well.

Granada was renewed, Rediffusion was merged with ABC, while Lord Derby and TWW lost their contract. Officially, this was because they were too London-based; unofficially, Derby had fallen foul of Lord Hill, the combative chairman of the ITA.

An early case for Granada involved another 'Friend of Arnold', Howard Samuel. Samuel was the chairman of MacGibbon and Kee, then a small and well-respected publisher. In 1961 Samuel tragically drowned while on holiday in Greece. His brother asked Goodman to find a purchaser for the publisher. He rang Sidney Bernstein to ask if he wanted to become a publisher. Bernstein bought the company and built up a small number of lists, including Panther Books and Paladin. He eventually sold out to Collins in 1980.

It was this background in media work, as much as the earlier contact through Bevan, that brought Goodman to Wilson's attention. Wilson was 46 years old and the most brilliant politician of his generation. While Goodman, after being demobbed, had been sitting in his coal-heated office at Kisch's, Wilson had been President of the Board of Trade in the greatest reforming ministry of the century and was about to perform as a highly effective Leader of the Opposition. Though he was not to get quite the swing he needed for a working majority in the 1964 general election, he still achieved what the Labour Party had failed to do for 13 years: he won power. He went on to win four out of the five general elections he fought as party leader and with each year that separates us from his premiership his historical stock gently rises. Goodman was three years older, a moderately successful lawyer who had begun to break into the world of politics and was already well known in the media and the arts. Though George Wigg had suggested he run in the 1945 general election as a Labour candidate in Hampstead he had not done so and indeed, as we have seen, he was reluctant to join a political party. (Labour lost in Hampstead in 1945.)

Wilson *made* Goodman. Without Wilson's patronage and need for consultation and a peculiar kind of friendship, Goodman would not have risen to the heights he did. After he became Wilson's lawyer, and especially after 1965, his career made him a unique figure in post-war British history. There are still small patches of patronage left in Britain's political system and in 1964 the PM had the pick of them. It bothered Goodman as he got older that his public stature was due to Wilson's patronage. His waspish references to him in his *Memoirs* reflect this annoyance that he, in a sense, owed it all to the younger man from Huddersfield. He recorded the moment of their meeting in his *Memoirs* thus:

> I met him for the first time ever when he took over the leadership of the party from the recently deceased Hugh Gaitskell in February 1963. He had heard of me from some of his colleagues and asked to see me to discuss the Labour Party's decision in relation to the litigation it had brought, with my guidance, against the Manchester *Guardian* as a result of the leaks from the National Executive. He was sitting in his chair, smoking a pipe, and my first reaction was not favourable. The Prime Minister designate obviously viewed me with suspicion, as being closely associated with his predecessor. He asked me what should be done about the action. I told him it was entirely a matter for him to decide: that the Labour Party was my client and I would proceed on its instructions. This single episode gave me a very good picture of Harold Wilson's qualities and defects. He discussed any issue, and particularly this one, with everyone he could think of and he continued to show throughout his political career an indecision that in some directions had dire consequences.[13]

Ben Pimlott's definitive biography of Harold Wilson sets a more realistic tone:

> One of Wilson's first acts as Party Leader was to instruct Goodman to discontinue the action [against the *Guardian*]. Nevertheless, he was sufficiently impressed by the encounter to consult Goodman on other matters in the summer of 1963 [in particular Goodman provided legal advice to the leadership during the Profumo scandal], and again in 1964 [during a strike] . . . Goodman was unfailingly helpful, calm, wise and – an aspect of importance – studiously non-partisan.[14]

The impression that Goodman tried to convey was that Wilson was the person being assessed for his suitability for a future role in Goodman's career. The opposite was, of course, the case. Goodman charmed and impressed Wilson but was entirely at his beck and call. It is hardly surprising that Wilson asked for more of him. With no family constraints and with a willingness to cancel meetings or break off dinners to do Wilson's bidding, Goodman became a close confidant. Throughout the 1964–70 government Goodman visited Wilson every week or every other week and sat opposite him in the Chancellor of the Exchequer's chair in the Cabinet Room, gradually displacing George Wigg as Wilson's sounding-board. Goodman was a more reliable confidant, a more Prime Ministerial factotum, than the odd Colonel.

Goodman entered the entourage of Harold Wilson when the politician was on the threshold of power. He immediately started coming into contact with Wilson's other advisers and, later, in Number Ten Downing Street, with the political staff. The most important figure was Marcia Williams. He later recalled:

> The only common factor was Mrs Marcia Williams (now Lady Falkender), his private and political secretary, of whom I saw very little, but I saw enough of her to realise the immense influence she exercised over Harold Wilson. As my own position with him became firmer, he aired occasional criticisms of Mrs Williams. I ventured on one or two occasions to suggest that he might find some way of dispensing with her services. He never reacted hostilely to any such suggestion, except to say to me that she was difficult enough in a friendly association and matters might be worse (his own words) if he took any action to remove her from his political scene. I witnessed on several occasions horribly embarrassing disagreements between Harold Wilson and Marcia Williams, but it was clear that his loyalty to her would not be disturbed by any difference of opinion or any show of temper.[15]

It was a political 'marriage' in which divorce was unthinkable. Williams had joined Wilson in 1957 and was both secretary and manager on an intimate basis that raised many eyebrows: it was not just the depth of the relationship between the two, it was also the style. Pimlott paints a vivid picture of the relationship as a 'sex-in-the-head' partnership that was indeed part marriage but also in part a case of a son and his domineering mother. If there was an actual affair it was short-lived and in fact the relations between the two were more profound than a mere sexual coupling. Mary Wilson, Harold's entirely unpolitical wife, eventually even came to rely on Williams. However, Williams was a demanding presence. She had Wilson all to herself for the first six years and, when they went to Number Ten, grudgingly allowed others access to him. The relationship and Williams's style of dealing with Wilson and other staff took its toll. There were frequent rows, shouting matches and worse. Other members of the entourage played different roles. Some, like Wigg, indulged Wilson's fascination with security; others, like Joe Haines in the 1974–76 period, were always available to talk about the press.

Goodman entered this odd little world at first simply as a lawyer. Wilson liked the fact that he was always available. He was also impressed by his all-round competence. One feature that Wilson treasured in Williams was her ability to go to the heart of a political problem and argue it through with him. Goodman was redundant in this respect, but was an excellent person to try out ideas on and had a logical mind, which often helped Wilson clarify his own thoughts. Gradually Wilson came to rely on Goodman. He was calm, funny and a reassuring presence. Because he was not a party politician he did not have the political investment in his relations with Wilson that even Wigg did. Moreover, Wilson quickly came to trust Goodman with confidences. In exchange Goodman offered his particular brand of cautious advice, his presence and help and a sustained flow of legal opinion – which was often listened to – and political thoughts – which were usually ignored. He was also a useful conduit for party donations. The solicitor Abraham Kramer had a client who, having previously supported the Conservatives, wanted to donate a substantial amount of money to the Labour Party. Kramer asked Goodman to see him. They discussed how the donation could be made without publicity and resolved it so that the Labour Party coffers were quietly filled.[16]

Almost as soon as the leadership election was over, Goodman was advising the new leader of the Labour Party on a fresh Tory scandal. The Conservative Secretary of State for War, Jack Profumo, had first met a prostitute called Christine Keeler when she was swimming naked in the pool at Cliveden, the country house of Lord Astor. At the same party was her friend Dr Stephen Ward. Ward had already introduced Keeler to Lieutenant Commander Yevgeny Ivanov, a Soviet naval attaché. The Secretary of State for War and the naval attaché thus shared a mistress. MI5 warned Profumo, who stopped seeing Keeler, but after a shooting incident at the flat she shared with Mandy Rice-Davies, *Private Eye* and the BBC's satirical television programme *That Was The Week That Was* began to drop heavy hints that a scandal was waiting in the wings.

More significantly, George Wigg claims to have received an anonymous phone call on 11 November 1962: 'Forget the Vassall case. You want to look at Profumo.' Wigg was soon involved in a parliamentary battle with Profumo over the condition of British soldiers in Kuwait.[17] In late November he asked questions in the House of Commons on the issue and at 6 a.m. the next morning

Goodman received an hysterical call from Wigg claiming that Profumo had lied in his reply and that therefore he was justified in pursuing the scandal. Goodman says he advised caution.[18] Wigg set out to investigate the anonymous phone call. He received more information from a former Labour MP, John Lewis, who was 'acquainted' with Keeler and had taped conversations with her, which he now passed to Wigg.[19]

By the new year the Keeler situation was an open secret in government circles. On 8 March Andrew Roth's political periodical *Westminster Confidential* carried an item on the stories that Keeler was trying to sell to the newspapers, in particular the *Sunday Pictorial*. On 10 March Wigg briefed Wilson on the possible security implications of the scandal.[20] Wilson wanted some insulation between himself and the making of the allegations and told Wigg to raise the matter himself. Wigg approached Goodman for advice on the wording he could use in the House under privilege to expose Profumo.[21] Goodman had already strongly advised him to stick to the security issues involved and stay off the sex, before making an intervention in the Commons. Wigg again consulted Goodman and checked what he proposed to say to ensure that nothing would be actionable outside the House.[22] On 21 March, at the end of the debate on the Vassall Inquiry, Wigg raised the matter of Profumo by outlining the rumours and the stories that were circulating, but he barely mentioned the security issues:

> There is not an Hon. Member in the House, nor a journalist in the Press Gallery . . . who in the last few days has not heard rumour upon rumour involving a member of the Government Front Bench . . . That being the case I rightly use the privilege of the House of Commons – that is what it is given me for – to ask the Home Secretary who is the senior member of the Government on the Treasury Bench now, to go to the Dispatch Box – he knows that the rumour to which I refer relates to Miss Christine Keeler and Miss Davies and a shooting by a West Indian – and, on behalf of the Government, categorically deny the truth of these rumours.[23]

Wigg's speech was backed up by three more Labour MPs – Richard Crossman, Barbara Castle and Reginald Paget. They were followed by a masterful speech by Harold Wilson on the substance of the debate on the Vassall Inquiry which linked the Labour Party to press freedom. The next day Profumo, speaking on the advice of government law officers, made a personal statement denying any impropriety in his relations with Keeler. This was sheer madness when he knew that the *Sunday Pictorial* had a letter from him to Keeler, on House of Commons notepaper, which began 'Darling' and strongly implied intimacy. On Tuesday 26 March Ward visited Wigg at the House of Commons and told his story. There was sufficient evidence in this and in early letters that Ward had written to Wilson – the significance of which Wilson's private office had failed to notice – to undermine Profumo's personal statement. Following the meeting with Ward, Wigg prepared a memorandum for Wilson, 'An appreciation of the Keeler case by George Wigg, 29 March 1963'. The content of this memo was to become crucial. There were two versions. Version 'A' read in part:

> In my opinion Profumo was never, at any time, a security risk. The intelligence services were aware of his meeting with Ivanov and with his subsequent meetings with Christine Keeler. It is equally true to say that the Intelligence services were aware of Ivanov's friendship with Ward and his general activities . . . According to Ward his association with Ivanov was harmless and Profumo's association with Keeler, as far as he knew, was equally harmless. He [Ward] made approaches to Profumo when he learned of Mann's [an associate of Keeler] efforts to tell the Keeler story to the newspaper. He met Profumo at the Dorchester, told him what was afoot and, if he is to be believed, the few letters that Profumo had written were either destroyed or put in a safe place . . . He, Ward, is convinced that Profumo has done nothing to compromise the security of the State and that there was no security risk in his contact with Ivanov nor with the girl, nor arising from the girl's contact with Ivanov . . . He came to me because he was worried about my suggestion that security was the main consideration and he wished to convince me that on this subject he was in the clear.[24]

Version 'B' stated:

> Mr. and Mrs. Profumo met Christine Keeler who happened to be visiting . . . A photograph of Profumo and the girl taken in the swimming pool had recently been stolen. Subsequently Profumo visited his [Ward's] flat on at least six occasions. He said that as far as he knew nothing improper took place. He said that the Intelligence services knew all about these visits and he had kept records and had supplied the

Intelligence services with full particulars of the visits. Ward said that he was certain that although Ivanov knew Christine Keeler had met Profumo this knowledge did not involve any security risk and never at any time had Profumo put himself in risk on security matters in his contact with Ivanov . . . He came to me because he was worried about my suggestion that security was the main consideration and he wished to convince me on this subject he was in the clear.[25]

The key difference between the two documents was that Wigg made clear his judgement that Profumo was not a security risk in the first, but that it is only Ward's opinion in the second. Version 'B', together with a carefully crafted covering letter by Wilson, was sent to Harold Macmillan.

The politics of the situation were irresistible. On 4 June, having confessed, in a letter to the Prime Minister, to having lied to the Commons, Profumo resigned from the government and as an MP. As a contemporary ditty put it:

> To lie in the nude
> May be rude
> But to lie in the House is obscene.

Wilson was in the United States and was asked to comment on the resignation: 'No comment – in glorious technicolour. And that's what I'm telling you; no comment in wide screen.'[26] Wilson made another brilliant but dishonest speech in the debate on the resignation on 17 June, linking the scandal to the decay of the government and the kind of society that the Tories had created. Although its whole security aspect was bogus, it was, overall, a piece of political management that secured maximum advantage for the Labour Party.

On 21 June the Conservative government established an inquiry under Lord Denning. Goodman advised Wilson that 'Denning should be told that everything to do with the case which had been received by any Labour Member of Parliament had already been sent to the Prime Minister, and that no further help could therefore be given.'[27] If Goodman did not know about Version 'A' at the time he gave this advice he was soon to find out about it. On 5 July the *Spectator* carried an article by Anthony West. This had been titled 'Thoughts of a Stranger Passing Through' but when Ian Gilmour saw the proofs, he changed it to 'McCarthy in Westminster'. The article provoked the following letter from Goodman Derrick & Co. on behalf of George Wigg:

In the course of this article the author imputes to our client conduct of a most discreditable kind in that he alleges that he is 'an industrious garbage collector' and that he is engaged in this country in the deliberate exploitation of the techniques and methods of the late Senator McCarthy for the purpose of vilifying and destroying the reputations of innocent men.

It is difficult to conceive a graver libel against a Member of Parliament.[28]

In November 1965, when documents relating to the case reached the *Spectator*'s solicitor, Peter Carter Ruck at Oswald Hickson, Collier & Co., both Version 'A' and Version 'B' were included, though they were listed as one document. It was a critical error by Goodman. It allowed the defence to insert a new paragraph in their Particulars:

The contents of the document headed 'An appreciation of the Keeler case by George Wigg 29 March 1963' and beginning 'In my opinion Profumo was never at any time a security risk' together with the fact that the Plaintiff continued after 29th March to carry out investigations relating to the conduct and resignation of Profumo and continued with the collection and collation of information relating thereto.[29]

Though the case continued until March 1968 and Goodman continued to insist that it was the most serious political libel he had ever had to deal with, his 'absurd hyperbole', as Gilmour described it, was now defensive. The matter was settled and a statement issued that accepted that the article was fair comment but apologized to Wigg for the suggestion that he 'had ever sought to put forward as fact matter which he did not sincerely believe to be well-founded'.[30] By that stage the priority for Goodman was to keep the Prime Minister, Harold Wilson, out of the affair. It was Wilson who selected the documents to be sent to Macmillan, who knew that not all the relevant documents had been shown to Denning and who knew during the Commons debate that Profumo was judged by his own key adviser on these things not to be a security risk. He judged that the destruction of an individual career was a price worth paying for the political advantage gained.

Goodman's role in the Profumo affair consolidated his position with Wilson, but it was his contacts in the television industry that allowed him to make his most important contribution to the Labour

Party. During the 1959 general election a bus strike had harmed Labour's prospects. As Labour approached the 1964 general election a strike was called by the Association of Cinematograph, Television and Allied Technicians (ACCT). The strike affected all the independent television companies, three of whom – Southern Television, Granada and TWW – were Goodman's clients. This put him in a slightly awkward position when George Wigg, who was trying to settle the strike on instructions from Harold Wilson, asked him to act as an intermediary between Jack Hylton, a leading member of the board of TWW, and George Elvin, the ACTT's general secretary.

The two sides were assembled at Goodman's flat at Ashley Gardens, near Victoria station, one of the first of the extraordinary negotiations that were to take place in his various apartments. In his account he devised a 'peace formula' that he thought would be acceptable to both sides. However, Wilson dismissed it as too 'legalistic' and wrote out his own draft. Goodman, 'as a matter of deference' to Wilson, presented the formula to Elvin, who rejected it. Goodman now laid the Wilson draft aside and presented his version. He then proceeded to push this in a further long meeting, going on well into the early hours of the morning. Finally Elvin, having consulted several members of his executive on Goodman's phone, accepted the proposal. This was the end of the strike and the technicians returned to work. Wilson, grateful and impressed, promised Goodman that his name would be kept out of the papers since, in Goodman's words: 'I had then, and retain, a keen dislike for gratuitous publicity.'[31] The key word is 'gratuitous'. Goodman was slightly worried that some of his television and other clients would not like the fact that their lawyer had been involved in the strike.

The postscript to the story eventually benefited everyone but came about in a strange way. Wilson told the press that a Mr X had helped to settle the dispute. This, of course, pushed the story up the news agenda because everyone immediately wanted to know who Mr X was. A few days later someone in Wilson's office, probably Wigg, leaked Goodman's name to the papers. The result was that the coverage of the settlement of the dispute, for which Wilson got credit, was carried over a number of days and Goodman, whose visibility had been enhanced by the *Spectator* case, became even better known. After the *Daily Telegraph* carried the Mr X story without naming Goodman, the *Financial Times* of 8 July 1964 ran the details:

The fact that there is still any doubt about whether Mr Arnold Goodman was or wasn't the Mr X of the television dispute is a considerable tribute to the loyalty of his friends. Goodman is not a man one would pick for his inconspicuousness – he stands six feet two inches in his socks, and though I cannot speak for his weight, an answer of over twenty stone would not surprise me. No one, however, does more good, covert work to spread peace and goodwill in a naturally fractious industry. If he tried to persuade you to take cyanide, you'd probably finish by doing it with a smile but of course that's not the sort of thing he works for. Charm, wit, and above all sheer persuasiveness are the qualities that most impress his friends. This is partly based on the reasoning power of an eminent, academic lawyer, partly on the fact that he is usually espousing good causes. His political background – he was Hugh Gaitskell's legal man, and a close friend of both Gaitskell and Bevan – has made him many friends in the trade union world as well as in politics and entertainment. All this qualifies him to be Mr X, and the closer you look, the better he fits the part. One of Goodman's earlier triumphs of mediation was between Mr Elvin's ACTT and the Boulting brothers. I can't say that Goodman was Mr X; but if he wasn't it must have been someone very like him.

Goodman's life managed to acquire layers of unnecessary complexity, but this was not always his fault. Wilson produced an excellent story which maximized the good publicity for the Labour leader as a peacemaker in industrial relations and provided a contrast with 1959 and the inability of the then Labour leader to fix a bus strike in the run-up to an election.

At the same time Goodman was settling the strike he was working on another front to keep Labour's involvement in further Tory sleaze out of the press. On 12 July 1964 the *Sunday Mirror* carried a story under the banner headline 'Peer and a Gangster: Yard Inquiry. Probe of Public Men at Seaside Parties'. The piece as it appeared on that first Sunday did not name the Conservative peer Robert Boothby but reported that the Chief Commissioner of the Metropolitan Police had ordered an investigation into allegations that a peer was linked to leading London underworld figures and had been involved in homosexual parties in Mayfair and Brighton, and was subject to blackmail. The *Sunday Mirror* also had photographs, which it did not use, of Boothby sitting with Ronnie Kray on a sofa in Boothby's flat. DCS Frederick Gerrard was said to be leading the inquiry.[32] The revelations followed a lengthy investigation by the *Sunday Mirror* into the activities of protection rackets and gangs in the East End. As soon as the story appeared it was denied by the Chief Commissioner because it was based on a leak from the inquiry. On 22 July the German magazine *Stern* reported 'Lord Boothby in Trouble'. Although he did not yet know it himself, Boothby's name was now in the public domain as the peer involved.[33]

Boothby rang Tom Driberg, the gay Labour MP, to ask him who the famous peer in these stories was. Driberg replied: 'I'm sorry, Bob, it's you.' The official version of the story, faithfully recounted in Boothby's authorized biography, was that as soon as he returned from a holiday in France he retained Gerald Gardiner and Arnold Goodman. The two lawyers advised Boothby to write a letter to *The Times* saying that the allegations were about him and were untrue. Published on 2 August, the letter stated that Lord Boothby had come back from France on 16 July to discover that Parliament, Fleet Street and other informed quarters were full of rumours that he had had a homosexual relationship with a leading criminal; that he had attended all-male Mayfair parties with this gangster and that he had been photographed with him in a compromising position. In his letter Boothby said that the photo had been taken with his consent at his office (which was in his flat) with three men who wanted his participation in a business venture, and that he had turned down their request. He specifically denied the *Sunday Mirror*'s allegations:

> I am not a homosexual. I have not been to a Mayfair party of any kind for more than twenty years. I have met the man alleged to be 'King of the Underworld' only three times on business matters, and then by appointment in my flat, at his request, and in the company of other people. I have never been to a party in Brighton with any gangsters, still less with clergymen . . . In short the whole affair is a tissue of atrocious lies . . . let them print it and face the consequences.[34]

The result came quickly: 'Lord Boothby: An Unqualified Apology' in the *Daily Mirror* on 7 August. The article was withdrawn and £40,000 [£600,000 at late-1990s values and one of the largest settlements of the day] plus costs was paid in compensation. The editor who had published the story was fired. Boothby's biographer, the late Robert Rhodes James, in his generally bizarre account of these events, accepts the substance of the letter as being true.

There are major holes in this official version. Was it merely a coincidence that a Conservative peer was retaining the same lawyer as the leader of the Opposition? Why did Boothby phone Tom Driberg to ask him about the story? In fact the *Sunday Mirror* account was 'broadly true'.[35] Boothby had known Ronnie Kray for a year. It was an Establishment cover-up, as the leading authority on the Krays puts it, which 'earned Lord Boothby a small fortune for his lies, stopped a Yard investigation in its tracks, and gave the Krays virtual immunity for several years – from the attentions of New Scotland Yard, from the British press, and from the politicians at Westminster'.[36]

The introduction of Kray to the Tory grandee, it soon became apparent, had taken place under the aegis of Driberg. Boothby's main interest was in the boys Kray could supply and the sex shows that he could put on for his benefit. Kray enjoyed the trappings of high society and realized that an ally like Boothby could prove useful.

Driberg told Boothby on his return from holiday that he was in danger, and tried to save him. Driberg convinced Wilson that Boothby needed to be saved and Wilson referred him to Goodman.[37] However, there was another motivation for Driberg to brief Wilson and warn him of the Boothby situation. Ronnie Kray had a further photo taken at the meeting at Boothby's flat. This meeting was attended by Leslie Holt, a cat burglar who had introduced the Krays to Boothby. Holt was Boothby's lover. Also present at the meeting was a crony of the Krays called Teddy Smith and Smith was one of Driberg's lovers. Driberg had met the Kray brothers at one of their nightclubs in Commercial Road in the East End in 1963 and quickly struck up a friendship with Ronnie, based on their sexual taste for young men.[38] 'The rumour that he [Boothby], like Tom, had been supplied with sexual playmates has been unusually persistent, though never proved.'[39] If Driberg were implicated in the story then the Tories could turn the sleaze on to Wilson and the Labour Party, nullifying the effect of the Profumo scandal.

Ironically the *Sunday Mirror*'s owner, Cecil King, had been keen to run the original Boothby story because it would produce another Profumo scandal during the run-up to the election and he thought this would help the Labour Party. The question is: did Goodman know the truth about Boothby and help in his denials? John Pearson, in his study of the Krays, states that Goodman had been convinced by Boothby of his innocence. This may well be true, but how much had Wilson told him about Tom Driberg? Driberg was a leading Bevanite, close to Nye and the Foots, and Goodman had moved in Bevanite circles since 1957. It is inconceivable that Goodman did not know that Driberg was gay. It was an open secret in Westminster. The suggestion in Boothby's official biography that Cecil King and Hugh Cudlipp folded because of lack of evidence is hardly tenable. They had photographs and witnesses. They could have made the story stand up if they had wanted to. Therefore somebody got to them. Boothby told Pearson that the person who got to the *Sunday Mirror* was 'the Little Man', Harold Wilson. Wilson did not want to save Boothby out of the kindness of his heart. Jack Profumo and his wife had been liked by Wilson but politics demanded that Profumo be exposed. Boothby was likeable but entirely expendable. The only logical explanation is that Wilson wanted to ensure that the scandal itself was killed. In these circumstances it is highly unlikely that once his own lawyer was involved he did not warn him. In my judgement, Arnold Goodman knew that Lord Boothby was lying in his denials. He knew that Driberg could be implicated, so he used his connection to Wilson to scare the *Sunday Mirror*'s management, who duly capitulated.

Boothby regarded the payout from the *Sunday Mirror* as 'dirty money' which he did not want to touch even though his own finances were not in good shape. He gave it away. The first donation was to the King Edward VII Hospital.[40] Boothby proceeded to enjoy giving away the money, mainly in covenants to members of his family and the children of friends for their education. In a letter to Boothby after the event Gardiner wrote:

> We were lucky in having Mr. Goodman's help, as he is one of the shrewdest bargainers in the business. It is, I think, the fastest and largest settlement of the kind ever made. And so it should have been.

Gardiner also apologized to Boothby for giving him such a hard time when interrogating him. Boothby later (December 1970) told Susan Crosland that he had given away his £40,000: 'the whole of it. I regret it bitterly now. But I felt I couldn't live with it. I hadn't earned it.' According to Driberg's biographer, Francis Wheen, Boothby sometimes: 'spun the same yarn to Tom [Driberg]; but on other occasions he hinted that he had used the money to buy a country house which he had always wanted. "Either way," Tom said, "he was wise to say that the money was entirely gone. Otherwise I might have tapped him.'" Overall, Boothby's behaviour over the £40,000 is more understandable if it was 'dirty money' earned by lying and the occasion for a guilty conscience in a silly rather than bad man, rather than a fair compensation for a vicious libel.

The Boothby case consolidated Goodman's position and his reputation. He had no contact with the Krays or the world in which Boothby was living his dangerous double life. However, in Fleet Street the message was clear that proprietors would do deals over the heads of editors when Goodman was involved and that Goodman had the ear of Wilson. When this was combined with his striking success in the *Spectator* case, the main justification for a 'fear of Arnold' was in place.

As the general election drew near the press attention on Wilson became intense. Goodman was on hand to keep journalists in line and also to keep Wilson's response to their stories in proportion. A recurrent theme was the rumour that abounded about the closeness of Wilson's working relationship with Marcia Williams. In 1961 Goodman had helped with the settlement of her divorce from Ed Williams. One of the rumours was that Wilson had nearly been cited as a co-respondent in this case. Goodman advised Williams free of charge and Ed continued with his career in the United States. But as the election loomed, so the rumours resurfaced, and they would not go away. The Profumo scandal had badly weakened the Tories and they were looking hard for a new scandal to use against Labour. At a Conservative Party meeting in March, Barbara Cartland had claimed that Wilson and Williams had been having an affair for the past 18 months. A coded account of the meeting appeared in the *Sunday Telegraph*.[41] The remarks caused an uproar at Labour headquarters. On 7 October Quintin Hogg responded to hecklers shouting about Profumo: 'If you can tell me that there are no adulterers on the front bench of the Labour Party you can talk to me about Profumo.'[42] There were only a few days before polling and the Wilson entourage was devastated by the attack because the last thing they wanted was the final days of the general-election campaign focused on such issues. Williams locked herself in her hotel bedroom and emerged 'tearful, red-faced and slightly hysterical'.[43]

Wilson was speaking in the Bullring in Birmingham. After the speech he retired to the Albany Hotel, where he was told that there was trouble with Williams. She was demanding that they issue a writ against Hogg. 'Harold is sucking his pipe, Marcia is in a state of hysteria, Mary is in a corner in tears, all sorts of things are being flung around the room. I hope to God it doesn't get out.'[44] It was probably on this intense night that Williams directly asked Goodman to issue a writ. Goodman refused, judging that a writ would only give more life to the story, and 'provoked an outburst of considerable ferocity'.[45] He then got on to Wilson and advised him against taking any action. Wilson agreed and enlisted Lord Attlee to deliver a powerful rebuke to Hailsham which swung the issue back against the Tories. It was a timely and important intervention by Goodman which prevented the story dominating the final days of the campaign, but it earned him Williams's lasting distrust because at a crucial moment his advice had been preferred to hers.[46]

Wilson himself remained highly sensitive on the issue. Anthony Howard and Richard West were writing a book about the general-election campaign, *The Making of a Prime Minister*, modelled on Theodore White's study of the American Presidential campaign of 1960. They had one meeting with Wilson as Prime Minister after the election, in the Cabinet Room in Number Ten. Overall, it was a strongly pro-Wilson book and caught much of the all too short-lived moment of optimism for the prospects of the first Wilson administration. However, there were sensitive parts of the story. As Howard remembers their meeting, Wilson was much exercised by Hogg's charge that there were adulterers on the Labour front bench and said: 'You know I must warn you that if you put a foot wrong it won't be a question of ordinary libel, it'll be a question of criminal libel and you can go and see Arnold Goodman if you like and he'll tell you the same.' It was apparent to Howard that Wilson had already talked to Goodman about this potentially dangerous aspect of the book, though neither of them had read it. So the entire conversation was a 'sort of high comedy really'. Howard and West ignored the advice and the book was published, without legal repercussions.[47]

Still the Williams story would not go away. In 1967 Tony Secunda, manager of the pop group The Move, decided to try a new stunt to help sell a single called 'Flowers in the Rain'. The idea was to market the single with a caricature of a naked Harold Wilson in a bath with two women present – one was meant to be his wife, Mary, and the other Marcia Williams. The Prime Minister was incensed and called Goodman. Goodman found a judge who issued an injunction against the band. With supreme irony, Hogg, one of the few barristers available in the long vacation when London was empty, represented the Prime Minister. The group and their manager offered no defence. The settlement was for all the profits of the record to go to Stoke Mandeville Hospital. 'Flowers in the Rain' got to number two in the charts and was the first record to be played on BBC Radio 1. It is still played today and royalties still go to the hospital. On the day The Move lost their case, the *International Herald Tribune* published an article on 'The Other Women in the Life of Harold Wilson'. Goodman was dispatched to New York. The magazine apologized and charities again benefited.

Polling Day, Thursday 15 October 1964, was the wettest of the autumn. The first result of the evening came in from Cheltenham at 10.02 and six further results quickly followed. There was initially a low swing but then, at 10.52, Labour gained Battersea South. Radio, television and the press ended the night predicting a Labour majority of 20 seats. The following morning Labour failed to win four or five seats that the previous night's percentage swing suggested they would take, and Wilson's forecast lead began to melt away. It was not until 2.47 p.m. on Friday afternoon that Labour won Brecon and Radnor and secured an overall majority. The Conservative Prime Minister, Alec Douglas-Home, resigned at 3.20 p.m. Labour had won the general election by four seats. It was a close-run thing but Wilson was now Prime Minister. And Goodman had played a key role. He had advised during the Profumo scandal and on the Vassall Inquiry, he had helped settle the television strike, kept Labour out of the Boothby scandal by killing the story and kept a lid on the Marcia Williams situation. All these were considerable contributions. In such a close election result many factors can have an influence. Goodman was one.

At the height of Goodman's political intrigues the Derricks were planning their twenty-fifth wedding anniversary. In the event it had to be cancelled when Derrick had a heart attack: he died on 30 July 1964. He requested in his will that his funeral should be fully choral and held at St Dunstan-in-the-West; the Rev. J. Satterthwaite wrote to his widow afterwards and said how difficult it was for the choir to sing at his funeral when they were all so upset at his passing. Derrick's death was a watershed. With Derrick gone and the gradual growth of the practice, the relaxed informality of the early Goodman Derrick days passed. The office became more like other lawyers' offices, though the range of clients and the style of its chief was somewhat different. Harold Wilson phoned on his first day in Number Ten to ask Goodman about the fate of the Royal Philharmonic Orchestra. This was Goodman's first consultation on Arts policy (and led eventually to the creation of the Committee on London Orchestras). The phone call was an early indication that Goodman was being considered for greater things; that he was on the inside track.

5

A Very English Sexuality

Marriage would interfere with my ordered life.
(Goodman in conversation 1993)

On 31 January 1959 Bertha died in University College Hospital of lung cancer, at the age of 71. The Letters of Administration were granted in 1960 to her son and solicitor, Arnold Goodman, whom she still called Abraham, and his brother Theodore. Philip Chody, a young lawyer at Goodman Derrick, dealt with the registration of the death. The estate left £5987 2s. 9d. (about £90,000 at late-1990s values). When Goodman's father had died, in 1940, he had been buried in the Orthodox Cemetery of the United Jewish Synagogue, but Bertha was buried in the cemetery of the Liberal Jewish Synagogue, the plot being bought when she died. The next plot to hers was taken for a single grave on 18 February 1959: Theo was later buried there. On 6 February Goodman had placed the following announcement in the *Jewish Chronicle*:

GOODMAN – on January 31, 1959, in the private wing of UCH, Bertha (née Mauerberger) widow of Joseph Goodman of 32 Platt's Lane NW3 (formerly of Oakdene, The Bishop's Avenue N2), dearly loved mother of Theodore & Abraham Goodman.

There is no mention of the moment of the death of either of Goodman's parents in his *Memoirs*, nor in the dozens of interviews he gave over the years. Death features a little in his conversations with David Selbourne, but with little reference to his personal experience of it. By the time his mother died Goodman was 45 and already set on a path of life characterized by emotional repression. He found no liberation in her passing and the pattern of relationships with women that he had already established was not altered. Bertha was the dominant emotional relationship of his life and in the years after her death he replaced her with a series of strong-willed widows.

Goodman's first mature relationship with a woman had come

during the war when he met an ATS officer called Pam Partridge. In the opinion of one of his closest and oldest friends, Frank Coven, and according to a sly hint in his *Memoirs* about an ATS officer, Pam Partridge was the love of his life. Perhaps this over-romanticizes. In the comparative quiet of life at Southern Command and in a period when he did a considerable amount of growing up, the element that is missing is love. Bertha was safely in London and could not supervise him, and yet his actions are not those of someone suddenly set free to explore whatever life has to offer. During the war he gave up drink and worked hard: these are not the actions of a person releasing the pent-up frustrations and emotions of a constricted childhood. Nevertheless, in war, as countless memoirs and diaries attest, the pitch of emotion is sharper and feelings more driven. Perhaps Goodman romanticized the feelings he had for this woman, in part because she, unlike many but not all his later female friends, did not become his mother in the end.

Pam Partridge was the daughter of a Church of England canon, which might have made life difficult had the relationship developed. Goodman and Coven met Pam at a drinks party at the officers' mess at Bridgwater, Somerset. This depot was where the RAOC dealt with the clothes, uniforms, helmets and so on. Weapons were dealt with at a depot at Didcot, and Coven remembers joking that a canon's daughter should really be based there. As he remembers it: 'she was the only one for whom I thought he had the normal, amorous feelings of a young man. I'm probably going too far. They were fond of each other.'[1] Years later Goodman recounted that he had had 'four intimate relationships with women consecutively . . . the first . . . with an ATS officer in the army. It was obvious that she had expected that I might marry her. But I hesitated, and she went off with someone else.' Selbourne asked him if he regretted this. 'I was regretful, but not for long.'[2] Later in the interview he summed up his views on marriage:

> I had opportunities to marry, but it always impressed me that marriage would interfere with my ordered life . . . marriage consumes a great deal of time that could be spent advancing one's career.[3]

As his ordered life had not really properly begun at the point at which he apparently loved and lost Partridge, it is perhaps to the second excuse that we must look for the failure of this first intimacy. He saw himself as an accidental bachelor, which implies not so much a conscious decision not to advance relationships as a failure to do so. He was still returning home regularly, had only lived away from home while in the army and was not yet established in emotional or professional independence.

In many ways his most intimate relationship was with his brother. Theo always remained a central part of Goodman's life and was his closest friend. To the public he was in Arnold's shadow, but in private the balance was reversed. Goodman looked after his elder brother, fussed over him and took him to events and meals. Though Theo had sexual partners over the years, he too relied heavily on Arnold. In addition to Theo, Goodman was always accompanied by a woman at social gatherings and became closely involved with at least five over the years. One of the closest of these relationships was with Sue Hammerson.

Mrs Hammerson was the widow of Lewis Hammerson, who had been invalided out of the army when he was 25. Both knew that he would not grow old and he died aged 42 in September 1958. In February 1957 Lewis had instructed Goodman to draw up his will and settlements. Sue met Goodman for the first time when she visited Goodman Derrick to sign the latter documents. By the time Lewis died the Hammersons had three teenage children and in the difficult period after Lewis's death Sue turned to Goodman for help with her own will. In July 1959 they met again and she was pleased to find that this busy lawyer remembered her. They became very close, phoning each other on alternate mornings at 8.15 a.m. He became a fixture in her life, bringing Theo to Sunday lunch and encouraging her children to call him Goody. He recognized that his appearance might be off-putting to children and asked Sue to let them come to him only if they wanted, never to insist. As well as a close friend, he remained her lawyer. He never charged her for his time, so she gave him gifts of silver: a silver tea service one time and a coffee service another. They talked of marriage for a while but she drew back and they remained friends.[4]

Of all the widows that Goodman was besotted with over the years, Jennie Lee, the widow of Nye Bevan and Minister for the Arts when Goodman was Chairman of the Arts Council, was perhaps the closest, in her personal style, character and personality, to his mother. Both were strong-willed, domineering and demanding. Unlike Bertha, Jennie was also a very sensual woman who intimidated men with her beauty, her brains and her consuming vanity. Goodman fell for her completely. He was constantly on the phone to her, popping into her flat and sorting out her problems. He wound up Bevan's estate and sorted out Jennie's finances, helping her become financially secure. He found a flat for her above his in Ashley Gardens. She would dismay her civil servants by bringing papers back to the flat and having Goodman go through them with her. According to her biographer: 'They would sit on the floor examining them, and Goodman would suggest suitable memoes that she might care to write to him, and suitable replies that she might care to receive from him.'[5] Throughout the late 1960s they were inseparable, and though Goodman maintained his links and relations with several others of his widows, Jennie was the diva of his affections. From his point of view she had everything and, according to her family, he would have 'married her fifty times over':

> What Jennie wanted, Arnold fixed, whether, as chairman of the Arts Council, it was money for the National Youth Orchestra, or, as her lawyer, a splendid and splendidly cheap house for herself. Friends speculated. They seemed so well suited, behaved so affectionately, and Arnold was so rich. Vincent [Jennie's ward] asked Jennie outright why she did not marry Arnold. 'You do not just marry the mind, you marry the body as well,' she told him. 'How can I love that body?'[6]

Anyway, Jennie had another lover who fulfilled her in these years. She asked friends not to tell Goodman of his existence; she needed him for more practical and friendly purposes, and this arrangement suited him fine.

At the same time as he developed his relationship with Jennie, he had moved, via his peerage and closeness to Harold Wilson, into the mainstream of politics. His proximity to events naturally attracted the attention of the society hostesses of the time and he began to get invitations to the various London salons. However, he was already well established with the leading hostess of the day, Ann Fleming, the widow of Ian Fleming, the creator of James Bond. The pattern of the beginning of their relationship was familiar.

Nineteen sixty-four, the year in which so much of Goodman's life changed, was also the year in which he met Ann. He was captivated by her. In turn, she used to say that he made her feel safe. According to Mark Amory, who edited her letters:

'A very large Jew' was how Ann described him to [Evelyn] Waugh, accurately, and one who had lived in a world apart from hers . . . For Ann he banished financial problems, a feat made easier by the unstoppable success of James Bond. Then he became the central figure of her life.[7]

The impact of Goodman on Ann's affairs was impressive. On 15 November 1964 she wrote to Waugh: 'Owing to my inability to understand legal gibberish and my folly in not taking the will to be translated when it was shown to me some years back, I am in the power of three solicitors . . . Bleak the solicitors say – the outlook is bleak.'[8] By 1966 she was recommending Goodman's services to Waugh:

> The only person who can save your trust is Lord Goodman, he admires your work, is clever and funny, he has done much for me and never sends a bill. He has saved me from the solicitors, found me a doctor . . . and can get tickets for the National Theatre. I seriously suggest you should seek his advice, would you come to lunch with him one day.[9]

Many of Ann's friends sought Goodman's advice, 'gratis',[10] and propelled him into the very heart of the social establishment. Ann had to compete with Jennie Lee on occasion and there was rivalry within 'Goodman's harem', but in the main he kept them, like other features of his life, neatly compartmentalized. Years later he was honest about the basis of his relations with women like Ann and Jennie: 'My successful relationships with women have been few in number. An aspect of the success has been the extent to which they have relied on me for advice.'[11]

For Ann, Goodman had a strong emotional appeal, he was funny and kind and supplied endless high-quality gossip from the court of Harold Wilson. For Goodman, she was a bossy, dominant and witty woman, who had streaks of Bertha and some of Jennie Lee, and who enjoyed the same games he did, but their relationship was not primarily physical. Ann once tested Goodman on the sexual side of his nature. According to her daughter: 'she made it clear that he could have slept with her if he'd wanted to'. He did not take up the invitation and the relationship settled into Goodman's usual pattern: close friendship, companionship and gentle conversational combat, but little more. They holidayed together each summer in the late

1960s and throughout the 1970s, but most of all they enjoyed each other's company and listened to opera together.

After Ann sold her house in Victoria Square and no longer had a settled London base, she needed a bolt-hole where she could spend the night; and after another arrangement fell foul of her liking for an occasional cigarette, she settled into an arrangement with Goodman whereby she shared his Portland Place flat whenever she came to town. It was never a proper second home and she did not move in, but after the opera she would stay the night. And so they became closer still.

Goodman's judgement on his failure to marry any of the women that he became close to was given to Selbourne some years later:

> There are indeed various types of bachelor, including the accidental bachelor, a category in which I would include myself. I am an accidental bachelor in the sense that I did not make a considered decision to remain a bachelor, even if all my instincts encouraged me to that . . . I have had many close women friends, and still have them. I also had opportunities to marry, but it always impressed me that marriage would interfere with my ordered life.[12]

In addition to Ann and Jennie there were other women who came and went in Goodman's life; and he was occasionally rebuffed. On three separate occasions he offered a lift home to widows after dinners or other social outings and made awkward verbal passes at them in the car.[13] In each case the offer was refused. Presumably in other cases it was not, but in no recorded case did a full-blown sexual relationship develop.

These encounters raise questions about Goodman's sexuality which go to the core of his character. If there is duplicity with respect to his sexuality, if the trophy widows were in some sense window-dressing for a different kind of life, then his integrity in other areas is suspect. We know there is a certain element of confection in the way in which Goodman constructed his identity, from the subtle change of his first name to the evolution of the way in which he presented his past. The question is: was he living a systematic lie?

The first element to consider is his opinion of the opposite sex. In his conversations with Selbourne, one of the more extraordinary chapters is 'Some Observations on Women'.[14] In the opinion of this 'late vintage' Goodman women are the inferior sex. They are more concerned with their status than men and have a built-in sense of inferiority which causes them constantly to be in need of justifying their existence. In turn this sense of inferiority leads them to assert their importance more aggressively than men and to defend their status through what Goodman called 'female argument'. Whereas men will give up on a bad position women will persist with it. He went on:

> The fact that I believe they are inferior intellectually does not mean that they believe they are inferior, even if their defensiveness may reveal that they have a sense of it. Indeed, it is unlikely that I could convince any being, whether a women or a dog that it was intellectually inferior. It would be a hopeless task; neither would believe it, nor want to believe it. Moreover, vanity, which is a characteristic of all human beings but of women in particular, prevents them acknowledging the fact . . . from the moment of birth, there stares at you the fact that women are in general intellectually inferior to men, it is not a prejudice to believe that fact.

Even though Goodman expressed these attitudes about women in general, he was prepared to concede that there were some who could measure up to men, but he would not admit to liking women in general. Then Selbourne asked him if he had ever 'suffered emotional turmoil caused by a woman, which made you unhappy'. Goodman replied: 'No, never. On the whole, my emotional sights are kept pretty low.' Nor did he think it was possible to have a true marriage of minds. He did not think women could hold a philosophical conversation, though he did say it was possible to like a women for her mind. But this was a rare pro-woman statement. A more typical observation from this conversation was:

> 'If you study the Bible, which I do not, the original arrangement was not to have Eve at all. I cannot think what was the inducement that persuaded God to create her.' As a 'helpmeet' for Adam, said I [Selbourne]. 'I do not see why He could not have designed him without the need for further companionship.'

Even allowing for some awkward attempts at humour, it must be said that his attitude to women was unreconstructed, though not untypical of men of his generation and social position. His attitude to sex itself was best described as squeamish: 'It is true that males have to fornicate in order for children to be produced . . . But fornication is a pretty minor process compared with the problems and labour of childbirth.'

Selbourne then asked, 'You used the word fornication, which in my ears has the sound of moral reproach. Do you have that sense of it?' Back came the reply:

> It is merely a word for a process. Copulation might equally do. I think fornication is the right word for a sexual operation involving both sexes . . . Bernard Shaw, in his play *Getting Married*, observed that the sexual process was sufficiently ridiculous to deserve being judged absurd . . . Whether he remained a virgin all his life must be a matter of fanciful speculation. His very elaborate description of sexual matters suggest [sic] that he did not repine at keeping his distance from them . . . because he might have found them easier to describe than to practise.

The question is, did Goodman practise, and if so, what? He described himself as a prude rather than a prig.[15] He rarely, if ever, condemned art in terms of obscenity and, though he was not on the extreme wing of the permissive movement, his views on censorship were not socially conservative. He once complained that he was unsure in his home life whether or not he could push his own interests. Later his emotional ties with both male and female friends were based on a combination of subservience, in the sense that they often sought his help, and dominance in the sense that he enjoyed the feeling of power that his ability to fix things gave him. There is little evidence to suggest that he consummated his relations with Jennie Lee or the other women to whom he was close. All this, taken together, might suggest that Goodman was a repressed homosexual or support the view expressed by Kenneth Rose that he was a 'troubled heterosexual'.[16]

What is the evidence that he was gay? He had a domineering mother and he never married. The physical evidence for some sort of psychological confusion is there in his compulsive eating and obesity. He befriended and helped a number of young gay men in the arts. On the other hand, the evidence we have for his sexual orientation suggests that he went in search of his mother in the series of women with whom he had long and in some cases quite intense relationships in his mature years: Ann Fleming, Clarissa Avon and Jennie Lee. They dominated him and allowed him to work through or perhaps re-create his complex feelings towards his mother. In the case of Clarissa Avon, the friendship seems to have been as much social as emotional, while in the case of other women like Sue Hammerson, the friendship was close and mutually supportive. Goodman could be good, warm, generous and loving to both contemporaries and people much younger than himself. In the end, aside from the odd kiss and cuddle witnessed by friends, we do not know of any sexual activity by Goodman with any individual, male or female.

We do know that he liked social recognition and standing. He was a snob who needed to be loved and loved to be needed. This was expressed most strongly in his relentless pursuit of friendship through contacts and work. Goodman was on the phone from the end of the Second World War until the last years of his life. He spent 45 years on the phone. This relentless quest for work, this unstoppable rate of advice, filled a void in his life which is usually filled by work as part of a collage of life which also includes home, family and children. For Goodman, work played many roles simultaneously. It was a means to two kind of ends. The first was money, to live in a style that suited him. But money in itself was not as important as the second end, social position. Goodman liked being the embodiment of the Establishment. He enjoyed it when people did things because he asked them to. After a number of years of success in operating like this he became increasingly confused and hurt when people refused to do what he wanted simply because he had asked them to do so. He was perplexed, when demanding that a musician behave in a certain way, if the person concerned was unimpressed by Goodman's allusion to the needs of important people. Being in the world of title, access, social cachet and influence, he was at sea with those for whom such things were meaningless or trivial. He accumulated social access like others make money or collect stamps. In isolation, such an underlying motivation for a life is trivial.

Selbourne, in an interview with Iris Freeman, compares Goodman favourably with Isaiah Berlin. Given the choice of dedicating your life to social success or to philosophy, one can understand why his friends might be defensive of the Blessed Arnold, but they presumably understand such aspirations. They will see Goodman's social success as a reflection of his standing in the world. For me, if this addiction to being at the centre of things were the sum of Goodman's motivation in life his character would be as uninteresting as that of Woodrow Wyatt. But there was another side to him. He was not only a snob. He did not only help those who could contribute to his networks or help him climb his social mountain.

His day would begin with a breakfast meeting on some commercial or later political matter, but would frequently end with him helping to settle problems in a friend's marriage, advising one of his many wards or godchildren or sheltering someone in trouble with the press. Often these people were neither rich nor powerful. These actions did not further his career or increase his client base but simply appealed to an old-fashioned streak of altruism that was part of his character.

While being kind to the great and the good and helping the ordinary and the obscure, he always sought out the intimate details of people's lives, and tried to solve their problems. He enjoyed knowing their secrets and while discreet about large things he was often indiscreet about small matters. There is something of the need for the 'comfort of strangers' in the way in which he lived vicariously through the problems and crises of others: the point is that the intimacy with clients' lives was a substitute for a real intimacy with people, as if he were unable to achieve intimacy with others except through the role of adviser and counsellor.

We need not look for a deeper or more defined sexuality lurking in Goodman. It is in the lack of a vocabulary of feeling; it is in the repression, the myriad of unresolved issues with his mother, his father, his brother; it is in his inability to form deep and lasting relations with women, that we find, not clues to the real and hidden nature of Goodman, but the nature itself. We have the emotional outline of his character, the scaffolding of his sexuality, but the building is overwhelmingly hidden. The best way of defining Goodman's sexuality is by placing it firmly in the midst of the ambiguities and repressions represented in this visible scaffolding. By which I mean that the clumsy passes at widows, the painfully awkward propositions, the many rumours of relations with men, are symptoms of what we might call a very English sexuality: born of the aridity of the emotional life of his parental home and forged in the serial compromises of self he had to make to shape the identity and social veneer he required for his chosen career. An English sexuality, that cannot be called clearly straight or clearly gay, but only confused and damaged.

★

The other side of Goodman's identity is not shrouded in mystery, nor is it ambiguous: 'It puzzles me that anyone should regard being Jewish as a problem', he told Selbourne, 'being a Jew is a fact of life, about which you need not worry.'[17]

His first practical involvement with Jewish affairs came in the army. Goodman had the special duty, while quartermaster-sergeant of his battery, of making arrangements that needed to be made for its Jewish personnel. They were not an overwhelming number. Apart from his old friend Dennis Lloyd – 'a loyal but wholly unreligious Jew' – there was a second lieutenant who was 'equivocal' about being Jewish to the extent of having described himself in his enlistment papers as a Unitarian. 'This was, of course, a philosophical truth since the Jewish faith prescribes a single undivided deity, but when I queried the description with him, he justified it on the ground that, if captured by the Germans, it would have been unfortunate for them to have known that he was Jewish.' Another was Sergeant Lazarus, of 'good, solid, middle-class Jewish stock, who in later years became a distinguished chartered surveyor, a leading member of his profession'. Then there was Gunner Cohen, who came, 'I think, from humbler origins, although with the Jewish community your social position is usually where you can contrive to place yourself.' Lazarus complained to Goodman that the battery had only bacon for breakfast.

> This had been a cause of satisfaction to me – to be able to claim that day after day the battery sat down to bacon and eggs, which I considered a masterpiece of provident provisioning. 'I have,' he complained, 'been breakfastless since I came to the battery.' I was moved and drove down to the NAAFI to enquire whether there was any breakfast food that did not involve the hated pig. 'We have,' said the manager, 'a nice line in kippers.' I was elated. Placing a continuing order for them, I returned to the battery with a large boxful to report this success to Lazarus, who gratifyingly expressed a great liking for kippers. All was well for some months until I encountered Lazarus in the courtyard of the elementary school, which was our headquarters, with a long face and an immediate grumble. 'I have,' he said, 'had nothing but kippers for breakfast for the last several months and I now hate the sight of them.' I rejoined at once. 'You are,' I said, 'an ungrateful wretch. I can do no more for you except to recommend porridge and toast!'

Gunner Cohen asked Goodman's help to observe the Day of

Atonement. The battery was stationed near Northampton. Goodman searched the main street until he found a shop called Molyneux Ltd: J. Rosenbloom, proprietor. 'Might I venture to ask whether – as I believe – you and I are co-religionists?' Goodman enquired. Mr Rosenbloom said he was indeed a Jew and Goodman asked him if he would be observing the Day of Atonement and if Gunner Cohen might join him. Rosenbloom agreed. 'I will come and collect him this evening, before the Kol Nidrei. He can join us at the pre-fast supper and come with us to the synagogue. We will keep him overnight; he can spend the day in the synagogue, break his fast with us afterwards and I will return him to you late in the evening.' To all this Goodman agreed.

> The plan worked admirably, with a slight hiccup that Cohen was not in fact returned to us for a couple of extra days! I recently gave a lecture on 'The Advantages of Being Jewish', but whatever the shortcomings of that great race – and I prefer to leave others to dilate on them – the spirit of comradeship and mutual help is unequalled in any other community.[18]

After the war Goodman's main contact with Jewish issues was through clients and through some private work with the Jewish Welfare Board. He did not become involved with the wider Jewish community until after his peerage. While still plain Mr Goodman, he once commented, he was unknown to that community, and it to him. Once he was made Lord Goodman, they became better acquainted. His first visit to Israel was in 1954: 'It is impossible for a Jew to visit Israel without being deeply affected by what he sees.'[19] He formed a firm friendship with Teddy Kollek, the Mayor of Jerusalem, but he was not an uncritical friend of Israel and attacked its government on occasion. In the main his professional involvement with Judaism was similar to the rest of his professional life. He spoke at functions, helped raise money for causes that he or key clients supported and chaired organizations like the *Jewish Chronicle*, the Institute of Jewish Affairs and the Liberal Synagogue.

Goodman did not feel that he had encountered prejudice in England, though he admitted that he had tried to avoid it. However, he had witnessed blatant anti-Semitism, though the prejudice he most often encountered was from Jews towards other Jews. What comes through from his conversations is a degree of competition between his English and his Jewish identities in different compartments of his life. He never denied his origins, never made any attempt to hide them – aside from the subtle post-war name change from Abraham to Arnold – but he also had a strong regard for England and the English and felt himself to have a dual identity. He told Selbourne: 'I am not a Englishman, but a Jew born in England, I owe a debt to England. I have had every conceivable reward in England that I could have hoped for, but I do not regard myself as an Englishman' and 'I like England. It is safe and secure here. Here Jews are in no way passengers. In many parts of the world they regard themselves as on approval.' Later, however, when he talked of Jews feeling ashamed to be Jewish, it was out of a sense of inferiority to English Christians, not to 'Turks, Eskimos and Hottentots'.

He was also adamant that Jewishness in no way affected his sense of patriotism. His culture was English, he was born in England, lived all his life in England, but he did not believe he had English prejudices. Still there were limits to his patriotism. 'Any Jew who believed in my country right or wrong would have to believe in every Jew right or wrong, how foolish that would be.' Goodman's philosophy was not to submerge his identity but to keep it gently in the background, a whisper not a shout. 'If you are a member of any minority the important thing is not to go looking for trouble, because if you do you'll find it' – a not unreasonable position for anyone.

Less happily he also told Selbourne: 'There is no anti-Semitism among the aristocracy. It is the upper middle classes who are the most fiercely anti-Semitic' – because they face professional competition from successful Jews. Goodman was as much defending the life he had chosen and the company he kept as making a considered judgement. Any analysis of the British Union of Fascists would illustrate the absurdity of the idea. In fact he admitted that many aristocrats would not have a Jewish doctor! Moreover, he later stopped offering advice to Sarah Ferguson, the Duchess of York, after she had visited an American country club which did not admit Jews.

His defensiveness towards the English was born of his social life and not derived from his home life. Bertha was more assertively Jewish and Zionist than his father, though she was also more liberal theologically. 'My life has not led me along specifically Jewish paths . . . I do not think I view anything specifically as a Jew,' he declared. There were Hebrew lessons at home and he could read Hebrew, he

claimed and understand 'synagogue prayers' better than most. The
two halves of his identity were not equal: the Jewish part was more
manifest in his being. To him the irreducible minimum of Jewishness
was the acknowledgement 'that you are a Jew, that Jews differ from
other people, and that you have a duty to the Jewish community and
to other Jews'. He felt the difference, he detected a difference;
between himself and Englishmen in a certain way of thinking. He
called it a reflex: 'the principal reflex is when you scent anti-
Semitism. However, it is necessary that that reflex should not operate
without proper justification. It is very possible for some Jews to go in
quest of anti-Semitism merely in justification for themselves in some
piece of behaviour.'

But while critical of Jews who used discrimination as a cover,
Goodman was also critical of those Jews who 'consciously left their
faith', ascribing this decision to 'cowardice, snobbishness and
ridiculous reaction to one's birthright'. When Selbourne asked him
about Disraeli and Heine, he turned both questions away with a joke.
On the former, who abandoned his faith, Goodman said that, unlike
Disraeli, he 'never had any aspiration to lead the feudal aristocracy',
nor did he think they would have followed him if he had. On
Heine's baptism in the hope of obtaining a chair, he replied: 'I do not
think anyone would be so foolish now as to abandon his faith for a
professorship.' He was always comfortable with other Jews, he said,
and when he wanted assistance he would seek out a Jew. Though he
admitted that he himself had made a compromise, perhaps feeling a
little that he would have disappointed Bertha, he compromised
between the rigours of traditional Jewishness and being 'sensible'. His
Jewishness was 'decent and not too onerous'.

In 1969 he formalized this approach when he and Theo joined the
Liberal Synagogue – perhaps, in doing so, disappointing the ghost of
their father. This balanced view, not denying his origins but not
being governed by them, was reflected in the significance that being
Jewish had in his life: 'I don't think that being a Jew is of paramount
importance to me'; nor, by extension, was it to his career. When
non-Jews spoke of Jewishness to him, he had the sense that it was
with 'covert hostility'; though those that loved Jews, whom
Goodman regarded as eccentric, would usually not raise the subject
for fear of offending. He believed that when there was a real
friendship between Jews and non-Jews, either could raise it. His
mentor, Harold Wilson, was certainly an example of an Englishman

who loved Jews and was a staunch Zionist. In later years Goodman was to be mildly critical of Wilson's attachments. In conversation with David Selbourne he said:

> He also had a penchant for associating with, and in the end honouring, rich and successful Jews. He need not have . . . The flaw was in himself. He was also the best illustration of the truth that anyone in public life, especially a prime minister, should be provided with a satisfactory income for his purposes. Because he was not. He was attracted by the clink of gold in the possession of undesirable people.[20]

His attitude to other Jews was mixed and not unreservedly positive. He told Selbourne that he hoped there was a hell, where Hitler is roasting on a spit: 'I do not think I would mind if Robert Maxwell were in the same condition.' But he did not think that Maxwell had inflamed feeling against Jews: 'If they think of him at all, it is as a born villain.' He generally thought that Jews had a greater proportion of intelligent people than non-Jews. Not that this meant all Jews were intelligent. When he heard a Jew 'enunciating Thatcherite doctrines' he would cheerfully have sent for a psychiatrist to certify him. In sum, Goodman's attitude to Judaism was a matter of loyalty rather than faith. As for the chosen people: 'the Jews are as good as any and rather better than most'.

Goodman had little to say about the spiritual side of being a Jew. The basis of his moral code, though in operation practical, was based on an individualistic theism. He acknowledged the existence of God because 'I always respect a widespread general belief. Moreover, most people would stop short of denying the existence of God out of fear that they might be wrong. If He should turn out to have the powers some people attribute to Him, He could visit dire retribution upon them for having denied His existence.' Goodman rooted his belief in a calculation of the odds – that most people believe and that the pattern of evolution suggests some kind of designer. 'While I pay lip service to a God, I am not entirely convinced of His existence.' And if he exists, then he must be responsible for the bad as well as the good: 'everything which is manifestly wrong with our lives could be attributed to His responsibility, or rather to His irresponsibility . . . If this planet is governed by a universal force, it is not governed as it ought to be.' Goodman, in this conversation at least, was both practical in his attitude to the possibility of a God and a little cynical in his justifications for his belief. For example, he believed 'on the basis that life is so short, and that only a mean force would have brought it into being without there being a further term'. His exasperation with the subject is quickly clear: 'All this is a mystical form of speculation which is alien to my nature. I am very agnostic about an after-life. But no one would want to dissent from promise of it lest they be wrong.'[21] In the end Goodman's views on God are straightforwardly Pascalian. In the opinion of an authority on the subject: 'He was betting on the favourite, without knowing the outcome of the race.'

By the early 1960s Goodman was approaching 50. His pattern of life was dominated by work. He was a very private man who kept the different aspects of his character rigorously compartmentalized. The compartment closest to him was his family. Then came friends from school, university and the army. Beyond this were the Friends of Arnold. The style of his relations with others was clearly established: people he met as clients, sometimes even as opponents, would seek him out after cases and become friends.

As he became more interested in the social rewards that came with acquaintance with titled people, he played a role with them which kept them rather distant from him. The result was that though the number of the Friends of Arnold increased, he became lonelier and was driven to make more and more contacts. Eventually the role he played for these people as adviser and counsellor became the person he was. This spiral of declining intimacy was augmented when illness made it harder for him to focus and he was in constant discomfort. The younger, funnier and more approachable Goodman could still be glimpsed in later years, but the more pompous and remote grand old man predominated. Though the circles of intimacy changed, his relationship with his cultural identity as a Jew was remarkably consistent. He became more of a public Jew in the sense that he played a full role in the affairs of the Jewish community; but the private essence of his Jewishness did not alter over the years. He always felt a dual identity as an English Jew and rejoiced in the nature of his difference. There was not an ounce of defeatism in his attitude to Judaism, but nor was it a defining characteristic.

6

From Mr X to Lord G

You will have nothing to do out here except commune with
the pigs.

(Goodman on visiting the proposed site for the
Open University)

Goodman had developed a strong interest in housing through his
association with the Centre Point development in London's West
End and other deals in which the Friends of Arnold had been
involved in the 1950s, and this interest in turn went back to his first
contact with property development at Kisch's before the war. In
1964 his old client Richard Crossman was made Minister of
Housing. Goodman became Crossman's unofficial adviser and
helped him subvert his formidable permanent secretary at Housing,
Dame Evelyn Sharp. The story is a classic of Whitehall manoeuvring
that could have come from *Yes Minister*.

A few days after his appointment Crossman telephoned Goodman
on a Sunday morning to ask for advice on an anti-eviction Bill, a
measure that was designed to build in some protection for tenants
against the corrupt practices of the landlords of the era. As Crossman
recorded in his diary:

> The draft Bill was sent down here late last night and I was asked to
> confirm the paper, which the officials obviously thought was a mere
> formality. But when I looked at it I was worried . . . there was no kind
> of protection for tenants during the period between the publication of
> the Bill and its being made law . . . I rang up first of all the Under
> Secretary at the Ministry who said no lawyer was available Sunday, and
> I then tried to get the Attorney-General, Elwyn Jones, who was not
> available. And finally I rang Arnold Goodman. That resourceful man was
> once again full of ideas.[1]

Goodman suggested a possible solution to the problem. The Minister
sent his civil servants to Goodman's flat in Ashley Gardens on the

same Sunday afternoon to take note of the solution. As Goodman commented: 'It was not for me to tell him how to treat his advisers.'[2] The measure was eventually passed as the Protection from Eviction Act, which prevented landlords of residential property from taking that property back without a County Court judgement. From that moment Goodman was seen by Crossman as a key adviser, but it took a battle with Crossman's new permanent secretary to have him accepted.

Dame Evelyn Sharp had entered the civil service in 1925 and was a formidable opponent: 'the daughter of a political clergyman, a keen walker and hiker. She is an expert on Town and Country Planning, a fierce opponent of litter and defender of green belts, and she has a reputation – very rare in Whitehall – for calling a spade a spade.'[3] Her complaints to the Minister were that an outsider had seen a draft of legislation and that her civil servants had been sent to get his advice on a Sunday. Neither complaint was unreasonable for the time, but her reaction must have been based on a fierce dislike of her new boss's methods, because she offered her resignation. Crossman told Goodman about Dame Evelyn's threats. Goodman's reaction was to lament that Crossman had 'lost such an opportunity' by not immediately accepting it.[4] By this time Dame Evelyn had been persuaded to stay on and a compromise was reached whereby independent, non-civil servant advisers – including Goodman and his old friend Dennis Lloyd – were allowed to work for Crossman. 'This concession having been wrung from Dame Evelyn, we were thereupon authorised to attend all meetings and to advise as though we had the accolade of civil service accorded to us.'[5]

But the civil servants continued to find ways of keeping things from Goodman. When the anti-eviction Bill was in draft a copy came to Crossman. Dame Evelyn told him that the draft was not suitable to send out to Goodman but that the Minister was allowed to see it. Crossman read it and decided that the only thing that made it unsuitable for Goodman was the word 'Secret', which the Dame had had put on the cover.[6]

Crossman increasingly leaned on Goodman for alternative advice and also for access to his business contacts. Part of the problem for the incoming Labour government was its lack of networks in the private sector. Part of Goodman's role was to bring the Labour Party into contact with industrialists. Before the election he convened an informal think-tank to advise Wilson on industrial policy, but his most direct intervention was on housing because such contacts are particularly necessary in departments like Housing and Local Government, which operate on the boundary between the public and private sectors. In the more corporatist days of the early 1960s the government's task was one of direct intervention, but, without the direct planning apparatus of the French, British Ministers needed to be able to talk and persuade people to take part in campaigns like the drive to build more housing. In the early days Crossman complained to his diary that all he saw was officials: 'I've got Arnold Goodman, who is introducing me on Monday night to a top director of Wimpey who might possibly be added to my staff as a director of the housing drive.'[7] Goodman's other main advantage to the new government was that he was, as usual, always available.

By November 1964 Crossman was describing Goodman as the 'centre point of his outside advisory group on rent reform'.[8] It was not conventional for a Minister to go outside his department for advice and his permanent secretary remained furious. Crossman, she argued, should have consulted her and not outside advisers. Worse was to come. Goodman arranged for Crossman to meet Harry Hyams, the Wimpey director:

> This evening I went to dinner with Arnold Goodman to meet Hyams . . . who Arnold thought was a possible adviser on housing or director of the housing drive. He turned out to be a man of thirty-six or so, dapper black beard and a nice, solid, tough wife, crude in his intellect, smooth and professional in his appearance. By the end of the evening he was trying to suggest socialist sympathies with me. It was clear after we had discussed things for a long time that he was prepared with his millions of pounds in the bank, his house full of Rembrandts and Picassos, to try Labour politics as an extra. I am still reflecting whether I should appoint him.[9]

Eventually Crossman brought Hyams in as a rather unsuccessful unofficial adviser.

Crossman persisted with his use of outsiders and set up two study groups to look at the issue of rent. The two groups met on 2 December, when Goodman and Dennis Lloyd presented a paper based on the idea of a fair rent. 'It says a good deal for Arnold Goodman's power of persuasion, but basically it was the idea of the fair rent that he had worked out that made it acceptable to this mixed gathering.'[10] Goodman's main role was in suggesting the creation of rent officers and in working on the various formulas for setting fair rents.[11] Overall the legislative achievement was considerable. The 1964 Housing Act set up the Housing Corporation to assist Housing Associations in providing homes and forced local authorities to take a more active role in home improvements. The 1965 Rent Act provided for the registration of rents, introduced the notion of a controlled 'fair rent' and allowed for security of tenure as long as the tenant met certain conditions. It consolidated the Protection from Eviction Act by ensuring that landlords had to get a court order to enforce eviction. For Goodman it consolidated housing as an interest and an area of expertise.

Crossman had first called Goodman for advice a few days into the new government's tenure. Wilson called him on his first day in Number Ten to ask about the Royal Philharmonic Orchestra. This was followed a little later by a call from Nye Bevan's widow, Jennie Lee, Minister for the Arts, asking him to chair a committee which was to report on the future of London's orchestras. The job was essentially a negotiating one and Wilson and Jennie had already seen how effective Goodman was at that.

The way in which Goodman wielded his skills as a chairman and a negotiator was to prove crucial in his ability to exploit the opportunity that Wilson's assumption of power afforded him. There were two key personal qualities that took this talented and well-placed lawyer from being another cog in the political and Establishment machine to being the universal fixer. The first was his style of negotiation: the ability to settle disputes and reconcile warring parties. The second was the time and effort he devoted to the needs of others in important places. His own description of his negotiating technique occurs in an interview with Naim Attallah:

> I'm immensely patient. In personal relations, I'm not so sure, but negotiation should be a continuous process until you have reached a conclusion. You should listen very carefully to what the other side have to say and make quite sure that they realise you do understand their point of view and that, if you are rejecting it, it must be for valid reasons.[12]

It is crucial not to be an impatient listener, he added: 'I'm very tolerant of nonsense because I'm very tolerant of the fallibility of human beings.' He saw his job as finding a 'tolerable solution acceptable to both sides . . . you arrive there by instinct'. Part of the secret of Goodman's success in these areas was the absolute confidence with which he expressed an opinion. Elliott Bernerd brought a case to him in the early days of Bernerd's time at the surveyors Michael Laurie and Partners. A young member of staff had approved, on behalf of a public company, a bid to purchase a business of 200 shops. He had not, however, made it clear to the vendor that this bid would be subject to contract. The vendor tried to get the practice to stick to the undertaking. Goodman said: 'This is a try-on, it's a nonsense. It will turn into nothing.' John 'Monty' Montgomerie, a partner in Goodman Derrick from 1963, took the young surveyors off to see leading counsel, who took the opposite view and advised them to prepare for a lengthy case. Monty reassured his clients that Goodman and not the counsel was right. It took many months of out-of-court negotiations, but in the end Goodman was proved right and Bernerd became a lifelong fan of Goodman and Goodman Derrick:

> Arnold from the beginning was robust, absolutely sure of himself and gave that warm comforting experience. His sheer physical presence and his soft voice – the thing about Arnold that was striking in his early days was this very large man – most people would have been frightened of him – but there was no bark, no growl – he was like Larry the Lamb – quietly spoken, softly spoken, very comforting.[13]

Unusually for a lawyer, however, he was not a detail man. As Bernerd puts it: 'You went to him with a very complicated issue and he said, "You need to do this."' He also wrote a good letter, going straight to the centre of a problem like a rifle with a telescopic sight rather than a scatter-gun. A partner from Goodman Derrick remembers:

> He had a fantastic brain. He was incredibly articulate, he had the most amazing command of English, and it was wonderful to hear him dictate. He could sit down and dictate almost word-perfect, a will, a complicated letter, pick out the guts of it, and he had a combination, which I'm sure a lot of the best solicitors have, which is an extremely agile brain, great academic intelligence, which he displayed for example when he was teaching law at Cambridge, coupled with the great practical pleasure in dealing with matters, getting to the bottom of a problem and then negotiating. So he had this, a lot of great lawyers are simply academics,

CHILDHOOD

1. Goodman's mother with her beloved Pekinese 'Pucci': the most domineering woman in the world?

2. Bertha's pride: Goodman (*left*) with his brother Theo, the most important person in his life, after his mother

3. The benevolent Widmerpool: Major Goodman, seated centre. Jim Gower is to his right

4. Goodman's quiet law partner and friend from Southern Command: Henry 'Mac' Derrick, with his wife Sybil and daughter Patricia

5. Reservoir Libel: Richard
Crossman, Nye Bevan, John
Baker and Morgan Phillips
leave the High Court during
the *Spectator* libel action, 1957

6. *Below:* Harry Hyams, the
property developer, clutching
his company's annual report

7. Lady Rayne, Rudolf Nureyev and Sir Max Rayne, who is holding a ballet programme

8. Ann Fleming and
Arnold with Lord
Drogheda and
Dr Paterno, 1971

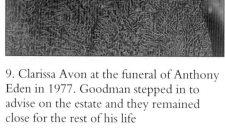

9. Clarissa Avon at the funeral of Anthony
Eden in 1977. Goodman stepped in to
advise on the estate and they remained
close for the rest of his life

10. *Right:* Goodman with his favourite
Royal, Princess Alexandra, 1986

11. *Below:* William Vassall arrives to give evidence at the tribunal investigating his spying, 1962

12. *Above:* John Profumo, who left the War Office after a sex scandal, 1963

13. *Left:* The cause of Profumo's downfall: Mandy Rice-Davies (*left*), Christine Keeler (*right*) and Penny Marshall (*front*) with osteopath Stephen Ward, 1963

14. *Right:* George Wigg, Goodman's old friend from Southern Command and Wilson's scandalmonger, leaves court after himself being charged – with curb crawling, 1976

POWER

15. *Above:* Three Goodman clients enjoy a joke *c.* 1968: Edward Heath, Jeremy Thorpe and Harold Wilson. Is Wilson offering to pay Goodman's fee?

16. *Right:* Little and Large: the finest double act of the 1960s?

17. Jennie Lee in the unusual situation of trying to get a word in edgeways: Goodman as chairman of the Arts Council with Lee and Lord Snowdon, 1970

18. *Below:* Goodman with members of the Council, Constance Cummings and Ben Levy, at the Wigmore Hall, 1969. He was the most effective chairman of his generation and his physical presence certainly helped

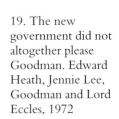

19. The new government did not altogether please Goodman. Edward Heath, Jennie Lee, Goodman and Lord Eccles, 1972

20. Goodman at the height of his powers in the 1960s

and others are not so intelligent but very good at negotiating, and enjoy the chess, or the legal cricket side of things, but he had both, in a unique combination, plus this amazing gift for English.[14]

Another witness to Goodman's skill as a lawyer was Edward Walker Arnott, later the senior partner at Herbert Smith, a major firm of solicitors in London. As part of the National Plan and the emphasis on technology in the Wilson years, the government was forcing a restructuring on the British nuclear industry. The government wanted British Nuclear Design and Construction and the Nuclear Power Corporation to merge into the National Nuclear Corporation. Goodman was the lawyer and chief negotiator for the Nuclear Power Corporation. Walker Arnott was advising the chairman of British Nuclear Design and Construction, who was conducting his own negotiations:

> The question to be faced was on what terms each of the parties would be prepared to go in. Goodman's mastery of essential points was outstanding. He had a stunning ability to make the parties see sense. He approached things tangentially, joking, making them feel warm and at ease. Then extracted concessions by good humour. He never put points doggedly, but made everyone see the funny side.[15]

Another long-standing client recalled simply that Goodman was the 'great comforter, who always poured oil on troubled waters'.[16] He brought these qualities to the complex world of London's orchestras.

There were four subsidized orchestras in the capital: the London Symphony Orchestra, the London Philharmonic Orchestra, the New Philharmonia and the Royal Philharmonic Orchestra. Many people felt that London was over-provided with orchestras in comparison with other capital cities and the regions, and that it was the Royal Philharmonic Orchestra (RPO) which was expendable. As Goodman recalled, this 'was regarded by the musical elite as being the least valuable and the least prestigious of the orchestras'[17] and it had accumulated a large debt. The Minister and the civil servants concerned could not simply make a decision on the merits of a particular orchestra, the level of subsidy or the overall need for subsidized music in the capital – a very difficult thing to quantify anyway – because of a political problem: Harold Wilson wanted the RPO saved, despite there being no additional money to save it. The

Arts Minister, Jennie Lee, decided that a committee should investigate the situation and that Goodman should chair it. The Committee on London Orchestras would be impartial. Paragraph 96 of her White Paper on the Arts states:

> The Goodman Committee has been asked to provide precise authoritative information on the proper cost of maintaining our great London orchestras, and the Government have made plain their recognition that additional funds may be required for this purpose.

The question which subsequently became a central feature of the debate on the Goodman Committee's report on London's orchestras was whether or not this paragraph committed the government to implementing the committee's recommendations. On the basis of the above wording, it is clear, as one of the civil servants pointed out, that it did not; but nevertheless the politicians, especially Jennie Lee, used it as an effective whip for action. The committee included David Webster, the director of the Royal Opera House, and Hardie Ratcliffe, the general secretary of the Musicians' Union. Its secretary was a young friend of Goodman's and at that time an Oxford don: Leonard Hoffmann (later to be a Law Lord). The committee met in the Arts Council's offices in St James's Square. Goodman rated Hoffmann very highly:

> He made an admirable secretary: he was good-humoured and patient and, what is more important, he had a rare skill in elimination. Obviously in the course of a commission of some kind a great deal of nonsense is bound to be said, and a conscientious but undiscriminating secretary will retain all this to the detriment of the ultimate report. Hoffmann had an instinct for selection that was near genius, and in the result the report was a highly impressive and convincing one.[18]

When the report was ready it was greeted, according to Goodman, 'if not with enthusiasm, at least with mild approval by that tiny section of the public interested in the wages and working conditions of musicians'. The substance of the report was to recommend the continuation of the four orchestras. It also recommended that there be an independent body – the London Orchestral Concert Board – run by the Greater London Council (which succeeded the London County Council in the mid-1960s) and the Arts Council, with representatives of the Musicians' Union and the Orchestral Employers' Association to coordinate programming and booking. The report said that £370,000 would be required for the four London orchestras – an increase in funding of £208,000.

The draft contents of the report were announced to the Arts Council at its meeting on 31 March 1965. In his *Memoirs* Goodman records that he was by now chairman of the Arts Council and thus reported to himself. In fact there was a short prologue to this. Lord Cottlesloe was still chairman when the recommendations of the Goodman Committee became known. He wrote to the key civil servant in the Department of Education and Science in some distress:

> To this must be added some special provision for the Royal Philharmonic. I will not rehearse the long and complicated story of this orchestra, but I think you will know it was decided, with the knowledge of the Treasury, to make a series of emergency grants to avoid a situation where the orchestra might be forced out of business before the Goodman Report was presented. Up to 31st March 1965 we had advanced £16,000 on the footing that this would be taken into account in any settlement arising from the Goodman Report. We are continuing to subsidise this orchestra at the rate of £1,000 a week, and presumably we shall be obliged to continue to do this until a decision is made on the Goodman Report's finances.[19]

Cottlesloe's letter also warned that, in the wake of the report, the estimated cost of pay claims from other parts of the theatre and music world amounted to £750,000. In contrast, Jennie Lee was pleased, because the report allowed her the scope to do what she knew Wilson favoured: 'I know you will have seen the Goodman Report on the London Orchestras by now. I don't have to tell you how delighted everyone in the arts world is by its contents . . . I hope very soon now to be putting proposals to you and I know I can count on your sympathetic consideration.'[20]

H. F. Rossetti, the civil servant responsible for arts funding, accepted Cottlesloe's reservations on salaries, and argued that representatives of the Orchestral Employers' Association and the Musicians' Union should be disqualified from voting in their own interests on the London Orchestral Concert Board. Goodman responded that he was 'quite content' with these points. By now he knew that he had merely to wait a month and he would then take the chair of the Arts Council and could reverse any changes. In addition to Goodman's impending arrival as gamekeeper, following his role as poacher on the committee, a joint internal response from the Department of Education and Science and the Treasury (probably written by Rossetti) argued that the White Paper 'virtually committed the government to accept whatever Goodman might recommend'. This would be the report's envisaged £370,000 per annum, divided between the four orchestras, and an element in 1965–6 for clearing accumulated debt, which was putting the RPO in danger. DES officials commented: 'It was largely the imminent bankruptcy of this orchestra whose management has perhaps been open to some criticism, which led to the Goodman Committee.' To clear debts 'would both have virtually limitless financial implications and would tend strongly to discourage the voluntary efforts by which most bodies keep themselves solvent'.[21]

The Goodman Report generated two kinds of opposition. The first came from civil servants who thought that its economics were simply wrong. The second came from people in the arts world who thought that the RPO was not worth keeping and that the money would be better spent elsewhere. Even after Goodman became Chairman of the Arts Council, civil servants were still questioning the detail and the general recommendations of the report. One DES official wrote that he disliked its implications and reopened the argument about 'the case for four major orchestras', saying that it was 'unconvincing', that the repayment of past debt was a 'thoroughly bad principle' and that in the light of the costed and uncosted pay claims: 'All this underlines the irresponsibility of the pledge to accept the recommendations of the Goodman Report, if indeed it was a pledge.' In June 1965 Rossetti returned to the fray, arguing that there were two problems:

> First, there is the weakness of the basic proposition in the Report, namely, that four symphony orchestras should be maintained in London . . . It is impossible, as I see it, to argue that a very convincing case is made out by the Goodman Committee for the maintenance of four orchestras. Secondly, there is the odd circumstance – at any rate to my mind – that this Committee dealt with the question of the appropriate income of orchestral players. In effect, what they have done is to play what will no doubt be a decisive part in the process of wage negotiations between the London orchestras and the Musicians' Union. I do not know of any precedents for such action but if there are I have never

heard of them. It is from the recommendation of the Goodman Committee that salaries should be around £2,000 a year that a good deal of the direct cost and almost all of the indirect consequences [result] . . . The whole situation is made even odder by the fact that the Orchestral Employers' Association and the Musicians' Union were both represented on the Goodman Committee. They were indeed half the Committee, apart from the Chairman . . . it really does strike me as a most bizarre way of conducting wage negotiations![22]

Rossetti's assessment of the Goodman Committee was shared, years later, by its secretary, Leonard Hoffmann:

It was fascinating to observe what went on there, because although in principle this was a committee to inquire into the London orchestras and decide what to do, in fact although I wrote a report, it was a union negotiation between Hardie Ratcliffe, the then general secretary of the Musicians' Union, an old Stalinist, splendid chap, and Jennie Lee on behalf of the Government as to how much money the Government could produce for the London orchestras, they and the GLC. Arnold simply brokered an agreement between them, and having ascertained how much money was available, we simply wrote a report saying that was the amount of money that ought to be spent.[23]

The Treasury broadly accepted the case put by the DES on the weaknesses of the report, its procedures and the difficulty of some its recommendations, like the repayment of debt and the open-ended commitment on pay. It then dragged its feet. In July A. F. Maxwell Hyslop of the DES Arts Division was asking plaintively: 'I don't suppose you've had anything from the Treasury yet?' Jennie Lee complained to the Treasury about the delay: 'I am becoming very disturbed at the Government's delay in announcing its decisions.' On 22 July Niall McDermott, the Financial Secretary to the Treasury, responded that they would accept the report but with four provisos:

1. That the GLC accept it and pay half the costs;
2. That musicians' pay should be decided normally by negotiation within the incomes policy and with regards to the £2000 figure, there should be no grounds for claiming it as government policy;
3. That there should be further reviews some years hence of the need for four orchestras;

4. That there should be more explication of the amounts of subsidy required. 'A point which need not be referred to in the public statement but which is of great importance.'

Before a public announcement could be made further economy measures were announced by the Chancellor, James Callaghan, so Jack Diamond, the Chief Secretary of the Treasury, and McDermott had to take a tougher line.

On 12 August a meeting took place between the Chief Secretary, Jennie Lee and Goodman. Lee insisted, in her own impetuous manner, that the White Paper had committed the government to implementing 'Goodman'. Jack Diamond was a Gaitskellite and the funder of the Campaign for Democratic Socialism, and not easily intimidated by Jennie Lee. He responded that the White Paper did not commit the government to anything specific. The Goodman Report was losing the head of steam that had been behind it earlier in the year and the danger was that it would be lost to cuts in public expenditure. Goodman decided to appeal to a higher authority. On 13 August he wrote to George Wigg from his office at Goodman Derrick, asking for help to bring the issue to a resolution. He told Wigg that in his view 'there is no doubt – if words have any meaning – that the White Paper contains a commitment on this subject' and that delaying the decision on the London Orchestras Board was putting the feasibility of keeping the RPO going at risk. 'A genuine crisis has arisen in the world of Art.' Wigg loyally brought the matter before the Prime Minister and on 19 August a Number Ten minute was dispatched with a copy of Goodman's letter. In the minute Wilson took the side of Goodman and Lee and agreed that the White Paper constituted a commitment to implement Goodman: 'He hopes that this will be honoured . . . The matter is of course now very urgent.'[24]

As a result the interim subsidy to the RPO resumed. This was short of the full subsidy Goodman had wanted but kept the orchestra going. It pleased Diamond because it avoided firm commitments in the austere climate of the summer of 1965. However, 'a subsidy on Goodman lines' was promised for October 1965, though there was no commitment on the £2000 pay level. The row was revived in November that year when the Arts Council asked for money for the remainder of 1965–6; the DES decided that if the Arts Council wished to do this it would have to find the money from economies elsewhere. The RPO struggled on without the permanent settlement in funding that Goodman wanted but with the administrative provisions of his report implemented, particularly with respect to the creation of the London Orchestras Board. In the short run a wage negotiation had been successful and the orchestras had survived, while in the longer run many of the arguments between musicians and management now had a suitable forum for debate. One of Goodman's better fixes.

Running in parallel with this work Goodman was helping Lee and Wilson in the creation of the Open University. The intention to create the 'University of the Air' was announced by Wilson on 8 September 1963 while Labour was still in opposition. It was a passion of Wilson's and, once he became Prime Minister, he was determined to use the resources of his office to get it started. It was, of all his achievements, the one of which he was most proud. His elder son, Robin, became an Open University lecturer while his younger son, Giles, took an Open University degree. Later Wilson said that the Open University was a 'brain child of mine, worked out by me in the early 1960s'. As one of his biographers, Ben Pimlott, points out, this was not quite the case. The idea had been widely discussed in Fabian circles and Michael Young had been impressed by the correspondence teaching that took place in the USSR when he visited in 1962 and wrote an article advocating the creation of an open university to give adults the chance to study from home.[25] Even though it was not purely Wilson's idea, he was determined that it would be a priority for his government and told the Shadow Chancellor, Jim Callaghan, that it would need money.[26]

The concept of the Open University evolved from the convergence of two major post-war educational trends and the ideological impact of progressive educationalists on planning. First, the provision for adult education, which had started to be built through the Workers' Educational Association in the interwar period, was now being widely discussed and implemented in other countries, including America and the USSR. Second, the growth of educational broadcasting, through the extension of the public-service provision to the new independent networks, revealed the potential for television to be used as an educational medium. Studies were being conducted by the Department of Education to see if a potential fourth television channel could be devoted to education, an idea which influenced Harold Wilson in particular. Moreover, a generation of politically active people were beginning careers in education and were influenced by the notion of spreading equality of opportunity. The higher-education sector was the most obvious bastion of privilege and elitism. The Open University promised a way of breaking down the barriers to higher education and inaugurating an era of mass access to university degrees.

All these developments linked up with Wilson's political beliefs and the rhetoric of modernization that he was so effectively deploying against the Conservatives. Moreover, an American friend of his, Senator William Benton, the publisher of the *Encyclopaedia Britannica*, had studied the Russian version of the Open University and was involved in distance-learning programmes in Chicago. These various influences, the opinions of Young and Benton in particular, were behind the message of the speech Wilson delivered in Glasgow on 8 September 1963 as part of Labour's pre-election programme. In this speech he proposed a set of nationally organized correspondence courses, primarily for technicians and technologists, designed for adults who had left school at 16 or 17 but who could reasonably be expected to acquire new skills or qualifications by working part-time at home. This was one of a series of speeches on the 'White Heat of Technology' theme. The idea was pushed hard by Wilson in the run-up to the election but the press, with the notable exception of *The Economist*, was almost unanimously hostile; for example, *The Times* disparaged the idea of a university that would provide qualifications for housewives. Jennie Lee's biographer quotes a verse sent into the *Listener* as summing up the reaction:

> We'll call every Tech a Varsity
> And overcome the scarcity
> Of buildings, by the Arm-chair University Degree
> The ethereal, Wireless Varsity Degree[27]

When Labour took office in 1964 the beleaguered government had no time to think of the Open University. It was only in February 1965, when Lee was appointed as Parliamentary Secretary with a dual mandate to sponsor the arts and create the Open University that Wilson really began to push the scheme. He decided to remove responsibility for Arts from the Treasury and offered it to Lee, who became Junior Minister at the Ministry of Works and then Junior Minister at the DES (Reg Prentice was Minister of State). In the reshuffle of March 1965 Wilson asked her to take on the Open University: 'For God's sake try to get this thing going. The DES is the most reactionary department in the Government: I can get no help from the senior officials or the ministers.'[28] Giving Lee this role isolated the Open University from other higher-education issues and from the normal bureaucracy of government. In turn corners could be cut, though only at the price of alienating, to some extent, those whose support would be required later. Lee was a politician of 'steely imperious will, coupled both with tenacity and charm', but she was not good at building bridges or attracting allies.[29]

Enter Goodman. Within a few days of Wilson's request she had, with his help, assimilated the PM's ideas and added her own. This intense briefing took place in the flat Goodman had found for her in Ashley Gardens. Once she had mastered her new brief she stuck to it without wavering. The Open University was to be an independent body offering its own degrees, making no compromises on standards, offering an opportunity to all, and without any entrance qualification. She scrapped the DES's scheme for a 'College of the Air'. She put the idea of a University of the Air to the Ministerial Committee on Broadcasting (a standing Cabinet Committee). This set up an Advisory Committee on Broadcasting to explore the educational functions and content of the University of the Air. The advisory committee's terms of reference were unusually specific: it was not to examine anything but the feasibility of a University of the Air as described in Wilson's speech of 1963 in Glasgow.

Lee insisted on being Chair of the advisory committee. It meant that, as the Minister responsible, she could not be independent of its findings. Throughout the short life of the committee she reported directly to Wilson. The general view was that, sooner or later, the idea of a University of the Air would be dropped. The committee first met on 8 June 1965 and its work was completed by 4 August. Its report was produced unchanged as Paragraph 8 of the White Paper *A University of the Air*, published in February 1966.[30] The report embodied principals laid down by Lee and offered a first outline of possible courses of study. It did not consider questions of resources or finance, which had been referred to the Official Committee on Broadcasting, composed of civil servants.

The conclusions of the Official Committee, which had been delivered the previous month, were that the 'University of the Air' would require the establishment of a fourth television network, at a capital cost of £42 million and an annual cost of about £18 million. The general tone of the report was negative and Lee's Cabinet opponents, armed with its conclusions, would be difficult to convince.

On 6 February, at a meeting of the Cabinet and the Labour Party's NEC, Lee presented her White Paper. According to Wilson, it was a moving occasion. No particulars were given of how this university would be set up, nor any date for its creation. Lee told her colleagues that the questions remaining were cost and the television channel: BBC or a fourth television network. Many members of the Cabinet suggested the hours 6–9 p.m. five days a week on BBC2 for this project. Lee agreed: 'I consider this the ideal solution. In these fifteen hours all the original programmes we needed could be presented and the repeat programmes could be offered on other channels.' She believed it was vital that the programmes should have a regular place in a single network – students should not be expected to jump around from one channel to another. On 8 February 1966 she wrote to Goodman:

> What we need now is a realistic assessment of the relative costs of launching the University of the Air on BBC2 and the fourth channel. The Cabinet are convinced that you are the best person to help on this and were unanimous in asking me to approach you.

This invitation to make an independent assessment of costs clearly overrode the report of the Official Committee on Broadcasting – annoying the relevant civil servants.

Lee had to fight a formidable body of opposition in Cabinet to get a firm announcement that the government would proceed. The Labour government was still working with a tiny majority. Lee was convinced that a fourth television channel must be available but the opposition was too strong and at a Cabinet meeting on 8 February she was forced to compromise. That day she wrote to Goodman that there was unanimous agreement that the University should be launched if it could be made financially possible.

But time was short. Wilson wanted a White Paper to be published before the election in March, and could not wait for Goodman's report. The White Paper *A University of the Air* was a compromise produced by the DES, shelving the two crucial questions of costs and the fourth television channel. The press reaction was at best lukewarm, while educators and broadcasters were doubtful. But Lee had succeeded in including in the election manifesto for March 1966 this statement: 'We shall establish the University of the Air by using TV and radio and comparable facilities . . . This Open University will obviously extend the best teaching facilities and give everyone the opportunity of study for a full degree.'

After the 1966 general election Lee returned to the DES. By July a sterling crisis had resulted in a bank rate of seven per cent, tax increases, credit restraints and a prices and incomes freeze. Throughout this period Goodman had been working hard to settle the two remaining questions of costs and the additional television channel. By 23 February he had seen Sir Hugh Greene, Director-General of the BBC, for preliminary discussions of costs. Greene was very cooperative. The BBC completed careful analyses of the overall cost of putting programmes on television and radio. It calculated that it could start broadcasting in 1968, and estimated that 32 hours per week could be made available on BBC2 at a total annual cost for production and transmission of about £2 million at 1965 prices. In addition it provided considerable detail on staffing and back-up facilities.

On 25 May Goodman's report was sent to Wilson. It recommended the use of the BBC to launch the Open University since no major costs would be involved, as there would be if a fourth channel were to be initiated. The report envisaged that the early years would be experimental and, if expansion were required later, there might be need to transfer to a fourth channel. The report advised firmly against the participation of BBC1 or ITV. The start was proposed for 1968, with ten hours of programmes per week on BBC2, rising to 30 hours in the third year. The estimated cost of the whole project would be £3.5 million annually. Initial capital expenditure would be just over £1 million.

Goodman subsequently admitted that he greatly underestimated the total costs.[31] In the Lords on 23 May 1974 he said: 'When I see the figure I mentioned and the figure it is now costing I ought to blush with shame.' He did not because it might not have been established except for his 'foolish miscalculation'. He took credit for having by accident made the Open University a practicable proposition. The Treasury was concerned that expenditure would be open-ended if entry were unrestricted and no qualification set. The first estimate of cost made by Goodman relied only on broadcasting time available on existing channels. The Treasury's suspicion of it proved valid.

Goodman's deeply flawed report was submitted to Tony Crosland, the Secretary of State for Education, who referred it to the Ministerial Committee on Broadcasting with a covering memorandum dated September 1966. Crosland asked his colleagues to announce the intention of establishing the Open University in 1968, or as soon as possible thereafter. Walter Perry, the first head of the Open University, thought the delay between May 1966 and September 1966 was primarily because the DES was not as convinced as Lee was of the desirability of re-submitting the project for Cabinet consideration.

Although there was early agreement between Sir Hugh Greene and Goodman about broadcasting, the BBC's own staff was sceptical about the project, in particular about giving up peak transmission times to educational programmes. In May 1967 Lee wrote to Goodman: 'The only thing holding us up, as you know so well, is finance.' She had agreed with Crosland that the new project must not penalize school-building programmes or other existing commitments. She was also anxious that the University Grants Committee should look upon the Open University as easing its problems, not creating an additional burden. No money was available within the funds available to the DES, and the Treasury was unwilling to vote additional funds to cover the new venture. Goodman had also been asked to see whether he could raise money from outside government sources to get the Open University established. Wilson suggested sources in the US from his own contacts: Senator William Benton and McGeorge Bundy, President of the Ford Foundation. So in February 1966 Goodman visited both men in the USA. He returned with expressions of interest but it was clearly too early to make any formal request for funds.

In May 1967 Goodman met Bundy again and told him it would be enormously helpful if the government could say the Open University had the support of the Ford Foundation, not only on financial grounds but in justification of its decision to proceed. Bundy invited the submission of a detailed request. In July 1967 Lee was making tentative approaches to people, with a view to forming a Planning Committee. She and Goodman had also submitted their bid for funds from the Ford Foundation. In July she wrote to Goodman asking him whether he was going to speak to Bundy again. On 31 July Bundy indicated by letter to Goodman that the bid was too large to be met by the Foundation alone. By the end of the month, the Cabinet having been won round, Goodman was able to tell Bundy that the government was willing to subscribe to the fund and ask the Foundation for a similar contribution.

At a press conference on Monday 18 September 1967, Lee announced that the programmes would be broadcast on BBC2 and the cost met from the funds of the Open University, not from licence revenue. The figures she gave were based on Goodman's of the previous year – capital costs of about £1 million and running costs between £3 and £4 million a year, when the University was fully operational. Students would pay fees comparable with those for correspondence courses. The rest of the money would come from direct grants from the DES.

Following the press conference, a planning committee was set up to oversee the launch of the Open University. Goodman, who sat on the committee, described himself as 'Solicitor; Company Director; Fellow of University College London; and Chairman of the Arts Council'. There were five Vice-Chancellors among its members. The committee worked from September 1967 to January 1969 and Walter Perry was appointed Vice-Chancellor of the Open University in May 1968.

On 7 June 1968 *The Times*, which had been hostile from the outset, queried the demand for such a university and also queried the budget. Not enough information had been made available, it said, for judgement to be made. Perry travelled the country talking about the Open University's future. Premises were an urgent necessity. He was invited to examine two sites within the proposed new city of Milton Keynes, and in mid-November 1969 he went to see them. It was a wild and wintry day and he saw the sites in the worst possible circumstances. One was a relatively small house, in poor repair, in a park of some 70 acres, bordering the River Ouzel. It had potential; Perry asked Goodman to visit. Goodman agreed it was a possibility but foresaw initial problems: 'You will have nothing to do out here except commune with the pigs.'

The site was chosen and the Open University founded. In part the credit for its creation must rest with Goodman's imaginative presentation of the funding figures: he gave the answer he thought most likely to move the project on. In this sense he was interested in delivering the goods for Jennie Lee rather than in making accurate assessments. This was not because of a personal political commitment to the Open University and the egalitarianism that this institution represented: rather he had 'clients' – Harold Wilson and Jennie Lee – and a case to win. His own political creed was more complex and more obscure than his actions usually suggested. Goodman's final judgement on the Open University, as on virtually everything that touched the magical couple of Jennie Lee and Nye Bevan, was warm and generous:

> The glum predictions from the established educationalists, most of whom were immensely hostile . . . have all been proved wrong . . . I will refrain from mentioning the number of distinguished left-wing Cabinet ministers who thought that such a project would muddy the universities' skirts . . . I regard the Open University as one of the major achievements of the Labour governments of 1964–70. I regard it as a great achievement by Jennie Lee and it is a matter of some pride to me to have been modestly associated with it in the early stages.[32]

The work on the London Orchestras report and the Open University consolidated Goodman's reputation as an all-round fixer. The regular evening visits to Number Ten took him deeper into the world of Harold Wilson. And he was not above showing off his access to Number Ten. On one occasion, sometime between October 1964 and July 1965, he was having a meeting with his old colonel from Southern Command, the architect Richard Seifert. As Seifert remembers it, the phone rang, as it did constantly in Goodman's office. Goodman announced: 'I must leave you, I have to go to Downing Street, to see the Prime Minister. He's having a terrible row with his wife! If I don't go down there they'll part.' Off he went, and later on in the day, finishing their meeting, Seifert, asked him what had happened. 'I've saved the marriage.'[33] Goodman's place in the Wilson camp was complete when on 12 June 1965 he was offered a life peerage.

He was introduced to the House of Lords on 20 July, standing at the door to the chamber with Lord Gibson and Lord Drogheda as his supporters. He must have loved every moment of arcane ceremony which followed and perhaps his mind turned to his father and the stories of Lloyd George's battles with the Lords. His recorded thoughts on the matter were not as disingenuous as some other passages in the *Memoirs*; after customary and only slight demurring, he wrote:

From Mr X to Lord G

Almost anybody who is offered an honour of some kind indicates that he has had a period of anxious, nay tortured reflection, but somehow inexorably arrives at the conclusion that duty demands – duty to his family, his wife, his children, his bank manager – that he should accept the honour. I am sorry to say that the same human impulses acted with me, particularly in relation to my bank manager, and I wrote a letter of acceptance.

Thus was Baron Goodman of Westminster born.

7

The Chair of Quangoland

In Jennie Lee's day, no one would have dared attack the arts in
the House of Commons.
(Goodman in conversation with David Selbourne, 1993)

Harold Wilson was in artistic matters a Philistine.
(Goodman in his *Memoirs*)

Jennie Lee called Goodman in April 1965 and asked him to become
Chairman of the Arts Council. The call came at a moment when
Goodman could not, in his own words, 'conceal my increasing
impatience and distaste for a legal system of almost demented
formalism where the ritual was far more important to the practitioners than any other element'.[1] The legal profession, in the
conventional way in which it was practised, was not enough.

Goodman had developed a number of laws of life which were not
in tune with the style of English legal procedures. His first law was:

Always go straight to the top. If you can not reach the top person
yourself then find someone in a position of power who has some
influence in the matter and get them to intercede on your behalf.

His second law was:

Should reason fail use humour. If humour fails use a threat but always
wrap the threat in the velvet gloves of charm and keep it vague.

Both laws worked well in unconventional situations which straddled
the worlds of politics and the media, but sometimes the 'thickets' of
the law disrupted Goodman's smooth passage. This he found
frustrating. So he looked for a world in which his own laws of life
could be useful but in which there was more freedom of action than
in conventional law. He found it in the realm of public service,
particularly in the grey areas of the committees and councils that
administered the expanses of the public sector that had grown in the

"I am aware of Lord Goodman's opinon that the British Legal System is 'Demented', nevertheless this boy did willfully commit the serious crime of acquiring sixpennyworh of sweets after legal shopping hours."

Sunday Express, September 27th, 1970

years since 1945; the institutions known as quangos and defined as 'the secondary institutions of the bureaucratic fringe'.[2]

The land of quangos was peopled by self-important committees charged with running a permanent but not a solid state. It was permanent in the sense that since the war the presumption had been that the role of the state would steadily increase and there would be an inevitable growth in areas of activity which were regulated and planned. It was not a solid state because its committees rose and fell as issues came up, organizations had to be self-perpetuating to ensure their survival and the individuals who ran this world of public service developed careers with structures, hierarchies and networks all of their own. In 1957 the writer William Cooper described the people of this world thus:

A dozen men are standing about in a nondescript room that contains a carpet, a desk, a glass-fronted book-case, possibly a picture, and a big table: a dozen men of not all shapes and sizes. Of all sizes possibly, but of a family resemblance in shape, heavily muscled, substantial, pretty masculine men, men who probably played games well in their youth and have certainly enjoyed sustained robust health ever since. The committee man is characterized by energy and stamina; he can go on for hours – he will never get his way if he cannot. His facial expression is sharp and intelligent but not given to sudden changes, least of all changes indicating passing emotion. His voice is loud – the committee man does not have to be asked to speak up. He stands around chatting genially, possibly jocularly, about one of that morning's letters to *The Times*, until the chairman's voice sounds unhurriedly above the rest. 'Well, gentle-men, shall we get round the table?' The committee man loves his job. It would not be unusual to hear two members of our type of committee reminiscing nostalgically about the days during the war when life was really lived to the full – when they went home at half-past nine instead of six! . . . Is the committee man who governs us a ruthless wielder of power? asks the beady-eyed, non-committee, governed man. The answer is that he may or may not be, in any case, that is not how it seems to him.[3]

Though Goodman was not the typical physical type, in everything else he became the British standard. The motivations, the politics and the influence of the people in Quangoland are difficult to untangle: it is a self-assessing world in which circles of contact and mutual admiration perpetuate careers. Amid the ego-stroking and the social climbing, some remarkable work is done and some sound and lasting decisions taken, structures created and reforms recommended. In other instances the committees and commissions are created to delay decisions, to avoid political difficulties and to contrive the impression of action without having to implement difficult or unpopular decisions. In other cases again, charities are run successfully by people who give up their time because they believe in something and are prepared to give of themselves. There are thus a number of competing species in Quangoland. The virtuous and the unremark-able are perhaps the most numerous and the paradoxes of their existence are many. In the first place their growth coincided with the growth of the state and yet much of the lifeblood of their existence is provided through volunteers who have more in common with the Victorian philanthropist than the Communist bureaucrat. Second, they are often without access to public money or spend the bulk of their time discussing ways in which public money might be raised. For success they need access, they need to be versed in the skills needed to implement Goodman's First Law.

The more politically connected committees in this era had access to public money and lobbied hard for more of it or for more access to the benefits of state power. This much smaller set of commissions, councils and committees was the real nerve centre of the corporatist age. Its task was to dispense the public money, honours and privileges of the state. As the state grew, so its tasks widened and the distinctions between it and elected representatives or administrators of the permanent state became greyer.

This complex world was not controlled by the structures of free election or the scrutiny of a democratic press. To succeed in it one had to be effective, one had to have access to people with political and financial power and have a network of contacts who could solve problems. Over the ten years from 1965 Lord Goodman was the chairman of Quangoland. The height of his reign was to be the Chairman of the Arts Council, but his presence was also felt at the Housing Corporation, on the boards of the English National Opera, the Royal Opera House, the Royal Shakespeare Theatre and the National Theatre; at the British Council, the Observer Trust, the Newspaper Publishers' Association and on numerous committees of inquiry.

Goodman maintained that the Arts Council job was one of the few public appointments that he would have seriously taken on. It is hard to evaluate this claim because he accepted all the invitations he received from the Wilson camp: what would not have been acceptable? Nevertheless, the work that was offered in the arts was certainly the most congenial to him, even if it was his skill as a negotiator rather than his reputation as a connoisseur which led to the invitation. Initially he was asked just to sit on the Arts Council, which met every two months.

Two weeks later the phone rang again. Jennie Lee asked if he would like to be the Chairman. He took little persuading and the confirmation came in a note from Tony Crosland, the responsible minister, at the end of April. The news leaked out immediately and the first press reports appeared in early April, though he officially took up the post on 1 May 1965. Here he was to set a standard of energy and success that leads people in arts administration in the late 1990s to talk still of a 'Goodmanesque approach'. He was lucky in a number of respects. He came to the job just as the Labour government got behind the notion of cultural expenditure and Lee was pushing through her landmark White Paper *A Policy for the Arts: The First Steps*. But the job also suited him.

Government involvement in the politics of cultural dissemination has a long history in the UK. Lord Melbourne once said: 'God help the government that meddles with art' and he was talking of a period before the private patron had been replaced by the patron state. Indeed in the 200 years before 1939 the role of the state in subsidizing the arts had been minimal and grudging. The British Museum was founded partly from a grant but partly from the proceeds of a public lottery and from 1753 until the middle of the nineteenth century the purchase of individual items was on an *ad hoc* basis. The birth of the National Gallery was similarly haphazard, that of the Tate a long and weary battle. Until 1939 no government money was devoted to supporting the performing arts and only a tiny amount to the commissioning of new art. The first real subsidy in this area had come towards the end of the First World War, 'when a few artists were paid to record with brush and pen the course of the war and the men who fought it'.[4]

The Second World War was the real engine for change in the relationship between the state and culture. Indeed much is claimed for the impact of the war as a catalyst for the collectivist age;[5] in terms of the attitude of the body politic to state action, the forging of a political 'consensus' on the provision of welfare and so on. In all these areas there were strong precursors in the developments of the 1930s or earlier. In state provision for the arts there was a similar set of changes in attitude but a much stronger resistance to the notion of a universal or open-ended commitment.

Once the war ended, the incoming Labour government decided to make the wartime Council for the Encouragement of Music and Arts (CEMA) a permanent feature of British life. The Arts Council came into being in August 1946. The position by the time Goodman took charge was that state patronage for the arts in Britain had developed into three main groups of activity. The oldest group of institutions were the national museums and galleries in London, Edinburgh and Cardiff, which were funded directly by the state and not through the Arts Council.

The second group of bodies receiving state patronage comprised principally the Royal Opera House at Covent Garden, Sadler's Wells and the Royal Ballet. These had been supported by subsidies on an increasing scale since the advent of the Arts Council. The support given to this group was around £500,000. The London County Council (LCC) also gave a grant to Sadler's Wells.

The third group consisted of major orchestras and regional and national organizations in other areas of the performing arts. By 1964 the Arts Council paid out £1.9 million in support of orchestral music. Most of this was allocated in annual grants to six symphony orchestras. Two of them (the London Philharmonic Orchestra and the London Symphony Orchestra) were based in London, but the Council's grant to the first was mainly applied to activities in the southern and eastern counties. The other four major orchestras (the Birmingham Symphony Orchestra, the Bournemouth Symphony Orchestra, the Hallé Orchestra and the Royal Liverpool Philharmonic Orchestra) worked in the provinces and were also supported by local authorities. The Arts Council gave an annual grant to the two principal chamber orchestras (the Philomusica of London and the Jacques Orchestra) and assisted some 500 amateur choral and orchestral societies and music clubs, either directly or through the agency of the National Federation of Music Societies. Help was given to the Rural Music Schools Association and to various festivals, including the Cheltenham Literary Festival and the Aldeburgh Festival. Annual grants were made to the Society for the Promotion of New Music, to the Music Section of the Institute of Contemporary Arts (ICA) and to the Central Music Library.

In drama, the Arts Council helped about 30 repertory companies, almost all outside London, through grants or guarantees or a combination of both. Financial help was given by the Council in approved cases in which productions were exchanged between repertory companies. Transport subsidies were given to reduce transport costs for those who came from areas at a considerable distance from any theatre, and a small sum was set aside for the promotion of new drama and for travel grants to producers. Continuing in the tradition of CEMA, the Council also funded a specially recruited team of actors, who travelled from London to perform classic and contemporary plays in the theatreless areas of Wales and the north-east of England. The Council was also supporting poetry and by the late 1950s it gave out grants totalling £1850 to promote readings, festivals and magazines.

In the visual arts the Arts Council's work was varied and wide. The exhibitions which it organized featured both traditional and contemporary art. Many of them were arranged for festivals and other special occasions in the provinces, others travelled regularly to museums all over the country. The Council's own collection was continuously on tour. The bulk of the annual grants went to the London Group, the ICA and the trustees of the Whitechapel Art Gallery. The Council acted for the National Gallery in sending pictures from the Gallery's reserve collection to provincial galleries. Some help was given to amateur art societies and grants were made occasionally towards the making of art films.

The election of the Wilson government heralded a new era in state expenditure on the arts. Their ministerial home was to be transferred to the DES from the Treasury: 'These functions are accordingly being transferred to the Secretary of State for Education and Science, who will delegate responsibility to one of the Joint Parliamentary Under-Secretaries of State in his Department.' In addition there was a phased increase in the funding allocated to the art. The Grant in Aid given to the Arts Council in 1963–64 was £2,730,000, in the year ending March 1965 £3,205,000, in the year ending March 1966 £3,910,000, in the year ending March 1967 £5,700,000, in the year ending March 1968 £7,200,000 and in the year ending March 1970 £7,750,000.

Though Lee's appointment was called at the time 'a wreath for Nye', because she was Bevan's widow and Wilson had been Bevan's follower, it was actually a strong indication of political backing for a more active arts policy. The appointment of a proper Minister for the Arts and the transfer of responsibility for the Arts Council from the Treasury raised a number fears in the arts community. There was a feeling that political interference was on the way, that ideology would in future determine the delivery of subsidy. Lee both further unsettled some and inspired others with the vision of her White Paper *A Policy for the Arts: The First Steps.*[6] It was a clear call for a new era. Hugh Jenkins, later a Minister for the Arts, called it a revolutionary document. It began:

> No one would wish State patronage to dictate taste or in any way restrict the liberty of even the most unorthodox and experimental of artists. But if a high level of artistic achievement is to be sustained and the best in the arts made more widely available, more generous and discriminating help is urgently needed, locally, regionally and nationally.

The White Paper went on to paint a depressing picture of the problems which the arts, especially the performing arts, faced around the country. For example, there was a shortage of suitable buildings, which made it impossible to take any of the leading national orchestras, operas or theatres to areas which lacked their own amateur or professional arts. The White Paper criticized the backward-looking museums, art galleries and concert halls that 'have failed to move with the times, retaining a cheerless unwelcoming air that alienates all but the specialist and the dedicated'; arguing that 'no greater disservice can be done to the serious artist than to present his work in an atmosphere of old-fashioned gloom and undue solemnity'. Quite simply, Lee wrote in her introduction, if getting the arts to people matters, then 'all this must be changed. A new social as well as artistic climate is essential.' There was an ideological underpinning to this drive for the popularization of the arts:

There is no easy or quick way of bringing this about, the more so as too many working people have been conditioned by their education and environment to consider the best in music, painting, sculpture and literature outside their reach. A younger generation, however, more self-confident than their elders, and beginning to be given some feeling for drama, music and the visual arts in their school years, are more hopeful material. They will want gaiety and colour, informality and experimentation. But there is no reason why attractive presentation should be left to those whose primary concern is with quantity and profitability.

The key word in this paragraph is 'best'. Excellence was not to be sacrificed in the name of access. The physical places in which art was presented could be attractive and still deliver excellence. But more than this, the White Paper envisaged centres that could provide a venue for 'both light entertainment and cultural projects' and thereby 'break down the isolation from which both artist and potential audience have suffered in the past'. For there to be a balance of artistic activity across all regions there needed to be an arts policy which matched the new national plan for the economy. Each region required centres of excellence; London would not be divested by such a regional development but each area would be given something in which it could excel. It was to be brought about, as it had been done since the Second World War, by 'the combined efforts of government and of regional associations that include representatives of industry, the trade unions and private donors as well as local authorities'. In other words there was not an assumption that the state could or would provide everything, but:

> If we are prepared to accept this challenge, we must also be prepared within the limits of the resources that can be made available to give expenditure for these projects a higher priority than in the past.
>
> The Government have decided therefore to advance by stages, at each stage making the necessary assistance available in support of the following objectives:
>
> (i) Today's artists need more financial help, particularly in the early years before they have become established. Their ability to develop and sustain a high level of artistic achievement lies at the centre of any national policy for the arts.
>
> (ii) The Government hope to see a great increase in local and regional activity while maintaining the development of the national institutions. They are convinced that the interests of the whole country will be best served in this way.
>
> (iii) The Government appreciate the need to sustain and strengthen all that is best in the arts and the best must be made more widely available.
>
> (iv) There is need for more systematic planning and a better co-ordination of resources.

When Goodman was appointed to head the Arts Council and implement this revolution, reaction was muted. One local newspaper neatly summed up the extent of public knowledge of him at the time:

> Mr Goodman, who first came into the limelight last year when he was revealed as the 'Mr X' who played a big part in settling the strike of television technicians, is already Chairman of the committee set up by the Arts Council and the London County Council to investigate the problems of London's orchestras. Aged 51 he is a leading partner in Goodman Derrick and Co. Solicitors of Bouverie Street, Fleet Street, London E.C. He also acts as solicitor for three independent television companies. He was present at many of the urgent talks which led to the end of the television technicians' strike which put ITV programmes off the screen. He has represented Mr Gaitskell and Mr Aneurin Bevan, and acted for the Labour Party during the Vassall Tribunal.[7]

The various national diary columns also mentioned the appointment, and Christopher Booker wrote a profile for the *Spectator* under the headline 'Mr X of the New Establishment':

At the beginning of this week the press spared no effort in giving coverage to the wedding of the man described by the *Daily Telegraph* as 'Mr Peter Raymond, so "Teazy-Weazy", the Mayfair hair stylist'. Meanwhile, under the modest disclaimer, 'I am not a public figure, and I have no desire to be one', Mr Arnold Goodman slipped past his appointment as the new Chairman of the Arts Council with but a couple of short interviews and a scattering of bare announcements. Which all goes to show that, even in this day, if you want to avoid publicity badly enough you can do so – even if you are, as Mr Goodman is, a fascinating figure, leading a highly active life, holding or about to hold at least two public appointments, and one of the great 'originals' of present-day London . . . only a novel could really do him justice.[8]

Goodman's response at the time was rather different from the diffidence about press coverage that he expressed in his *Memoirs* in connection with the original Mr X stories. Booker had worked in Goodman Derrick and was worried Goodman might not like the profile. But Goodman replied:

I endeavoured to telephone you when I received your letter this morning as I was anxious to make it clear – before I saw your piece – that I would love you none the less and bless you with my usual fervour, whatever you had written about me. Since then I have seen the *Spectator* and cannot understand your having the slightest misgivings . . . No one can know whether a portrait – except as to physical details – tallies with one's own character or behaviour, but I am sure whoever the original of this particular cameo may be, he cannot fail to be hugely flattered. Moreover – as you have taken pains to put in all the addresses, the name of the firm and only negligently omitted the telephone number – it must be hugely good for trade. Law Society rules prevent me from paying you a commission.[9]

The main Arts Council consisted of 16 members, with four separate panels: Visual Arts, Drama, Music (including opera and ballet) and Poetry (which became 'Literature' six months after Goodman's arrival). Each panel had its own director, who presided over a sub-committee of experts or enthusiasts interested in its field. The Council's permanent staff were headed by a secretary-general, who effectively ran the Council as the Chairman was frequently only in attendance for one day a week. (Indeed Lee had promised Goodman that the commitment of time would be strictly limited.) There was also a deputy secretary, who was responsible for financial matters. Before venturing into the offices as Chairman, Goodman met with his predecessor, Lord Cottesloe, to be briefed. Cottesloe had been a member of the Visual Arts Panel from 1956 until 1959, when he replaced Kenneth Clark as Chairman of the Council. He served a full five-year term in this post, was a kindly but shy man and was replaced before being given the opportunity to make any real progress in the problems with arts provision that Lee's White Paper had identified. Goodman and the outgoing Chairman met for tea at the Travellers' Club, where Cottesloe told him: 'You will find that the staff are all a very good lot and that the secretary-general is quite splendid.'[10]

Nigel Abercrombie, the Council's secretary-general, had indeed served his previous Chairs well. That was largely because they had allowed him to run the place. Relations with Goodman and with the new dynamic Minister for the Arts were not so smooth. There had been early indications that life under the new regime was going to be different. Lee had attended the meeting of the Arts Council on 31 March 1965, the minutes of which recorded: 'The Chairman said it was without precedent to receive at a Council meeting the Minister responsible for the Arts Council's Affairs.' Into the comfortable world of gentlemanly business strode Lee. Shuffling in just behind her was Goodman.

The next meeting of the Council was set for 26 May 1965 at 2.30 p.m. It was to be the one hundred and twenty-fourth meeting. The incoming Chairman, having been briefed by the old, visited his new domain at 4 St James's Square. The Georgian house had previously been the London home of the Astor family. Goodman arrived and was shown round by Abercrombie, with a distinct coolness. He was conducted to the Council chamber, which had been the first-floor drawing-room. He turned to the secretary-general and asked him where the Chairman's office was. 'The Chairman has never had an office, but my secretary will always type any letters you want to write.' 'Well', replied Goodman, 'I think this room [Abercrombie's] looks just about right to be my office and my secretary will want somewhere next door.'[11]

It is difficult not to feel some sympathy for Abercrombie. In the space of two months he had lost a tame Chairman and inherited a Minister who attended meetings and a new Chairman who wanted his office. It is also a neat illustration of Goodman's capacity to be both bully and charmer. In the months that followed, having established who was in charge, he tried to soothe his secretary-general. He had little success. As he put it:

> Abercrombie for a long time could not be mollified, and if I had not had an invincible optimism and a buoyant confidence in my own notions, he would have reduced me to a state of hapless despair within weeks. The cold water he poured on my plans would have filled the reservoirs of the Water Board. But – sometimes very contrary to my real feelings – I maintained an attitude of kindly understanding, which must, I think, have driven him to almost homicidal lengths.

Abercrombie was a civil servant who had been seconded from the Admiralty to the Arts Council at a time when, according to Goodman, 'it was felt strongly that a civil servant was needed to install proper notions of discipline and control in the ranks of Bohemia'. A staunch Roman Catholic, he was cold and distant, could not really cope with Goodman and had no time at all for Lee: he told the *Daily Telegraph* that he 'hoped she would be spending much of her time encouraging local authorities to support the arts' – that is, out of London and out of his hair.[12] Goodman's assessment of him was, in the end, kind: 'He was precise, careful, just, eminently decent, but he was not terribly interested in and somewhat supercilious towards youth and experiment. He had absorbed civil service techniques and wrote letters of superlative clarity. The Arts Council could have done a great deal worse, but he was not the secretary-general required for a vastly expanding scene, with a Chairman and a Council anxious to seize the opportunities made available by increasing funds.'[13] It took Goodman two years to move him out of London, but eventually Abercrombie became a regional adviser and organizer, and rather a successful one in the Chairman's view.

Having established an office, assessed the staff and been briefed on the functions of the organization, Goodman was ready for his first meeting. According to his *Memoirs*, as he arrived a young man jumped out of a car: 'I have come to tell you I cannot come.' The young man was the Earl of Snowdon, one of the members of the Council. Goodman took a shine to him straight away (and Snowdon would use Goodman as a lawyer on a couple of occasions in the 1970s as well as during his separation from Princess Margaret). His first contact with the Royal Family had been made. Goodman assessed Snowdon, through ermine-tinted spectacles, as 'a useful member of the Council, remaining silent about matters in which he was not especially interested, but very vocal and emphatic about things he was concerned with – photography, architecture, urban design, and a multitude of other things'.[14]

As pleasant as the story of Snowdon's alleged first meeting with Goodman is, it could not have been the 26 May meeting, unless the minutes are wrong, because they record him as being present, along with T. E. Bean, Constance Cummings, C. Day-Lewis, Colin H. Mackenzie, Henry Moore, Myfanwy Piper, Dame Lean, Roberts, Hugh Willatt and John Witt.

The first meeting commenced. Goodman signed the minutes of the previous meeting, though he had not been present, and surveyed the Council.

> The first image to collide with my glance was Henry Moore. There sat this legendary artist – and sat was the word since for the first three or four of my meetings not a sound emerged from that splendid head – benignly and contentedly. He was never late, never appeared remotely bored, and departed the moment the proceedings concluded. He radiated a welcome which I found out later was an expression of a considerable degree of goodwill. At the end of my first meeting, Henry Moore came to me and said that I had handled the meeting as though I had been in charge of the Arts Council for generations. I found this a very pleasing compliment, although I have some doubts about how justified it was. As a member of the Council, Moore had no faults. He listened attentively, agreed with all rational proposals, and made no otiose sounds.[15]

Hugh Willatt, later the secretary-general of the Arts Council, shared Moore's praise of Goodman as Chairman. He enjoyed the way in which Goodman would initiate a dialogue with the members of the Council and join in and keep the debate going. He was witty and usually talked a great deal of good sense. Goodman's assessment of Willatt was correspondingly favourable; indeed he pressed him to take over from Abercrombie when the latter was moved out to the provinces.[16]

Next to Henry Moore sat Cecil Day-Lewis, 'a splendid head, a fine person, the Chairman [director] of the Poetry Panel and an informed advocate of the proposals his Panel urged upon us'.

Goodman admired him and favoured him for the position of Poet Laureate. Then there was Myfanwy Piper, the wife of John Piper, 'an open-faced, vigorous intellectual with qualities rarely found in the middle classes. Her heart always led her towards the side of justice, the side of progress and the side of liberty, and she was an immensely useful member.'

The meeting started with a welcome from the vice-Chairman, Sir William Coldstream, a portrait painter, whom Goodman did not rate highly but tolerated:

> As the vice-Chairman Coldstream had qualities, but they were not easily to be perceived. His most alarming quality was invariably at a meeting to take the opposite point of view from that which he had taken up in private. You went into a meeting convinced that you had his full support, only to find that since had spoken to him his views had swung through 180 degrees. Frequently I would telephone him before a meeting to sound him on some controversial issue and would find that we reached unanimity with the greatest of ease. But how misleading. At the meeting the unanimity vanished without any compunction or shame on his part.[17]

At that first meeting Coldstream 'welcomed Mr Goodman as Chairman and said that members of the Council were looking forward to working under him'.[18] The first piece of business was to endorse the decision of the Executive Committee that the Report of the Committee on London Orchestras be published as soon as possible. Goodman was, as Chairman, endorsing his own report. Another item, which also revealed his work in the background, was the discussion of the feasibility study on the building of a new opera house in Manchester, which would establish a permanent home for opera and ballet in the north. The cost of the survey had been borne by Granada TV. At the meeting Goodman said: 'There was evidence of strong local feeling in Manchester and he would not like the enthusiasm to be damped.'[19] He enjoyed the meeting and rated his Council members highly:

> Anyway, these and others constituted the members of the Council. We met every two months, with an Executive meeting in between, but it was clear that we had too much to do and in the end we met monthly, sitting from 2 to 5 p.m. or even later on the last Wednesday of every

month. The attendance record was remarkable. Most such Councils find difficulty in summoning a 50 per cent attendance. It was rare for us not to have 80 per cent and by no means uncommon for us to have 100 per cent. The Council enormously enjoyed the meetings, they loved the discussions and the airing of viewpoints, and they came early and they stayed late.[20]

The Arts Council was in its twentieth year when Goodman took over. This was not only a period of political change, it was also a culturally rich period that had begun in the late 1950s as the icy grip of post-war austerity was finally released. By 1964–5 a cultural blossoming was in full swing, which inspired and in turn was nourished by the financial and political commitment of the Wilson government.

In that first year, in which Goodman overlapped with Cottlesloe, the Royal Opera House completed its re-staging of Wagner's *Ring*, Kenneth Macmillan's *Romeo and Juliet* entered the repertory of the Royal Ballet, Sadler's Wells produced Janáček's *The Makropulos Affair*, the National Theatre – about the only nationalized enterprise created by the Wilson government – completed its first year at the Old Vic and touring. It had given well-received productions of *Othello*, *The Crucible* and *The Royal Hunt of the Sun*. Bookings at the Old Vic were at 89 per cent capacity. The Royal Shakespeare Company had 'astonished the world' with Shakespeare's seven history plays and *The Marat-Sade*. Forty thousand had visited the Miró exhibition at the Tate, nearly 90,000 Peggy Guggenheim's exhibition. In other words the administrative and political framework being reformed by the Wilson government was connected to a cultural industry that was booming in the one field that no politician or administrator could control or influence – creativity.

However, the physical structures for art were also being created at an unprecedented level. The Hayward Gallery was being built. Plans had been announced – subject to financial approval – for a permanent home for the National Theatre as well as for an opera house on the South Bank. (The second idea was later dropped.) The City of London Corporation had published its plans for the development of the Barbican site, which would include a theatre, concert hall, cinema and exhibition space. A new concert hall and theatre had been built at Croydon and new theatres were underway at Chichester, Guildford, Leicester, Nottingham and Southampton.

All these regional works had been completed with only 'token assistance' from the Arts Council. This was set to change with the capital fund, first announced in Lee's White Paper, to help regional and local authorities develop arts spaces. The Arts fund had reached £618,000 per annum by the time Goodman stepped down.

Goodman's first full year in charge was 1965–6. His first major innovation came in July 1965, when the Poetry Panel was converted into the Literature Panel and Frank Kermode, Julian Mitchell, C. V. Wedgwood, Angus Wilson and a young publisher would be asked to join. Aside from these administrative changes, high-level meetings were being held on the progress of the National Theatre and Goodman gave the advancement of this project a high priority.[21] The new style was soon in evidence. Goodman suggested, at only his second meeting as Chairman, that they dispense with the executive meeting and gather the whole Council monthly. It was the beginning of a much more intrusive Chairmanship of the Council. 'I was never aware of how much power a Chairman could wield,' said Tony Field, 'until Arnold Goodman arrived.'[22]

In October Goodman could finally firmly report that the Goodman Report had been accepted in principle by the government and that the London Orchestral Concert Board was to be established. The financial position, as we have seen, was still not yet absolutely clear. The following month Sir David Webster was appointed the first Chairman of the Board. Goodman now set about putting heads together. He reported to this October meeting that he had chaired a meeting of the London Festival Ballet and the Royal Ballet to explore a merger of the two. His reasoning was pragmatic: the Festival Ballet was virtually a new organization after recent changes and it was costing an increasingly large amount to maintain them as separate units. It was curious perhaps that in the case of ballet the question of merger was fully supported but in the case of orchestras not even entertained. Harold Wilson had not expressed a view on the future of ballet.

In January 1966 Goodman's pragmatism caused some dissent when he suggested the Arts Council suspend discussion of the aesthetic quality of a proposed design for the Glasgow Arts Centre because of the urgent need for the scheme to be approved. But his practical knowledge and firm hand was more popular and useful when he chaired a joint meeting between the National Theatre and the Royal Shakespeare Company at which there was discussion of common interests: salary scales, joint use of certain services and touring plans.[23]

The structure of the Council was not keeping pace with the increase in volume and scope of the work. Goodman asked for a working party to redraft the charter so that the number of members could be increased from 16 to allow greater coverage. By January 1966 he was firmly in charge and steering the Council in a number of new directions; he was spending about two days a week on arts work. The London Orchestral Concert Board was incorporated as a non–profit–distributing company limited by guarantee. Under pressure from the DES the initial grant to the orchestras was cut from £40,000 to £30,000 but at least the new structure was now in place.

At the January meeting, heavily influenced by Lee's experience of meeting and visiting young artists, Goodman announced that he 'had a notion' that the Arts Council was out of touch with the young. He proposed that an advisory panel of 'really young people' should be appointed. Sir William Coldstream's view, conveyed by John Witt, was that Goodman should approach the idea with caution. 'Speaking as one who spent much of his time teaching, he felt young people were not particularly successful in knowing what they wanted or how it should be obtained. He preferred to have a greater number of young on the advisory panels and possibly on the Council.' But he did not want them to have a forum of their own. Goodman's view prevailed.[24]

His technique for handling the Council and the government soon became clear: he had a direct line to the Minister for the Arts, his friend Jennie Lee. With her as a neighbour, and a supper partner on Sunday evenings, there was a continuous dialogue. The relations between Minister and Arts Council Chairman have never been so close: he was in love with her: 'He rang her every morning, sent fresh flowers every week, gave her a birthday party every year. He escorted her, scolded her, cuddled her, sorted her finances, and cherished her in sickness and in health. What Jennie wanted, Arnold fixed.'[25] It was a reciprocal relationship. The Minister benefited from having such access to the Chairman of the Arts Council, but the Chairman had the ear not only of the Minister but also of the PM through his weekly or twice weekly meetings with Wilson. It was a political and personal triangle the like of which has not existed in British politics before or since.

They did not always agree. Goodman was more socially

conservative than Lee. He accepted the avant garde as an intellectual necessity in a free society, but he did not embrace it and at times he opposed grants that would support it. He was also hostile to elements of the youth culture that had developed in Britain since the new affluence of the mid-1950s. He disliked drugs and overt sexuality. Occasionally Lee would take exception to a work but in the main she was more liberal and more permissive than Goodman. For example, Arnold Wesker's experimental theatre Centre 42, which was based at the Roundhouse, in north London, with which Jennie had been involved for some years before the election, was refused an Arts Council grant. Wesker had asked for £10,000 towards the conversion costs of the former locomotive turntable shed. Goodman thought the Council should be very cautious in reaching a decision: 'The Council should not give a token sum to encourage others, unless members really believed in the enterprise.' It was unanimously agreed that the Council was not prepared to give funding until it could consider the merits of work performed in the Roundhouse. The Arts Council never funded Wesker and Wesker in turn fell out with Lee and Wilson. Usually, however, Goodman and Lee agreed on strategies and worked closely together. When she was moved on he wrote an appreciation of her for the *Evening Standard*:

> . . . once in an eon there is universal and unpolitical regret at the departure of a distinguished public figure . . . I have rarely met such unanimity of regret expressed in so widespread a circle as at the end of Jennie Lee's House of Commons career. But she will not encourage any elegiac note. Miss Lee is not one to promote wakes in her lifetime . . . For one of the amazing achievements of this remarkable woman has been to take the area of her parliamentary activity almost entirely out of politics . . . There was a universal recognition enhanced by her policy and her own attitudes, that public sponsorship of the arts – on a scale, although still modest, exceeding anything that had previously been practised by any previous government – was only respectable if it was freed from political direction or control . . . Above all, I would pay tribute to a rare and generous gift of friendship of which I, and countless others, have been grateful beneficiaries.[26]

The heart of the Lee–Goodman project was excellence. Priority had to be given to the great artistic institutions, because they feed everything else and set the standards for everything else. The first-class opera of Covent Garden and the ENO, the national theatre in

London and Stratford, the great orchestras, established standards which would influence the whole country. They set the tone for the cultural life of the nation. It was not therefore, according to Goodman, a simple matter of arithmetic. But it was also not the case that this metropolitan provision was only providing cultural outputs for a small élite. Goodman took exception to

an article that I read last Sunday, in a newspaper that ought to know better, dealing with the question of subsidizing the arts. That particular newspaper raised the question of how the money was to be found, and it again used this popular phrase about 'providing arts for a small elite'. But this is by no means the case. We have recently engaged a statistician, and between us we have done a little work. We have never arrived at a satisfactory conclusion, because there is a highly conjectural element in the arithmetic concerned. But if you take into consideration the audiences that attend concerts by all the nine symphony orchestras that we subsidize in England, the audiences that attend the sixty-odd repertory theatres we subsidize, the audiences that go to the Opera House (which I believe holds 2,300) each evening, eight performances a week; and if you take into consideration the audiences that go to the National Theatre and to the Coliseum (holding 2,700 people), you will, I think, find that, far from there being a small elite, there are many millions of people who have a direct interest in, and who benefit from, the activities of the Arts Council. So it is great nonsense to regard this matter as one that affects only a small elite and that the mass of the population should show resentment because money is spent in this fashion.

He concluded with one of his favourite analogies:

150 years ago, when a great many people believed that the percentage of literacy in our population had been predetermined by the Almighty – it was, I believe, ten per cent. Happily, there were dedicated people, enlightened people, who did not accept these statistics and who were firmly convinced that if education were made available that statistic could be altered for the better. Time has shown how right they were.

In the same way the money spent on the arts would produce a similar artistic literacy.[27]

Goodman told William Emrys Williams that he would not, as Chairman of the Arts Council, be a policy-maker. 'I shall be a chairman and not generalissimo . . . Like any sensible ship's captain, I shall keep out of the engine-room.' In fact he tried to run the Council just as he did his legal practice, with a gentle authoritarianism. On one occasion he was pushing for a particular decision. He went round the room and asked each member of the Council for their view. Each disagreed with him. When the vote was 19 to one he announced that the Council had reached an impasse. The matter was held over for another meeting. He usually, though not always, got his way.[28] Such arguments were the exception: he was usually arguing for positions with which most of the council agreed. He governed firmly but with the flow of the consensus and not against it. Things might have been different if he had had a genuinely different agenda of his own. He was also helped by the fact that, amid much bleak political news for Wilson in the late 1960s, the arts developed well and were a focus of national attention.

Nigel Abercrombie had written in 1963 that he was against the transfer of the Arts Council to a spending department because of the potential for political interference. But it was exactly the kind of impetus needed to energize the arts that would also politicize them. Goodman once told Jennie Lee that she could be popular if she spent £1 million. She replied: 'To descend to your crude level, how many votes?'[29] The conflict between politics and art in this era was plain in two main areas of debate: regionalism and censorship. These issues dominated Goodman's tenure at the Arts Council.

8

The Catfish Murders

A young artist to Goodman: 'You're all a very old lot.'
Goodman: 'It's just the light, my dear. Don't let it worry you.'

Goodman was firmly in favour of keeping the arts centralized, as much as possible, in London. In the debate on her White Paper, Jennie Lee had made plain her views: 'Before we arrogantly say that any group of our citizens are not capable of appreciating the best in the arts, let us make absolutely certain that we have put the best in their reach.'[1] To which sentiment Goodman privately responded: 'It is idiotic that the regions, which are pretty barren of talent, should run the show. You can't find that in Wigan or Warrington. They need a hard centre.' In public he put things rather differently. In his House of Lords speech in 1967 he said: 'Nothing will arouse greater resentment than that we should probe about all over the place telling parts of the country that they are insufficiently cultured and that they need some particular cultural activity.' But he went on to put out the right message:

London is a capital city; it must have the furnishings of a capital city. A civilized country must have a great and good quality opera house. It should have a fine national theatre, fine concert halls. These I would not really regard as counting towards the total sum at all, because they are available to everyone, and to talk as if England was a country where it was necessary to travel for seven days on a camel in order to reach London is, I think, a rather absurd presentation of the picture. But the fact remains that it is in the regions that actual inspiration and growth arise. Leaving aside the question of the furnishings of a great capital city, I think the most important work that we can do today is to promote regional artistic activity. We shall not find in London a sufficient coherence of population to be able to do that sort of thing. In London you promote and support individual artistic effort. In the regions there is a community effort which can be supported and can be brought to a rich fulfilment and blossoming. This is something which we have to bear very prominently in mind. The expenditure on the regions, leaving aside the great centres, leaving aside the National Theatre, the Opera House, and so forth, has now outpaced and exceeded the expenditure one finds in London. I do not think the regions have any legitimate cause for complaint at all.[2]

Lee was genuinely interested in devolving arts administration and had a much wider and richer experience of the country than Goodman. When the Arts Council needed new offices she suggested it look for them in Manchester. Goodman would not consider it. More money would be spread out across the country, but control would stay in central London. This was part élitist ignorance of the world north of Watford and partly convenience. Goodman still had a legal practice to run and the Prime Minister to meet. He needed to be close to the action.

In April 1968 the dispute over the regional versus central role of the Arts Council erupted with an argument over the funding of the Renaissance Theatre Trust Company in Barrow-in-Furness, Cumbria. The Council agreed to offer half the sum of £3000, which it was told would clear the debts of the theatre and give it possession of the theatre building. A letter from the Town Clerk of Barrow suggested that the money could clear the debts but would not allow the company to purchase the theatre. Goodman suggested that a letter be sent to the Town Clerk saying that the Arts Council was anxious to maintain live theatre in Barrow but could not contribute to paying off the company's debts. Hugh Willatt, the chair of the Drama Panel, considered that the present situation in the town was due to under-subsidy and argued that if Abercrombie felt there were a moral case to do more he would bring the matter back to the council.[3] In May 1968 he did so. The Mayor of Barrow had told the Arts Council that the theatre building would be a liability to the company rather than an asset. He asked them to join Barrow Corporation in clearing the company's debts, suggesting that it then remain in existence to act as an agency for presenting cultural events in the town. Willatt thought that a contribution of £1500 from the Council would be matched by the local authority, thus avoiding a great deal of bad feeling. Goodman, not happy with this, wondered if the Council could spend £1500 on live entertainment in Barrow, leaving the Corporation to clear the debt. He was told that this was not an option but he blocked, at this stage, the payment of the debts.[4] At the 31 July meeting the 'moral obligation' view prevailed and it was agreed to follow Willatt's proposal to provide a pound-for-pound grant matching the contributions of the local authority.[5] In most similar arguments for money to leave the capital, Goodman was reluctant and tight-fisted.

The experience of Barrow-in-Furness coincided with the proposal, made at the May 1968 Council meeting, that a Theatre Investment Fund should be created. A delegation led by Peter Saunders, John Gale and other theatrical managers had recently visited Lee, with Goodman in attendance, to ask for support for the commercial theatre, which was finding it harder to compete with the subsidized sector.[6] Goodman discussed the plan with Anthony Field, the Council's finance officer, and suggested that a capital sum could be invested of £10,000 for each of around 20 new plays.[7] If five were a success there would be a return on the money. The Council members of the subsequent committee were concerned about the prospect of money being awarded to another body to dispense according to its own judgement. They were also worried that the commercial activity would undermine the Council's charitable status. Goodman's response was that if the Council put in £100,000 he would find the other £150,000.

The Theatre Investment Fund was finally established in 1972 with £100,000 from the Arts Council and £150,000 from private investors and charitable trusts. The bulk of the funds was obtained from charitable trusts, in particular Max Rayne's. 'Months were lost in negotiations with the Treasury to ensure that the private investors were not subject to discrimination. As it turned out, this was of minimal importance in view of the insignificant nature of the private support, and when all the taxation problems had been resolved the TIF finally began operating in 1976.'[8] The investments were concentrated in the West End and by the early 1990s well over £1 million had been put into the by now booming commercial theatre.[9]

The London-versus-the-regions debate continued to rage throughout Goodman's tenure at the Arts Council. His views were set out in a speech in the House of Lords in 1969:

We did not decide to establish an opera house in London ... We now have ... two splendid opera houses in London, and it is quite right that we should have them. But these were existing established institutions. Once there, they had to be paid for. One could not shut them down in order to enter into some academic distribution of the money on an arithmetical basis per capita throughout the country. It would not make sense to send to everybody in England a 2s 6d postal order and say: 'We have shut down every artistic institution in all parts of the country but this may be used by you exclusively for artistic purposes. Here is a list of Penguin books of an artistic nature for which the voucher may be changed.' In a sense that is the logic of the regional argument, if carried to its conclusions.[10]

Despite Goodman's instinctive, though usually only privately expressed, rejection of the regionalist argument, a mirror of his overall belief in cultural élitism, the Arts Council did become much more sensitive to regional needs under his chairmanship. The reason was simple: Lee wanted it that way. It was a recurrent feature of Goodman's life that his clients, whether professional, personal or, like Lee, both professional and personal, got their way. Years after the event he tried to rationalize and justify virtually all his actions to show the extent to which he had been in the right and his clients wrong, but the reality was that either he frequently did not have a particular view of his own at the time or he subordinated that view to the wishes of his clients. Such attitudes highlighted the limitations of his ability to apply his gifts as a lawyer to the different demands of playing a role in public life. The job of the lawyer is be able to switch from client to client and represent their interests to the best of her or his ability. This is not to say that lawyers do not have beliefs but that their training is to keep these firmly in the background, behind the needs of their clients. As Goodman once put it: 'Look at me as a taxi for hire.' But he was not content to see his life as just that of a lawyer. The more he was involved in public life, the more he wanted to justify his actions with principles and consistency and the less, in a way, he wanted to be that legal taxi.

Another recurring theme of the time was censorship. The wave of creativity which had begun in Britain in the 1950s was reaching a peak by the mid-1960s. Across all cultural fronts the barriers of conformity and respectability were being challenged. The structure of law was considerably behind the content and direction of much of this creativity. When the law was challenged by artists, this involved the Arts Council. There were two areas of censorship which touched on Goodman's domain. The first was in literature. The Obscene Publications Act 1959 had been inspired by prosecutions in 1954 for obscene libel of established literary works by well-known writers, which had resulted in two convictions and three acquittals. The Obscene Publications Act allowed expert witnesses to defend the content of a book on grounds of its artistic merit. Ironically, it was the passing of the 1959 Act which encouraged Penguin to proceed with the publication of *Lady Chatterley's Lover*. This led to the company's prosecution, with debate during the trial focusing precisely on the issue of the work's artistic merit or lack of it. An amendment to the Act 'gave the publisher the right to a trial by jury, rather than making him submit to the decision of a magistrate as to whether or not the book should be condemned'. Donald Thomas, the historian of literary censorship, judged that the 'first case before a jury was misleading'.[11] The 1959 Act, which had been designed to allow great works of literature to be published by updating the law on obscenity, had led directly to the prosecution of the publishers of *Lady Chatterley*.[12] Thomas writes: 'despite the greater hostility in the tone of counsel for the prosecution than has been customary since, the Crown presented a weak case. No witnesses were called to rebut the expert evidence given for the defence and many of the defence witnesses were not cross-examined.' Penguin won.

The second area of censorship was the role of the Lord Chamberlain's office in censoring plays, as the then Home Secretary, Roy Jenkins, wrote: 'a court official who may exceptionally have an intelligent playgoer's knowledge of the stage but never has anything more, possesses powers of absolute censorship over all the theatres of London'.[13] Goodman held out against the recommendations of various Arts Council committees and the Jenkins Committee on censorship, for the retention of a voluntary system of control. He argued:

The 1966 Committee received evidence which, so far as it was rendered orally, was sparse in number and almost uniform in character. But it did not lack excitement or entertainment, usually hinged on moments when it was investigating not the abolition of pre-censorship of plays – which was taken almost for granted from the outset - but possible safeguards to management. One such was a voluntary system of censorship, a course recommended by the 1909 Committee (which, in justice, had itself as its main recommendation called for the abolition of the censor) ... It would be a legitimate reproach in democratic affairs if the unanimous opinion of a wholly representative committee did not emerge on the statute book.[14]

As the Council had submitted evidence which was entirely in line with the consensus view that censorship should simply be abolished, he had, of course, to be forthright in his praise of Jenkins. Lee was four square behind the Home Secretary. But Goodman's natural conservatism was evident in the remainder of the article, in which he gently differed with his Minister and outlined a position of his own: the country should reconsider and adopt his proposal for a voluntary system.

His argument for second thoughts on the issue of censorship was based on a further legal decision. Calder and Boyars, the publisher of *Last Exit to Brooklyn*, by Hubert Selby Jr, was prosecuted in 1967. The prosecution called a number of witnesses to challenge the expert evidence given for the defence and the jury found that the novel was obscene. Goodman Derrick was acting for Calder and Boyars at the Old Bailey. The counsel for the defence on that occasion was, Goodman recalled, 'one of the most gifted lawyers in the country, Patrick Neill QC':

> However, after we had failed to convince the jury, I thought that an approach of less orthodoxy might be more successful and we instructed Mr John Mortimer to conduct the appeal. For this purpose he invented as a criterion the 'repugnance' theory, which was swallowed hook, line and sinker by the Court of Criminal Appeal. The theory was very simple: that if a book was so obscene as to revolt the reader, it was not consistent with corruption and on that extraordinary score the Court of Appeal allowed *Last Exit*'s appeal.[15]

Donald Thomas judges that in the first hearing:

> Counsel on both sides, as well as the judge, made it clear to the jurors that they might be disgusted by the book, it might make them feel physically sick, but that was not enough to condemn it: it must deprave and corrupt by inciting its readers to act as the characters in the novel acted. Even if the book was obscene by those standards, the jurors must still consider whether its publication might not be in the public interest as being of benefit to literature, science, or learning.[16]

The problem with the 1959 Act was that it was left to juries to judge what might 'horrify, shock, disgust, and nauseate' but would 'still be uncorrupting'. 'The difficulty is that this asks of jurors a type of objectivity not universal even among literary critics and very rare among ordinary readers.'[17] On 31 July 1968 the Court of Appeal allowed *Last Exit*'s appeal. The trial judge had failed to put to the jury Goodman's defence on the alleged obscenity of the book. 'Particularly that he had not given sufficient direction on the question of whether, even if the book was obscene, publication might still be for the public good.' Even on appeal, though, the court stressed that: 'The Jury must set the standards of what is acceptable, of what is for the public good, in the age in which we live.'[18] The basis of Goodman's critique was inherently that this application of the ordinary legal process to the business of censorship was inappropriate. Writing before the appeal was allowed, Goodman argued that:

> The 'Last Exit' decision has, of course, reinforced the misgivings of those who do not regard the ordinary processes of prosecution, and the ordinary prosecuting authorities, as appropriate to deal with matters of the mind. This is not the place to argue again the 'Last Exit' case, though in my opinion by no literate standards was the work obscene. The decision was arrived at by what is described as 'the robust common sense of juries' and not by literate standards. What caused the damage was one simple fact: that a jury – whatever its robust common sense – could not fail to ask itself why one book out of hundreds of thousands found itself pilloried in the dock at the Old Bailey. From this damaging vantage-point only a classic like 'Lady Chatterley', written by an author long dead and of immense and increasing international renown, had any comfortable prospect of acquittal. The moral of the 'Last Exit' case is not that the Lord Chamberlain's departure should be delayed (and in saying this it would be wrong not to pay tribute to the enlightened exercise of his office by the present incumbent) but to ensure that the legislation recommended in broad principle in the Committee's report should obviate major risks to the theatre. A parallel provision should be enacted for literature, whose present censorship dilemma has been brought into such conspicuous relief by the unhappy fate of 'Last Exit'.

He advocated two safeguards:

> First and absolutely foremost, that no book or play should be prosecuted without the approval of a literate official or body such as an ad hoc Home Office Committee specially selected for the purpose . . . Second, a requirement which should, I think, be antecedent to any prosecution of a play or book: notice of the matters complained of in the play or

book must be served before any such prosecution is launched. The management or publisher should be entitled to discuss the notice with the prosecuting authority; and if so minded (but only if so minded) make appropriate changes which would in ordinary circumstances debar prosecution. There is manifestly no perfect solution to this problem. Pre-censorship of books would today be a totally unthinkable notion. Voluntary censorship is rejected by most of the thinking elements in the professions concerned. If, therefore, the matter is to be left to the post-censorship of the courts it is of cardinal importance to writers, managers and publishers alike that ill-judged prosecutions (the cost of which must be forbidding and may be ruinous) are avoided by sensible preliminary safeguards.[19]

As Goodman's article made clear, the pressure on censorship and control was as much in evidence in the theatre as in publishing. Indeed he connected the two. The decision in the *Last Exit* case encouraged him in his view that the removal of the Lord Chamberlain's licence would lead to an atmosphere of greater fear and reservation rather than greater boldness:

But one or two afterthoughts are very relevant, particularly in consequence of the recent 'Last Exit to Brooklyn' decision at the Old Bailey. Those who, like myself, were canvassing the possibility of a voluntary system, were not concerned with the dangers to public morality which might arise from removing restrictions on freedom of production. To a man, we regarded this as an acceptable risk which would in any event be controlled 'more than adequately' by the obscenity laws to which the stage was now to conform. The emphasis is on 'more than adequately'. Our fear was that the removal of censorship would produce not a more liberal but a less liberal theatre, with managements inhibited by the fear of prosecutions and, deprived of the insurance of a Lord Chamberlain's licence, adopting a policy of greater timidity: that plays now and previously presented in the West End and elsewhere would not see the light of day – which, with the recent decision restricting the operation of club theatres, might mean that effectively they would be produced not at all.

The Arts Council was heavily involved in the moves by Roy Jenkins towards the abolition of the censorship of plays by the Lord Chamberlain. Goodman had established an inquiry, headed by his old friend Max Rayne, into the issue of theatre censorship in

September 1967. In June 1968, when the inquiry reported, Goodman convened a conference of organizations concerned with the arts to consider the problems of obscenity. He presided over the conference, which decided to set up a working party, under his Goodman Derrick partner John Montgomerie, 'to investigate the country's obscenity laws'. In June 1969 'Monty' joined the Council's meeting to introduce his report. The Lord Chamberlain's office stopped licensing theatre productions in September 1968. The obscenity laws were more problematic and Goodman differed markedly from the Drama Panel, from the conclusions of the report and from the majority of the Council. Monty – 'who possessed one of the shrewdest legal minds in the country [and] was as taciturn as a Trappist monk, hardly uttering a word where he regarded it as unnecessary'[20] – recommended in his report the repeal of the existing laws on obscenity. Sir Leslie Scarman, a Council member, said that his experience led him to believe that 'the man-in-the-street was particularly concerned about anything tending to deprave or corrupt the young and did not want pornography to intrude upon himself or his family as they went about the streets'. Hugh Willatt felt that the working party had perhaps gone beyond the strict field of the Council's concern. Monty responded that though at present the law was administered liberally, the climate of opinion could change at any time. Therefore the Council should work for the repeal of the law.[21]

Goodman concluded the discussion by saying that it was not the job of the Council to reduce the number of sexual offences though it would be 'an excellent thing if such a thing resulted from activity designed to encourage the arts' and he expressed his view strongly that 'however much one disapproved of the existing laws relating to obscenity, it would be a total waste of time to recommend their repeal since no government would repeal them'.[22] Goodman's flippancy at the close of the meeting was born of this firm belief that repeal would not go through the Commons – 'let alone the Lords'.[23]

The following month the report was again debated and the Literature director reported enthusiastic interest in its findings. The meeting debated whether to publish the report as a paperback through a printer or to bring it out as a hardback through André Deutsch. The DES questioned whether the Arts Council should be spending its money on this sort of activity, but the meeting decided that the report should be published commercially, with a hardback edition at 25s., of which the Council would purchase at least 500 at a discount of 50 per cent for circulation. The Council also decided that the report should be sent to the Home Secretary, 'with our personal recommendation that the proposals should be enacted'. Goodman concluded his account of the report: 'In fact, from that day to this nothing more has been heard of it.'[24] While it is true that the case for the abolition of all obscenity laws was very much the product of a particular cultural moment, the debate that was generated about the meaning of obscenity and freedom of expression has continued. What is striking here, as in his general taste and demeanour, is the conservatism of Goodman. This was in part born of pragmatism – why push for a reform that you know does not stand a chance? – and in part of his own social conservatism on matters of taste. Ironically, after Labour lost the 1970 election and Lord Eccles became Minister for the Arts, Goodman found himself in the position of being the more libertarian and defending the Arts Council's work from Eccles's criticisms.[25] Also revealing was his private view that he did not see the point of spending time, as Monty had done, on a report that stood no chance of being implemented.

Goodman's general attitude was liberal within limits. This was in part a function of the Council's position and in part the result of his natural instincts. But he was not a prude and, as ever, he managed to inject a little humour into his Council work. The theatre director Sir Bernard Miles had decided, in September 1971, that the text of *Othello* demanded a naked Desdemona. Letters of complaint came to Goodman, who wrote to Sir Bernard:

My Dear Bernard,
    The Arts Council exercises no form of censorship but occasionally proffers some common-sense advice. Do drop this nonsense about a naked Desdemona. You have extracted all the fun from it – got all the possible publicity – and to continue with it would really be unworthy of you and your theatre. You have such a good Shakespearian reputation that to belittle the Bard with a silly and totally unjustifiable gimmick, which puts the play completely out of perspective and furnishes you with audiences of slobbering yahoos instead of the excellent quality you now attract, would be to expose yourself to serious long-term injury for the most trivial present advantage – even if you get one at all. Needless to say, this is a private letter, which I shall not publicise in any way – nor shall I make any public comment on whatever your decision may be.

157

But, do think again and do not be driven to take an unwise stand out of sheer defiance at the volume of criticism.

Yours ever, Arnold

Sir Bernard replied:

Dear Arnold,

> Iago: Or to be naked with her friend in bed
> An hour or more, not meaning any harm.

> Othello: Naked in bed Iago and not mean harm
> It is hypocrisy against the Devil.

– in other words, husbands and wives naturally and habitually go to bed naked, but dear God, 'with her friend.' This is one of the biggest daggers pushed into Othello and the tact and delicacy with which it is handled and the quite justifiable horror that it adds to the scene in my opinion more than justifies it. Josephine and I are both puritans, or we would never have done what we have done in such a personal and partly sacrificial way. We have three children and nine grandchildren. The Director, Peter Oyston, has an adored wife and two small children. The Othello, Bruce Purchase, has a beloved wife and three small children. Julius Gellner is a Czech Director of many years experience and not a little renown. The scene is handled with the greatest delicacy and tenderness, with only a very fleeting glimpse of nudity.

In a play which contains a frightening description of male ejaculation and of the semen pouring back out of the woman: 'the fountain from the which my current runs, or else dries up' – then the frightening hint of necrophilia 'Look thus when thou art dead, and I will kill thee and love thee after' – for which many of our modern and highly-prized dramatists would have used the word fuck, instead of love – these and many other violent sexual images which make *Sons and Lovers* sound like a Methodist tea party, do, I believe, totally justify the conception we have – which I think is most beautiful. I would only add that as an Honorary Fellow of my old college, a member of the City Livery Company, and of the Worshipful Company of Wheelwrights, Parish Clerk of the Church of St Mary Mounthaw and a practising adherent of the Salvation Army, you must please believe I am to be trusted in this matter.

To which Goodman, perhaps a little demob-happy as the end of his Arts Council tenure approached, replied:

The Catfish Murders

My dear Bernard,

I have now received your letter. I do not believe you are a pornographer. I do believe you are an immensely experienced, sensible and responsible theatrical producer, but it is a tragedy that it is this particular textual discovery that you should have made at this moment. If you had made the discovery that Iago was Desdemona's father, that Othello was the original leader of the Black Panthers, that the whole play was an argument in favour of Welsh nationalism, you could have revealed them triumphantly and with the loudest blast of trumpets, but suddenly to discover that undressing a pretty girl is a remarkable textual achievement at a time when the London theatre – bankrupt of other ideas – is stripping them all like plucked hens, is unfortunate and ill-timed. However valid the argument in favour of doing it – and I am singularly unimpressed by the argument – this is a tragic moment for doing it without associating yourself with people who are out to use any contrivance to make money at the box office. Hence my final appeal to deck the poor lady in any raiment. Bourne & Hollingsworth and C & A are open and I will immediately sponsor an additional Arts Council grant for the purpose. Or use my Credit Card at Harrods.

Love Arnold

The production went ahead as planned but it is doubtful if any other Chairman of the Arts Council would have tried to exert influence with quite such style.

The debates on censorship and its implementation were both more abstract and more interesting than much of the work of the Council's meetings. For instance, in September 1966 Goodman was approached by the owner of an art gallery who complained that the police had seized, without warning, a large quantity of exhibits, suspecting that they were obscene. Goodman had discussed with Lee the view to take and they decided to advise the police that in future they should seek expert advice before mounting a raid. In the main, however, there were two kinds of discussion at almost all the meetings: finance and the development of plans for buildings and institutions. At the same September meeting and earlier in July, the effects of the government's cuts in public spending were a worry, especially its wage freeze, which would effectively block an increase agreed for the members of provincial orchestras. Goodman characteristically had to be persuaded by the civil servants from the DES that the increase could not go ahead. These constant money worries accompanied the project-management issues.

In September 1966 Goodman met Sir William Fiske, leader of the GLC, to discuss an architect's proposal for a cheaper plan for the South Bank's new art gallery to meet the Arts Council's requirements. The total cost – unlikely to have been more than £10,000 – would be borne by the GLC. Goodman liked the idea of saving money but he liked the idea of building a prestigious gallery more. He told Lee that there should not be a financial strait-jacket on the scheme but rather that they should find the right building and then the plan should be costed. Such attitudes endeared him to the arts world because at such moments he was led by the aesthetic rather than the practical considerations.

In February 1967 the new Charter for the Arts Council received the Royal Assent and four new members could be added. Goodman used the existence of the Charter to underplay the closeness of his relations with Lee, saying in the House of Lords: 'We are subject to no governmental control; we would not respond to governmental control, and it is desperately important that we should make a selection of members of the Council that manifests this matter beyond any peradventure. I hope that we have done this.' In these appointments Goodman was conservative but in his recommendations for panels he tried, urged on by Lee, to bring in some new blood. Since becoming Chairman his other new recruits had been Sir Edward Boyle, Lord Harewood, Sir Joseph Lockwood and Angus Wilson. But many of the older staff and civil servants were dismayed by some of his other recommendations for appointments: 'experientialists, non-conformists and conformists, the unconventional and conventional, the fashionable and the unfashionable'.[26] After the renewal of the Arts Council's Charter the panels included:

Visual Arts: Edward Lucie-Smith, Bryan Robertson, Roy Strong, David Sylvester.

Drama: Judy Dench, Michael Elliott, Bamber Gascoigne, Jonathan Miller, John Mortimer, Peter Shaffer.

Literature: Melvyn Bragg, Richard Holmes, Karl Miller, Peter Redgrove, Frank Kermode.

Music: Richard Rodney Bennett, Harrison Birtwistle, John Drummond.

Young People's Theatre: Frank Dunlop, Richard Eyre, Terry Hands, Harold Pinter, Diana Quick.

A new director of the Music Panel, John Cruft, was brought in. He took a dim view of Lee, believing that she knew nothing of the arts but wanted people to be enabled to consume culture and not instructed or edified. But he had a 'fairly cordial' relationship with Goodman and was generally on the chairman's side. Anthony Field, the finance director of the Arts Council and the person constantly bringing these worries to the meetings as well as some imaginative schemes of his own, rated Goodman very highly. For Field this was a golden age in which artistic and financial decisions were in remarkable harmony. The panels chose the recipients and the accountants assessed how much each would receive in subsidy, though Goodman had reservations on some issues. For example, he was unconvinced of the artistic merit of Centre 42's work at the Roundhouse and was suspicious of the Royal Shakespeare Company's potential to develop into a second national theatre for which there was simply not the financial support. But relations between the Council and the administrators of the Hallé, the RSC, the Theatre Royal at Stratford and the Roundhouse – especially after Arnold Wesker's departure from the latter – were generally 'sympathetic and constructive'.

In a House of Lords debate on the arts in April 1967 Goodman welcomed the increased expenditure on the arts but made it plain that he did not expect a blank cheque. The Council was:

> . . . not here to administer and control the artistic life and effort and output of the country. It would be a horrible thing if any bureaucratic organization had that function . . . if the day comes when an author has to turn to the Arts Council before he can write a book, or a dramatist before he can write a play, or a manager before he can present it, I should not wish to be administering the affairs of that body . . . We are an auxiliary body, and we shall remain an auxiliary body. We are not here to control artistic output; we are not here to regulate what artists are doing; we are not here to promote artistic activity all over the country.

In essence then he was repudiating the ideological underpinning of the nationalization of cultural policy. He defended the intention, but is clear that the policy was not to create a country with a particular cultural outlook through social engineering or to centralize all artistic creativity. He wanted local councils to use the funding at their disposal to subsidize more local arts activity and not bring their requests always directly to him. He went on to argue that local councils should be forced by law to spend a certain amount of their locally raised funds on locally produced arts. But his primary concern in this speech was to defend the expansion of the Arts Council's expenditure and refute two kinds of criticism. First, the former Chairman of the Council, Lord Cottesloe, argued that as the work of the Council expanded so it would be more difficult to ensure the quality of the work that it subsidized. Second, as this work grew, the Council should be much more concerned with the kinds of things that are produced and much more censorious of the absurd and bizarre. Goodman's response to these two criticisms, encapsulates the essence of his and Lee's philosophy of arts expenditure:

> I do not regard it as the function of the Arts Council to judge the quality of every performance in every part of the country. This I regard as the function of the organizations to which we give the money. I think it of the greatest importance that we should not seek to establish from St James's Square a censorship over all art. All the organizations which receive money from us should know that they are autonomous and are free to do what they like with it, subject to the qualification that there is proper accounting and that, in the end, there is sufficient public service benefit – sufficient value to the public for the expenditure of that money. This is a very difficult question; it is a matter of degree. If you have a poet, he may be the most obscure poet and he may attract only a few hundred people to his readership, but he may be a man who is well worthy of support, and it would be wrong for a civilized country not to support him. If you have an opera company, a totally different consideration arises. It would be wrong to continue to subsidize an opera company which was producing operas that played to empty houses night after night. This is the sort of consideration that weighs with us. It has to be considered individually in respect of each application. There are no rules that can be laid down, no criteria that can be applied, except the criterion of common sense. This is what we try to do, in a fallible way. What we have to seek to avoid desperately is the notion that within St James's Square we have the best answer as to what the artistic values are: that we know what is good art and other people do not. Obviously we have experts; we can provide sound judgments; but, if we look at the matter historically, how many generations have succeeded in identifying all their geniuses in their own time? What a piece of arrogance and folly it would be on our part to believe that we possess this faculty, when nobody else has possessed it previously. Plainly, we must take the widest possible spread to ensure that we avoid, not the danger that we may waste money on a non-genius - this, where we are spending one-

hundredth part of the expenditure on scientific discoveries, seems to me a trifle – but the danger that we may not subsidize the genius. That is the danger we must seek to avoid.

In pursuing these aims – devolution on the assessment of the outcomes of the subsidized work and the pursuit of excellence and genius – the production of absurdity was a risk worth taking and the ridicule of these absurdities a ridicule worth enduring. 'If we were spending great sums of money on these absurdities there would be legitimate cause for complaint, but it is bound to happen that over the edge there will seep a little money to things which may seem extravagant, too avant garde, too "with it". This must be the price you pay if you want to win the confidence of artists.' The Arts Council therefore existed to promote excellence to enable artists to take chances and to create an environment in which institutions could, over a long period, produce good work. The question remained of why such activity mattered and why it mattered to Goodman. Actually his views on this changed over time, but in 1967, influenced no doubt by Lee and Wilson, he was clear that there was a connection between the cultural products of a society and the health of the people in that society. In his peroration to this speech, he stated that:

> I believe that there is a crucial state in the country at this moment. I believe that young people lack values, lack certainties, lack guidance; that they need something to turn to; and need it more desperately than they have needed it at any time in our history – certainly at any time which I can recollect. I do not say that the arts will furnish a total solution, but I believe that the arts will furnish some solution. I believe that once young people are captured for the arts they are redeemed from many of the dangers which confront them at the moment and which have been occupying the attention of the Government in a completely unprofitable and destructive fashion. I believe that here we have constructive work to do which can be of inestimable value.[27]

Goodman's vigorous defence of the work of the Council from the attacks from those who condemned its support of the avant garde should not leave the impression that he was seen at the time as the champion of radicalism. In fact, he was attacked by some of the artists he defended. He commented later: 'Many of the young people clearly did not like the Arts Council and did their business with it only because of the allure of money and its premises.' (Presumably, by 'premises' he meant the Royal Opera House and the like.) These opponents produced magazines containing caricatures of Goodman drawn as an octopus. His only comment was that the tentacles were 'too few and too short'.[28] Such direct attacks seemed to wash off Goodman's back and he could also hit back. The literary magazine *Ambit* had been offered an Arts Council grant of £120 for four issues. In the second, it had announced a 'Drugs and Creative Writing Competition'. The Literature Panel advised that in its opinion the magazine had some merit and that some of its members might resign if their view were not accepted. Goodman was adamant. The Arts Council was a public body, dispensing public funds and must not be associated with a magazine advocating anti-social and irresponsible behaviour. The case had already attracted undesirable publicity and he proposed the grant for the year should not be restored. On a vote, this was accepted.[29]

There were further cases in which the Council was embroiled in controversy as artists were pushing at the boundaries of taste and decency. There were a number of fixed ideas in Goodman's world view which were both characteristic of his age in some respects – the attachment to a rather abstract notion of freedom, for example – and in others distinctly old-fashioned. 'I certainly believe in a moral code which distinguishes between right and wrong, a distinction which is necessary to civilisation. One of society's troubles is that a generation is growing up for whom the distinction is not sufficiently defined.'[30] This attitude to his times, to the new generation that had pushed through the boundaries of the cultural and artistic conservatism of the post-war era, was thus mixed and, again, entirely conventional. At times the libertarian was to the fore, as in 1971, when he commented: 'It is heartening to see how many young people are taking to more elevated interests . . . there has been almost an avalanche of interest by young people in cultural matters.' At other times, and in other moods, his was a much more reactionary voice: 'The higher standards of the arts were in desperate danger of being destroyed by young people who found it easier to appreciate lower forms of art, Lord Goodman yesterday told the annual meeting of the Composers Guild . . . He said that young people did not take the trouble to understand the higher products of the human mind.'[31] Or, in later conversations, he could simply be tortuous:

If you believe that things were worse in the past – obviously a false argument – this could lead you to the equally false assertion that the present situation approaches perfection. Conversely, the argument, also false, that things were so much better in the past might suggest that a quest for present improvement is unrealistic.[32]

Or even, largely nonsensical, as the following example from *Private Eye* shows:

English Language

Time Allowed: 15 mins

1. There is a kind of Teutonic thoroughness about this approach which might commend itself to a number of people, except that it is totally demented that one should seek to apply a Teutonic thoroughness to writers which has the same relevance and the same kind of effect as it will have to machine grinders or whatever operation is necessary, important and is carried on in shops under the control and supervision of trade unions
    Arnold Goodman, House of Lords, 11 March 1975
    Re-write the above passage in correct and easily intelligible English. Send your answer to the Master, University College, Oxford (to await arrival)[33]

Goodman did have some strong convictions and his thinking was not often confused. His more considered view on the morality of his age was again straightforward. Indeed he did not like grand statements of moral purpose. His response to the idea that life could be dedicated to the pursuit of truth was to call the statement ridiculous: 'It means that when you wake up and even before you have breakfasted, you must consider how to pursue the truth in the coming day.'[34] Thus it was to a practical operation of a moral code that Goodman looked and not to the abstract or philosophical contemplation of these questions. Indeed as a good liberal he disliked elaborate philosophical systems of thought, was frightened of the misunderstandings that they could lead to and dismissive of the profession of philosopher: 'in a hard and ruthless world there is very little time to brood over philosophical matters'. The nature of truth was essentially practical and the nature of lies distressing, but in a somewhat abstract sense: 'All honest people desire an unqualified practice of the truth . . . any situation where bad behaviour is involved causes one distress. Telling lies is not good behaviour, even if the entire political world, for instance, has become inured to it.'

These liberal and socially conservative views influenced his handling of cases which came before the Arts Council. One classic example involved the very British obsession against cruelty to animals. A member of the Council, Dr Thorpe Davie, referred, at the meeting held on 29 September 1971, to an article in that day's edition of *The Times* about an exhibition at the Hayward Gallery titled 'Eleven Los Angeles Artists'. In the ordinary run of business it was the Visual Arts Panel of the Council and not the Council itself which assessed exhibitions, so this was the first that the Council had heard about the event.[35] The director of this panel, Robin Campbell, reported that one of the items was a portable fish farm. This contained catfish, shellfish, crabs, lobsters and so on, and it was intended that at regular intervals an electric current should be passed through the water to kill them, and the catfish eaten in the style of an American catfish feast. The artist's message was that life was hard. As Goodman recalled: 'He certainly established the point that it was especially hard for a catfish which fell into the hands of a Californian artistic innovator.' The first catfish execution would be at the opening party the next evening, when those present would be guests of the Contemporary Arts Society and the Arts Council.

Campbell felt it was possible to make a perfectly good artistic defence of the activity, bearing in mind the conception of this artist's exhibit as a whole. Sir John Pope Hennessy said the organizer of the exhibition was a 'thoroughly responsible person' and the exhibition included other works which were of a non-controversial nature. Professor Lawrence Gowing said that the point was that 'in the view of the artists concerned the fish farm was a work of art'. He thought it right that the British public should be able to see what was being put on in Los Angeles. The Council decided to go ahead with the opening.[36]

The next morning Goodman went down to the Hayward to see for himself. He found Spike Milligan, a former client, trying to break the glass windows with a small hammer. He told Milligan the hammer was too small for the window. A 'wild-eyed' woman approached him and asked: 'Will the catfish live?' Longer than your morning kipper, Goodman says he replied. He went into the gallery to find the artist, Newton Harrison, who was with a coterie of advisers. They attacked Goodman: this was art because the artist defined it as art. Goodman replied that anyone could call themselves an artist but that did not entitle him to murder catfish. The argument grew heated. The world, Goodman recalled, seemed divided between 'the majority of artists who saw in any interference by the Arts Council the philistine hand of bureaucracy' and the rest of the world, who viewed the murder of catfish as 'further evidence that the artist today was a fraud and confidence trickster'. He suggested that the conceptual artist give an oral demonstration of his ideas, a proposal which was scorned by Harrison, who, like most conceptual artists, had extremely banal concepts behind his vivid physical expressions.[37]

Goodman assembled an emergency meeting of the Council at his flat to decide the fate of the catfish. He was for censorship. He wanted the exhibition and the public execution of the catfish prevented. Pope Hennessy and a large majority of the rest of the Council argued that it should not interfere with free artistic expression. Goodman, in a small minority, still forced a compromise on his colleagues. The catfish would have to die, but the RSPCA would kill them and the catfish would be served to the public as a kind of bouillabaisse.[38]

The Council issued a press notice:

> The exhibition 'Eleven Los Angeles Artists' at the Hayward Gallery will open at noon today Saturday 2nd October. Concern has been aroused by one aspect of Newton Harrison's 'Portable Fish Farm.' A special meeting of the Arts Council yesterday evening decided that it could not accept the killing of fish in public as a feature of this work; and the artist, who had already indicated his willingness to eliminate the feature, has agreed to adapt the work accordingly. He has also agreed that all the arrangements relating to the fish in the exhibition will be carried out in consultation with the RSPCA.

Goodman insisted that the Visual Arts Panel take steps to ensure that issues of this kind, 'which had a high publicity content', were in future brought to its notice well in advance. Peter Hall, the theatre director and Council member regarded the whole thing as a classic demonstration of the folly of a liberal conscience, but Goodman was unrepentant and maintained that there had been a genuine dilemma involved in the case. The catfish, being killed twice a day in the name of art, would probably have agreed.

9

Operatic Deficits

There's one of those nitwits from whose disastrous advice I'm
forever extracting Jennie.
(Goodman on a senior civil servant)

The antibody in our time is Lord Goodman. A man who has
never held elective office, he wielded more power than anyone
in the country, except for the Prime Minister in the last decade.
(Kenneth Tynan on Goodman)

Most of the activities of the Arts Council went largely unnoticed by
the press – so much so that in April 1967 Goodman suggested that
the media be admitted to Council meetings. Other members of the
Council had strong reservations about such access and thought that
it was better for Goodman himself to give a press conference after
each meeting. Goodman responded by suggesting that the minutes
of meetings might be made available.[1] This too was opposed by the
Council. He raised the issue again the following month and again it
was opposed. He was keen that the press should be in the position
to write about the Council's work on a regular basis and not just
when something controversial occurred. He complained later that
the Council was largely ignored by the press. This was true in
respect of the routine work that took 95 per cent of Goodman's
time, but it was not true of the new committee he had recently
created.

The expansion of coverage allowed under the Council's new
Charter had resulted in a rapid increase in the volume of applications
for grants from non-traditional arts enterprises such as arts
laboratories, theatre groups and what Goodman described as 'loosely
knit bodies of young people operating in halls and basements'.
Goodman's problem was not that he was resistant to helping these
bodies but that many of them came under no clearly identifiable Arts
Council heading. As he put it: 'They were not precisely drama or
music or literature or belonging to the visual arts, but it was clear that

there were surface stirrings all over the country. And it was clear that their practitioners took them seriously.'[2] Some could be put to particular panels, but for the rest a new committee was created called the New Activities Committee. Its original membership included Michael Astor (formerly a Conservative MP) as Chairman, Lord Harewood, Sir Edward Boyle MP, Sir Joseph Lockwood, Peter Hall, Jack Lambert (the literary editor of the *Sunday Times*) and – at the instigation of the Committee itself – a number of the new arts activists.

It was the presence of these activists that caused many of the difficulties. On one occasion, Peter Hall recalled, the door burst open and three or four 'street people' came in, 'one in a yellow jumpsuit with yellow tubes emerging from his head'.[3] They demanded a grant for their performance Art of Protest. 'Until they received it, they would occupy the premises. Lord Goodman was charm itself, thanked them for coming and ushered them out without a golden handshake.' The activists who were supposed to be present as part of the Committee also caused difficulties:

> The new activists did not think as did their older colleagues; the problems of communication and interpretership were considerable. Much time was occupied, for instance, in discussing whether the proceedings of the Committee should be tape-recorded in view of the new members' obvious mistrust of any record or minutes produced by a human being and not a machine. In fact, the new activists movement is characterized as perhaps one would expect in this age, by its superior confidence in machinery over people.[4]

The Committee was set up to investigate and produce a report which would provide a basis for assessing the worthiness of new projects for Council funding. The press coverage of the New Activities Committee neatly showed the way in which the Council was trapped. On the one hand condemned for being dull and Establishment-minded by an expanding radical arts scene, it was condemned on the other by the *Daily Mail*'s 'Middle England' when it supported avant-garde art which was not considered decent. The impression, wrote Goodman, was that the Council had taken leave of its corporate senses and engaged in a policy of nihilistic destructivism. The middle course adopted was somewhat random in its allocation of resources. Goodman acknowledged this:

The test of eligibility for support is easier to sense than to define, but in broad terms the beneficiary objective must have merit or promise of merit, appeal or prospect of appeal, and must satisfy a discriminating need. The importance of an audience response is a variable factor. If it is a commodity which depends for its survival on the response of an audience – such as a theatre or a concert hall – it is a nonsense to subsidize an activity that produces no such reaction. But it is equally wrong to measure its value solely in audience terms. Hence if a repertory theatre which performs a range of relatively popular plays fails to draw an adequate audience, it is plain that it should be re-sited or change its policy, or even, as the final decision, be closed. But if subsidy is for a poet, his recognition by a single perceptive mind can amply justify support to maintain an activity which can rarely find an adequate public.[5]

Despite his conviction that it was important to encourage new work, Goodman had little time for much of what passed for art in these avant-garde movements, though he was sympathetic to the individuals concerned. On one occasion a woman appeared in front of the Arts Council demanding a grant to put on an exhibition on the trees in Green Park. 'The bemused and amused Goodman gave her £75. When she reappeared a week later for another sub to place particular pictures on the trees he asked her her principles of selection. "Random choice," she replied. "I will exhibit anyone who brings a picture." Her request was refused.'[6] The New Activities Committee later became the Experimental Projects Committee. During Goodman's reign, a little against his own instincts, though not completely, there gradually developed a dominance of the avant garde and 'new' over the conventional or traditional, particularly in definitions of what should be supported in art. The debate intensified around the time of the general election of 1970. Although the dominance by the avant garde varied between art forms, the Conservatives abolished the Committee after they won the election.

The subtlety of Goodman's position in supporting the right of individuals to experiment but being personally offended by some of the results, was born of his view of the role of the artist in a civilized society. This view was well illustrated in his stubborn support for a Public Lending Right (PLR). In April 1967 he began pushing for reforms through the Council. He based his case, first and foremost, on the reward due to one person by another person's use of his or her intellectual property. 'When you have a book you buy that book for your own use. No canon of natural justice should entitle you to let it out to 150 different people and make no payment of any kind to the man who had originally written the book.'[7] He proposed a small amendment to copyright law so that a small fee was charged by the library or other lending body when the book was handed out. This would not destroy the notion of the 'sanctity of the free library' because the library would remain free to the subscriber; the cost would be borne by the community.[8]

There was a working party on possible reform and Goodman urged the Council to concentrate on getting something on the statute book. Anthony Field raised the administrative and financial difficulties involved in making such a change. Goodman put his pen down quite forcibly and said: 'Just because we cannot achieve justice, there is no point in going on with absolute injustice. We must take the first step, with all the imperfections, we must make a start.'[9] They decided to proceed and a meeting was arranged for July 1967 with Jennie Lee and her officials. At this meeting, which was also attended by members of the Literature Panel, they pulled back from some of the more controversial aspects of the proposed PLR but decided to push forward with the attempt to establish the principle that authors should be paid. Goodman suggested that the Council ask for a separate earmarked sum of £2 million to kick-start the scheme. This was rejected by the government on financial grounds.

The need to act on the PLR issue was something that Goodman cared about deeply. The practicality of the reform appealed to him, as did its potential to bring a small relief to poor writers and allow them some independence. He realized that it would also be good for the Council. But more than this, he had an idealized view of the artist and the artist's role in a community. In defending the need for reform of PLR in the House of Lords in 1969 he made this idealism plain when he said that, in his view: 'The artist is of course the most important man in any civilized society. He is the man who counts for most and who brings the greatest pleasure, to whom we owe the greatest debt of gratitude.'[10] But these artists could only be encouraged by the exertions of society; they could not be mass-produced by the state. However, society had a duty to make their living conditions better for artists. In fact 'we owe it to ourselves, as a civilized community, to see that the working conditions of artists are tolerable and that they do not live in penury and in circumstances of difficulty'.[11] The scheme that was eventually introduced did

171

considerably more for the most popular authors than for poor ones, but worked well enough.

Such high-minded interventions were balanced with the occasional piece of traditional fixing. Goodman's control of the Council was considerably tightened once he finally managed to shift Nigel Abercrombie into regional management. Goodman was relieved to replace him, but there was a problem finding someone to take his place.

Hugh Willatt was a solicitor from Nottingham whom Goodman had made chair of the Drama Panel. They had disagreed and argued over a number of issues but Willatt was much more to Goodman's liking than Abercrombie. Goodman and Willatt were engaged in an argument over the Nottingham Playhouse. According to Willatt's recollection, he rang Goodman and asked if he could come and have a talk. 'Of course, dear boy, any time,' he was told, but the only time that fitted Goodman's schedule was after a dinner party at 11 o'clock. Goodman had by now moved from Ashley Gardens to Portland Place.

In the dead of night a heated argument ensued about the future of theatre in Nottingham, with Goodman resisting further regional aid to complete the project. After talking each other out, Goodman suggested they have a drink. Willatt had a whisky; Goodman had a Perrier, then said: 'The question of the secretary-generalship is coming up. Are you wedded to the law?' The job had to be advertised, but Goodman thought that Willatt should have it. Willatt went home and talked it over with his wife, who told him, 'You're cut out for it.' So Willatt agreed. The advert still had to be placed and the charade of selection gone through.[12] In his *Memoirs* Goodman inverts the order of events:

We naturally advertised the job in the press. I take the view that a job of any importance should be advertised. It should not be suspected that a small coterie has perpetuated its power by replacing one place man by another place man. The advertisement, however, brought a most pitiful response. We had only about a dozen replies. The selection committee, appointed by the Council, interviewed each candidate carefully. The most promising candidate was a semi-retired civil servant who certainly had the intellectual ability and seemingly the imagination to discharge the work. But somewhat cautiously I made a point of reading one of his few publications. It turned out to be a sustained attack on the operation of public subsidy for the arts. On that score alone he did not seem to me ideally suitable to supervise the day-to-day working of the Arts Council. But him apart, there was no suitable candidate.[13]

Goodman's version was that at this point he had an idea:

I invited Hugh Willatt, a practising solicitor who had been the chairman of the Drama Panel for many years and was one of the most influential, although rather taciturn, members of the Council, to supper one evening in my home. I then asked him whether he would consider taking on the secretary-generalship.

At the Council meeting in June 1968 Goodman mentioned that one of the applicants had 'become aware' that an application from the Council was contemplated and had objected to this as a kind of insider dealing.[14] Goodman said that he had given an assurance to the Department that 'the appointment had by no means been a foregone conclusion'. Indeed Willatt was a very successful secretary-general. The interesting point is Goodman's sensitivity to the charge that he would fix the job. The order of events comes down to a choice between two memories: Goodman's and Willatt's.[15] On balance, someone who is asked to give up a partnership in the leading solicitors Lewis Silkin & Co. to take a job that would combine his passion for the arts with a new career is more likely to have an accurate memory of events than someone for whom this was one fix among many.

Whatever the mechanism of the fix, the result was a more harmonious Arts Council and a wider suspicion of Goodman's powers. These more informal interventions were a key aspect of his tenure at the Council. There were three layers to his style of operation. The first was the political layer, composed of his access to Lee and Wilson. Except on the occasion of the investigation of the Arts Council by the Estimates Committee, this almost always worked to the advantage of the Council. The second layer was his professional network in the arts and television, which gave him an enviable set of personal contacts. The third layer, which overlapped with the first two, was the Friends of Arnold. The three together allowed him to solve problems himself. As Noel Annan put it, when he needed help for some venture he was involved in, he could count on Goodman: 'He introduced me – which was invaluable to me – to some of the great benefactors, such as Max Rayne – that was absolutely invaluable. Whenever I wanted money I could always phone Arnold and say, "Is there any hope?" '[16]

A few examples will give a flavour of Goodman in action. The choreographer Richard Buckle was trying to set up a theatre museum and Goodman was keen to help. The opportunity arose to purchase a backdrop that had been painted by Picasso for Diaghilev. The museum was not fully developed but the chance could not be missed. Goodman persuaded the Council to advance the money to purchase the curtain, and then raised this amount from the Friends of Arnold in order to pay the Council back. On another occasion the ICA galleries were moving slowly in their preparations for opening because of a lack of funds. Again Goodman raised the money, from Max Rayne and others.[17] In 1963 Lina Emery had founded the English Bach Festival with a small Arts Council grant. After Goodman became Chairman he backed the Festival strongly and when it needed money he came up with an anonymous donation, which Emery always thought was from Goodman's own pocket.[18]

In the spring of 1970 the wage rates of musicians again came to the fore. Goodman was personally sympathetic to the Musicians' Union's resistance to possible redundancies among its members at Sadler's Wells. He made it clear at a meeting of the Council that it was not the Council's policy to reduce musical employment and that there were instances where increased employment opportunities had resulted from the Council's actions. He could also point to instances in which his intervention had helped to save entire orchestras. Later that year there was a threat to the future of the Bournemouth Symphony Orchestra. On Goodman's initiative – he arranged and chaired the meeting – representatives of the local authority, the Bournemouth Symphony Orchestra and the Musicians' Union met and reached an agreement which saved the orchestra.

While all these interventions were successful, Goodman's unconventional techniques could sometimes backfire. The most important instance was his personal initiative in transferring the Sadler's Wells opera company to the London Coliseum in St Martin's Lane, to form the English National Opera. Goodman and Willatt realized that moving Sadler's Wells would be very expensive. As Goodman recalled:

For some months my principal concern at the Arts Council was to procure the funds for this important artistic change, and I was involved in long and complicated negotiations both with the owner of the Coliseum and with others to whom it was possible to appeal for what was plainly an important national cause. Financial help and encouragement were received from an astonishing number of opera supporters, and it was a source of great satisfaction to me when the hour arrived for Sadler's Wells to become the English National Opera, as it did in 1974, and establish itself as one of the cornerstones of artistic activity in the capital.[19]

Willatt cites this move as one of Goodman's great personal achievements and one which he did virtually alone.[20] However, the method of funding it was questionable. The way in which it was done reflected a slightly relaxed view of financial arrangements. As Lord Harewood puts it: 'In his day at the Arts Council, you were not allowed to put away money for a rainy day. When a rainy day comes, they said, we will see you are all right. We don't pass your budget unless we think you should reach your target box office figure.'[21] The Council allowed Sadler's Wells to run up a deficit of £300,000 and the Council allocated an extra £75,000 for the move, money which the Welsh National Opera claimed should be theirs.

The Estimates Committee of the House of Commons took a less relaxed view of Goodman's imaginative presentation of the figures. The Auditor-General had noted the irregularity of Sadler's Wells's deficit and the way in which the management of the capital grants fund had been altered. Neither was particularly serious and both would have been rather hard to spot in the normal course of things. There was a strong suggestion that someone had shopped the Council. The suspicion in Goodman's mind was that the Conservative MP, David Eccles, later Minister for the Arts, was behind the inquiry.[22]

Goodman was very upset that an inquiry had been launched and was adamant that he had to defend the Council. It is revealing that in his *Memoirs* he ridicules civil servants' response to the inquiry. He always maintained a disdain and rudeness towards civil servants, learned from Jennie Lee. Civil servants represented the conventional and ordered way of doing things, whereas he liked the direct and, frequently, the chaotic. He did not much mind what rule he bent to achieve his objectives. There is room for a very small number of

Goodmans in the arts world; not much would happen without a large number of arts administrators and civil servants.

As Anthony Field remembers, Goodman rode right through any bureaucracy that stood in the way of getting the right decision for the arts. To an extent this was true, but in the case of Sadler's Wells the Auditor-General gave him a pretty good run. When the possibility of an inquiry was first raised Goodman exercised his First Law and told his officials he wanted to speak directly to the Auditor-General. He was told that nobody speaks to the Auditor-General.

> . . . in due course a rather rasping voice came through saying, 'Yes?' 'Sir Bruce,' I said (I think that was his name), 'I wanted to talk to you about the Arts Council because this suggestion that we should appear before the Public Accounts Committee [sic – in fact the Estimates Committee] could do a good deal of harm to our fund-raising activity.' 'Can't help that,' he snapped. I persevered slightly but soon observed that I was up against a brick wall, and being one who lacks the physical resources for destroying brick walls, decided that on the whole we had better proceed with the matter.[23]

Having failed to circumvent the procedures for ensuring that potential corruption and impropriety were reported to parliament, he prepared the material required by the Estimates Committee of the House of Commons.

Field attended the first meeting, along with Abercrombie and Willatt. A 'little chap' came and sat with them. 'Who are you?' The man replied, 'I'm your accounting officer.' 'Where are you from?' 'The Ministry of Agriculture and Fisheries.' He told them that when the Council was set up under Royal Charter a civil servant had to be the accounting officer and he was it. He had never been near the Arts Council.[24] When the committee began to question him it became obvious that he knew nothing, and he was replaced as accounting officer by the secretary-general. It was he who would then have to present the Council's case to the Estimates Committee. The Auditor-General now raised an objection to Harold Lever, chair of the Committee. According to Goodman's *Memoirs*, he said: '"Mr Lever, do you think you ought to preside over this committee since I believe that Lord Goodman is rather a pal of yours?" To which Lever replied, "A pal? . . . No, he is not a pal of mine, he is a very dear friend."'[25] The Auditor-General then concentrated on the procedural point that only the accounting officer should appear. Goodman consulted Harold Wilson, who had been chair of the Public Accounts Committee in opposition, and Wilson reeled 'off a list of hearings before this committee when a chairman [of an organization under investigation] had appeared'.[26] They compromised and allowed Goodman to sit next to Field, the witness called from the Arts Council. Goodman rated Willatt highly but was worried that he would be bullied by the Estimates Committee. Lever kept reminding Goodman that it was supposed to be the accounting officer and not he who was doing the talking. Field remembers the whole thing as a terrifying experience: 'You get to the room, with police standing at the door and you really feel if you give the wrong answer you'll be taken to the Tower.'[27]

> The trial took place in a Committee Room in the House of Commons, under conditions that would have horrified Judge Jeffreys. The public was totally excluded and even a Member of Parliament who sought entrance was brusquely discouraged – notwithstanding that he was a member of the Arts Council. The Minister for the Arts, Jennie Lee, racing to defend her fledglings, was turned from the door like Queen Caroline from the Coronation. The actual proceedings resembled an Asian bazaar far more than a judicial tribunal. The members of the committee arrived and departed haphazardly throughout the proceedings, so that I doubt if any member was in attendance for the whole performance.[28]

The first main charge, arising from the formation of the English National Opera, was that the Arts Council had made financial commitments on capital projects for which it did not have the resources. Goodman strongly denied that he had made any such commitment.

> 'But,' they said, 'you told these people that you would give them the money.'
> 'Yes,' I said, 'but only on condition that we would give it to them if it was voted to us.'
> 'Was there not then a legal commitment?' they asked.
> 'Certainly not. I speak as a lawyer and you can consult any other lawyer you like, and I also have the authority of Mr Justice Scarman that this is the correct view.'
> 'Well then, was there not a moral commitment?'

'Yes,' I said, 'there was a moral commitment; had we been given the money and not given it to the local Council we would have behaved very improperly.'

'Wasn't there something midway between a legal commitment and a moral commitment?'

'Alas,' I said, 'I do not know of anything midway between legal and moral commitments and due to shortage of money we are unable to employ any Chinese metaphysician to deal with the situation.'[29]

On the claims of the Welsh National Opera for the additional funding that had been given to the ENO, Goodman was just as dismissive:

> First of all, the Welsh Arts Council said we used £75,000 to move Sadler's Wells to the Coliseum which could have gone to the Welsh National Opera. This was absolute poppycock because the Welsh Arts Council is an autonomous body that gets its own grant. At the beginning of the year they arrive with their mules and camels, we count them out their ingots, they put them in their bags and off they go over the hills with their money. They spend their money, we spend ours and Scotland spend theirs. If we were to spend £75,000 of their money there would be the most colossal to-do in Wales and the massing of troops on the border would be terrifying.[30]

This was an entertaining though disingenuous answer because at issue was an allocation of additional funds and not a part of the existing grant for Wales. However, the overall result after a bravado performance by the Arts Council, completely dominated by Goodman, was more than satisfactory from Goodman's perspective. The report vindicated the Council. He could not help crowing in the Annual Report:

> During the year there has been considerable and ever-increasing Arts Council activity at hand. First and foremost we had to deal with the investigation of the Estimates Committee. That Britain is no longer 'the country without music' (or any of the other arts for that matter) is largely due to the patient work of the Arts Council over the past twenty years or so in supporting and encouraging performing, and to a lesser extent, creative artists. It must surely therefore appear a more than usually odd paradox that the nation spent as much in 1965–66 on military bands as

178

was given to the Arts Council, even after the substantial increases in grant. These increases were absolutely and proportionately considerable, but it is clear that there is still a long way to go, even if the road has an end. The Report has not merely vindicated the exertions of twenty-one years – a mere five so far as I personally am concerned – but has, I believe, achieved a healthy public purpose in dispelling, through the eyes and mouth of a completely objective and impartial body, a number of the legends and myths with which we are beset. First, it is immensely satisfactory to find that, although the ambit of the Committee's inquiries extended to a great many Arts Council subsidized organizations (the Committee were prepared to receive evidence from anybody, however disgruntled – the gruntled rarely give evidence), not a single instance was brought to their notice, or suggested, of extravagance or wastage by Arts Council customers. And there was not a vestige of a suggestion – as indeed we should hope would be the case – of anything but the most proper and scrupulous use of the funds which we so widely disburse into so many quarters. It is an immense tribute to the artistic beneficiaries of this country that an investigation of this kind should conclude with a totally negative result on these scores, and it would be wrong if we did not react to these conclusions with a faint suggestion of pride and even of trumpet-blowing. But, of course, the thrift and probity of financial administration, necessary as they are, do not vindicate the ultimate use of the money. What was no less satisfactory was the emphatic conclusion arrived at by the Committee that what we were doing needed to be done, and, what is more, that the sums of money we were administering were inadequate, and should be augmented on a scale which we ourselves had never had the temerity to suggest. But we shall, now.[31]

Goodman did not try similarly fancy footwork in the other big move, of the National Theatre to the South Bank, which was developed under his chairmanship.

In 1848 Effingham Wilson, a London publisher, put forward the first proper proposal for a National Theatre in the UK. The unsteady relationship between the arts and government and the still rather less than respectable reputation of the theatre compared with that of the popular brands of Victorian science represented in institutions like the Natural History Museum, resulted in little progress for the remainder of the century. In 1903 Harley Granville-Barker and William Archer published a book outlining definite plans for the creation of the national company housed in its own building. In the event the company was created before the building.

The first major step in creating the new building for the National

Theatre came in 1945 when the London County Council offered a site (later changed) for the theatre to be built on. The National Theatre Bill followed four years later, but little progress was made. Pressure by the LCC under the Leadership of the late Sir Isaac Hayward culminated in its offer in 1961 to find the sum then needed to meet the balance of the cost. By this stage the company had been assembled under the direction of Laurence Olivier and another company had been formed, based at Stratford–upon–Avon, to produce new Shakespeare interpretations. This second company – which eventually became the Royal Shakespeare Company (RSC) – was under the direction of Peter Hall.

The site for the new home was changed a number of times in the 1960s. As the late Nicholas Tomalin pointed out: 'the National Theatre foundation stone has been ceremonially laid in at least three – arguably four - temporary positions'. The logic of placing the National Theatre building within the area which would eventually include the Royal Festival Hall and the Queen Elizabeth Hall, the Purcell Room, the Hayward Gallery and the National Film Theatre was a powerful one, but the location, like virtually every other aspect of the development of the National Theatre, was heavily contested.

Goodman's first involvement with the National Theatre had come when he was still an ordinary lawyer. In 1960 Emile Littler, an impresario in the West End, recommended to Lord Chandos, the chairman of the board engaged in planning the National Theatre, that Goodman would make a good solicitor for the project. Goodman's first impression of Chandos when they met was 'of a slightly burlesque, patrician figure, with more than a touch of arrogance and as profound an ignorance of the theatre as was possible for one man to marshal in a lifetime'.[32] Goodman was duly appointed and charged with drafting a constitution for the new National Theatre in London. On 21 March 1961 Selwyn Lloyd announced that the government had decided against a National Theatre. As Peter Hall's biographer puts it:

> Lloyd's announcement contained wonderful news for Stratford. Instead of paying for a National Theatre, he said, the government proposed spending £400,000 a year to subsidise the Old Vic, regional repertory theatres, and Stratford. Quite suddenly, the principle of subsidy seemed to have been accepted, and in the absence of competition from Olivier's as yet unformed company, Hall would be running what was effectively a National Theatre.[33]

Chandos did not favour such an outcome. He attacked Lloyd and other Tory Ministers, 'making a charge that establishment figures use only *in extremis* – that the Chancellor had insulted the Queen Mother, who had laid the foundation stone of the National Theatre in 1951'. Three months later 'Lloyd announced a U-turn: the National Theatre would happen after all' and announced that the funds for building would be released and set up the South Bank Board to build the theatre on a 4.7-acre site. The LCC had offered to put up more than £1 million itself, and Lloyd asked the Council and the LCC to come up with a new scheme which would spend an annual subsidy of £400,000 on the opera and ballet as well as on the theatre. The South Bank site was to have an opera house as well as the National Theatre. Lloyd's message suggested that, having changed its mind, the government was determined to crush any mavericks.

> If any one of the three organisations concerned should not participate in the scheme, any annual subventions would have to be reconsidered, and the Government would be under no obligation to contribute monies for the improvement of their existing premises.[34]

Lord Cottesloe, then Chairman of the Arts Council, now informed Hall that the National Theatre project would take all the subsidy that the Council was planning: there would be nothing for the RSC. 'Perhaps Cottesloe did not intend it as such, but to Flower and Hall this was a declaration of war. They seemed to relish the challenge.' Into this theatrical battle of egos stepped Goodman with a constitution for the new National Theatre. The National Theatre's secretary, Kenneth Rae, asked him to take the draft around the organizations that would make up the proposed new institution – Sadler's Wells, which would be replaced by the new opera house on the South Bank, the RSC and the planned National Theatre Company. 'Sadler's Wells presented little difficulty. Jimmy Smith was then the chairman and an immensely amiable, kindly and gentle figure. Stephen Arlen was the director, and the document was agreed without trouble.' Peter Hall and Fordham Flower were not to be so easy. Goodman set out for Stratford accompanied by Jane Samuel, the wife of a close friend. He intended to see Ian Bannen in *Hamlet* and meet Hall and Flowers to look over the constitution.[35] The weekend was not a success. According to Goodman, Jane Samuel was 'rather highly-strung' and 'collapsed at various points all over Stratford, particularly at the very beginning of the play so that I had to cart her back to the hotel, have her attended to and dash back to the theatre for the next two acts'.[36] (Hall's biographer has Samuel merely slipping on some steps.) However, the meeting with the RSC team had been even less successful:

> Sir Fordham Flower, the chairman, much beloved, effective, simple and nice; Peter Hall, much beloved, effective, complicated and often nice; and various other faces including Mr Patrick Donnell, later the administrative director of the National Theatre, to whom I explained the document in the naive belief that the principle had been agreed. They looked at the document with lack-lustre eyes and minimal interest. Who, they said, is to be the head of the organisation? I coughed slightly, since no one had told me, but I opined that it was likely to be Sir Laurence Olivier. There was an exchange of glances, and faces which had never been wholly welcoming became rather distant. It was clear to me within seconds that on the basis of the leadership of Laurence Olivier, to whose qualities they paid tribute of unstinting eloquence, there was going to be no Stratford included in the new entity. They told me that they wished to consider the matter further; that there were complicated reasons why it might be difficult for Stratford to become absorbed, and I departed from lunch firmly convinced that we had seen the last of them, at least while Sir Laurence dominated the scene.[37]

Flower later 'refined to three the reasons why Stratford backed away from the idea of amalgamation. One was the fear that Stratford would quickly become the poor relation in the partnership; another was that, "to put it very bluntly, we didn't like the set-up"; the third was his belief that public opinion was opposed to the idea.' Goodman returned to London and was politely dropped by Chandos as solicitor for the National Theatre, and was replaced by a City firm. Four years later, the National Theatre having been established at the Old Vic while it awaited its permanent home on the South Bank, Goodman returned to these matters as Chairman of the Arts Council.

The South Bank Board was given the initial development role, and was responsible for the building of the theatre, which, when finished, would be handed over to the National Theatre Board. A Building Committee, under the joint chairmanship of Sir Laurence Olivier and Norman Marshall, designed the three stage areas.

Goodman spent many long hours in meetings with architects and administrators, advising Jennie Lee. The architect chosen was Denys Lasdun, who had designed the Royal College of Physicians in Regent's Park (1960), the University of East Anglia (1968) and the flats in St James's Place overlooking Green Park (1958). Finally, on 3 November 1969, the new theatre was inaugurated by Lee, as Minister for the Arts.

The overall cost of the project came to £16 million. This was paid in part by central Government, and in part by the GLC. In the end, after much negotiation, the GLC contributed a fixed sum of £5.7 million. The National Theatre started to operate in the new theatre with an Arts Council subsidy of about £2 million and with a GLC subsidy of £300,000 in its first year. The plan at the outset was that when the National Theatre was operating fully, just under half its total costs would come from box office and other National Theatre receipts, and just over half from subsidy.

Goodman's critical contribution to the process of getting the National Theatre built was in separating the project from the building of the new Opera house on the same site. Together with Jennie Lee, Goodman stopped the building of a second London Opera House and though this entailed a set of redesigns and new expenditure, it meant that the National Theatre could be built. Amid the endless meetings with architects and the boards of the various bodies concerned, Goodman defended Lee and watched out, as a National Theatre Board member from 1968, for the interests of the Arts Council. Though the building has never been a success, the National Theatre itself is one of the major legacies of the Lee–Goodman era.

One of Goodman's late interventions as Chairman of the Arts Council drew heavy fire from the critic Kenneth Tynan. Tynan's opinion of Goodman was representative of a small minority of writers and artists who flourished during this period and likewise took a negative view of him. Tynan thought Goodman typical of the 'tyranny of the middle way', the *éminence grise* behind many a reform movement of the period, and a 'fanatical compromiser'. His rage was provoked in particular by Goodman's role in finding a replacement for Laurence Olivier at the National Theatre. In 1971 Goodman made what Kathleen Tynan, in her biography of her husband, calls a 'secret approach' to Peter Hall. Goodman sounded out Lord Drogheda, who was employing Hall at Covent Garden, on the possibility of a change. Lord Chandos, the Chairman of the Board of the National Theatre, with whom Olivier said he could no longer work, was being replaced by Max Rayne in August. Goodman decided that Hall would make the perfect replacement when Olivier stood down. After Rayne was in place, so was the fix. Though Hall denies that he knew about it, Kathleen Tynan claims that Hall made it clear that he would not come in as Olivier's assistant. Whatever the truth of the matter, Rayne told Olivier on 24 March 1972 that the Board favoured Hall, and Olivier, according to Tynan, felt the decision was a *fait accompli* and 'acquiesced as gracefully as he could but felt a sense of outrage at his treatment'.[38]

Olivier agreed to resign when the new National Theatre was fully open. His outrage was not, apparently, communicated directly to Goodman. In his *Memoirs* Goodman records Olivier coming to see him at the Arts Council to 'thank me for the consideration I had shown in relation to his resignation'.[39] The bitter pill was sweetened when Wilson, probably at Goodman's suggestion, offered Olivier a peerage. Kenneth Tynan's reaction to these events was bitter:

> I hate the most important decision in the administrative history in the English theatre being taken by a property tycoon (Rayne) and a lawyer (Goodman) without full word from the people who planned, created and evolved the national theatre.[40]

His broader judgement on Goodman is also worth quoting:

> when it actually seems as if real democracy might be about to exert some genuine influence on the nation's life, the ruling class produces an antibody to counter it. The antibody in our time is Lord Goodman. A man who has never held elective office, he wielded more power than anyone in the country, except for the Prime Minister in the last decade.[41]

The hyperbole of this attack, which was echoed by others that he had bested over the years, appealed to Goodman. He quoted the remark in full in his *Memoirs*, commenting: 'I find this allusion highly flattering, although alas untrue.'

The contingent nature of his own power and influence was clearly demonstrated in June 1970. If Harold Wilson had not forgotten about the purchase of two jumbo jets which were included in the balance-of-payments figures, he might have won the 1970 general election. In the end he lost to Edward Heath, the builder's son from Kent whom Goodman had met before the war. He was personally sympathetic to the arrival of Heath at Number Ten, commenting that the Prime Minister had 'installed a musical instrument which cannot be operated mechanically', i.e. a piano.[42] This was a view in sharp contrast to his assessment of Wilson as a philistine in artistic matters.[43] But the effect on Goodman's world of the arts was immediate and not pleasant. He lost, in Jennie Lee, a Minister with whom he had the closest possible relationship, as well as a Prime Minister who was also a client. The new government was a slightly unknown quantity but the new Minister for the Arts, David Eccles, was neither trusted nor liked by Goodman. On his prospects, Goodman allowed a hint of sarcasm to enter his Annual Report that year:

> At the Arts Council we shall contract astigmatism by keeping our eyes fixed on him with steady and unwavering hope. He is a cultivated man who has established his personal love for the arts, and our first encounters with him have been stimulating. Since we believe that what we are doing is good and necessary, it is gratifying to find him of the same belief.[44]

There was a certain worry later in his report:

> Inevitably a change of government, involving more than anything a change of social and political philosophy, must cause questioning about State support for any activity. We have frequently repudiated the extremists who regard the State's as the only appropriate purse to finance artistic projects. It is inconceivable that such a notion should be acceptable in a free society. But we are unrepentant in our belief that whatever the political faith of the government administering us, there is an area of artistic activity that must wither and die without help from the public purse.[45]

There were reasons for Goodman's sense of unease. In March 1969 he had reported to the Council on a session of the Conservative Party seminar on the arts, at which Eccles had suggested public spending on this area might decrease and incentives be given to the private sector to increase its support. The Conservatives' general-election manifesto pledged the Party to:

... continue to give full financial support and encouragement to the Arts. The Arts Council will be strengthened so that it can take a more active role in stimulating regional co-operation and in establishing effective regional arts associations. Local authorities will be encouraged to play a larger role in patronage of the Arts. We recognise the vital importance of private patronage. We will devote special attention to those areas of artistic life such as museums and music colleges which face particularly acute problems.

Goodman responded to these new policy directions with some trepidation. He told the Council that the uncertainties of the policy 'could have a profoundly discouraging effect on artistic activity'. His response was to argue again that the Council should try to increase the publicity which surrounded its activities so that more people would understand what it was doing.

But the writing, however vague and general in tone, was on the wall. Once the new government was in place the Council set about debating the ways in which it could increase funding from private sources. Goodman was reluctant to see change. He did not think that the Council should engage in fund-raising activities on its own account, but was prepared to consider how it might formalize what it was already doing in a small way to assist its clients in raising money from the private sector. He was aware of watching the costs of the Council itself. When it was proposed to make two new appointments to the publicity staff he queried whether they were necessary, but he was not prepared for a change in the underlying nature of the Council's operation. In the event, little actual policy changed under the new government; however, the personal relations were worse and though Goodman's term was extended for an additional two years, he did not stay beyond this.

Labour's loss of the 1970 general election created a new role for Goodman in his relations with Wilson. As soon as an election result is announced the losing Prime Minister has to move out of Number Ten. Wilson had a considerable overdraft and there was a conflict between his desire to stay close to the action and Mary Wilson's desire to withdraw a little after six years in the limelight. The compromise was that they sold their house in Hampstead Garden Suburb and purchased, for £21,500, Grange Farm in Buckinghamshire and, for £20,000, a short lease on a house in Lord North Street, near the House of Commons.[46] Wilson also wanted a proper office.

Management consultants were brought in and they, writing to Marcia Williams's brief, assessed the cost of a proper office at £25,000 per year.[47] Wilson secured £300,000 from the advance and serial rights to his account of his first administration.[48] But there was need for more. Two trusts were established after the election. The first was a political research fund, contributed to by the Rowntree Trust and organized by Sigmund Sternberg. This provided the so-called 'Chocolate Soldiers' who did research for Shadow Cabinet Ministers.[49]

Goodman was brought in to help organize a second trust specifically for Wilson. Wilfred Brown, an industrialist and junior minister in his government, assembled a group of wealthy donors known to Wilson. In addition to Goodman, these included Rudy Sternberg, Samuel Fisher, Jarvis Astaire, Donald Gosling, Arieh Handler and Cyril Stein.[50] Rudy Sternberg and Fisher later received peerages from Wilson; Wilfred Brown already had one. Rudy Sternberg was suspected, by Wilson himself, of being involved with the Soviets and at the time of his death his house was being watched by the security services.[51] Arieh Handler was the manager of the International Credit Bank of Geneva,[52] which was linked to the Israeli security services and was forced to close in October 1974.

The stories of this trust, which was actually quite modest in scope and to which Wilson himself was the largest single contributor, merged into the allegations, which appeared in *Private Eye*, that Wilson had been paid by the raincoat manufacturer Sir Joseph Kagan for a consultancy. In fact Kagan had made donations to help with the costs of Wilson's political office during the premiership but had not employed Wilson while he was the occupant of Number Ten.[53] Wilson wrote to Goodman on 11 November 1971 asking for him to get an 'apology, a clear retraction, costs and an undertaking about the future' from *Private Eye*. He got most of what he asked for. This was the second writ of the year that Goodman issued for Wilson. On 16 July 1971 a writ was issued against the BBC. David Dimbleby had alluded to Wilson's financial arrangements in his film *Yesterday's Men*. In addition to a bitter exchange with Wilson himself on the serialization deal, Dimbleby had not told contributors what the programme would be called, and in introducing Wilson had said that the former Prime Minister had used his privileged access to government documents to profit from the secrets of government.[54] Three years later the *Eye* revealed the details of the funding of

Wilson's private office in opposition, but this time no proceedings were taken.

Goodman's own view was that Wilson was being extravagant in the way in which his office was funded. Even so, he issued the desired writs and the 1970s began with Goodman facing the unknown quantity of a new government but still playing the familiar role of looking after Wilson.

10

Hot Dogs and Diaries

I prefer a bad agreement to a prolonged disagreement.
(Goodman in his *Memoirs*)

Goodman, at his height, had access to the political leaders of all three
major parties, connections in the forms of a network of friends and
contacts in the highest level of business and the arts, and the ear of
the Establishment. However, he did not possess vast amounts of
capital, he did not make laws, control the lives of thousands or daily
influence the fate or opinion of nations. The power that he wielded
and the influence that he had painstakingly accumulated were based
on perception. His was a world of smoke and mirrors. Those who
claimed that he was a major force in the land were usually people
such as James Goldsmith whom he had thwarted in some way and
who responded by elevating his status to explain their defeat. (In
Goldsmith's case this preoccupation extended to trying to hire a
journalist, Bruce Page, to write an exposé of Goodman's role in
public life.) So long as people believed Goodman had power and so
long as he behaved as though that power were within his grasp, the
legend held. The power was mainly reflected from the flame of
Harold Wilson: while that glowed brightly, the 'Fear of Arnold'
flourished and his influence was something to behold. As Wilson's
light dimmed, so Goodman's reflected brightness dulled. But he had
a good run and his repute reached its height during his secret
diplomacy missions to Rhodesia.

There was a moment in Goodman's early life when he had
contemplated emigrating to South Africa to practise the Roman and
Dutch Law that he had studied at UCL and Cambridge. There might
also have been pressure from Bertha because of the eminence and
success of her brother Morris and the Mauerberger family in their
business in South Africa. But the war intervened and by the time it
ended Goodman was set on establishing his own practice in London.
But southern Africa was to return to play a role in his life: privately
in the 1950s and publicly in the 1970s.

Goodman's first trip to southern Africa had been in connection with his uncle Morris, who had joined the family's South African interests in manufacturing and retailing, emigrating there before the First World War. Sometime in the later 1940s, while still working in Kisch's practice, Goodman received a telephone call from his uncle. This was not particularly welcomed by him. Morris was a difficult man, who made enemies, was a bully and, according to Goodman, particularly enjoyed estranging those close to him. Largely uneducated, he had a quick, agile business mind, formidable powers of mental arithmetic and a practical man's contempt for formal education – he prevented his five children from attending university. For these traits and for his meanness with money, Goodman's father, Joseph, particularly disliked Morris.

Bertha had introduced Morris to his wife Helen, the daughter of one of her oldest friends, and the marriage, largely through Helen's inertia, was a success. Goodman recalled his formidable uncle after meeting him in London in 1930:

> I recollect in conversation with him, when he was staying at a luxury London hotel, his query about why I needed to pay a visit to Rome. 'You can,' he said, 'see it all in postcards. Why take the trouble and expense of going there?' It was, I believe, Whistler who, when asked to explain one of his paintings to a counsel engaged in his cross-examination, told him that it would be as futile as trying to explain a Beethoven symphony to a deaf man. An even greater futility would have been to try to explain to my uncle anything relating to the splendours of human thought.[1]

There was another side to Morris. Before he died he established a charitable trust to put much of his fortune to work and, recognizing the limitations of Joseph Goodman's money-making capacity, he settled an income on Bertha, as well as supporting Theo during her lifetime. As Goodman recalled: 'He was, I must confess with pain, a horrible man. In consequence of his horribleness, my father, who was sensitive and scholarly, loathed him and was very reluctant to admit him to the house. My mother, whose universal love of mankind could extend even to this pestiferous brother, insisted on seeing him when he came to London, and in justice to him he had a sufficient sense of family solidarity to bestow on her a minute income, for which he exacted a very full price.'

Because of his father's distaste for Morris, Goodman and his uncle rarely met in Goodman's early years. It was therefore a shock when Morris telephoned to ask him to come out to see him. 'I need legal advice and there is no lawyer in South Africa I can trust,' he said. Goodman replied: 'I am afraid it is an impossibility. I am heavily involved in my practice and my much older partner would be very unwilling to let me go.' 'Tell him I will make it worthwhile,' he said. 'It is not a matter of money,' Goodman replied. 'But come you must,' Morris said. 'You have never been to South Africa and you will enjoy a visit.' 'I will talk to my partner and send you a cable.' 'Make sure you come.' Kisch did not object and Goodman set off on his first visit to South Africa. Morris collected him from the airport and took him to a hotel to explain the situation. His son and heir, Joseph, had been married to an Egyptian Jewess but had fallen for a young Englishwoman who was working on the cosmetics counter of a department store in Cape Town and now wanted to marry her. Morris regarded the woman as a gold-digger, but Joseph would not budge. So Morris forced him to sign away his fortune. Joseph was now suing his father for the return of the share of the family fortune in the form of shares. Goodman advised Morris to settle. To which Morris replied: 'Settle! I will see him at the bottom of the Bay!' Goodman met Joseph and the young woman, and it was clear that neither of them would change his position.

I concluded my visit by making various legal recommendations in consultation with South African counsel – for the conduct of the law suit. It seemed to me, knowing my uncle, that time would heal the situation – as indeed it did. I recommended a course of action that would have taken at least five years and during that time both sides could come to their senses . . . On my final day Uncle asked me to come into his study where he was sitting at his desk with a large cheque-book, which gave rise to interesting expectations. 'I must,' he said, 'pay you a fee.' I went through the characteristic motions of a slight demur – unwisdom in the extreme. Before I had even faintly demurred, Uncle said, 'Well, if you do not want a fee, that is all right,' and closed the cheque-book. In the end I returned to England with a second-hand Remington typewriter, without a lid, and with a dinner-jacket manufactured for me by a local tailor, to enable me to travel respectably on a Union Castle boat, still maintaining the conventions of Empire.

Some 20 years later Goodman returned to southern Africa as the

envoy of the British Prime Minister, Harold Wilson, to try to broker
a solution to one of the worst residual sores of Empire. In the late
nineteenth century Zimbabwe had been invaded by speculators
based in South Africa and led by Cecil Rhodes. It was fully
incorporated into the British Empire as a British Protectorate in
1891 and in 1923 was granted a measure of autonomy known as
'responsible government'. This was technically not the same as
Dominion status but the British government virtually never used the
powers it held in reserve to overrule the Parliament of Southern
Rhodesia (as Zimbabwe was then called). The white minority ran
the institutions of state on the basis of an electoral franchise which
had a property qualification which virtually no black Africans could
reach. In the 1960s there were about 250,000 whites and nearly five
million blacks. Gradually, as in South Africa, racially discriminatory
laws and regulations affecting growing areas of social life and the
state were introduced. Rhodesia was firmly on the road to full
apartheid.

As a self-governing territory in the British Empire with a white
minority regime, Southern Rhodesia was in an anomalous position
when, in the early 1960s, decolonization started in earnest. In 1953
it became part of the abortive Central African Federation. In
1963 the Federation was wound up and a year later Malawi (formerly Nyasaland) and Zambia (formerly Northern Rhodesia)
became independent under straightforward majority rule. The white
Rhodesian government had applied for independence in 1960 but
Britain wanted an assurance of eventual democratic majority rule.
The constitution of 1961 was a tiny step in this direction. The
franchise was extended, with a complicated system of two electoral
rolls depending on property, and the apparatus of a Declaration of
Rights and appeals to the Privy Council in the event of constitutional
dispute. It was claimed, with disingenuous optimism, that under this
constitution majority rule might arrive in 15 years. In reality it would
have taken most Africans centuries to reach the property threshold,
assuming, of course, that ownership laws allowed them to do so. The
bottom line was that the whites were not about to surrender their
hold on power. In December 1962 the relatively liberal Rhodesian
governing party lost an election to the more right-wing Rhodesian
Front Party, which favoured apartheid and independence under
completely white rule.

When Ian Smith became Prime Minister of Rhodesia in April

1964 the chance of a reasoned compromise or a gradual evolution became still more remote. Smith emerges from his memoirs as a deeply flawed individual, capable of breathtaking hypocrisy. He was also a gambler, set on a high-risk course, in which compromise which conceded the central point of democracy was not an option. Smith was ready to die in the last ditch. He was also an extremely shrewd operator who knew his constituency well: he played the British government for the next decade or so and, partly because of much misguided and racist support in the UK, managed to run rings round it. The first set of inconclusive negotiations had been taking place on the linked issues of independence and majority rule from 1963 to 1965. In these first set of talks, the Wilson government, building on the work of Alec Douglas-Home's government, codified the 'Five Principles' that should govern a settlement:

1. The principle and intention of unimpeded progress to majority rule already enshrined in the 1961 constitution would have to be maintained and guaranteed.
2. There would have to be guarantees against retrogressive amendment of the constitution.
3. There would have to be immediate improvement in the political status of the African population.
4. There would have to be progress towards ending racial discrimination.
5. The British Government would need to be satisfied that any basis proposed for independence was acceptable to the people of Rhodesia as a whole.

After an election landslide for Smith's party in 1965 and more talks, Smith unilaterally proclaimed Rhodesia independent on 11 November that year. The Unilateral Declaration of Independence (UDI) was denounced by Britain as illegal under international law, and sanctions (the Wilson government decided firmly against military action) that became progressively tighter were introduced, including oil restrictions, in December 1965. The sanctions, applied first by Britain and then by other countries, were not effective. Rhodesia was supplied by South Africa and through the Portuguese colony of Mozambique; and there were flagrant breaches of the sanctions by many multinational companies.

New negotiations took place after the 1966 UK election (at election times Labour policy was for 'No Independence Before Majority Rule', but in government Wilson actively sought a compromise solution) and this led to the talks on HMS *Tiger* in December 1966. The sticking point was the transition arrangements, particularly the interim powers of the British governor. Smith showed no enthusiasm for the scheme and it was turned down by his Cabinet.

By his own account, Goodman was no expert on Rhodesia or Africa before becoming involved. A leading historian of British policy in Rhodesia, Elaine Windrich, wrote of him:

> Presumably his selection for this mission was based upon the premise that Rhodesia was merely another problem to which he could apply his obvious talents as a negotiator. It was also possible that his choice for the task was due to the fact that, having no political constituency to which he was responsible, he had no prior commitments which would either inhibit his freedom as a negotiator or offend those with whom he was obliged to negotiate.[2]

His interests in Africa were limited to family connections with the South African élite in the form of the Mauerberger family and an involvement with South African business interests as a director of a firm called Gee Marine from 1962 until May 1971.[3] Wilson did not judge this lack of expertise to be a drawback and Goodman's first exercise in secret diplomacy was authorized in August 1968. Lord Beaverbrook's heir, Sir Max Aitken, had commanded Ian Smith in the RAF in Egypt during the war and was still a friend; he arranged for Goodman (who was his friend and legal adviser) to travel incognito to Rhodesia and meet Smith to arrange an agenda for another set of talks with Wilson.

The initiative for the 'Aitken–Goodman' mission was, according to Kenneth Young's pro-Rhodesian history[4] and Ian Smith's self-justifying memoirs,[5] with Aitken. However, according to Goodman's account it had been instigated by Wilson when he asked Goodman for advice about how to get talks started and who might make a suitable intermediary. What is clear is that Smith trusted Aitken in a way that he did not trust Wilson.[6] Aitken and Goodman visited Wilson at Number Ten on 30 June. Wilson indulged in his love of intrigue:

Sir Max said I looked well. I replied that I was, 'apart from this appalling deafness'. This was news to him, but I explained it by saying that, for instance, I had thought he had said he would shortly be visiting Rhodesia. No, he said, I must have misheard. Then realising what I was after, he said that I heard correctly, and went on, 'Did you hear me say I was going?' (Full marks to Sir Max.)[7]

From this exchange it would seem that Wilson had indeed instigated things but did not want to be identified at the time as the person who had done so.

As well as the personal link, Aitken had the traditional Beaverbrook prejudice in favour of the white Commonwealth, as reflected in the *Express* newspapers' stance on Rhodesia. As Smith put it: 'the *Daily Express* and the *Sunday Express* had always adopted a realistic and honest approach to the Rhodesian problem.' The initial moves took place in April 1968, but Wilson activated the mission in August on condition that it was secret and looked unofficial. Wilson wanted Goodman to go with Aitken on the mission.[8] According to Goodman, Aitken brought a girlfriend.[9]

Goodman still had a considerable practice to run and shuttle diplomacy tended to interfere with the smooth running of his office. Moreover, he could not tell his staff precisely where he was going, but he had to tell them something so that if the press called they had some sort of answer. Goodman Derrick partner Leighton Davies remembers:

He used to say to me I'm going to count the penguins in Iceland. And I knew what he meant, and that was what we always told any newspaper that rang. They had to speak to me, and I used to say he's gone to count the penguins in Iceland. And they would say, 'Ho, ho, ho.' But they couldn't get anything else. And we had a method of contacting him, we had a contact in the Foreign Office who I could ring and tell him that I needed to talk to Arnold urgently on some business or other, and the message would get through to him and he'd ring. But apart from that we never knew what was going on.[10]

There were no direct flights to Rhodesia because of sanctions, so Aitken and Goodman flew to Johannesburg and then to Salisbury. Smith provided full security. Wilson's memoirs record: 'Their aircraft was grounded some distance from the terminal, and on leaving it they were surrounded by as many security guards as Mr Nkomo would have attracted, and whisked off by car to a guarded suite at the hotel.'[11] Goodman waited while Aitken went ahead and then was summoned after Aitken reported that Smith would see him. Smith saw Wilson's motivation for allowing Goodman to undertake the mission as being of use to the British government: 'Anything which would help to divert attention from all the local problems which were closing in on the government.' But such a view underestimates, as Smith and many others did, Wilson's real political convictions in this area and is anyway entirely contradicted by the secrecy of the mission: how could a secret mission help with Wilson's domestic position? If unsuccessful, there would be no bad press. If successful, it would be a major diplomatic coup. More accurate is Smith's assessment of the problem of secrecy: 'It was difficult to keep Goodman under cover, because he was a large man, both in height and mass, with prominent features and large, husky, black eyebrows, dressed in the dark suit associated with members of the British legal profession.'[12]

Goodman had a first conversation with Smith, having resisted Smith's efforts to keep him waiting.[13] This first talk Smith described as constructive and he felt himself 'subjected to incisive analysis by the clear, well-trained legal brain of a man who was highly rated by his profession in Britain'. Goodman then telegraphed Smith's responses straight to Wilson via a specially secure cipher to Downing Street and then to the Prime Minister's holiday home in the Scilly Isles.[14] The ground was laid for another round of talks before 'Goodman (who carries a lot of weight) became seriously ill, a victim of Salisbury's 5000ft altitude. But thanks to Aitken's administrations of brandy, the teetotal Goodman got home safely.'[15]

The August talks with Smith produced a nine-page memorandum which Goodman took back to Wilson. Secrecy was impressive: other than a reference in the Rhodesian press to 'two mysterious persons from England', nothing leaked. Further talks took place: 'a series of coded messages from Hot Dog [Aitken] and Friend [Goodman] to Old Mate [Smith]'.[16] It proved promising enough for more contacts to be made at an official level and for Wilson to meet Smith again, this time on HMS *Fearless* at Gibraltar in October 1968. At this meeting Smith appeared ready to accept the Principles (a sixth had been added since 1966: that there should be no oppression either of a minority by a majority or vice versa). However, the *Fearless* talks produced a formula that was weaker than *Tiger* on several counts. One of these regarded the composition of the body which was to examine racial discrimination, while another concerned arrangements for a Rhodesian Front majority on the transitional government. Among other measures, Britain agreed to provide aid for educational programmes to increase the number of black voters. Despite Smith's initial acceptance, the proposal still failed to win support from the Rhodesian Cabinet and Smith attacked the continued appellate jurisdiction of Britain's Privy Council. Goodman thought that he could have done better; his exclusion from the *Fearless* delegation he felt had been 'a mistake'.[17] The proposals remained on the table, but Rhodesian intransigence continued.

A new constitution was produced in 1969 and became operational in March 1970. There were 16 black African seats out of 66, and a formula for extra representation linked to income-tax payments which would produce parity (majority rule was not permitted) in possibly several hundred years. The new constitution also prevented the Declaration of Rights from being justifiable in courts of law, which curtailed the influence of the Privy Council.

Goodman's role in relation to these two sets of talks illustrated the strengths and the limitations of his skills. Few others could have managed Smith in the preliminary sets of conversations, because few could have inspired the level of trust necessary on both sides for the process to begin. Goodman enjoyed this position simply because of the promiscuousness of his friendships and client base: the Aitken–Wilson link gave him the ability to be comfortable with both sides. The bottom line for Smith was the impossibility of majority rule; the bottom line for Wilson was that majority rule was essential to any settlement. There was a good reason for excluding Goodman from the *Fearless* talks: this was not a dispute in which a complex compromise would work in the long run. This was, in the final analysis, about principles and power politics, and Goodman was wrong to lament his exclusion, but deserves praise for his role in the initial feelers towards talks. After the talks on *Fearless* had broken down, the Rhodesia problem receded from British politics for a year or so.

The Heath government elected in 1970 was committed to making another attempt to solve the problem. Goodman was again called upon — he had told Heath in the late 1960s that he would be prepared to try again if the Tories won the election.[18] Miles Hudson, Douglas-Home's political secretary from 1971 to 1974, records:

'Well chaps, we've had the weekend to assess our positions
and frankly, that's the position I'd like to see you in . . .

This was a brilliant choice as not only was Goodman a supreme
practitioner of the art of negotiation, but he had performed a similar
function for Wilson, and Labour Party political criticism of his role could
not be strident. Apart from his intellectual ability which was very
considerable, Goodman had three invaluable attributes. He was
consistently optimistic and never downcast by an apparently total
impasse; he had a great sense of humour which again and again brought
a sense of proportion at the vital moment; and he was a very nice man,
courteous, understanding and friendly to everybody whatever their
views or position – he was as polite to the African servant scrubbing the
floor outside his room at Meikles Hotel as he was to Smith or to
Douglas–Home.[19]

Goodman made a secret visit to Salisbury in April 1971, again under
the auspices of Max Aitken and with the blessing of the Conservative
Foreign Secretary, Douglas–Home. This was not disclosed until
September — another example of the cloak-and-dagger trappings
with which all the Goodman missions were surrounded.

Goodman's second secret visit on behalf of Douglas-Home was on 9–10 June; he observed the availability of fuel and consumer goods in Rhodesia and concluded that sanctions were a fraud. As with all his trips, he was given the authority to talk only to Smith, and not to enter into discussion with black leaders: indeed in all his dealing with the Rhodesian question he heard only the white case in detail. His talks were sufficiently encouraging that they were announced in the British press on 16 June and a publicly reported trip was arranged for the end of that month. On this occasion he was accompanied by an official team: Philip Adams from the Cabinet Office, Philip Mansfield (the Foreign Office Rhodesia officer) and Gordon Smith QC, a Foreign Office adviser on constitutional law.[20]

Perhaps Wilson's passion for secrecy on the earlier mission had been justified by the complications caused during these talks, which started on 28 June. On 1 July there were student protests outside Smith's office before Goodman arrived that morning, and coincidentally some harsh sentences were announced that day against school pupils who had previously been protesting. Because the talks were in the public eye they were linked to the sentences. According to Goodman, he raised an unofficial protest with Smith by calling the caning sentences 'potty' and they did not go ahead. The talks adjourned for the weekend, and some of the party flew to Victoria Falls, while Goodman went to Durban to witness the July Handicap and visit the Mauerbergers. Rumours started at once that this was a pretext for secret discussions with South African government representatives, and the Foreign Office was rushed into a denial.[21]

On 4 July Goodman returned to Salisbury and further discussions took place ('everything is convivial')[22] before he returned to London on 8 July, a day earlier than planned with a memorandum from the rebel government and his own account of the proceedings. The June–July talks were very much Goodman's show: he had been given more or less a free hand by Douglas-Home and did not have to report back daily.[23] It was probably at this talks marathon that he conceived the regard for Smith – 'essentially a worthy man' – which he later expressed in his *Memoirs*.[24] He came to like Smith, and when they were both left out in the cold (Goodman not consulted, Smith on the defensive) during the Lancaster House process in 1979 had a convivial lunch with him and Max Aitken. Smith for his part also appreciated Goodman.

The content of all the Goodman discussions in 1971, however, remained unknown to the public, though the statements of Douglas-Home and Smith about the Principles remained far apart and Smith was under pressure from those in his party who wanted a firmer entrenchment of apartheid. Goodman and Douglas-Home developed a good working relationship of mutual trust. During the visits questions were asked about who would be paying Goodman's fee. Douglas-Home called Goodman to ask him what his fee would be. Goodman characteristically said that he considered the trips – he made five in all – to be a public service, which Douglas-Home saw as the perfect answer. They continued to meet through July before the process was paused to avoid entanglement with the European Community negotiations also taking place. Goodman's memorandum was not presented to the Cabinet in July,[25] and it was not until the end of August that it was decided that he should return.

Goodman was back in Rhodesia from 16 to 18 September 1971 ('Lord Goodman . . . appears to have been given a season ticket,' was the *Daily Mail*'s comment)[26] and made sufficient progress to allow an official delegation to visit in November. According to Miles Hudson, he managed to get the Rhodesians to agree that the 1969 constitution was unacceptable and that a transition to majority rule should occur in the foreseeable future; much remained for the final sessions despite overoptimistic press accounts of a 'breakthrough' in Goodman's September discussions. In fact there was no indication that the grass roots of Smith's party had budged an inch on the principle of majority rule.

As Goodman arrived back in England from the world stage that September, he was confronted with an unpleasant domestic problem. His impressive record of helping his friends and clients make money in television and property deals had been extensively chronicled in the press. But his own finances were something of a mystery to Fleet Street. Goodman was notoriously bad at billing people but also acquired the reputation of being very expensive. His rule of billing seems to have been one of social discrimination: he wanted money only from those that did not contribute to his expanding social web and the building of the legend. Duchesses did not, in the main, have to pay. Goodman was also a very generous man. The question the press asked was: did the accounts add up? Occasionally Goodman's record-keeping and the sheer volume of his involvements led to mistakes and caused extreme embarrassment; his accounts might, if they had been investigated by the Law Society at the time, have led him into even deeper trouble. As it was, when the press got on the scent of a Goodman story they ran with it as far as they could before the writ arrived: *Private Eye* was always at the head of the pack in Goodman-baiting.

In September 1971 a file detailing accounts controlled by Goodman and held at Barclays Bank appeared in the offices of *Private Eye*. On 24 September the following item appeared in the magazine:

> The newspaper proprietors have missed the negotiating skills of Lord Goodman, their chairman, while he has been away on other negotiating business in Rhodesia. When Lord Goodman returns from Salisbury he will, no doubt, be up to his neck in the press crisis and will not have time to answer the increasingly hysterical letters from officials at Barclays Bank in the Strand where Lord Goodman's private account is overdrawn by nearly £20,000. The overdraft has crept up from the £14,000 mark since 1967 despite scores of letters and telephone calls begging Lord Goodman to make it good. Barclays head office have always allowed the overdraft to stand. Lord Goodman, it is noted on the top of his account, 'has introduced very useful business in the past'. Even so, an internal Barclays note earlier this month commented: 'The time must be fast approaching when we will have to consider making a formal demand.'

Goodman was landing at Heathrow from his short visit to Rhodesia which had started on 16 September when he was handed a copy of *Private Eye*. He immediately phoned the *Eye*, demanding a meeting in his office that afternoon. The editor, Richard Ingrams, called his lawyer, Geoffrey Bindman, who advised that he and Paul Foot, who had written the article, should attend as requested. Foot had lunch with his father the same day in a restaurant in St James's Street. Goodman was also dining there and spotted them. He spoke to both courteously and said to Paul: 'I'll be seeing you later on.' So that afternoon Ingrams, Foot and Bindman duly presented themselves at the basement office in Little Essex Street, off the Strand. They sat around the large table and Goodman told them that they had committed a crime and that he wanted *Private Eye* closed down. Bindman replied that he did not see in what way the magazine had committed a crime: it had simply been given the documents. It may have been that there had been a breach of confidence, but that was a matter for the bank. Then Goodman, in Bindman's words: 'went absolutely mad, and said to Richard, "I strongly advise you not to take the advice of your solicitor". He was incredibly pompous, spoke in this amazingly Victorian lawyer style – he was absolutely furious, probably partly because he realised there was nothing he could do about it. In fact he did not do anything about it.'[27]

Goodman's problem was that the account was a Portman family trust account and he was the sole trustee. He should have responded to the letters: why had he failed to do so? Why was the account overdrawn over such a long period? At the least Goodman was failing as a trustee, at the worst illegitimate use was being made of clients' funds and the bank statements had exposed the practice. What else would explain his level of rage, or his failure to take action? If he had sued *Private Eye* or the bank he would have had to prove that the trust fund-holder had been spending the money. If he could do that, then why not sue? The answer, it seems, is that if he had sued the *Eye* on this occasion he would have had to admit that mistakes had been made in the handling of clients' accounts and his reputation would have suffered even further damage. Despite the fact that Goodman was not going to take action, the magazine decided that it would be prudent to print an apology and a correction, which it did in the following issue. It was the second crack in the façade of Goodman's professional standing, though, like the earlier Estimates Committee investigation, the Fear of Arnold contained the damage in the short term.

The *Private Eye* débâcle was dealt with, but the Rhodesia crisis rumbled on. Douglas-Home led a delegation, including Goodman, to talks with Smith which took place on 15 November. Before leaving England Douglas-Home had persuaded Lord Pearce to head the Commission that would test the acceptability of any settlement to the black African community. Goodman would have preferred the former Lord Chancellor, Viscount Dilhorne, as the Commission's head.[28] His later judgement, given to Douglas-Home's sympathetic biographer, D. R. Thorpe, was that Douglas-Home's contributions smoothed the way: 'In the negotiations, Alec showed exemplary patience, was devoid of partisan feeling, dispassionate and represented his government's viewpoint without fear or favour.'[29] When it was clear that an agreement would be reached, Goodman flew home. Douglas-Home wrote to him: 'We concluded only a few minutes after you left . . . The final product is as good as I think we had any right to expect and a good deal better than often seemed possible.' He went on to thank Goodman for his 'tireless energy and unmatched ingenuity'.[30]

An agreement was signed on 24 November 1971. To Windrich, and to most Labour, Liberal and Church opinion at the time, it was 'the Salisbury sell-out'; for Lord Caradon the worst constitution in the world. The agreement conceded even more than *Fearless* and bore a dubious resemblance to the Six Principles. The Rhodesian leaders thought the prospect of majority rule under its provisions remote: the provision for the creation of new institutions was hedged about with too many conditions and hurdles, and in any case would probably not arise until some time in the distant future, although Goodman estimated that it might come sooner than most people thought. The property qualifications for black voters were higher than in the 1961 constitution. The Declaration of Rights would be enforceable again once the State of Emergency was lifted and the repressive laws introduced since 1962 would stand. Apartheid as such was out, although there were weak provisions about official racism and land tenure which would mean, in effect, that the pace at which black Africans would reach of the property qualifications necessary for voting would be fixed by the government. Miles Hudson defended the deal as reversing the trend in Rhodesian policy from moving towards apartheid to a recognition of human equality and an eventual trend to proper democracy, but the hurdles remained and there was no real acceptance of the principle of majority rule.[31]

After the conclusion of the deal, Goodman spoke in its favour in the House of Lords in December. It was the speech of a good lawyer defending a deal: pragmatic and defensive.[32] However, his private attitude could be expressed differently. According to *Private Eye*[33] and the white Rhodesian dissident Judith Todd, his real view was disapproving and cynical. At private meetings on 30 September and 6 October 1971, Todd maintains that his view was that the settlement would serve mainly to increase black resistance (as its collapse probably did) and that it was time Rhodesian blacks and white liberals stopped having illusions about Britain coming to the rescue. He might in this conversation have been playing to his audience, but his realism in this private talk is in marked contrast to his optimism in public.

An agreement may have been reached, but the fifth principle, concerning broad acceptability, still had not come into play. The Pearce Commission, which took evidence in the first half of 1972, was the device chosen by the British government to measure Rhodesian opinion. The disenfranchised Rhodesian blacks were overwhelmingly hostile towards the agreement. This was clear as early as the second half of 1971, when Goodman was dubbed 'Lord Badman' by black leaders. The fact that the weakness of the agreement was not painfully obvious from the outset is an indication of the desire on the part of the British government to get some kind of deal that would extricate it from the situation. According to Goodman, Smith was convinced that the tribal chiefs could deliver the African vote: 'No one warned me that the idea the chiefs could control the tribes was wrong. The tribes controlled the chiefs.'[34] In Britain some on the right attempted to argue that the result of Pearce was unrepresentative but, as Goodman in his 1972 Lords speech makes clear, it was not. The deal could not proceed. The result should have surprised fewer people than it did.

In public Goodman defended the deal and used his influence to help Douglas-Home. By now he was Chairman of the *Observer*'s Board of Editorial Trustees and used his position to try to influence the paper's owner-editor, David Astor, but without much success.[35] More directly, Goodman Derrick forced the removal of references to Douglas-Home's 'Munich in Africa' from Granada's *What the Papers Say* in December, but other than this there was little Goodman could do to save the deal or even just improve its reception.

Goodman's pragmatic endorsement of the 1971 deal in December, in terms that seemed to say that despite the flaws any deal was better than none, was reflected by his philosophical response to the Pearce Commission's findings in the House of Lords on 21 June 1972. He felt that the result 'was that people who were politically dominated for years seized the opportunity of being treated as free men for a few seconds to utter a cry of defiance' and that distrust of Smith was the main reason. He personally claimed not to take 'the view that he would seek to renege on the agreement'.

> Speaking purely as an individual, it is a profound disappointment to me and it would be hypocritical not to say so. But all is not lost, and if we maintain the authority that I believe the Pearce Commission have given to us, if we maintain the faith of the African people that we are still there to see justice done between them and the people who they believe are dominating them, something good may still come out of it.

In his *Memoirs* he summed up the key point to him: 'I prefer a bad agreement to a prolonged disagreement.'[36] The problem with this view is one of proportionality. The lawyer's pragmatism works, and Goodman's worked in many instances when there was a choice between two lesser evils or in disputes which were essentially the bickering of two parties over inessentials – the ownership of television franchises springs to mind: so what if one group of capitalists wins a contract rather than another. In such cases our rotund Henry Kissinger was safely within his own depths and many of the people around him were out of theirs. But put him in at the deep end, in matters of life and death, in the choice between an evil and a good, between apartheid and democracy, and then the pragmatic deal-maker was not the person to send for. The fixer's actions have consequences and in this respect 'the architect of the Rhodesian settlement', as he allowed himself to be described on the sleeve of a book of his speeches published some time after the agreement, cannot avoid some of the guilt for the outcome.

In 1972 the African Nationalist forces started to wage a guerrilla campaign against the Smith regime – there had been sporadic incidents in the late 1960s – and by the late 1970s it had escalated into a full-scale civil war which killed 16,000 people. After Mozambican independence in 1975 the main supply route for white Rhodesia was cut. The Smith regime produced an 'internal settlement' in 1978 which gave formal majority rule but left whites with a veto on constitutional change and control over most public institutions. This failed to satisfy the British, and in 1979 the Lancaster House accord was signed. UDI was rescinded and the British took back formal control of the country to expedite a transition to majority rule, which was completed by 1980. In the light of this prolonged and bloody process the 1971 deal might be seen as something of an arcane historical detail. With hindsight, even if implemented sincerely by the Smith regime, it could not have been a lasting solution because there was a basic difference of principle which could ultimately be resolved only through conflict. But, in its own terms, Goodman's mission had not been a failure. He had succeeded in finding common ground between the Smith regime and the Heath government, and that was his task. However, any such formula would probably have been unacceptable to the black majority by 1972. Goodman (and the Pearce Commission) demonstrated that the diplomatic route had been exhausted. The larger question must be whether he was the right man to send and whether the deal that was struck, a typical pragmatic compromise, was the right deal to make. The evidence suggests he was the wrong man, given the wrong job, who came home with the wrong outcome.

"CURIOUS! I SEEM TO HEAR A CHILD WEEPING!" . . . AFTER WILL DYSON

'Every twitch,' the historian and constitutional expert Peter Hennessy has written, 'in the fortune of Cabinet government under Wilson Mark I [the Labour government 1964-70] was lovingly recorded by Richard Crossman, the would-be Bagehot of the twentieth century.' Crossman had been keeping detailed diaries since the early 1950s and part of the motivation behind his political career was to see these published and the inner workings of the British political élite exposed. That élite resisted the publication with vigour. The British constitution, they argued, was based on the notion of collective Cabinet responsibility. This was defined by Lord Salisbury in 1878 thus:

> For all that passes in Cabinet every member of it who does not resign is absolutely and irretrievably responsible and has no right afterwards to say that he agreed in one case to a compromise, while in another he was persuaded by his colleagues.

Moreover, though there can be a 'full and frank' exchange of views, once a decision is taken a Minister must give 'loyal support' to that decision and it must be considered 'as being made by the Government as a whole'.[37] If the internal workings of the Cabinet were recorded and published, then this notion would break down, and for some this would mean not just a threat to an important convention, but an attack on a 'reality and an important part of the constitution'.[38] Graham C. Greene, who, as Managing Director of Jonathan Cape, was to play a key role in seeing Crossman's diaries published, remembers lying awake at night during the controversy, wondering if what he was doing would undermine the British constitution.[39]

Crossman planned on a leisurely pace for the publication of his assault on the British Constitution. His plans changed in November 1973, when he was diagnosed as having a terminal tumour and given only a few months to live. On the same day he told Tam Dalyell: 'I'd better get on with organizing the Diaries.'[40] He visited his old friend and publisher Graham C. Greene to arrange his literary executors. Crossman's wife Anne and Greene himself were to be two of the executors. The third was to be Michael Foot, who, Crossman judged, was unlikely to be in the government if Labour were to win an election in the near future. Crossman was wrong about this and when Labour formed an administration in February 1974 Foot was appointed Secretary of State for Employment. Therefore a member of the current Cabinet was the executor for the publication of diaries that would reveal the inner workings of the previous Labour Cabinet. Crossman drafted a letter telling his executors:

> The immediate task of the literary executors, if I die before publication of my ministerial diaries is complete, would be to supervise this and make sure that the pressure, which will undoubtedly be brought to bear both from Whitehall and from Westminster to prevent publication of parts of the manuscript, is completely rejected. I hold this to be of the greatest importance since it is the publication of the diaries as a whole which will provide a unique historical record of how British Cabinet Government operated in the 1960s.[41]

This opposition from Whitehall and Westminster would come because the material he had produced challenged the notion of collective Cabinet responsibility and would alter perceptions of the nature of contemporary British politics by casting light into many of the hidden corners of British government.

On 10 May 1974, in accordance with the established convention that memoirs written by politicians are vetted before publication, the typescript of the diaries covering the period 1964–6 was sent by Greene to the Cabinet Secretary, Sir John Hunt. Hunt had been Cabinet Secretary since 1973 and was already operating in ways that would lead Peter Hennessy to judge his tenure 'the zenith of the power of that office, certainly since the Brook–Churchill years of

1951–5'. Hennessy quotes one anonymous assessment of Hunt as a:

> Fascinating man, a Jesuit with a total belief in the state and its objectives. Nothing, neither friendship nor anything else, would come before that. In many ways he was a frightening man in his devotion to the Hegelian concept of the state. He was only interested in two things – the [Roman Catholic] church and the state. He had extraordinary energy. He pulled power to himself and the Cabinet office. He intervened in twice as many things as Robert Armstrong [his successor].[42]

Or, as Harold Wilson's press secretary, Joe Haines, more succinctly put it: 'Sir John Hunt made the Secretary to the Cabinet the most powerful man in Whitehall.'[43] Hunt was constitutionally responsible for the business of the Cabinet and therefore took the lead in the negotiations with the publishers. In the midst of the battle he told Anthony Howard that it would be a 'tragedy for his reputation' if they were to be published.[44]

On 10 June 1974 the proofs of the book version of the diaries were forwarded by Cape to the Cabinet Office. Having read these, Hunt requested a meeting with the executors. On 21 June the executors gathered in his room in the Cabinet Office to be informed that the manuscript as it stood could not be published for 30 years and that an edited version was also unacceptable. A letter was dispatched to Greene the next day confirming that the diaries could not be published and that no amount of editing or cutting would alter his view.[45] At this point Greene phoned Goodman.

According to Hugo Young, Greene's initial judgement was that the opposition to publication being offered by the Cabinet Office presented a political rather than a legal issue – or rather a quasi-legal problem that existed in a grey area, partly legal and partly political. This was Goodman's domain.

In a letter to the executors from Hunt on 7 August, the formal case against publication was presented in terms of 'parameters'. These were (a) accounts of Cabinet discussions and the 'blow by blow . . . revelation of differences between members of the Cabinet', (b) accounts of advice given by civil servants, (c) discussion about senior civil servants' appointments, (d) conversations about members of the government which were clearly intended to be private.[46] Hunt's task was to enforce these parameters, which represented the legal front of the battle. However, the Prime Minister, Harold Wilson, would in the end make a political judgement about how far to go in trying to stop his former colleague breaking through the existing rules. Greene's judgement was that: 'If, in the end, Wilson himself was to have the casting vote in any decision to mobilize the ultimate deterrent – a court action to stop the book or prosecute its executors – it seemed sensible to begin working without delay at the semi-political level somewhat esoterically occupied by Goodman. The very ambiguity of his role might prove fruitful.'[47] Goodman's view was that Hunt's real target in trying to stop publication was not to prevent the revelation of any particular secrets contained in the diaries but to ensure that Crossman's comments on senior civil servants and other colleagues would not be revealed.[48] The Cabinet Office's fears were, of course, well justified. Michael Foot summed up the diaries at a Crossman memorial meeting on 15 May:

> The diaries, I'm glad to say, have exactly the degree of malice required for the purpose. They are laden with revelations and I've no doubt that the Cabinet Office over the next few weeks is hardly going to be able to give its mind to any other matter at all.[49]

The sensitive point on Civil Service appointments and advice was a real issue but not the central argument. This was that the diaries would undermine the fiction of collective Cabinet responsibility and that their publication would undermine the 30-year rule on the disclosure of official documents.

Goodman held his first meeting with Crossman's executors on 25 June 1974 in Foot's room in the House of Commons. He advised them the whole question of publication was much riskier than Crossman had supposed because the government could ultimately evoke the Official Secrets Act and claim a civil breach of confidence which would result in injunctions. He persuaded the executors to try again to reach a compromise with Hunt. Naturally Goodman was confident that what was at stake here was essentially open to compromise. If offending passages were to be removed, he was sure that Hunt would allow publication. It is not clear quite why he simply ignored Hunt's insistence at his first meeting with the executors that no amount of cutting would be acceptable. The Goodman confidence was clearly in evidence. Hunt agreed to see a revised version of the diaries but only if the executors agreed to show him any material they intended to publish 14 days before publication.

This would, of course, have given the government ample time to issue injunctions to prevent publication. Indeed it is a little unclear in quite whose interests this advice was offered. On 10 July 1974, Hunt, with little to lose on the terms Goodman offered, agreed to view an edited version of the MS. The Goodman Derrick partner John Montgomerie was given the job of trying to produce the edited version, and this was sent to Hunt on 6 August 1974. This new version 'pleased no one, for all its considerable ingenuity'.[50]

The publishers and the *Sunday Times* – who had agreed to serialize the diaries – disliked the new version and thought it was well short of the kind of record that Crossman wanted to publish. Foot, in particular, was adamant that this version was a cop-out. It was irrelevant anyway because, even in the revised form, it fell foul of Hunt's parameters. Hunt rejected the edited version in early August and all that had been achieved was that independence of action had already been compromised.[51] Goodman now suggested, at a meeting at his flat on 25 September 1974, that the executors could sever legal connections with the *Sunday Times*, which had not been party to the undertaking to Hunt to give 14 days' notice. Foot and others opposed this on the grounds that it was 'too transparently deceptive' and Greene disliked the gimmickry. The *Sunday Times*'s lawyers thought it would make their case harder. Hugo Young's judgement was that 'a typically Goodmanesque ploy foundered on the high mindedness of his clients – although it was to be revived a few months later'.[52]

Goodman meanwhile handled the correspondence with Hunt and continued to look for a compromise.[53] However, while the executors and the *Sunday Times* remained as a team they continued to be restricted by the 14-day obligation. In January 1975 Goodman revived the idea that the *Sunday Times* go it alone. He argued that the executors responsible for the Crossman estate would be failing in their duty if they risked publishing against legal advice. As Goodman later put it in his *Memoirs*:

> It was no secret that Michael Foot – believing that he had a duty to the late Dick Crossman to procure the publication of the diaries – was courageously prepared to accept the risk and bare his breast for the dagger. (I may say that Barbara Castle declined to give evidence on our behalf. It would be unkind to attribute this decision to her intention to publish her own diaries.)[54]

Foot's loyalty appears all the stronger considering that he himself disliked the idea of diary-keeping by active politicians and was distinctly of two minds about the issues of substance concerning Cabinet collective responsibility. Castle's reluctance to become involved remains curious given that she already had a contract for the publication of her own diaries.

The *Sunday Times* was losing patience with these endless complex manoeuvres by Goodman. Foot had already suggested that they simply write to Hunt telling him that they would publish anyway. The result was a combination of these two approaches. The executors gave the *Sunday Times* a licence to publish and on 20 January 1975 Goodman wrote to Hunt informing him that his clients and the *Sunday Times* both rejected the 'parameters': 'They see a difference in your attitude as compared with that of your predecessor [in evidence to the Franks Committee on the Official Secrets Act] in the drawing of a distinction between matters of national security, which Ministers have, in the past, deleted on request, and other matters which may be properly drawn to a Minister's attention but which, in the end, are left to his own discretion.' Goodman went on to inform Hunt that the *Sunday Times* was, from then on, acting alone.[55] Hunt responded with an ultimatum that the *Sunday Times* give him seven days' notice before publication. This was sent on 23 January 1975 but with a request for the notice to begin from Monday 27 January. Sir John's bizarre oversight gave the newspaper a unique chance to start serialization on 26 January without contravening any undertaking to give notice. In great secrecy and still having arguments with some of his own executives who urged caution, Harold Evans, the paper's editor, prepared six extracts, which began to appear on 26 January; at first they covered safe material already seen by the Cabinet Office, but then their scope widened.

By 16 March six extracts had appeared in the *Sunday Times*, and the paper had put 85,000 words into the public domain, including the most controversial section about the July 1966 economic crisis. On 2 April Goodman wrote to Hunt on behalf of the literary executors 'clearly expecting to go through only minor formalities before the book was published'. The reply came not from Hunt but from the Treasury Solicitor, Sir Henry Ware, and stated that 'the Attorney General [Sam Silkin] does not accept that the position has been changed by the serialisation in the *Sunday Times*'. They were therefore still opposed to publication of the diaries in book form because this would still violate Hunt's parameters.[56]

Goodman replied on 23 April 1975:

> I hope you will not regard it as flippant if I say that the Attorney General must be one of a very select band of people believing that the serialisation in the *Sunday Times* has not materially altered the position. Several matters that would clearly have come within your previous parameters now appear in print in a serialisation greatly exceeding the highest expectations of publishers.

However, Goodman again renewed the 14-day undertaking to inform the government of publication but this time threatened to withdraw it if Hunt continued his obstructiveness. Greene instructed Goodman to issue the notice to publish. Goodman advised strongly against it and insisted that Greene get letters from both Foot and Anne Crossman. Greene did so and the notice was finally issued on 5 June 1975.

The *Sunday Times* was angry that the Attorney General had let the serialization pass but was now attacking the weaker party, the literary executors. They increased the stakes on 22 June by provocatively publishing 'The Jigsaw of Truth', which contained Crossman extracts not seen by Cabinet Office plus recollections from other ministers and comparisons with Harold Wilson's book on the 1964–70 government. On 26 June an injunction was served, drawn so widely by lower-level lawyers that almost any political journalism would fall in it.[57] It was clear that the government was determined to take the matter to court. The Appeal Court discharged the injunction on condition that the *Sunday Times* undertook to publish no new Crossman material until after the trial.

Goodman had worked hard to prevent the affair reaching this point. He had warned the executors all the way through that the government would resort to the Official Secrets Act to prevent publication and that they should compromise to prevent such a confrontation. In fact the government's lawyers did not intend to use Section 2 of the Official Secrets Act, because prosecution of Foot as a serving Cabinet Minister would have been too bizarre and a defence of Crossman's ministerial 'self-authorization' would have been available. Crossman's death would also complicate the status of the information. This was not, of course, known until after the trial.[58]

Despite his efforts to prevent things going this far, as the case began Goodman told Greene that if it were lost he would find money for the defence's costs.[59]

The publishers and executors were represented by Goodman favourites: Brian Neill QC, Gavin Lightman and Leonard Hoffmann. But James Comyn QC for the *Sunday Times* was to dominate the trial. Sam Silkin, the Attorney General, led for the government. The grounds were civil breach of confidence, a much weaker weapon than the Official Secrets Act. On this, as Goodman described it, undefined rule of confidentiality, Lord Gardiner gave an affidavit for the Attorney General arguing against publication.[60] In response the literary executor's team of lawyers assembled affidavits from Godfrey Le May (Fellow and Tutor in Politics, Worcester College) on collective responsibility, John Mackintosh MP, H. W. R. Wade (Professor of English Law, Oxford), Harold Evans, William Rees-Mogg and Peter Jenkins on political journalism and discussions between journalists and ministers, Lord (Douglas) Houghton, Jeremy Bray MP and Jo Grimond on secrecy not held to be in the public interest, from Sir Anthony Nutting on his book on the Suez crisis, *No End of a Lesson*; from Roger Graef and Brian Lapping – on filming Whitehall committees during the progress of the Fair Trading Bill in 1973 – and finally from the historian Keith Middlemas on political memoirs. Various figures more closely connected with the diaries also gave evidence, including Greene, Anne Crossman, Janet Morgan and John Montgomerie of Goodman Derrick.

The government's case on confidentiality rested on Argyll v Argyll 1967. In this case the memoirs of the Duke of Argyll revealed details about the private life of his wife. The judge, Ungoed-Thomas Jr, held 'that a contract or obligation of confidence need not be expressed, but could arise independently of any right of property or contract'. The point was that there are special relationships which entail a contract of confidentiality.[61] Hunt and Silkin had a generally bad time. The Prime Minister had stayed publicly neutral in the whole affair and this tended to weaken the Cabinet Secretary's position. Neill, who led for the executors, concentrated on the public interest, the question of a breach of confidence and the nature of the injunction the government was seeking. There was also plenty of historic record that Hunt's parameters had been breached frequently, not only in the famous example of Anthony Nutting's book on Suez but even in Wilson's own record of the 1964–70

Labour government. The Public Records Act could not be invoked because it has never applied to comments on politics but only on documents as physical property of the Crown. As a result there was no precedent on the confidentiality of what ministers said. Moreover, the diaries of Hugh Dalton, a Cabinet Minister for most of the period from 1942 to 1951, had never been submitted to the Cabinet Secretary and were freely available in the LSE library. As Goodman later recorded:

> The government ... took its stand on the position that the confidentiality rule operated between members of the Cabinet and in the general context of a minister's official duties, and that it could be invoked in a court of law to restrain revelations of Cabinet and other officials ... the defendants took the view that the rule ought not so to relate and that such discussions should be free for publication without restraint or inhibition. The social desirability of either position was not really an issue, although needless to say it was copiously referred to. The matter the judge had to decide was whether, if there were confidences, there was any legal prohibition preventing their publication.[62]

There was general surprise that Lord Chief Justice Widgery ruled in favour of publication of *Volume 1* of the diaries, arguing that Crossman clearly agreed with collective responsibility and that:

> A Minister is, no doubt, responsible for his department and accountable for its errors even though the individual fault is to be found in his subordinates. In these circumstances, to disclose the fault of the subordinate may amount to cowardice or bad taste, but I can find no ground for saying that either the Crown or the individual civil servant has an enforceable right to have the advice that he gives treated as confidential for all time.[63]

Goodman's role as lawyer for the executors involved complex questions of constitutional propriety and well-balanced argument and always looked likely to be resolved by a deal. That the Crossman affair ended with Goodman's side, a little unexpectedly, getting everything that they wanted, was in part down to his advice. The Rhodesia episode and the Crossman affair displayed some of the best and some of the worst sides of the universal fixer at work.

11

The Fear of Arnold

Editors are no longer fully literate. They do not read.
Newspapers have been permitted to be sold to entirely
unsuitable people.
(Goodman on the press to David Selbourne, 1993)

Lord Goodman is a very good friend of mine, but can cause
Brobdingnagian confusion.
(Michael Foot on Goodman, 1974)

For the first six years of the 1970s Goodman was at the heart of the
newspaper world as Chairman of the Newspaper Publishers'
Association (NPA). Max Aitken, who had inherited the Beaverbrook
papers from his father, and David Astor of the *Observer*, together
nominated Goodman for the job in 1970. He held it until 1976. His
public views on the membership of the NPA were uncompromising:
'the most impossible body of men that could have been assembled
outside the League of Nations'. His private view, as expressed to
Donald Trelford, then deputy editor of the *Observer*, was even more
forthright: 'If I was to choose a cricket team of the most unreliable
villains I've ever come across in my life, I think some of the
newspaper owners would be on there. I can think of several, Max
Aitken . . . would be opening batsman.'

Goodman liked to give the impression that his relationship with
the British press was like that between a mother and her difficult
children. The children could not help but misbehave and the mother
had reluctantly to apply measures of discipline in increasing degrees
of severity to get the required outcome. Sometimes he only needed
to drop a hint of the terrible consequences if the misbehaviour
continued and the miscreants would come into line. At other times
a harsher verbal assault was needed, followed by a writ. The result of
such a self-image was that when the gentlemen of the press refused
to do Goodman's bidding, or indeed attacked him directly, he was
hurt as much as angered or exasperated. Such attitudes were actually
childish rather than parental.

Goodman's judgement in his *Memoirs* was: 'Few people today would claim any great credit from an association with the "newspaper" world.'[1] He actually seems to have enjoyed newspapers and naturally, once the door was ajar, his driving ambition and energy propelled him to the centre of yet another world: to the law, the arts, property and politics was now added the press. The newspaper with which he was most closely associated was the oldest and most liberal Sunday paper of the era, the *Observer*. He first met David Astor through his friend Ifor Evans, whom he had in turn met through Harold Wilson. In 1966 Evans was Chairman of the Board of Editorial Trustees of the *Observer* (known as the Observer Trust) and he recommended that Goodman become a member. Evans's plan seems to have been, from the outset, to make Goodman Chairman of the Observer Trust and in 1968 Goodman replaced him. In turn, Wilson, who frequently consulted Goodman about honours, gave Evans a peerage.

Astor became a second Wilson in Goodman's world. He 'played a large and influential part in my life and in my career . . . Within a few months of my first board meeting . . . David had developed an admiration for my qualities, wildly undeserved and totally excessive'.[2] In many ways the pairing was unlikely. Astor had been born with a silver newspaper in his mouth. He was part of the liberal establishment but had made the *Observer* the premier newspaper of the 1950s with his determined radicalism on subjects such as decolonization and Suez. Astor combined such radicalism with the social position and contacts that Goodman had worked hard on acquiring. They differed, after the 1967 war, on Israel, but on little else. Goodman's influence at the *Observer* was based on his access to Astor and he gradually became part of the fabric of the paper and of Astor's life.[3] From the late 1960s, if Astor became involved in a project or a cause, so did Goodman. Frequently Goodman came to see it as his role to protect Astor from people trying to take advantage of his good nature.

Goodman was interested in helping the paper, but he also had something to gain in that his access to it could be helpful to his friends: sometimes his interventions worked and sometimes they did not. On one occasion the paper wanted to run an article telling a famous story about George Brown, who was Foreign Secretary from 1966 to 1968. Brown had unsuccessfully propositioned a female guest at a lunch given by the French Ambassador and he then asked her if she had not received such invitations previously. She replied that she had, but not before the soup. Brown's long-suffering first wife was still alive and Goodman was worried that she would be offended by the story. He asked Astor to spike it but he refused to do so. Goodman threatened to resign – 'the one and only time I uttered a genuine threat of resignation'.[4] Astor gave in and pulled the article. Though this might have been the only moment Goodman 'genuinely' threatened to resign, it was not the only occasion he tried to spike stories and used the threat of his leaving as his weapon.

His *Memoirs* mention two occasions on which he intervened to keep a story out of papers other than the *Observer*. He implies strongly that these were the only times on which he tried to interfere with press freedom. As he put it: 'Time and again I was approached to suppress some item that would cause embarrassment or distress, and time and again I refused.'[5] Notice the assumption that of course he could have suppressed the items if he had wanted to but was loath to become involved. Such false modesty does not preclude the possibility that on other occasions he was asked and he did all he could. In other places in his *Memoirs* he states that he was also loath to become involved in libel actions. It is a little harsh to say that Goodman wanted to reinvent his past as he got older, but he certainly wanted to smooth out the rougher edges of that past. Naturally, as an old man he wanted to look back on what gave him pride and neglect a little of what he found distasteful.

The following two examples are revealing. In the first case: 'I passed on an appeal that I had received from a distinguished public figure about the intended publication of a piece of gossip about the illegitimate child of one of his relations.' Goodman succeeded in keeping the story out of the papers – Harmsworth at the *Daily Mail* and Aitken at the *Express* each agreed to sit on it if the other did. Though he does not mention the name of the public figure, it was in fact Lord Portman.

The second story concerns the land deals scandal which engulfed Wilson in 1974. The passage in Goodman's *Memoirs* about his role in this is cleverly crafted, the implication being that he simply told the *Daily Mail* that the story – about a letter which implicated Wilson in shady dealing involving members of Marcia William's family – was untrue. It cites an attack by Harold Evans, the editor of the *Sunday Times*, on Goodman for helping to suppress the letter in the run-up to the 1974 general election, thereby ensuring a Labour victory.[6] The letter was indeed a forgery but the incident was not, as the *Memoirs* suggests, an exceptional instance of Goodman working to keep something out of the press for Wilson. In fact it was a routine intervention.

Goodman Derrick had specialized in media work since Goodman's involvement in the independent television franchise bids in the 1950s and 1960s, but he developed his more specialized skills in media manipulation from 1964. The Goodman technique in these interventions was different in style, though not in tone, from his usual method in negotiating. Normally he was brilliant at finding the exact point at which there was the chance for two sides to agree. In cases involving Wilson he always applied Goodman's First Law: go straight to the top. He had long been fascinated by newspaper proprietors, asking Michael Foot to take him to meet Beaverbrook in the 1950s. Astor was an early client and was followed by Aitken and Rupert Murdoch. Goodman had a direct line to each of these men, although they differed in their response to his requests. If an approach to the proprietor did not work, or if there was no direct contact on the newspaper in question, he would approach the paper's editor. He rarely spoke directly to the journalists. Frequently, when editors or journalists heard that Goodman was involved, they caved in and told him what was going to be in the story, or even sometimes delayed publication or removed it altogether. His considerable reputation for securing victories for his clients nearly always succeeded and in turn helped build the legend of his almost mystical power and influence. He was mostly unsuccessful in preventing stories based on established facts from appearing, though even his discovery of what was in a piece could be useful in itself to his clients. The fact is, he had exactly as much power as he was perceived to have by editors and other journalists; this in turn was determined often by the intrusiveness of the proprietor in the affairs of the paper.

On one occasion Goodman was wheeled out after a bizarre encounter between Astor and Richard Crossman. In the last days of the 1964–70 government, Crossman had had lunch with Astor, throughout which he attacked Wilson. As Astor told it afterwards to Donald Trelford, his successor as editor: 'His portrait of Harold Wilson and what's going on in the government was devastating.' Later that day Astor told Trelford that Goodman had been on the phone, at the request of Wilson, to find out what was going on and what was going to be in the *Observer* that Sunday. Apparently

Crossman had left lunch and gone straight to Number Ten to tell Wilson that Astor had been attacking the government and to warn him that terrible things would be in the paper.[7]

Sometimes two of the key Friends of Arnold would square up against each other. In October 1973 it was Astor and Sidney Bernstein of Granada. Through the 1960s the *Observer* had frequently attacked Granada's programming and Astor and Bernstein had kept up a 'slightly fractious correspondence'.[8] On Sunday 7 October 1973, in an article headlined 'The £25 million Barranquilla scandal', there was the assertion that 'Lord Bernstein now owns 64.2 per cent [of the shares] through his master company Granada group, as well as having the lion's share of the 7.4 per cent personally owned by the Barranquilla board'. The following day Bernstein issued a writ. He did not have a single share in the company. The case dragged on for 18 months before the High Court awarded damages of £35,000 to Bernstein. The *Observer* appealed. Goodman, 'in his role as friend indicated tentatively that it might be wise, now that Bernstein's name was vindicated, to settle out of court'. Bernstein refused and Lord Denning in the Court of Appeal upheld the verdict and damages. It was a notable failure of Goodman's ability to smooth troubled waters.[9]

Later the *Observer* was considering naming the fifth man in the Cambridge spy ring and Goodman rang, at the prompting of the person concerned, to urge the paper not to because it had it wrong. It had already decided not to publish. According to Trelford: 'He'd ring up really just to find out what was happening on behalf of a friend. Sometimes he would say, "Well, you ought to be aware that he's in a very difficult position at the moment and I think adverse publicity would be very damaging to him; and since he stands on the same side of life as the *Observer* does, I can't believe you really want to hurt somebody like that." Never a direct threat.' There were difficulties later when the *Observer* attacked the Chairman of the BBC, Marmaduke Hussey. On one occasion Hussey asked Goodman to sue. Goodman undertook to stop him doing so if the *Observer* promised to lay off for a while. However, Trelford does not 'remember any occasion where you had a good story, true story, and Goodman said, "Pull it" and we pulled it'.[10]

When Goodman, at his height, really wanted to keep an article out of the newspaper he could be more of a bully than Trelford allows. In 1967 Anthony Howard was the *Observer*'s US correspondent.

Howard came back on leave. A story was breaking about the television franchise deals and he stayed on in England to write an article about one aspect of it.[11] He put together a piece, with information from his friend John Morgan, on the TWW franchise deal. This intimately involved Goodman and his friends and clients.

In the autumn of 1956 TWW was the first consortium to throw its hat in the ring. TWW was a merger between several groups that had applied for the franchise for Wales and the West but not been able to raise sufficient money the first time around. The consortium was headed by Lord Derby, the entertainer Jack Hylton and Mark Chapman-Walker of the *News of the World*, all of whom were Goodman Derrick clients. The application took the form of a letter from Goodman Derrick. Goodman handled most of the arrange-ments for forming the consortium,[12] at the same time acting as an adviser to Southern Television. Goodman's involvement in television continued over the next 11 years. In 1967 the franchise for Yorkshire Television, the fifth major ITV region, was also opened to applicants. Prominent among the candidates for the Yorkshire franchise was a consortium called Yorkshire Independent Television, which also represented the fusion of two earlier would-be applicants, one led by *Yorkshire Post* Newspapers in association with the local picture chain, Star Cinemas, and a London-based one made up principally of EMI, the *Daily Telegraph*, Penguin Books and British Lion films, which Goodman had brought together. In the event rival bidder Telefusion won, on condition that it recruited more or less the Yorkshire element of the Goodman–*Yorkshire Post* coalition.[13] Goodman was much later, in 1981, also responsible for introducing Rupert Murdoch to Brian Hayes, a television producer who owned Satellite Television plc. The result was Sky Television. For nearly two decades he was thus in the thick of the television bidding wars.

Howard's *Observer* article, 'How the West was Won', told the story of how a group of 'amateurs and play actors' put together a consortium – Harlech Television – and defeated Lord Derby and the *News of the World* in the bid for the franchise. The piece was handed in on a Friday. It was 2500 words and was to have prime placing on the review section's front cover. Howard heard nothing until 6.00 p.m., when David Astor came out of his office scratching his nose, which was, according to Howard, 'always a bad sign'. 'I want to have a word with you . . . I've got Arnold Goodman in my office and he's very upset by what you've written.' The young Howard, then 33, was ushered into Astor's office to confront Goodman. 'I've been reading your article. I'm very disappointed in it,' growled Goodman. It is not clear how often he read the paper before it was put to bed. It is likely that he had been tipped off that something affecting one of his commercial interests was going into the paper and that Astor had then allowed him to see it in advance. Howard asked: 'Well, what's the trouble?' Goodman rather cryptically replied: 'Wickedness has been committed and wickedness has not been exposed.' There followed a 'very unpleasant' interview until Howard was asked by Astor to leave. Later that evening Astor approached Howard again. 'What if I told you that Lord Goodman says he will resign as chairman of this paper if I publish your article, what do you think I should do?' Howard replied that this was not a matter for him. Thirty years on Howard still remembered the whole affair as rather strange.

> I don't say he would necessarily have followed my advice, but my brusque response was to say really that's not a matter for me. 'What I have written I have written, now you must decide, your decision as editor, whether you want to publish it.' I don't know if those were my exact words, but it was still very odd. You have to understand what David was like to see why he said this, but I fear I sent him away, as it were, with a flea in his ear, and the article duly appeared. Whether Goodman had said, 'I'll resign', I don't know.

Goodman did not resign.[14]

Later, after Astor had been succeeded as editor by Donald Trelford, Goodman would still sometimes ring the *Observer*. If Trelford were away he would get on to Howard, by then deputy editor. The editor's secretary would come out and whisper, 'Tony, I've got Lord Goodman on the line' and Howard would come to the phone and say, 'Ah, good afternoon, my lord, what can I do for you?' 'Oh, a very delicate matter,' Goodman would say, 'one of my clients is led to believe there may be something appearing in the *Observer* and I wonder whether you would be kind enough, if such is the case, to read it to me.' Howard would answer, 'Well, I'm not sure I can do that.' The response was always in a velvet glove: 'I think it might create difficulties were you to follow that course of action.' The threats were gentle, never improper, and the aim was to pre-empt. Sometimes it worked and sometimes it failed.

Goodman's involvement went far beyond merely interfering with stories. Trelford and others give Goodman the credit for saving the paper in the early 1970s, when it went through some very harsh years. The honour must be shared with the leading journalist and broadcaster Kenneth Harris.

The crisis at the paper came to a head in 1975 with redundancies and massive cost-cutting. The roots of the paper's problems were in the general state of the market but also in the particular circumstances of the *Observer*. Astor's weakness as a business manager, even as he triumphed as an editor, was exposed by the cutthroat competition from the other Sunday papers, most significantly the *Sunday Times*, edited by Harold Evans. The commercial problems were compounded by the general economic situation, which hit both advertising revenues and sales. The adverse effects of the industrial-relations record of the newspaper industry in these years also contributed to heavy costs.

The *Observer's* independent position was guaranteed by two trusts. The publishing trust owned the buildings and most of the stock in Observer Holdings, the operating company. The Observer Trust, chaired by Goodman, selected the editor and was responsible for maintaining the paper's editorial character.

In 1966 the Thomson organization bought *The Times* from Lord Astor of Hever – an uncle of David Astor. The *Observer* had been printed on *The Times*'s press, which was housed in New Printing House, and the implications for the paper were potentially serious. David Astor had earlier tried and failed to put together a consortium to buy *The Times*, and out of that process Goodman possessed a valuation for New Printing House. In his *Memoirs* he claims that this was crucial in allowing him to make a split-second decision, though three years had elapsed between the valuation and current crisis. Their own bid having failed, Goodman, Astor and the *Observer's* business manager, Tristan Jones, approached Roy Thomson. They demanded safeguards for their printing contracts. Thomson replied that they did not need them. It was at this point that, according to Goodman, they 'blackmailed him'.[15] They said they would be hostile witnesses before the Monopolies and Mergers Commission (MMC) if he did not give an undertaking that the *Observer* would have a five-year-notice clause in its printing contract. Thomson agreed, through clenched teeth. Three years later his editor-in-chief, Denis Hamilton, visited Goodman to inform him that the Thomson organization was serving the notice. Hamilton told him that it was going to sell New Printing House. The *Observer*'s lease gave it an option to buy. Goodman asked how much. Hamilton was surprised and, in one account, produced the figure of £5 million from the top of his head,[16] and, in another version, from a valuation that he had in his pocket.[17] Goodman, judging the price on his three-year-old valuation, decided it was a good one and said the *Observer* would buy. Hamilton asked where the money would come from. Goodman replied, 'I am sure the Astors can always find a penny or two.' As Trelford put it, only Goodman 'would have had the chutzpah'.[18]

Astor and Goodman set to work raising the money. It was a complex property deal. At the crucial meeting to finalize the details and get the Observer Trust's agreement, a member of Rothschild who was representing one of Astor's sisters, questioned the quality of the transaction: 'Look, Arnold, I think we could do better.' Goodman was rattled by the younger man challenging a deal that he described in his *Memoirs* as 'the business coup of his career'. But the man threw away his initial advantage, as hundreds of negotiators had done before, by giving Goodman an opening for humour. He said, 'Arnold, can we just forget that the *Observer* is a newspaper and work at this as a straightforward property deal.' Goodman paused. 'All right. Let us imagine that my mother is a Number 11 bus. Carry on.' Everyone laughed and the young man's position was lost.

In the short term the purchase of New Printing House was a solid financial success for the paper but the industrial relations set-up it inherited was to be Astor's undoing. The print unions at the building had agreements for working six days a week; the *Observer* was printed only once a week. The resultant huge costs led to some drastic solutions being proposed, one of which involved moving the printing out of London. As the historian of the *Observer* in this period puts it, this would have been 'predating the Wapping agreement by ten years'.[19] With crippling print costs and poor industrial relations, and against the background of a wider slump in newspaper sales, the future of the *Observer* was under serious threat. After long and bitter negotiations the paper underwent a comprehensive restructuring: 25 per cent of staff were shed, but it was still losing £500,000 a year. Finally, on 30 September 1975, Astor announced his resignation as editor, though he did not go until January 1976, and the Observer Trustees began looking for a buyer for the paper.

Wilson suggested to Goodman that the *Observer* make an approach to IPC, the group which controlled the *Daily Mirror* and the *Sunday Mirror*. IPC refused and Wilson contemplated a direct intervention by the government. This evaporated after Wilson's resignation and the financial crisis of 1976, so Roger Harrison, one of the *Observer's* management team, suggested approaching Rupert Murdoch.

Goodman had known Murdoch longer than most players in the British media. In 1957 Goodman Derrick had been housed in offices in the *News of the World* building, which Sir William Carr, the paper's owner, rented to them. In turn Goodman represented the *News of the World* in the failed TWW television franchise bid. In 1968 Robert Maxwell attempted to buy the *News of the World* and tried to enlist Goodman's support. Goodman developed an intense dislike of Maxwell and refused to work with him. Murdoch heard about the Maxwell bid for the *News of the World* and flew in as a white knight for Sir William. The resulting battle produced the first of many confrontations between Maxwell and Murdoch at shareholders' meetings. Maxwell phoned Goodman to ask him not to appear on the platform against him. Goodman was not directly involved in the battle, which Murdoch won,[20] but was further irritated by Maxwell's request.

With Murdoch in charge and intent on expansion, Goodman Derrick moved to new offices in Little Essex Street. In turn Murdoch hired them as his solicitors in London. His key worry was that Wilson would refer future purchases to the MMC. Goodman proved useful in introducing Wilson and other politicians to Murdoch and letting them know more about him. Between November 1969 and the election of 1970, Wilson lunched at Goodman Derrick's offices in Bouverie Street, and on 17 June 1970 the *Sun* advised its readers to vote Labour. Four years later Goodman arranged a dinner with Harold and Mary Wilson and Murdoch.[21]

When the idea of asking Murdoch to buy the *Observer* was suggested, Goodman was in a good position to judge it. Harrison and Astor both favoured the approach, which finally took place in September 1976. Murdoch immediately flew to London. Richard Cockett, in his account of these transactions, suggests that Goodman was initially hostile to Murdoch but came round. This seems unlikely given Goodman's role as Murdoch's lawyer. Whatever the truth of the matter, Goodman now backed him and continued to represent him over the following 15 years in a number of key deals.

Murdoch told the *Observer* team that he would want to bring in Bruce Rothwell, a former editor of the *Sunday Australian*, as editor-in-chief and Anthony Shrimsley as editor. Journalists on the paper were disturbed by these developments and they were leaked to the *Daily Mail* on 21 October.[22] A delegation of journalists met Goodman and the Trustees and opposed Murdoch's involvement. There were noisy protests and questions in the House of Commons. Murdoch did a mock withdrawal and the hats of new buyers, Maxwell and Jimmy Goldsmith included, were thrown into the ring. Goodman rejected out of hand any deal with Maxwell or Goldsmith, going so far as to say that Goldsmith was not a fit person to own a national newspaper.[23] Other bidders materialized and dematerialized or were rejected, including Tiny Rowland of Lonrho, Oleg Deterding, who wanted to make the *Observer* more whimsical, and Sally Aw Sian from Hong Kong.[24] On 12 November the Trustees met in Goodman's flat and decided to recommend the sale of the paper to Murdoch. Astor said it was like attending a funeral.[25]

This was when Kenneth Harris stepped in to save the paper. He was having dinner with an American friend, Douglass Cater. Cater had strong links with Robert Anderson, Chairman of the American corporation Atlantic Richfield. Following his dinner with Harris, Cater asked Anderson if he would be interested in acquiring the paper and Anderson said he would. Harris duly called Goodman. Goodman spoke to Anderson and the deal was done. Over five years Anderson pumped £8 million into the *Observer* and Roger Harrison and others described him as a model owner.

Even with Atlantic Richfield backing the paper, it continued to lose money. Anderson became impatient with the paper's management and wanted to advance his own people to the top of the organization to make sure that he knew what was going on and that they were in place to do his bidding. He particularly wanted to promote Kenneth Harris. As Trelford remembers it, this caused problems:

> ... there were I think at the time two managing directors, joint managing directors, as well as an editor and an editor-in-chief, and we felt that to have another line of command, and a chairman, all operating in London, would be very confusing.[26]

Goodman told Trelford that Anderson was 'determined to make Harris chairman or vice-chairman or editor-in-chief or editor. I'm not sure what role he has in mind for Kenneth but he quite clearly wants him to have a senior position.' Trelford further questioned Goodman, who revealed that Harris had been to see him about the matter. There are conflicting accounts of what transpired at the meeting between Harris and Goodman, and disagreement about whether, before the fateful board meeting, Goodman had given Anderson his agreement to the proposal. Harris denies that the editor-in-chief's post was ever offered to him.

Goodman's own account of this meeting is as follows. In September 1979 Harris and Goodman had breakfasted together. Harris told Goodman that Anderson was considering making him editor-in-chief. Goodman felt that, although Harris was a gifted journalist, he did not have sufficient experience for such a position.[27] Trelford's account is more or less the same:

> Well, I think what Goodman said was something like, 'People see us in a certain way at a certain time in life and the way they see us may be fair or unfair, but it has a lot to do with the way we've lived our lives. And I may be the most suitable person in the world to be a prima ballerina, and I may know it, but the fact of the matter is the world will never see me that way. And I'm afraid, Kenneth, the same is true with you in this sort of role.' Whether he used exactly those words I don't know, but that certainly was the insulting spirit of what he said.[28]

Harris's view of what occurred is somewhat different, but the gist was that Goodman was clearly opposed to his appointment. Indeed he flew to New York at his own expense and met Anderson. Thornton Bradshaw, the outgoing Chairman of the Observer Trust, strongly supported Goodman and the idea was shelved. In Trelford's opinion, it was only a reprieve because Anderson had already decided to get out and the Harris dispute simply gave him the pretext.

In February 1981 Anderson asked Goodman to breakfast at Claridge's. He was now proposing that he himself would become Chairman and Harris Deputy Chairman. As Anderson would be in the USA most of the time, this would mean that the paper would effectively be under Harris's control. Goodman said that if such a resolution were implemented then he would resign and he felt that Astor would too. His account is that Anderson then stated in those circumstances that he would not put forward the proposal. Goodman was clearly not convinced, because he informed Trelford of what was being proposed and Trelford contacted Conor Cruise O'Brien, who was then the paper's editor-in-chief, and told him that they had a problem. O'Brien was just as opposed as Goodman and immediately offered to resign, but Trelford suggested that all he needed do at the relevant board meeting, when the subject came up, was to say, 'I think it'd be better if the matter was discussed in Mr Harris's absence.' The feeling was that if Harris left the room, they would win.[29]

Accounts of the actual board meeting which sealed the fate of the *Observer* differ. In Goodman's version the opposition to Harris was voiced while he was still in the room. In Trelford's account Harris had been asked to leave. Whichever was the case it was clear that Goodman, Astor, Trelford and O'Brien successfully opposed Harris's promotion. Anderson withdrew from the meeting to tell Harris what had been decided. Astor turned to Goodman and said, 'The likelihood is that he will now sell the *Observer*.'

Frank Stanton, who was an important American on the Board of the Observer Trust and on Atlantic Richfield's board of directors, in addition to being one of Anderson's friends and a former president of CBS, stood up and said: 'I've got to go for my plane now, boys, but I warn you, I've never seen Bob Anderson crossed at any board meeting in my life. You guys had better watch out.'[30]

A week later Goodman received a call from Anderson to inform him that he had sold two-thirds of his interest in the paper to Tiny Rowland of Lonrho. Anderson had prepared the ground by buying out the remaining Astor-family interest as early as January 1980. After that earlier sale Goodman was merely a courtesy director. Goodman's response to the sale was one of perplexity: 'I really was speechless – you will be astonished to hear that I could be reduced to that state! I said virtually nothing and telephoned the news around.'[31] He now fought as hard as he could, through the MMC, to oppose the deal. He succeeded in having an independent board created in order to retain some of the character of the paper, but the sale went through.

Even as Rowland took over the *Observer*, Goodman was working for Murdoch again. In 1981 Murdoch launched a hostile takeover bid for the publishers William Collins. Ian Chapman, Chairman of Collins, lined up to defend his company against Murdoch and Goodman represented the interests of Murdoch's News International. Chapman had met Goodman at various times in the 1970s and had been to his box at Covent Garden with Mark Bonham Carter, a one-time director of Collins, but he knew Goodman more by reputation than through personal acquaintance. Nevertheless, Chapman agreed to meet to discuss the merger. It was a typical Goodman ploy to try to personalize relations between the two sides and find common areas of agreement and social connection before the hard bargaining began.

Chapman had referred the Murdoch bid to the MMC in an attempt to prevent it. The picture was further confused because Robert Maxwell had built up a 9.6 per cent stake in Collins. Also, Murdoch and Maxwell were in a dispute over the printing costs of the *Sunday Times*'s colour supplement. Murdoch had run up a considerable bill with Maxwell. Maxwell now phoned Chapman and asked for a meeting. Chapman said, 'Yes, if we both have our professional advisers present.' Collins's merchant bankers were Schroders, while Maxwell was being advised by Sir Robert Clark at Hill Samuel. An arrangement was made to meet for lunch, but Maxwell arrived without Sir Robert, saying he had hurt his shoulder. He then insisted that they get straight down to business. 'You have three options,' he said. 'First of all I'm either part of your problem or I'm part of your solution. I can mount a bid, or I can decide to sell, but it's up to you to do what you want to do.' Chapman replied, 'Let's take these three things. First of all I thought you were already part of my solution because you have backed my board and me in the columns of the national press, in that you regard Murdoch's bid as outrageously low. As to whether you might mount a bid, that's nothing to do with me. That must be your decision. What do you mean you'll sell? Do you mean you'll sell to Mr Murdoch?' Maxwell thumped the table. 'If I live to be as old as Methuselah I would never sell to that Australian bastard.' Sixty-six hours later Murdoch and Maxwell went into a private meeting which lasted six hours. Maxwell agreed to sell Murdoch his stake in Collins and Murdoch settled the dispute on the printing of the *Sunday Times*'s colour supplement.[32]

The deal went against the Stock Exchange's code of practice on takeovers and Chapman challenged it. As he remembers, he was then presented with the spectacle of Goodman, as Murdoch's lawyer, now being on the same side as Maxwell. 'Arnold hated Maxwell with a passion. He didn't hate many people and he certainly didn't reveal his hatred very often, but Maxwell had certainly tried on several occasions to cosy up to Arnold. Arnold had told me that. But there he was, sitting shoulder to shoulder with Maxwell, which amused me intensely.'[33] The dispute went before the Takeover Panel.

Characteristically, Maxwell could not keep quiet and it became obvious that he was about to put both feet in it. Goodman cut him short and then, according to Chapman: 'made one of his most brilliant speeches. The panel recessed for 35 minutes, which was very unusual, and I was absolutely certain we would win. But we lost. We would not have lost if it had not been for Arnold, he absolutely saved the day.' It is a mark of Goodman's style that it was his opponent on this occasion who judged his performance as 'brilliant'.

Goodman's most important and sustained intervention in the history of newspapers in this era was his passionate opposition to the trade-union legislation of the second Wilson government, 1974–6. The key bill, which was designed to replace the Tories anti-union legislation with a pro-union framework for industrial relations – the Trade Union and Labour Relations (Amendment) Bill, or TULRA – was introduced by the Secretary of State for Employment, Michael Foot, in May 1974. The story of the passage of TULRA is a classic of twin-track politics: the style of the public debates in both Houses of Parliament indicated the thin Labour majority in the Commons and the private discussions reflected the balance of power in the industry. The purpose of the Bill, as it related to the closed shop, was to restore the position which had existed before Edward Heath's Industrial Relations Act of 1971 had set out to outlaw restrictive practices; it was not designed to enforce a closed-shop system. As Foot put it in the Commons: 'We have not imposed the closed shop. We are neutral about the closed shop. The government are not encouraging people to form a closed shop, but they are not forbidding them to form a closed shop.'[34]

Goodman had argued against Equity's operation of a closed shop in the acting industry which ensured that only union members could perform, while both at the Arts Council and now he led the charge against the closed shop in Fleet Street, whereby only union members could join the staff of papers as journalists. He insisted that his stand against this Bill was one of principle and was therefore not connected with his position as Chairman of the Newspaper Publishers' Association. Indeed in his *Memoirs* he calls it 'the battle for freedom of the press'. His belief in this freedom was sincere, but he was also the mouthpiece of the newspaper proprietors; and although he tried hard to keep his campaign separate from his work for this group, for which he was effectively a paid lobbyist, he did not succeed.

Goodman had known his adversary Michael Foot for many years. Foot was a client and friend who had first used Goodman as a lawyer in 1958. As editor of *Tribune*, he showed him a pamphlet on the Bank Rate Tribunal which alleged corruption by Conservative Ministers during an increase in interest rates. Goodman read it and told Foot that it was definitely libellous but that he should definitely publish it.[35] Foot did, without repercussions. In 1974–6 Goodman was also acting for Foot in his role as one of the executors of the Crossman estate in the battle with the Cabinet Secretary. Client and solicitor faced each other on opposite sides of an argument across the two Houses of Parliament.

The problem of the closed shop focused most sharply on the press because of the claim that the National Union of Journalists' (NUJ) monopoly supply of journalists was a challenge to press freedom. The whole debate was odd because if the closed shop were a threat to press freedom, then how had a free press operated before 1971 when there had been a closed shop? Moreover, the real power in the industrial relations of Fleet Street was in other hands. On the union side it was the print unions that were the real militants, rather than the NUJ or the much smaller Institute of Journalists. On the owner's side it was the new generation of proprietors like Murdoch and Maxwell who threatened the editorial independence of papers, rather than the old-style owner-editors like David Astor. Thus the wrong heroes were fighting the wrong villains. The nitty-gritty of the battle is the story of a consummate parliamentarian, Foot, being given an initial run for his money before out-distancing the 'non-politician' Goodman. In terms of political class it was an unequal fight, as Goodman admitted: 'success might have attended on us if I had had more political experience and subtlety'.[36]

Goodman's first critical intervention was actually a considerable help to the government. Under the Conservatives' old industrial-relations legislation the Amalgamated Union of Engineering Workers (AUEW), led by Hugh Scanlon, had its assets frozen on Monday 6 May 1974 after an industrial dispute with a Surrey engineering firm, Con-Mech. The union was fined £65,000. AUEW members demonstrated outside the Industrial Relations Court and its president, Sir John Donaldson, released enough money for their wages to be paid. It was clear that there would be a showdown between the powerful AUEW and the Labour government. The next day Scanlon used his casting vote to break a deadlock in the union's executive and called a national strike in defiance of the Court. Ministers were informed. At 5.30 p.m. the dispute reached Fleet Street when the engineers met to discuss their response to the AUEW's call for a national strike – only the *Daily Express*, *Daily Mail* and *Daily Telegraph* appeared the next day. Gradually British industry began to close down and the potential damage to the government was immense. Brian Neill, acting for a firm of London solicitors who had a client prepared to pay the union's fines, made a submission to the Court, which in effect gave the union a victory: though the Court had ordered the union to pay, it had not paid. Sir John Donaldson retired to consider the application. At 1.20 p.m. he announced that he was prepared to accept the offer and allow an outside interest to pay the fine on the union's behalf. At 3.30 p.m., following a meeting with Foot, Scanlon announced that the strike was over. Despite much speculation at the time, the identity of the firm of London solicitors and the secret benefactor was not revealed. It was, of course, Goodman representing the Fleet Street proprietors, who stood to lose a fortune from the strike. Foot recalls Goodman paying the fine, then proceeding to oppose him in the passage of the legislation which would abolish the very Industrial Relations Court that had provoked the strike.[37]

The battle against the closed shop in journalism was soon publicly identified with Goodman's name. As talks with Foot were leading nowhere, David Astor decided to make Goodman's role more public and wrote to him as Chairman of the Observer Trust and of the Newspaper Publishers' Association, appealing for help. Referring to the existing deal between the NPA and the NUJ, which already eroded editors' freedom to recruit staff, Astor told him, 'You obviously cannot make the NPA militant over a situation they themselves largely created.' Denis Hamilton, editor-in-chief of *The Times*, welcomed Goodman's involvement. He had heard him, at the Annual Dinner of the Printers' Charitable Corporation on 20 November 1974, speak of the grave threat to press freedom in the government's closed-shop policy. 'If people imagine that you can create some instrument that enables an interference with that freedom, in the belief that the people possessing that instrument will not use it, they are making a grave mistake. History throughout the world has proved the contrary.'

Goodman's view was that the argument had nothing to do with

industrial disputes but with the potential for unions to operate censorship of newspapers. Foot told the Commons that, in some matters, Goodman was 'a babe in arms'. Nevertheless, Goodman's experience of printers' disputes made him aware how unions used their monopoly to gain concessions. Though the NUJ was seeking only a post-entry closed shop, Goodman suspected it would be just a first step. In the Lords he imagined editors saying they could not accept a drama critic who had never heard of Ibsen, and the official replying, 'But he is a paid-up member of my union.' However, by linking his stance directly with the proprietors' position, he undermined his own chosen role as a mediator above politics. For example, he stated: 'On behalf of the management side of the industry, I will give an undertaking that we will negotiate forthwith.' Was he an independent voice in these matters, battling for the right to freedom of speech or was he the paid lobbyist of the newspaper proprietors? Both moderates and extremists on the union side claimed that when rich people like Goodman pretend to be defending cultural interests, they were using 'fancy language to conceal material interests'. Goodman was surprised and hurt when he found himself being treated as the spokesman for money-grabbing tycoons, though only he could have even half believed in his own ability not to confuse his heroic struggle for freedom with his job as head of the employers' association.

Goodman did not attempt to use the Prime Minister against the Bill, which shows some political realism, though it also illustrates how their relationship cooled during Wilson's second term. He told the journalist Nora Beloff, who wrote a rather deranged book on the passage of the Bill reflecting her anti-unionism (which stemmed from her resignation from the NUJ in 1974 when a chapel meeting delayed the printing of the *Observer*, where she then worked), that 'a few casual comments at social gatherings convinced him that Wilson had no intention of getting embroiled in the argument'. He contacted Wilson only once on 'a procedural point near to the end of the struggle'. Wilson was never going to back Goodman against Foot, who was as loyal a colleague in government as he could be a difficult maverick out of it: 'This is Michael's Bill. You should talk to him.'

Another dimension of Goodman's weakness was his ignorance of the depth of feeling in the unions against the Industrial Relations Act of 1971. In particular he did not understand 'the hostility of unions to the judges being involved in industrial matters': he knew nothing of the history of the Labour movement. Time and again he tried to shift the debate away from these realities towards what mattered to him. In a radio interview he said: 'I can think of no greater enormity . . . than that a man has something to write and is prevented from doing it because of industrial organization.' Larry Lamb, the editor of the *Sun*, thought Goodman spoke above most people's heads and should have concerned himself less with Ibsen and more with chapel power in the news room.[38]

Goodman's proposals for exempting journalism by law from the monopoly of a single union foundered when the NUJ – backed by Foot – proposed a voluntary Press Charter, including a Code of Conduct. The Charter was drafted by Alastair Hetherington from the *Guardian* and Ken Morgan of the NUJ. The Charter was designed to reconcile press freedom with trade-union rights. The editors rejected it and leaked garbled accounts of their private meetings with Foot to discredit it. The NUJ tried to negotiate a compromise. Goodman and most editors regarded a voluntary agreement as totally inadequate. Astor's managing editor, Ken Obank, told Goodman, 'You might as well resolve that both parties subscribe to the principles of truth, beauty and goodness.' On 29 January 1975 a dinner was held at the *Observer*, principally for Labour peers, which was intended to strengthen support for statutory measures for enforcing the Code of Conduct by law, including penalties if the unions broke the Charter. It had the opposite effect. In the Commons, the Liberal leader Jeremy Thorpe proposed talks to discuss the Code of Conduct, though Goodman warned him that his intervention might make matters worse. Lord Pearce chaired a series of meetings at the NPA's headquarters in Bouverie Street, but still no agreement was reached.

Eventually, on Goodman's advice, the editors abandoned their proposals to amend the Bill and concentrated on improving proposals for the Press Charter.[39] Their aim was to ensure guaranteed editorial freedom enforceable by law. The battle in the Lords was protracted and Goodman played a much more active role than at any other time during his membership of the House. Goodman said he was 'enthusiastic to a point of positive passion to find a solution . . . which did not involve confrontation'. His proposal to resolve the dispute was meant to revolve around four principles:

1. Editors would be under no obligation to join a union.
2. Editors would have the right to commission, publish or not

publish any article free from pressure of industrial action.

3. All journalists, including editors, would have the right to join any union of their choice.

4. Journalists would have the right not to be arbitrarily or unreasonably expelled from union membership.

The drafting of amendments to try to include elements from the four principles in the Bill was entrusted to Leonard Hoffmann, the lawyer who had acted as secretary to the Committee on London Orchestras, who acted more out of personal loyalty to Goodman than conviction. Goodman tried to rally all-party support by recruiting key individuals to his cause who might attract more voters. He successfully lobbied Lord Evans and Lord Longford but failed to persuade two normally right-wing peers, Lords Pannell and Gordon Walker. The last chance to block or change the Bill came in the Lords debate set for 10 March 1975. Goodman visited Lord Hailsham to ask him to whip the Conservative peers to defeat the Bill. However, a week earlier, on relatively minor matters, Goodman had accepted a government-inspired amendment without consulting Hailsham – a breach of etiquette which Hailsham made Goodman pay for by refusing to back any amendment which included the four principles.

At the Report Stage on 24 March, Goodman tabled various amendments which would make the breaking of the Press Charter actionable in court. There were 125 votes in favour to 48 against, but it was a change which the government could not accept because it would have brought the judiciary back into industrial relations. On 10 April Goodman, Astor and a deputation of editors tried to win the support of Mrs Thatcher. At first she was unconvinced, especially when she asked them if they were united and Vere Harmsworth let slip that he could see nothing wrong with a closed shop for journalists. As Goodman put it: 'There was no time to strike him to the ground and trample on him', but he nonetheless managed to persuade her to support them.[40] He then went to see the right-wing Manifesto Group of Labour MPs. Clearly exhausted after a long day, he infuriated some of his audience by haranguing them. It never occurred to him that his earlier reception by Mrs Thatcher, which the MPs had by now heard about, meant that their actions could be used in the party battle. Even so, he had some success with Labour MPs, to the extent that Foot no longer expected an easy passage for the Bill. Sensing a possible opportunity for compromise, Goodman asked Hoffmann to draw up a new formula, toning down the question of going to court if the code were broken. Foot countered with his own suggestion to amend the Bill to meet 'the vital question as to the position of editors and contributors'. Goodman with Hoffmann, Denis Hamilton, Astor and Frederick Fisher, editor of the *Financial Times*, called on Foot on 9 July. The meeting produced nothing.

After the summer recess Parliament reconvened. Foot accepted Goodman's invitation to tea and listened courteously to yet another new proposal for making the Charter legally enforceable. Goodman still sought compromise, falling back on a suggestion by a Home Office barrister that an amendment be inserted into the Bill that would protect journalists and would be acceptable to the government. At a dinner in Goodman's flat at which Hoffmann, Lloyd, Hamilton and Astor and Nora Beloff were present, Goodman was not keen on the idea but thought it might get 'if not a toe, at least a toe-nail' into the door of legal enforceability. With Hoffmann's help, he hurriedly drafted the new amendment. On Monday 10 November Goodman called on Carrington, the Conservative leader in the Lords, to explain it. Hailsham, hearing of this, accosted Goodman as he left Carrington's office and told him that he 'had played false and was ready to settle for a meaningless compromise'. Hailsham demanded that Goodman come into his office immediately to discuss what possible validity the new amendment might have. 'Goodman said he'd come after lunch and Hailsham roared back: "You don't need any lunch. You're fat enough already".' Goodman then went into Hailsham's room 'and did some shouting too'. This probably paved the way for the following year – 1976 - when Hailsham deprived Goodman of votes he needed in his last effort to defy government.[41]

When the Bill came back to the Lords that afternoon, Goodman had little support from Labour. Lord Cudlipp, former Chairman of IPC, proposed that given the government's hostility to his campaign in the upper house, Goodman's epitaph would be: 'Here lies the man who failed to defend the press by statute but succeeded in abolishing the House of Lords.' Wilson now took a hand and instructed the Lord Chancellor, Elwyn-Jones, Foot and the Leader of the Lords, Lord Shepherd, to make a final effort at agreement. By Sunday Goodman had heard nothing and so phoned Wilson, who made it clear that he did not want to intervene but suggested Goodman ask Elwyn-Jones to discuss a possible compromise. On Monday Elwyn-

Jones said the government would not accept judicial intervention in industrial relations. Goodman insisted on further talks. At 5.30 that evening (10 November) Goodman met Elwyn-Jones, Foot and Shepherd, together with senior officials and parliamentary draftsmen. Later that evening officials called on Goodman at his home. Also present were Goodman's old friend Lord Lloyd, Brian Neill QC, Leonard Hoffmann and Denis Hamilton. After long technical discussions Goodman argued that, with some cosmetic changes, he would accept the officials' new formula. Though he did not recall it, the officials said he had seriously suggested that the Queen should be asked to delay the prorogation of Parliament to give more time for talk. Next morning Goodman rang Shepherd expecting an agreement. Shepherd put him on to Elwyn-Jones, who told him that they could not go along with the proposal discussed because it conceded too much in terms of enforcing the code of conduct. Goodman went to *The Times*, where Hamilton had assembled a dozen editors, expecting a deal. From there at 11.00 a.m. he again phoned Elwyn-Jones, who said the proposal was rejected.

Defying the conventions of confidentiality, Goodman gave his version of the past 24 hours in the Lords. In the Commons, Foot hit back at once. Goodman's account of that 'night and morning is completely wrong . . . The fact is that the discussions broke down on the same point on which they had broken down over previous months – that is, that Lord Goodman wanted to make the whole business legally enforceable and we did not accept that view.'[42] In effect Goodman engineered a situation in which it appeared that the government was being intransigent. Foot and others maintained that no agreement had been reached at the evening meeting and that it was Goodman who had stopped the search for a compromise. Foot accused Goodman of rejecting the compromise proposal and Wilson endorsed the view that it was Goodman who had broken off negotiations.

Even so, Goodman's speech had its effect and, with the support of the Liberals, Tories, a majority of cross-benchers and Labour's Lords Lloyd, Fletcher, George Brown and Baroness Gaitskell, the clause concerning the Charter was defeated. The Lords had defeated the clause but the Commons could reintroduce it. Goodman did not obstruct the Bill when it came back to the Lords. During the first weeks of 1976 he was in hospital with early signs of the problems with his feet and legs that were to plague his last years. While there he decided that, since the government refused to amend the guidelines for a Charter to make it enforceable, the industry was better off without one. He began to canvass the editors and found that most agreed. He invited Hailsham to his bedside and tried to convince him that the Tories should follow the route of now opposing the Charter. On 24 February Goodman was not well enough to go to the House and so conveyed his view in a letter to *The Times*. His arguments dominated the debate in the Lords. A fortnight later, defying the advice of his doctors, he delivered a passionate speech against government proposals to the House:

> During the last debate the noble Lord, the Leader of the House, perhaps understandably, displayed a slight impatience with the fact that we had devoted so much time to this question. I am totally unapologetic on that matter. I can think of few matters of higher importance which justify greater attention and expenditure of time. We are dealing with fundamental liberties.[43]

He decided that he would accept the Bill only if the government agreed that the Charter should not be drafted by Foot but negotiated with the NPA. In an effort to push through this final amendment, Goodman, Hamilton and Astor appealed over Hailsham's head direct to Mrs Thatcher. Goodman's appointment with her was scheduled for Tuesday 10 March at 10.30 but he arrived late and Hailsham informed Thatcher that it was too late to whip the peers. Goodman lost by 128 votes, with only the ever-loyal Lord Lloyd and Baroness Gaitskell voting with him. The Bill finally received its Royal Assent on 25 March 1976.

In typically Goodmanesque style, his relationship with Foot recovered from the long and bitter fight, and indeed during the ensuing debate on the Lords amendments Foot paid personal tribute to Goodman's campaign against the Bill: 'I am sure that it derives from a genuine belief that something wrong is being done which he ought to resist. I never questioned his good faith.' And when Goodman left the NPA, Ken Morgan of the NUJ wrote: 'We will miss you on the other side of our particular table and I would like you to know that you will carry the best wishes of all our side with you.'

Goodman usually managed to wear his many hats, as a lawyer, as a public figure or a member of various organizations, without confusing them. For example, in a dispute over pay-beds in the NHS, during which he managed to infuriate Barbara Castle, the Minister of Health and Social Security, with his insistence that meetings take place at his flat and by going over her head direct to the Prime Minister, he represented the private health insurance company BUPA. Because he was acting as a conciliator rather than a lobbyist, he did not take a fee.[44] In other instances the sheer number of hats he wore simultaneously should have caused him to pull back from an overt involvement or at least to declare an interest. He rarely, if ever, did either. His general geniality, together with his self-belief, convinced him that he was above the codes of conduct that applied to others. Parliamentarians should declare the interests they are representing when presenting a case. Goodman was, in effect, a lobbyist for one side of the dispute on freedom of the press, but he presented himself as motivated by an Olympian detachment from the sphere of politics and a love of free speech. He did indeed hold the views he espoused but his involvement was professional as much as principled; it was political as much as philosophical because he would not have made the stand he did had he had not been at the NPA.

Goodman never again attempted such a parliamentary fight and it is revealing that this, his longest and most significant intervention, was in the cause of his client, the newspaper proprietors, though he tried hard to present it as being really about 'press freedom'. Had journalists in the 1970s been asked if the name Goodman was most clearly associated with freedom of the press they would have laughed.

12

The Fall of Jeremy Thorpe

I have the three most powerful pillars of the state on my side,
Harold Wilson, Lord Goodman and MI5.

Jeremy Thorpe, 1976[1]

The greatest British political scandal of the post-war period, the
Jeremy Thorpe case, was also the greatest challenge a legal-political
fixer could have faced. It required action in the courts, in the press
and at the highest political level. Goodman's problem was that
without knowing what was actually going on he could not really
contain the situation. Indeed when he finally found out, he ran a
mile. In such a situation there was little chance that he could have
pulled off another 'Boothby' but he was part of the reason that
Jeremy Thorpe survived as long as he did.

After the Orpington by-election in 1962 it seemed for a moment
that the long-delayed Liberal revival was on the way. The energetic
organizational genius Jeremy Thorpe was the leading political
figure in the resurgent Liberal Party and naturally he wanted the
top political lawyer to advise him, which Goodman did, first on a
libel action in 1957, then regularly from July 1967 onwards on the
Scott affair and a DTI investigation into London and County
Securities, of which Thorpe was a director. Thorpe's youth and
driving ambition seemed perfectly fitted to the times and he was a
shoe-in when the ageing Liberal leader Jo Grimond retired as leader
of the party in 1967. But Thorpe's relentless political energy and
showmanship was mirrored by a breathtaking recklessness in his
private life. He was an active homosexual at a time when this was
still illegal. Other politicians were active in similar ways to Thorpe,
among them Tom Driberg in the Labour Party and the
Conservative Boothby, but none reached such a high position in
their party while leaving so many hostages to fortune; and none was
to go to such lengths to protect himself as Thorpe did. Various of
his sexual adventures might have caught up with him, but in the
end it was his brief affair with Norman Scott, lasting between

November 1961 and February 1962, which came back to destroy him.

For years after his affair with Thorpe, Norman Scott, a one-time male model and devoted animal lover, suffered from depression and his life was in constant disarray. He continually appealed to Thorpe for help and money. Finally, in desperation, Scott wrote a 17-page letter to Thorpe's mother:

> For the last five years, as you probably know, Jeremy and I have had a 'homosexual' relationship. To go into it too deeply will not help either of us. When I came down to Stonewalls [Thorpe's mother's house] that was when I first met him. Though he told you something about the TV programme and Malta. That was all not so true. What remains is the fact that through my meeting with Jeremy that day I gave birth to this vice that lies latent in every man.[2]

In the face of such behaviour an increasingly desperate Thorpe had recruited the assistance of a fellow Liberal MP, a womanizer and failed businessman named Peter Bessell, in an effort to placate and silence Scott.

In 1967 Thorpe and Bessell had tried to send Scott to the United States and were dismayed to find that he had spent the hush money fruitlessly – on a psychiatrist – and was still in London and still demanding help. Thorpe called Bessell and told him he had decided that it was time to see Lord Goodman. According to Bessell's account, he himself arranged an appointment for the following day:

> Arnold Goodman or, to give him his full title, the Baron Goodman of Westminster, was Britain's best-known lawyer, a solicitor who specialised in criminal law [sic]. Jeremy knew him well ... Arnold Goodman's office was surprisingly small, whereas he was large and a trifle oily. It was my only meeting with him and he and Jeremy did most of the talking. Jeremy suggested that on the basis of Scott's letter to his mother and the one I had received, which I brought with me and which J had read in the taxi, Goodman should write to Scott. Neither letter constituted libel since they had not been 'published' and Scott's admissions to Father Sweetman and Dr. O'Connell [a priest and a psychiatrist who had heard Scott's tales] would have been regarded as privileged. Jeremy wanted Goodman to issue a tough warning coupled with a hint that Scott was at risk of being charged with blackmail.[3]

21. Goodman spent much of the post-war period on the phone, sometimes – as in this picture – at his desk but also, from the start of the day, from his bed

RHODESIA

22. *Facing page:* Legend has it that moments after this picture was taken on 22 September 1971 at Heathrow Airport, Goodman was handed a copy of *Private Eye* which alleged that his bank account at Barclays on the Strand was hopelessly overdrawn. After a memorable shouting match with Richard Ingrams, Geoffrey Bindman and Paul Foot, an apology appeared in the magazine

23. *Left:* Ian Smith bids farewell to Goodman as a negotiator

24. *Below:* Douglas Home allegedly told Goodman to remain inconspicuous in Rhodesia. Here he is hiding, almost unnoticed, among his team of negotiators, 1971

25. If looks could kill: Robert Maxwell and Rupert Murdoch on the day that the *News of the World* was sold to Murdoch, 2 January 1969

26. Goodman centre-stage as the *Observer* is saved from the clutches of Rupert Murdoch and sold to Atlantic Richfield. David Astor, Douglass Cater, Goodman and Donald Trelford, 1975

27. The *Private Eye* boys kept on Goodman's trail for thirty years. Here Richard Ingrams, Willie Rushton, Christopher Booker and Nicholas Luard are outside the high court during a libel action, 1963

28. *Below:* During the Rhodesian negotiations Goodman's codename was 'Hot Dog' and Max Aitken's was 'Friend'. Here Hot Dog and Friend take on Michael Foot and the NUJ closed shop for the Newspaper Publishers Association, 1975

29. James Goldsmith with his wife Annabel (*left*) and Marcia Williams, 1979. Goodman judged Goldsmith unfit to own a newspaper and Williams to be the reason Harold Wilson was not a great PM

THE GOODMAN

30. The closest Goodman got to a hammer and sickle: cutting the ribbon on a Housing Corporation development, 1974

31. Goodman with the first owners of Motability cars, 1978

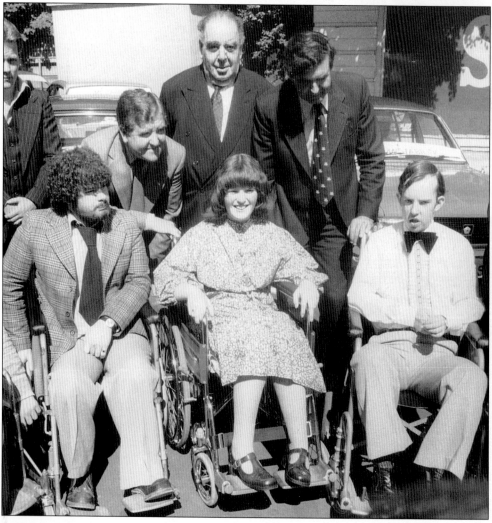

32. Goodman tried and failed to save the one-time Liberal leader Jeremy Thorpe. Here, Thorpe with his wife Marion and his mother celebrate inappropriately on the day of his acquittal, 1979

33. Goodman is rewarded for twenty-five years of writs with the 'honour' of being the *Private Eye*'s cover girl, 13 February 1981

34. Lord and Lady Portman on their wedding day, 1966. Portman was later to accuse Goodman of misappropriating £10m of his money

35. The most distinguished citizen outside government: Goodman in the 1980s

Goodman considered Thorpe's request and then 'dismissed the proposal', pointing out that Scott might consult a solicitor who would tell him to call Thorpe's bluff. If they then failed to prosecute Scott, he could use Goodman's threat and subsequent inaction as evidence of Thorpe's guilt. Goodman agreed that the best plan was for Bessell to see Scott and try once again to arrange his departure for the United States. According to Bessell, Thorpe showed no embarrassment while talking to Goodman. He neither admitted nor denied Scott's allegations. 'Goodman seemed understanding and sympathetic.'[4] From this consultation onwards Goodman became increasingly involved in the case. Thorpe was to call on Goodman over the next decade whenever he was worried about Scott's story being published; as Goodman was the recognized expert at keeping damaging material out of the press, Thorpe could not have been in better hands. Tom Dale, Thorpe's assistant, had instructions to contact Goodman whenever journalists asked about Scott[5] and David Holmes, a close friend of Thorpe, did the same later during the February 1974 election when Scott was causing trouble in Thorpe's North Devon constituency.[6] As Holmes remembers it: 'I told Goodman what Scott was doing in North Devon and said that Jeremy's agent was worried about the effect that this might have on the campaign. Very wisely he advised us to ignore the man.'[7] Goodman was extremely impatient and felt that Holmes and the agent were fussing; on other occasions, especially when the requests came directly from Thorpe, he responded much more effectively.

However, Goodman's calm counsel could not stop Thorpe from worrying about the threat from Scott, and more drastic methods than a quiet word with editors were discussed and eventually used, without Goodman's knowledge. In late 1968, according to the most recent account of the case, Thorpe began to consider the idea of having Scott murdered. On several occasions between 1968 and 1971 his close friend David Holmes and co-conspirator Peter Bessell were able to stop anything of the sort happening.[8] It was not until 1974 that Holmes was converted to the idea that something had to be done. He had tracked down some of Scott's incriminating documents, including love-letters, notes and postcards from Thorpe to Scott. Scott had passed a selection of these to a West Country doctor for safe keeping and others he had given to the Metropolitan Police as far back as 1962, though they had taken no action over the illegal homosexual relationship implicit in the letters. Holmes now purchased the collection held by the doctor for £2500 and burned them in an Aga stove, only to find that Scott had given copies to Gordon Winter, a freelance journalist, and to the Liberal Party itself. In fact this particular collection, which Scott called his 'dossier', was mostly harmless. Holmes, in buying the material with a cheque, had merely become deeper involved in the conspiracy.

In November 1974 a new set of incriminating letters and photographs was found and sent to the *Sunday Mirror*. Believing them to be part of an attempted blackmail, the paper copied them and returned them to Thorpe. Thorpe now told Holmes that Scott had 'to be eliminated'.[9] Holmes was a weak man, essentially in the power of Thorpe, and he agreed to do as Thorpe asked. As a respectable business consultant, Holmes did not know any violent criminals, but through friends of friends he found a bungling fantasist, Andrew Newton, who would be prepared to do the job for money. Thorpe swindled the cash from a well-meaning donor to the Liberal Party called Jack Hayward.[10] Newton told Scott that he would protect him, but in fact drove him on to Exmoor on the night of 24 October 1975. Newton met Scott, who arrived with his Great Dane bitch Rinka and refused to leave her behind. Newton hated and was frightened by dogs and shot Rinka before the gun apparently jammed. Newton fled the scene. The question that has never been fully answered is whether the shot that jammed was intended to kill Scott or simply to scare him. Newton's efforts to conceal his identity were so poor that he was arrested within 48 hours. He demanded more money from the conspirators to keep silent, and his flimsy cover story, that he had met Scott through a sex magazine and arranged to meet him thinking he was a woman, stayed in place during his trial.

On 29 January 1976 Thorpe saw a lot of Goodman. In the morning the long-awaited Department of Trade and Industry (DTI) inspectors' report into a crashed secondary bank, London and County Securities, was published. Thorpe was blamed for a serious error of judgement in lending his reputation to such a dubious concern, but cleared of being involved in any of the fraudulent accounting practices that had taken place. The Liberal MP Cyril Smith recalled that: 'In giving evidence before the DTI inspectors Thorpe said he had been advised by his solicitor Lord Goodman throughout most of the affair.'[11] The embarrassment Thorpe faced through his brush with City regulators was dwarfed by the outburst from Scott, who used a hearing in Barnstaple Magistrates' Court on social security fraud charges, held on the same day as the DTI hearings, to blurt out his allegations against Thorpe under privilege. These allegations had been refined over many years of obsession: Thorpe had ruined his life by perverting him to homosexuality and had stolen his National Insurance card, which prevented him from earning a living.

Cyril Smith tried to track down his leader and tell him the news; he found him at Goodman's office.[12] Goodman's advice to Thorpe was to keep it simple: 'If you are accused of stealing an apple, it's best to simply say I didn't steal it. If you elaborate and say I could not have stolen the apple because I was in New York at the time and in any case I don't like apples, that leaves room for more questions.'[13] Accordingly, Thorpe issued two terse statements that day. The first concerned the bank: 'I placed total reliance and faith in quarters where it is now, alas, all too clear that confidence was wholly misplaced.' And on Scott: 'It is well over twelve years since I last saw or spoke to Mr. Norman Scott. There is no truth in Mr. Scott's wild allegations.'[14] The press now began to pick up the story in earnest, for all Goodman's keeping things simple. Auberon Waugh, a near neighbour of Thorpe in the West Country, led the charge and wrote an early account of the whole affair. He was particularly incensed by Thorpe's insensitivity towards the death of Rinka and he closely followed the case, even standing against Thorpe as a candidate for the Dog Lovers' Party.

Goodman continued to work to limit the damage to his client, but political pressure built up and Thorpe could no longer contain himself.[15] Tom Dale, Thorpe's assistant, was blunt about Goodman's role: 'We knew he [Scott] was a nuisance. We knew he was saying that Jeremy had stolen his insurance card. As far as we were concerned he was a dangerous nut. Lord Goodman would threaten an injunction if anyone intended to publish anything. That always stopped the story.'[16] Goodman's advice was always to simply ignore or deny the allegations. But Thorpe wanted a more wide-ranging denial. With Goodman's reluctant help he recruited the *Sunday Times* to his side and the result was a defensive piece, 'The Lies of Norman Scott, by Jeremy Thorpe', published on 14 March. Goodman checked the copy item by item. It was not only a pack of lies but included the denial of accusations which had not yet been aired, as *Private Eye* was quick to point out.[17] If Goodman had not known what he was dealing with before the *Sunday Times* article, he must have began to suspect now.

While Goodman and Thorpe were trying to use the press to fight off Scott, another strand in the story was unravelling. Harold Wilson wanted to protect Thorpe because he was convinced that it was the South African secret service which was persecuting the Liberal leader because of his party's anti-apartheid stance. In a speech to the Commons press gallery on 12 May 1976, Wilson said publicly that South African plots were behind Thorpe's tribulations. He repeated this, and the justifiable suspicions he harboured against MI5, in more lurid form to Barrie Penrose and Roger Courtiour ('Pencourt'), two journalists who were on Thorpe's trail, over drinks at his house in Lord North Street, Westminster, later that same evening. Wilson offered to be the 'big fat spider'[18] watching over their investigations; unfortunately for him, Pencourt found little evidence of South African involvement but instead unravelled the case against Thorpe.

After this initial meeting with the former Prime Minister, the material dried up. Penrose was convinced that Goodman had persuaded Wilson not to help him and Courtiour any more and talked wildly about Wilson's resignation and Princess Margaret's divorce, both of which they claimed, wrongly, had been 'orchestrated by a sinister lawyer called Lord Goodman, who serviced the rich and powerful, to distract attention from Scott'.[19] In fact Marcia Williams's version of this particular story is probably closer to the truth. When Wilson had informed the Queen, on 16 March 1976, that he was to resign, she asked him to time his announcement to take some attention away from the royal divorce.[20] There was certainly no connection between the Prime Minister's resignation and Newton's trial at Exeter Crown Court. Goodman did not trust Pencourt and strongly advised Wilson to stay clear of them, even hinting that Pencourt were actually agents of the South African security service Boss.

Pencourt wrote pieces for the *Observer* on Wilson's disillusionment with MI5 and on the Thorpe case. Goodman now worked hard behind the scenes to try to stop stories appearing. In some cases stories by Pencourt and others were kept out of the papers altogether. Goodman's usual line with editors was that Thorpe was an honest man and Scott a proven liar. He also had to get Wilson under control. He disliked intensely Wilson's intriguing over the Thorpe case and it was a contributory factor in the cooling of their relationship from the mid-1970s. The result of Goodman's interventions was that the *Observer* threw away a series of scoops from Pencourt on the Thorpe situation but managed to publish some of the Wilson and MI5 material. However, they did not publish the fact that at the height of the plot, by some elements in MI5 opposed to Wilson, the Goodman Derrick offices were twice 'raided' by rogue members of the security services in search of documents that might incriminate Wilson.[21] Aside from trying to block coverage of Thorpe, Goodman also acted for Thorpe when a new development broke.

In May 1976, backed by the *Daily Mirror*, Scott announced that he was going to sue the Metropolitan Police for the return of the letters which he had given them in 1962. The letters were deeply incriminating for Thorpe and revealed the intimacy he had shared with Scott. Goodman immediately demanded the return of the letters, which he claimed as the property of his client as the author. Scotland Yard was under heavy pressure to avoid or delay this delivery, but on Friday 7 May told Goodman it was going to return the letters to 'Scott without a court hearing and probably sometime the following week'.[22] However, they sent a set of copies to Goodman. Thorpe and Goodman decided to pre-empt Scott by offering the letters to the *Sunday Times* in the hope that in this way they might be able to control their release. On 7 May the paper's then editor, Harold Evans, was attending a press awards lunch when he received a call from Goodman asking him to come to the Goodman Derrick office. There he found Thorpe and Robin Salinger, Thorpe's financial adviser. Goodman told him he could have two Thorpe–Scott letters for publication provided 'the letters were not presented in a blatantly hostile way'. A contemporary account said:

> Thorpe was glum and took little part in the discussions beyond asking occasionally and embarrassingly for assurance that the letters were completely harmless. Salinger suggested that perhaps not all of each letter need be reproduced: some parts might be misunderstood. Evans, with Goodman's support, resisted; it was all or nothing, though he agreed he would not present the letters in a hostile way.[23]

In exchange for the letters and an interview with Thorpe, it was finally agreed that the paper would not highlight Thorpe's failure to deny his homosexuality nor would the content of the letters be spelt out in the paper. One of the key letters read:

Lord Goodman

My Dear Norman

Since my letters normally go to the House, yours arrived all by itself at my breakfast table at the Reform, and gave me tremendous pleasure. I cannot tell you just how happy I am to feel that you are really settling down, and feeling that life has something to offer . . . In haste. Bunnies can (and will) go to France.

Yours affectionately

Jeremy

I miss you[24]

The effect of the publication of the letters was instant. On 10 May Thorpe resigned as Liberal leader.[25]

The major source for the revelation of the Thorpe story was Peter Bessell, who had been telling journalists he trusted such as Pencourt and the BBC's Tom Mangold that Thorpe had planned Scott's murder in the late 1960s and that Holmes had admitted that the plans had been reactivated in 1975. Journalists became interested in Andrew Newton, who had been convicted for shooting Scott's dog and was serving two years, and the Thorpe team became worried about the gunman's capacity for discretion. Even at this late stage they were still using Goodman's name to suppress evidence. John Le Mesurier, a Welsh carpet salesman who was the alleged middleman between Newton and Holmes, told Dave Miller, another minor character in the drama, that:

> All the arrangements that we made with Andrew stand. We want Andrew to know that because, if the press get hold of him, he starts blabbering . . . the geezer involved in this lot is fucking Lord Goodman . . . defending solicitor. These writers already have letters from Lord Goodman threatening them if they mention Holmes's name, they'll be sued for libel, criminal libel fucking slander. Not from some little solicitor tucked away . . . this will be Lord Goodman's office . . . so they ain't playing with the boys, you know they've got the money, the real money to go up.[26]

The reference to Goodman in this context is somewhat puzzling, because Goodman was not Holmes's solicitor. Goodman's fame, and the intimidating power of his reputation, had reached into unlikely corners of British life – but it was no longer enough to ensure compliance. When, in the summer of 1977, Newton was released

246

from prison, he collected his hush money from the Thorpe team and then started talking about a contract to murder Scott. At a chaotic news conference on 27 October 1977, Thorpe defended himself. An uncomfortable John Montgomerie, representing Goodman Derrick, had to step in to advise Thorpe to refuse to answer a question about whether he had been a homosexual.[27]

In August 1978 Thorpe and others were arrested and charged with conspiracy to murder, and Thorpe additionally with incitement to murder. Peter Bessell was to be the main prosecution witness at the trial, so the main thrust of the defence was to discredit his character. After the trial Bessell wrote a book, *Cover Up*, which was published privately in the United States because there was no chance of it passing the British libel laws. Bessell's credibility in Britain had been reduced to zero by a concerted campaign, on which Goodman advised, but since the trial, as other participants have corroborated much of his story, it has steadily risen. In 1996 the publication of Simon Freeman's absurdly titled *Rinkagate*, the fullest account to date of the Thorpe affair, was a belated and posthumous vindication of Bessell's account, if not of his life and character. As Bessell's story began to come out, Goodman handed over Thorpe's defence to Sir David Napley, who had more criminal experience. It must have been a considerable relief to him to get rid of the Thorpe case, given the harsh light that had already been shed on Thorpe's conduct, the sordid nature of a case involving South Wales low-life and, not least, Thorpe's abuse even now of Goodman's reputation in order to persuade his own associates to go along with his schemes. But Goodman was still not free of Jeremy Thorpe.

First, there was Pencourt. Their investigations of Thorpe fell foul of letters Goodman sent to Charles Curran, the Director-General of the BBC, complaining that filming interviews with Scott amounted to harassment of his client, and drew complaints from other political figures.[28] As so often, the Fear of Arnold worked and the journalists were isolated, then moved out of the BBC and began operating independently. It is worth bearing in mind that only the South African element in Pencourt's stories, fed to them by Wilson, has not stood up: in all other particulars they were right.

Having been forced out of the BBC, they got a contract instead from the publisher Secker & Warburg, and a serialization deal from the *Observer*. The newspaper ran its story on Wilson and MI5 in the summer of 1977 but held off on the much larger collection of

Thorpe material. Pencourt watched, frustrated, as the press now published allegations of the murder plot from Newton and Bessell and they were scooped. The *Observer* dithered about whether to serialize the book and in January 1978, under heavy pressure from Goodman and other Establishment elements still defending Thorpe, finally decided against doing so. This did not help Thorpe, because the *Daily Mirror* ran the story instead. Penrose suspected that Goodman had tried to scupper their investigation; it is certainly extremely improbable that Goodman had argued in favour of publishing the evidence they had accumulated.

In November, when the case began, Napley insisted on a full–scale committal hearing at which the prosecution evidence was laid out. One of the defendants allowed reporting restrictions to be lifted, and a media circus descended on the Magistrates' Court in Minehead to hear a lurid account of murder plots and gay sex. Part of Bessell's evidence involved an occasion when David Holmes visited him in January 1976. Holmes's task was to enlist Bessell's help in a scheme to concoct false evidence to keep Scott's allegations out of the impending court case in which Newton was charged with a firearms offence relating to the shooting of Scott's dog. According to Bessell:

> He told me Jeremy had consulted Lord Goodman, who had agreed with his analysis that the situation was dangerous and Scott must be prevented from mentioning Jeremy's name in court. I was impressed. If that was Goodman's opinion then my arguments fell automatically and it was time for me to stop scoffing.
>
> 'All right, that's different,' I responded, 'is there some way I can help?'
>
> David answered promptly that there was. He alleged that Goodman had suggested to Jeremy that I write a confidential letter to Scott's solicitor saying that long ago Scott had blackmailed me also. Goodman would then inform Scott's solicitor that if he refrained from mentioning Jeremy in court I would take no further action. On the other hand, if Scott brought Jeremy's name into the case I would swear an affidavit and my evidence, taken in conjunction with the pilot's [Newton], would result in Scott's arrest, trial and a probable jail sentence.[29]

Bessell's evidence to this effect led to extensive press coverage, probably none so inflammatory as the front-page headline that appeared in the *Evening Standard*, 'Goodman's Advice to Thorpe'. Holmes told Bessell that it was Goodman's advice and Thorpe's wish that Bessell write a letter explaining away the payments that Bessell had made to Scott years earlier. In essence Goodman was advising the conspirators on how to conduct a cover-up. He was enraged and wrote a brief letter to *The Times* saying that he could not comment until after the proceedings were over. In fact he could hold his tongue only until later that night, when he spoke to the *Daily Telegraph* and vented his spleen against the 'demented allegations' from the Minehead courtroom. According to the paper:

> Lord Goodman reacted last night to the Bessell allegations in court with the 'righteous indignation of a man convinced of his innocence'. He declared, 'I do not think I can say anything. There are technical difficulties and I am taking advice on whether an innocent man is able, under our legal system, to repudiate allegations made against him. It is apparently the case that one is unable to defend oneself against not only baseless, but demented, allegations made against him. But who in the world would believe that a sane man, of blameless reputation, who over the years has rendered no insignificant services to his country, could be guilty of allegations which no small kindergarten child would believe?' Lord Goodman said he was especially concerned at headlines in most morning newspapers suggesting that there was direct evidence that he had urged Mr Bessell to write an untrue letter. 'In fact, all that is being said in this court is what one man said to a second man about the advice given to the first man by a third.' Lord Goodman, a practising solicitor, said he had been consulted by Mr Thorpe for a period of two years. But his advice to him did not remotely relate to those matters discussed in court so far.[30]

The last two sentences of the statement were untrue. Goodman had been involved with Thorpe for at least 11 years and had acted for him in areas which were directly concerned with the case. The splenetic incoherence of the rest of it – the contradiction between his righteous indignation and his admission of what Bessell had actually said – leads one to wonder whether he was protesting too much. Like his behaviour towards *Private Eye* in 1971, he seemed to lose control only when there was substance behind any attacks. Yet nowhere, not even in his book, did Bessell allege that Goodman had indeed urged him to lie. Peter Taylor, for the Thorpe prosecution, pointed out that they were not making allegations against Goodman, but Goodman was lucky that his statement to the *Telegraph* and reference to the evidence of the Crown's main witness as 'baseless' and 'demented' did not lead to proceedings for contempt of court. One is tempted to say that this would have happened to anyone else.

In 1993 the incident still rankled enough for Goodman to devote more than half of the brief discussion of Thorpe in his *Memoirs* to 'a weird and rapidly discounted suggestion that I had given certain advice of a character in which impropriety and idiocy vied with each other'.[31] It seems most likely that Thorpe lied about Goodman's advice. Simon Freeman and Barrie Penrose say that Goodman had told Holmes that, legally if not morally, Bessell could say anything he liked, which sounds like vintage Goodman and can be interpreted as showing that Goodman originated the idea of the letter only in the most indirect way.[32]

Goodman's involvement with Thorpe was the least successful of his relationships with the three party leaders of his era. At one point in the mid-1970s he was Wilson's personal lawyer and chair of the trust that funded his private office, Heath's negotiator in Rhodesia and one of Thorpe's main advisers. In the first two cases both sides seemed to benefit in different ways; in the third Goodman's reputation was the clear loser. Thorpe, however, gained much from associating himself with Goodman. Goodman was useful in delaying the appearance of the fullest version of the story in the *Observer* and Goodman's name was useful in suppressing stories and scaring witnesses, but Thorpe's folly was so monumental that not even Goodman could have contained it. Moreover, much of the main thrust of the cover-up was occurring ten years after the Boothby case, at a time when Wilson's political stock was much lower and the deference of Fleet Street a much less bankable commodity – though the BBC proved predictably spineless.

Goodman's judgement on the case in his *Memoirs* was circumspect:

> [I] was gratified that Jeremy Thorpe was acquitted. It was unworthily pusillanimous that law officers and prosecutors were willing to rely on the tainted and corrupt evidence available to them – which it was clear no jury would accept – because of a fear that it might be said they had failed to prosecute on account of the public prominence of the individual concerned. Public prominence should not place you at any advantage over the rest of mankind, but it is a craven society where it is allowed to place you at a disadvantage.[33]

Which is all well and good but does not account for Thorpe's failure to testify on his own behalf. In such a situation the jury relied on the judge's summing-up. Mr Justice Cantley described Scott as a crook, fraud, sponger, whiner and parasite, and Thorpe as a 'very distinguished national figure'. Thorpe was acquitted on 22 June 1978.

13

The Great and the Goodman

I am glad of the realisation that people need my support. It is a
compliment that they feel I am able to supply it. And in a small
way I can encourage their good behaviour.

(Goodman in 1993)

Any honour I received was never sought. I would be sitting
quietly at home and a letter would arrive from the Prime
Minister offering me this or that honour. On one occasion, I
was even offered a choice.

(Goodman in 1993)

Throughout the 1970s the pace of work that Goodman set himself
was relentless, but it was not all political. As the years passed
Goodman lived his life in a number of different compartments. Aside
from Theo, the Friends of Arnold were the compartment which was
closest to home. They nurtured his growing sense of self-importance
and self-belief, they encouraged him in his predisposition that the
ordinary rules did not apply. More than this, they defined the
parameters of his actions: he did nothing major if it was not in some
way connected with one of his networks or would benefit one of his
circle or one of the charities that he chaired. The exceptions to this
rule were the personal and private acts of kindness to individuals,
usually young people at the beginning of their career. All the
evidence suggests that these were straightforward acts of altruism:
Goodman no doubt enjoyed the moment at which he could grandly
announce that the money for the flat was not a problem or that a job
could be found, but there was no gain for him. Such acts and his
longer-term involvement with charities raise significant questions
about his motivation in particular and the notion of altruism more
generally. Goodman's self-image was as the last great Victorian
philanthropist, though his kindness was not usually with his own
money. To an extent this picture is accurate; but nobody does
anything unless they will gain from it, even if it is only by feeling a
little better about themselves.

The best idea Goodman ever had for a way to help other people was Motability. This charity was launched in 1978 'for disabled drivers or passengers to procure cheap finance, discounts and insurance'. In 1979 one-seater tricycles, which had been the main form of transport available to the disabled, were replaced by a taxable Mobility Allowance of £5 per week, which by 1982 was increased to £16.50. The purpose of this benefit was to enable people to have a choice of transport and in the first three years it was taken up by nearly 200,000 people aged between five and 65 who had severe trouble walking. Motability offered adults the chance of a car.[1] Four motor manufacturers, British Leyland, Talbot, Ford and Vauxhall, offered discounts on their vehicles. A disabled person applied to the charity to lease or buy on hire purchase a new or second-hand car. Motability Finance, owned by the London and Scottish Clearing Banks, charged well below the market interest rate. On a leased car Motability paid maintenance and service costs and the first £80 of the insurance. The disabled person paid for any necessary adaptations to the vehicles but Motability provided grants from its charitable fund of £750,000. Since 1981 Motability had helped disabled drivers to purchase second-hand cars that had been approved by the Automobile Association, thereby providing much cheaper deals. Outdoor powered wheelchairs could also be bought at favourable rates.

There were persistent rumours about the financial arrangements of Motability and Goodman fought at least one libel action against the *New Statesman*, which alleged that the charity allowed him and his associates to make money out of it. But what if they did? They also supplied thousands and thousands of disabled people with cheap transport. Pure altruism it was not, but it was certainly, as Goodman says in his *Memoirs*, 'the most successful achievement of my career and the most fortunate thought that ever came into my head'.[2]

Another area in which Goodman was heavily involved over the years was property. His involvement took two forms. On the one hand he was an early and successful property lawyer, working closely with some of the most successful property developers of the post-war era, like Harry Hyams of Oldham Estates and Max Rayne of London Merchant Securities. The great profits made in property and the activities of some who worked in the residential field, like Peter Rachman, led the term 'property developer' to become one of abuse. A Goodman client, John Gaul, added to this unfavourable image.

Gaul's company, Sun Real Estates, owned £3 million worth of flats, offices and shops. In 1962 Gaul was fined £25,000 for living on the earnings of prostitution in Soho. On the other hand, once established in the political world, Goodman chaired the Housing Corporation through its period of greatest growth.

Goodman himself was also indirectly involved with property development from 1954, when he reorganized the Portman Estate. One of his first and best clients had been the Portman family. The 7th Lord Portman died in 1949, leaving two sons, Gerald, and a younger brother called Michael, who was also known as Winkie. In addition to much of Dorset, the family owned a chunk of central London. They also had land north of Portman Street because a much earlier Lord Portman had been told when ill that the only cure was goat's milk and, to ensure a regular supply, he bought a farm on which to keep goats in that then outlying area.

The fallout from the death of the 7th Lord Portman was considerable. In 1954, to raise some of the £7.5 million of death duties needed, the 'goat's milk-producing' Portman Estate in London was reduced from 258 acres to 108 acres. The remaining land included Portman, Bryanston, Montagu and Manchester Squares and the north side of Oxford Street between Edgware Road and Great Portland Street. After the resolution of the issue of death duties, Goodman reorganized the family's finances into trusts and managed the investments and loans from these trusts. He avoided future death duties by resettling early on heirs.

Goodman also acted for developers. Harry Hyams was one of a group of key clients who stayed with him when he left Rubinstein Nash to establish Goodman Derrick in 1954. The timing of the move was crucial because in November of that year the Minister of Works in the first post-war Conservative government, Nigel Birch, in line with a manifesto pledge to give more freedom to private builders and with the final ending of wartime controls and rationing, removed building licences and the effect was immediate. The post-war property boom was on. A week before Birch's action Hyams, in an extremely shrewd move, had purchased a piece of land in Grafton Street, off New Bond Street, from Gabriel Harrison for £59,000. Harrison sold because he could not get a building licence and did not, as Hyams did, anticipate their imminent demise. As soon as these licences were abolished the value of the land shot up. Hyams got planning permission for an office building of 40,000 square feet. Ten years of building followed the relaxation of restrictions. Then in 1965, George Brown, the Secretary of State for Economic Affairs, placed a cap on further office building in London, so the value of existing properties increased with no risk to the developers. Moreover, so long as the developers did not sell a building they did not incur capital gains tax on its value as an appreciating asset. Hyams had been trained as an estate agent and turned the Oldham Estates from a tiny concern with assets of £20,000 in 1959 to one worth £39 million by 1966 (about £500 million at late-1990s values). Oliver Marriott wrote in his 1967 account of the great property boom of the 1950s:

> [a] cornerstone of the Hyams formula was that he surrounded himself with some of the finest talent available to a property developer. Richard Seifert was his architect. As his number two in Oldham he had William Allen, a solicitor's clerk recognised to have one of the best brains in London on the conveyancing of property; the giant Oldham was run by a full time staff of two men and three girls. His accountants were Silver, Altman, wizards on tax in relation to property. He had several shrewd estate agents working for him on various projects; two of the partners in Jones, Lang, Wootton, the brothers Eric and Noel Taylor, and two lesser known agents, William Grainger of Hamptons and James Gray of Waite and Waite.

In the original version of the book published the next paragraph read:

> His lawyer was Arnold Goodman of Derrick, Goodman [sic], another mystery man until elevated to public posts and the peerage by the Labour Party, which he supported. Arnold Goodman suddenly shot into the limelight as the 'Mr. X' who solved the television technicians' strike of July 1964. All these men were extremely loyal to Harry Hyams and almost all of them had a handsome reward.

It went on to make allegations that suggested Goodman may have been guilty of insider dealing – not perhaps as serious an allegation in the late 1960s as it is today, but nevertheless one to which Goodman was extremely sensitive. Marriott, perhaps sensing this, actually went out of his way to state that 'There is no trace on the shareholders' register of Lord Goodman's owning any shares in Oldham but he and others might do so through some of the nominee holdings.' But this was not enough for Goodman. There followed an exchange of letters in which Goodman denied that he had received any shares and asked for a paragraph to be inserted in the 1969 edition of the book, the revised version read as follows:

> On rereading the references to Lord Goodman, they might carry a meaning I did not intend, particularly as he has never owned a single share in any of Mr Hyams' enterprises – or for that matter ever been engaged in any property transactions – and his firm was one of several solicitors employed by Mr. Hyams and never in the capacity of financial or business adviser – nor did they act until the company was already a firmly established entity. I should emphasis that the phrase 'mystery man' did not intend to convey that there was any mystery about his professional or other activities but only that – like all reputable lawyers – he avoided the limelight until he was reluctantly dragged into it by the television strike.

Goodman played a key part in the Centre Point deal. Richard Edmunds was a Goodman Derrick client and chairman of the London County Council Town Planning Committee. The LCC wanted to enlarge the junction of New Oxford Street, Charing Cross Road, Tottenham Court Road and Oxford Street, but its efforts to purchase the land required had got bogged down in legal wrangling with the owners of some of it, the Pearlbergs. Hyams offered to buy them out, as well as the owners of other surrounding property and give the LCC the land it needed in return for allowing a greater density of development on the remainder of the site. In 1956 the LCC approved a plan to modify the road pattern at this major intersection. After the failure of negotiations to purchase leases on key properties, the LCC served notice of compulsory purchase. The matter then went to the Lands Tribunal, where the argument centred on whether the notice was valid. The matter was adjourned until October 1958 and it was clear that the case could drag on for years. The LCC despaired of ever starting work. Shortly after the adjournment Richard Edmunds was called by Goodman and asked to come into the Goodman Derrick office:

> When I arrived a reddish-faced young man with a beard was already with Arnold Goodman. 'This is Mr Hyams,' said Goodman. 'He thinks he may be able to help you on St Giles' Circus'. Hyams said to me,

'You're in trouble with St Giles' Circus'. And I replied, 'Yes, we certainly are'.[3]

Hyams then produced a solution. His company would buy out the Pearlbergs at a price which the LCC could not afford and make a 'land for planning permission' deal with it. In this way the LCC would get its land for the road improvements and Hyams would get planning permission for the rest of the site. Moreover, the plot ratio – the number of units that could be built on the area – would include the area taken up by the road: which is why Centre Point is so disproportionately tall compared with the surrounding developments.

The 1969 edition of Marriott's book, as well as redefining Goodman's role, has an additional sentence, inserted after the description of the meeting between Edmunds, Hyams and Goodman:

> Apart from this introduction of Edmunds to Hyams, when the matter was already under way, Lord Goodman played no part in any financial negotiations connected with the Centre Point deal.[4]

However, Goodman was present, always standing at the back, throughout the planning application hearings. As the architect, Seifert, recalls:

> He was acting for Harry Hyams, one of the major property developers, mainly on Centre Point. Goodman was a shy man but he always came into the discussion at the last moment with some brilliant idea, which impressed everyone, and one thing which was very good about him was that when there was a planning enquiry he would always stand in the background; I don't know why he would never sit down. He was always in the background, and he used to pass little notes to me, whilst the discussion was going on, or whilst I was giving evidence. I'm very sorry I never kept those notes because they were giving excellent advice.[5]

The planning application was made on 12 August 1959. Four days later it became illegal to make applications for development without ownership or without the knowledge and consent of the owner. Under the old system people could be bought out without knowing that the value of the land had been increased by the granting of planning consent. This is exactly what happened in this case. The existing tenants, who included the tailors Cecil Gee, were told that they would be subject to compulsory purchase by the LCC and that they would get a much better price from Hyams – a perfectly legal move at the time it was made. Also, unusually, when the LCC was given the freehold (by Hyams) Hyams's company's ground rent was fixed for 150 years at £18,500 per annum. Hyams defends the deal in a letter reproduced in the 1969 edition of Marriott's book on the grounds that the land had been gifted to the LCC, whose direct interest was only a small part of the site.[6] Goodman's extreme sensitivity on the subject by the late 1960s was in part because of his then well-established public role and the continuing controversy that surrounded Centre Point. The building proved difficult to let and stood empty for much of the sixties following the controversy over the way in which it had been built. This coincided with an upsurge in concern over housing that was in part inspired by television programmes like *Cathy Come Home*, first broadcast in 1966. Concern focused on inner cities and the renovation, rather than mass clearance, of older housing. This was an area of expertise of housing associations, particularly those related to the churches. At this time housing associations could claim government subsidies similar to those available to local authorities. There was concern in the early 1960s about the dramatic decline of private renting in the face of unscrupulous landlords like Rachman and the corresponding rise of council housing and owner occupation. The general view in the housing world was that what was needed was a 'third arm' of tenure other than owner-occupation and renting from local authorities. Existing housing associations were thought to be a suitable vehicle and the sector was to be greatly expanded and receive government aid. The forms of non-profit ownership were simplified into housing associations, and the vast bulk of funding of their acquisitions and renovation work was routed through the Housing Corporation.

The function of the Housing Corporation was to keep a register of, and supervise and control, housing associations, and to act as the agent of the Secretary of State for the Environment in paying grants to registered housing associations. It also, in general terms, promoted the voluntary housing movement. The Corporation's funding for its running costs came from a levy charged to registered associations. In fact it was a quango with a very large budget and was not subject to much accountability for its decisions. The National Building Agency was a separate and slightly mysterious quango which gave technical advice to the Housing Corporation. Between 1964 and 1974 the Corporation was involved with 'cost rent' schemes, but after rising and changeable interest rates in the late 1960s and 1970s these schemes were no longer viable. The Corporation was also involved in 'co-ownership' schemes aimed at middle-class renters. It gave money to 'housing societies', which established cost-rent or co-owned developments – many such societies were offshoots of housing associations, builders and local authorities. This bipartisan policy survived the February 1974 general election. The core of the idea had been evolving under the Labour government in 1968–70, was worked up into a White Paper by the Conservatives in 1973 and became the Housing Act 1974, passed under the minority Labour government.

In April 1973, immediately after a White Paper had set out a new expanded role for the Housing Corporation, Goodman was summoned by the Conservative Secretary of State for the Environment, Geoffrey Rippon, and asked to chair the Corporation and the National Building Agency. He joined at a time when increasing activity had to take place in advance of the extra powers that the Housing Act would bring, and extra staff were needed to conduct the extended consultation during 1973–4. Under Goodman's chairmanship the Housing Corporation Board was directly responsible for policy, and the Corporation took the initiative in pressing housing associations for new large projects that could be implemented quickly, and asking for schemes that could come on stream as soon as the 1974 Act allowed. The Corporation also sponsored working parties to lessen delays, for example with contractors. There were imaginative deals done to secure land; for example: 'Following discussions with the British Rail Property Board, Lord Goodman obtained the consent of Paul Channon [Housing Minister in 1973] to an agreement under which land would be offered for development by fair rent associations in exchange for nomination rights for transport staff to some of the resulting homes.'[7] The expansion managed to achieve an increase of nearly 300 per cent in approvals for new social housing: 10,000 to 38,000 between 1972–3 and 1974–5. It was likely that the rules were bent if not broken, although in a way the government undoubtedly condoned.

Goodman's approach to housing problems and his role as

chairman were credited by professionals and colleagues at the time as being a significant element in the success of the Housing Corporation before and after the 1974 Act. At the least his presence ensured that the quango retained the support of government ministers. At the first board meeting in 1973 Goodman announced that he had already been talking to people and thinking about ways to achieve the main objective of building more houses. In addition to chairing the Housing Corporation Board, he took many meetings with officials from associations and councils across the country – the Corporation's own history credits him with starting the Scottish community-based housing sector after discussions with Glasgow City Council. His main imprint on personnel was to ensure that the Housing Corporation had a Chief Executive whom he liked and could work with. His choice was astute and successful – Dick Madge, a Department of the Environment civil servant was persuaded to take the job. As Madge put it: 'I was hijacked by Lord Goodman.' Madge stayed as Chief Executive until 1984.[8]

The 1974 Act's reorganization of the Corporation entailed changes in its registration and monitoring functions. These were decentralized and approval for individual schemes passed to regional offices – the exact opposite of the administrative structure of the Arts Council, which Goodman vigorously defended against regionalism. In 1976 the growth of the Corporation entailed a move from Sloane Square to larger offices in Tottenham Court Road. There was also an increasing concern, which originated in the Corporation rather than the Department of the Environment, about 'special needs' housing for disabled and elderly tenants (which in turn reflected the charitable roots of the housing association sector). The Housing Corporation Board sponsored studies and as a result decided to earmark 25 per cent plus funding for such housing.

By the mid-1970s the Housing Corporation's overall budget had levelled off after expansion and the worsening public-spending situation of 1976 led to the introduction of spending ceilings. But Goodman devised a scheme, using the Friends of Arnold, to gain access to private funding which raised £50 million in two years through a subsidiary, Housing Corporation Finance Company Limited, which was formed with City help recruited by Goodman. The pattern was the same as with Motability, and similar questions were asked about who gained from the arrangements, but again the initiative was effective. However, the sheer volume of increased money and activity, and the need to monitor the actions of several thousand local organizations, produced problems. The speed of the increase that Goodman as Chairman encouraged resulted in insufficient control and monitoring procedures and, as a result, some suspect associations were supported and there was a lack of accounting clarity at the centre. Goodman's old friend the Estimates Committee investigated the Corporation in 1979 and found that 'there were grounds for concern in three areas: the thoroughness of the Corporation's vetting of housing associations before registration and of its subsequent monitoring; the high proportion of associations which were late in submitting their annual accounts; and the quality of management of the associations themselves'.

Goodman was very stretched in these years and his role as overseer and auditor of the Corporation was sacrificed to what he could do better: help with expansion by getting things done. The problem was that the Corporation faced two ways – as paymaster (and encourager of growth) and policeman. It was a potential conflict of interest that Goodman characteristically denied. Despite the economic crisis, housing approvals were able to increase to 40,000 a year by the late 1970s, although the rationing process that had been introduced in 1976 caused division between the regions.

In 1976 Goodman was persuaded by Tony Crosland, on the very day that Crosland was preferred by James Callaghan to Roy Jenkins as Foreign Secretary, to stay on for an additional year. He finally resigned as Chairman in 1977. His personal involvement in housing did not end there, for he was thereafter on the board of two housing associations. The Cyril Wood Trust was intended to provide village accommodation for retired artists and craftsmen; Goodman's involvement must have seemed like a good idea at the time, as he was someone with experience of housing, the arts and resolving problems (the Trust's programme was running behind schedule) but his personal relations with the other board members were poor. He resigned after he failed to persuade the Trust to buy Stoke Bruern Manor, in Oxfordshire, which Michael Astor was trying to sell; the housing scheme was eventually opened in 1989, but Goodman did not attend the ceremony.

Overall the Housing Corporation, though it had a much less glamorous client group than the Arts Council – touring building sites on provincial housing estates was not the same as taking Jennie Lee to the opera – was a great deal more obviously worthwhile.

Goodman took a serious interest in its role and focused on the important matters – how to get more houses built for people who needed them, and the nature of the existing housing problems. This focus and his generally good relations with Ministers and the City, as well as his open-minded approach, steered the Housing Corporation through an important and stormy period. Goodman's involvement with it was a great success. Between 1974 and 1978 2750 housing associations were registered; by 1978 the annual grant to housing associations stood at £650 million. The Corporation succeeded in establishing a third sector in housing that was to play a progressively greater part in social housing in the next 20 years – a significant policy development which Goodman had overseen in the crucial first few years.

In 1973, about 18 months before the Master of University College, Oxford, Lord Redcliffe-Maud, was due to retire, about 35 Fellows met and discussed the succession. A number of names were suggested. Michael Yudkin, son of Goodman's old school friend John Yudkin, was a Fellow at University College and thought Goodman would be suitable for the position. He put forward Goodman's name, and other Fellows became interested in the idea. Names were added to the list, others taken off. No one had at this stage approached Goodman directly, but knowing he was now 60 Yudkin wondered if 'he wanted to do something else'. Goodman had maintained links with academic life since his undergraduate days, lecturing at University College London and Cambridge over the years and clearly enjoying it.

Yudkin was sure enough of the potential interest to press Goodman's case and eventually the Fellows agreed that a preliminary approach could be made. The understanding was that Goodman was to be asked if he was interested but told that nothing had been decided. Yudkin visited the Portland Place flat and Goodman told him that he had refused Downing College, Cambridge, some years before because he wanted to stay in London. However, he had still been Chairman of the Arts Council at that stage. Now he agreed to be considered. By now the short-list was down to three or four names. It was decided to invite the candidates to the College for drinks at 6 p.m. with the Fellows, followed by dinner at 7.15 p.m. By 6.30 Goodman had not arrived. At 6.40 a rather embarrassed Yudkin walked out of the building to see if he could spot Goodman.

He discovered him and his chauffeur outside asking a passer-by where University College was. The evening was not a great success, but the Fellows still decided that Goodman should be offered the post.

The Fellows were concerned that some heavy persuasion might be needed to secure Goodman and in February 1975 a delegation was assembled to lobby him. They sat going through their lines as they waited for his – inevitably late – arrival. Professor Wyndham Albery, later a Master himself, was the youngest don on the delegation and he assigned his colleagues to specific tasks. David Cox, the Senior Fellow, was to talk about the constitutional side of the Mastership, Tony Firth, the Dean, the social side and entertaining under-graduates, Maurice Shock, the former Estates Bursar, the finances and Albery himself, as Tutor for Admissions, the academic side.[9] They waited. They had a gin and tonic and ran through their roles again. Goodman arrived. 'Gentlemen, I know why you've come and the answer is yes!'

The duties of a Master are poorly defined, but in general terms he is not necessarily expected to take a highly active part in the governance of the College but rather to represent it in the wider world, to raise funds and perhaps aid in the settling of internal disputes. It is hard to imagine a job better suited to Goodman's tastes. In addition there was a social role of entertaining and a pastoral role with undergraduates. 'Influence but no power' was Goodman's own description of the role. During the 1980s contacts with rich potential donors also became a desirable feature of the post. Fellows like a Master who brings in money and famous guests while leaving them to run the place; Goodman was by all accounts a highly popular choice.

As soon as he agreed to take on the position he arranged for the Master's Lodgings, a Victorian building on the south (Merton Street) side of the College, to be redecorated and he enjoyed having a stream of decorators and designers to shape it to his own tastes. The finance for this work came mainly from a farewell gift from the Newspaper Publishers' Association. If ever there was a stage set which suited Goodman it was the Master's Lodgings at 'Univ'. There was a large hall, panelled in dark oak with a broad staircase, with carved-oak banisters, lit by a large window with inset stained-glass crests. Above the fireplace was a tapestry, commissioned by Goodman, in which the College seal figured prominently. There was a large kitchen (and a housekeeper's sitting-room) where Miss Sullivan, who looked after Goodman, prepared the meals, with occasional help from the College kitchens. There was a large sitting-room hung with green damask curtains; a Steinway grand piano looked small in this room, where recitals were often given. A door led from here to the conservatory and garden. Goodman's dining-room – which could seat up to 16 – also contained the Master's library, the books still on the original oak shelves. In a semicircular bay window with a window seat stood a smaller, round table which could seat a lesser number. A marble-topped serving table and display shelves also graced the room, and over the vast stone fireplace hung a Victorian painting of Alfred the Great. Upstairs were the Master's bedroom and a bathroom with a large bath equipped with a platform by which Goodman clambered in and out; and two guest rooms. Goodman's bedroom looked across to the Alington Room, where the Fellows took their lunch, and down the walled garden. When he left the College many of the furnishings stayed in the Lodgings.

Personally, Goodman had little to gain from the Mastership. His annual stipend of £11,000 was more or less consumed by the expenses of keeping a house and a housekeeper and the heavy load of entertaining that went with the job. For University College, his Mastership was a paying proposition. Its coffers were in need of replenishment after the construction of new accommodation (in Staverton Road, away from the main College buildings) and the impact on its investments of the property and stock-market crash of 1973–5. The balances were higher when he left than when he arrived, and several construction projects went ahead, including renovation and safety work on student accommodation overlooking the High Street. The Friends of Arnold were tapped for cash, some more successfully than others. Max Rayne became an honorary Fellow and gave money. Goodman tried to get a donation of around £100,000 from the Wolfson Trust but was disappointed to obtain 'only' £25,000.

Goodman raised money for several fellowships, a clue to the sources of money being contained in their names: the Beaverbrook Fellowship in English, the Sir Jules Thorn Fellowship in Physiology, the Rayne Fellowship in Theoretical Physics, the Hammerson Fellowship in Plant Science. After Goodman's retirement his name was given to one of the law fellowships, being partly funded by donations by his friends. Despite these successes, the Wolfson grant and his failure to obtain a donation from Armand Hammer, one of his clients, rankled with Goodman and dented his self-image. 'If he was applying himself to something, he wanted to come out as the wonderful successful man,' declared one of the Fellows, and in his *Memoirs* Goodman dwelled more on Armand Hammer, who was a 'failure' of his more than on Rayne or Thorn, who were successes. His passage on his efforts to raise funds gives a flavour of his work:

> My successes were achieved on the whole with minimal effort. It required . . . only one letter to a friend who happened to have a charitable trust for substantial sums to be forthcoming. One trust gave us £300,000, another the same amount, a third trust gave us £200,000 and one benefactor . . . gave us £100,000 of shares in his company, which in the event became worth £350,000. So all in all I cannot claim to have been unsuccessful. But the requirements of an Oxford College are . . . an absolutely bottomless pit.[10]

The failure with Hammer was not for want of a stylish try. Princess Alexandra, Goodman's favourite member of the royal family, was laid on for a dinner at the College when Hammer and his wife were in the country. The evening was a great success and Goodman followed up with a personal approach through a mutual friend in the United States. Even though Hammer retained Goodman as his UK solicitor, he never actually used him. He is said to have paid a retainer to Goodman Derrick just to ensure that he never had to face Goodman as an opponent. His regard did not, however, extend to making a donation.[11]

For Goodman, the move to Oxford was not an abandonment of London and his legal practice, at least not in the first five years of his Mastership. Though the College statutes required him to spend a considerable part of the year there, the Fellows accepted that Goodman would split his time with London so long as he was available when they needed him for meetings. His style in chairing College business would have been familiar to anyone who had witnessed him on a quango: 'probably not always the best prepared for meetings, he had the ability to spot the difficult or controversial items'.[12] Despite being mostly an absentee Master, he made an effort to attend College meetings. At his first meeting there was a long discussion over whether the assistant librarian should receive one or two free lunches. Goodman had the casting vote. Two lunches won the day.

Socially Goodman was in his element as the central figure in the social life of the College. Surprisingly, as he records in his *Memoirs*, the first time he was ever a guest at high table at either Oxford or Cambridge was when he was being wooed by the Fellows of University College. High table is a formal dining experience of a peculiarly English variety and Goodman was unimpressed by the culinary standards of Oxford. While Master he called in some contacts in Forte to examine the kitchen procedures, and by his account this both saved money and produced better food.[13] The Master's social role also involved meeting every student and hosting various dinners and drinks parties, which Goodman enjoyed: 'At Christmas he would hold court for a week or more; evening after evening, a mixture of Fellows and the great and famous would be entertained.' He also used his contacts in the arts to bring some of the finest musicians in the world to give concerts in the College, including Yehudi Menuhin and Henryk Szeryng. Some at College felt that this was an all-too-rare recognition of the world of academia, while to others it seemed more than a little patronizing: 'Behind all the words, I don't think he actually cared for our society.'[14]

Goodman's life at University College produced his sharpest confrontation with *Private Eye*. The issue of 18 January 1981 contained two items mentioning his name; the first made unfounded allegations about David Burgess, former chaplain of the College, and the second read as follows:

> I am glad to hear from Oxford friends that the Blessed Arnold Goodman is still living up to his name 'Two Dinners'. Apparently he haunts the Old Parsonage Hotel, Banbury Road, with young undergraduate friends. And the waiters are now used to the Blessed Arnold's habit of crying 'Same again, please!' as he wipes his plate clean.

Goodman sued, and the issue was resolved by a grovelling apology in *Private Eye* on 5 November 1981 and the payment of substantial damages. Goodman, and the apology, stated that the article had been 'an obvious suggestion that Lord Goodman was a homosexual', though the suggestion appears far from obvious, and in any case hardly 'so serious and so offensive that an apology might seem futile'. The allegations against Burgess were rapidly dismissed, but the snippet about Goodman led to a year of legal shadow-boxing, perhaps unwisely stoked by *Private Eye*'s encouragement of correspondence from readers about the causes (primarily obesity) of the hiatus hernia from which Goodman suffered in spring 1981.

His colleagues at University College never for a moment believed that Goodman was homosexually interested in students. In any case, ironically, his term as Master saw the first admission of female students, in October 1979. Under Redcliffe-Maud, this initiative had been postponed on the 'unripe time' argument, but Goodman found the majority of the Fellows were actually in favour, as was he. The College statutes were accordingly amended in 1978. Goodman reacted against the more bizarre aspects of academic sexism: he was heard to say to the head of another Oxford college that 'the Fellows are interested in electing the best candidate solely on merits, but they do not add that one of the necessary qualifications is that the candidate be a man.' In the case of the Univ Fellows, at least, this was wholly unfair and led to some anger: 'He loved to say witty things regardless of the truth,' said one contemporary, confirming the principle that some of the anecdotes Goodman told were indeed too good to be true.

College gossip about Goodman did not focus on the students; even a bitchy, enclosed academic community was prepared to accept that he was motivated by benevolence. He was, as one might expect, good at fixing problems that faced students, from a quiet psychiatric referral to a job to keep someone from being sent back to apartheid South Africa. Instead the glamorous widows whom he paraded through College are remembered. He was introduced to Clarissa Avon, Anthony Eden's widow, during his University College years, though his main companion was Ann Fleming, who seemed to some of the Fellows to be cold and snobbish. But Goodman loved her and uncharacteristically showed his feelings of loss and distress when she died. In 1981 he was photographed at a fancy-dress party, in the costume of Friar Tuck, accompanying Diana Cooper, who was dressed as a nun. Jennie Lee also came to high table, although she was not a success with the Fellows.

In 1983 Goodman reached the retirement age for Masters, 70, but was asked to stay on for another two years. This testament to his popularity and success as a Master was further reflected when he did retire, to general benediction and praise from most of the Fellows. For the rest of his life he was fêted with a College feast on significant birthdays. He had not been involved much in university politics or administration, had done a little for the Oxford Arts Society and had arranged for a grant from the *Observer* to the Oxford Playhouse, both nominally town rather than gown activities. But he was instrumental in raising money for the Oxford Union, which named a library after him. After leaving the Lodgings, he bought an ugly modern house in Headington, a suburb on the road from Oxford to London. It possessed a swimming pool, which Goodman enjoyed using.[15]

After retiring from the Mastership, he returned to Oxford frequently and kept up with a circle of friends in the city, for example lunching with Isaiah Berlin and his wife.[16] Of all the jobs that Goodman held, the University College post was in many ways his most successful and the one that suited him best. Outside Oxford the clash of politics, law and the media produced questions, disputes, arguments and difficult ethical decisions for him, and his tendency to cut corners led to charges that his style of working was inappropriate. But in his role at the College there was never a question mark and the universal fixer had a ten-year stretch in a congenial and satisfying post.

However, if Oxford provided a happy resting-place, in other aspects of his life the period was not as content.

14

A Man? No, Lord God[1]

> I'm not intolerant of mediocrity, since you ask, or one would
> be intolerant of 99 per cent of the human race.
> > (Goodman in conversation with Naim Attallah)

From 1964 to 1970 Goodman had seen Wilson most weeks for their
late-evening chat. When Wilson, a little unexpectedly, returned to
Number Ten in 1974, the same pattern of involvement in the Prime
Minister's life was not re-established and the centre of the political
world began to shift away from Goodman. This process was
accelerated after Labour lost power to the Conservatives in 1979.
The corporatist establishment of the age of Harold Wilson was in
terminal decline in the second half of the decade. The self-
destruction of Jeremy Thorpe was emblematic of a new era coming.
The part of Goodman that always felt ambivalent about being in the
spotlight welcomed the change. Another part of him wanted to cling
to the wreckage of his life at the centre of politics. But the last two
decades of his life were to witness a gradual decline in his health and
his public standing, along with an increasing sense of isolation as old
friends died and Thatcher turned Britain into a free-market island of
philistinism and unrestricted capitalism. The fall of Lord Goodman
began with his break with Wilson.

There had been strains, not directly between Wilson and
Goodman, but between Goodman and Marcia Williams [later Lady
Falkender], whose domineering tendencies were even more marked
in the second administration. Goodman could not stand Williams
and even went so far as to say that, had it had not been for her,
Wilson might have been a great Prime Minister.[2] In his conversations
with David Selbourne, Goodman summarized his view of the
Wilson–Williams relationship thus: 'Harold Wilson, for example,
started off with virtuous ideas, but did not stay with them for long
... He succumbed to undesirable influences ... such as Lady
Falkender.'[3]

Wilson's antics over the Thorpe case, particularly his attempt to brief Pencourt, infuriated Goodman, but Goodman's feud with Williams was the real sore in his relations with the PM. The feud extended to Wilson's resignation honours list in 1976. James Goldsmith, who was to be offered a peerage, and others who had been within Williams's circle, appeared on the original list. Goodman told Naim Attallah:

> It couldn't have mattered twopence to Harold Wilson whether some unworthy businessman was going to get a knighthood or a peerage, so he had no great personal advantage to get out of it. He had a certain weakness towards particular influences, and he didn't have the strength of character to resist them. I think the 'Lavender List' did him great harm, but I'm equally sure that there was no element of corruption in it and that he was doing it because he thought he was obliging someone or other. He should have had a stiffer resistance to obliging people.[4]

Goodman offered direct to Wilson his advice on what he saw as an 'unwise and reckless list' and then leaked the list to the *Daily Express* to try to stop some of the least-deserving awards. There was considerable uproar in the press and Goldsmith ended up with just a knighthood.

Goodman's acceptance of the Mastership of University College, Oxford, also contributed to the cooling of his relations with Wilson. As Goodman later told the story, during Wilson's last days in office he had asked Goodman to help *him* become Master of University College. 'It was one of the most awkward moments of my life, since I had in my pocket at the time a letter from the Fellows of the College offering the job to me.'

In the years after his break with Wilson, Goodman also endured the death of two of his closest friends. The first was that of his brother Theo in 1977. Goodman had trailed behind Theo in the galleries and museums of interwar London, and learnt from him the importance of art and creativity. Their frequent trips to the opera and their intense regard for each other had been fixed points in Goodman's life. On 22 February 1977 Theo died of a coronary thrombosis while attending a concert in the Festival Hall with Cynthia Gladwyn. He collapsed during Britten's *Sinfonia da Requiem*. Jeremy and Marion Thorpe were sitting a few rows behind and Marion phoned Goodman and told him that his brother had been taken to St Thomas's Hospital. As soon as Goodman heard the news of Theo's death he called his old friend Frank Coven, who immediately came round to Portland Place.[5] It was a deeply felt blow and for once Goodman did not hide his feelings. In a friendship lasting over 50 years, it was the only time that Coven saw Goodman cry.

The second blow came when Ann Fleming died in 1981. Ann had become seriously ill three months before she died and had gone to Ireland to stay with her son. With Ann away, Goodman turned to Clarissa Avon. He had first got to know Clarissa when Ann had recommended him as the solicitor to deal with Anthony Eden's will in 1977. Ann was not best pleased to be replaced with such alacrity. As Fionn Morgan, Ann's daughter, remembers it, there was 'something endearing, almost comic, about my mother's fury about the fact that Arnold had been taking out Clarissa while she hadn't been well'. Ann seems to have given him a hard time. He loved it. The most important thing she did, in a similar way to Jennie Lee, was keep his feet on the ground, affectionately tease him and puncture, yet affirm, that sense of his specialness that had been carefully nurtured since his boyhood.

In his prime Goodman was at his best with people who challenged rather than deferred to him. The problem, as he got older, was that fewer and fewer people were prepared to contest what he said or tease him for his frequently ridiculous way of saying things. He began to believe his own myth. Fionn Morgan remembers going to dinners at Portland Place after her mother had died and of the fun having gone out of Goodman. He became:

> slightly more pompous, and those were the times I think when there was too much bowing and scraping. Other people round the table were treating him too much like a god. And there again, it needed somebody like my Mama, who would not have let him get away with the things he would sit there saying. I remember thinking somebody should be answering back and arguing with this man a bit more, not allow him to just pontificate in this way.[6]

Moreover, as he got older Goodman covered the mental impact of his physical discomfort behind walls of pomposity. The sparkling humour, much of it self-effacing, which once accompanied his grand ego, was replaced by a seriousness that concealed much physical pain.

By the mid-1980s Goodman was beginning to think about writing some kind of memoir. Ian Chapman and André Deutsch were both interested in publishing such a book. Even the former *Observer* editor Donald Trelford became involved: 'I went with André Deutsch more than once, I went with Ian Chapman more than once. And we were all persuading Arnold. There would be lots of talk and then I discovered that André had actually got him to dictate a lot of material.' Goodman doubted if Deutsch could match the commercial power of Collins. In the end it came down to money: 'He was talking quite big money at that time. He was talking six figures, well over six figures, I mean not just £100,000, more than £100,000.'

Goodman produced a draft outline which was extremely good. Discussion continued. Murdoch succeeded in buying Collins in 1989 and Chapman left to found his own company. After his departure Collins did the deal with Goodman and paid him a handsome advance. When he finally delivered a manuscript, Collins demanded significant rewrites. After protracted negotiations Goodman cancelled his deal with Collins and took the manuscript to Chapman. Already ill, Goodman was not up to the task of rewriting, so he called an old friend from the Arts Council, Charles Osborne, and asked him to do it. When the chauffeur arrived with the script Osborne thought that he had been sent three copies so that he could scribble on them, but it turned out to be just one copy of the whole manuscript. He spent three weeks cutting this to a manageable size. Then he went to tea with Goodman and after they had talked for a while he said, 'Well, shall we go through the script?' and Goodman said, 'What for?' 'So you can see what I've suggested,' Osborne explained. 'If that's what you suggest, that'll do,' Goodman replied. The script went straight to Chapman.

Chapman next proposed that Goodman do a face-to-face interview with Trelford. Goodman agreed, but at the last minute he cancelled, as he was already giving a series of interviews to David Selbourne for *Not An Englishman*, which appeared in 1993 at about the same time as Goodman's *Memoirs*. When the *Memoirs* appeared, many reviewers were kind, but many others shared Trelford's view that they were 'just a shadow of the book he could have produced in his prime. The humour had gone, his memory had largely gone.' The problem was compounded by *Not An Englishman*, which, even though he was paid for his involvement, was a mistake. The younger Goodman would never have agreed to the publication of Selbourne's conversations. The result was that the *Memoirs* were reviewed alongside the conversations, and his reputation suffered. As Trelford remembers it: 'We all loved Arnold, and in a sense we set aside normal publishing judgements because in a way we wanted to help him get his life down on paper because we thought it was important he should. Not because by then we thought there was any money in it for anybody.'

By the early 1990s Goodman's professional performance was also a shadow of what it had been, but still he could not resist trying to help. In July 1992 he tried to carve a niche for himself in the sorting out of the Maxwell pension crisis. Between November 1991 and March 1992 the size of the hole that Maxwell had left in his companies' pension fund started to emerge. There were 32,000 pensioners, and a high-profile lobby group headed by Ken French was demanding action. The group pointed to the government's acceptance of responsibility in the Barlow Clowes insurance scandal, which had been very expensive. There was strong pressure on the Attorney General to take over the cases of individual pensioners, as he had with Barlow Clowes. Goodman arrived on the scene and seemed to be working for the Newspaper Publishers' Association – though it was never clear who his client was. At any rate he was accompanied by Clive Bradley, the Chief Executive of the NPA, and his old friend Professor Jim Gower, who gave him advice on the Financial Services Act. Goodman was immobile by this time, so people would visit him at Portland Place. He managed to get a meeting with the Prime Minister and Peter Lilley, Secretary of State for Trade and Industry. He was treated courteously, but by now he had no influence at all and was not able to be of much help. He did not get a single contribution to the £6 million fund eventually raised.[7] It was an indication of the extent to which the world had moved on.

Nineteen ninety-three brought Goodman's eightieth birthday and a potentially damaging attack on his carefully protected reputation. He made a public intervention in the libel case that the Prime Minister, John Major, brought against the *New Statesman* over allegations of an affair with a Downing Street cook. Goodman wrote an article for the *Evening Standard* arguing that Major had been wrong to sue and agreed to make one of his rare appearances on television to discuss the case. He made the mistake of choosing to go on a live programme, *Newsnight*. Over the years he had given a number of interviews and managed to have them edited, though never actually stopped. It was as if his vanity could not resist the initial request but his solicitor's reticence then rebelled against the publicity. Or perhaps it was simply that once the interview was done it was out of his control: the defence of his reputation, the thing that mattered to him most towards the end of his life, was out of his power, and he hated that. Live television would not even allow an edit. Still, he could not have known that Anthony Howard had spotted hypocrisy in the position that he had taken, and had decided to get him.

The issue, whether Major was right to sue, was central to disputes over press freedom that had dogged Goodman for many years. Howard decided that he was going to challenge Goodman. 'I sort of came along, working out in my mind an insult I was going to say at some time, whatever he said − "Come, come, Lord Goodman, you've got a record as long as my arm" sort of thing − and I duly said all this and it just bounced off him.' As the discussion developed, Goodman, clearly tired and feeling unwell, repeated the line he had been putting out for much of the 1980s and on which he had rarely if ever been challenged. He said that he had always advised politicians against suing. This was not the case because, though he often advised them not to sue, there were many other occasions on which he encouraged them to do so. Howard took his chance. 'Lord Goodman, that sounds to me rather like a deathbed repentance.' Goodman, never as robust as he appeared, was deeply upset by the remark. After the cameras were turned off, Howard, who by now realized that he had really hurt him, tried to apologize. Goodman turned his chair away and asked to be taken home.[8] Later he gamely told *The Times*: 'It was vigorous. I would willingly have a rematch.'[9]

Having survived Howard's insults on *Newsnight*, Goodman's reputation now came under much heavier and more sustained attack from the unlikely quarter of one of his oldest clients. The Portman family had been a fixture of his professional life for 40 years, yet he does not mention them by name in his *Memoirs*. The reason, as revealed by the *Independent* in January 1999, is that on 29 July 1993 Edward Portman issued a writ against Goodman and Goodman Derrick. The four main parts of the Lord Portman writ were a demand for a full accounting of Goodman's management of his family's money. The writ read:

274

1. Delivery to the Plaintiff of a cash account, in relation to all transactions since 1955 to date, in which the Defendants or either of them has acted as Solicitor for the Plaintiff
2. Payment to the Plaintiff of all money in the custody or control of the Defendants or either of them on behalf of the Plaintiff
3. Delivery to the Plaintiff of all securities in the custody or control of the Defendants or either of them on behalf of the Plaintiff
4. All such further accounts and enquiries as the Court shall consider fit.[10]

When the story broke, Lord Portman was constrained in what he could say because of a confidentiality agreement covering the final settlement. Though he did talk to the press, it was Lady Portman who was quoted as explaining the motivation for issuing the writ. 'It was very difficult to discover anything about our own money,' she remembers. Lord Portman had been asking questions about the management of his funds for a number of years but had been 'bamboozled' by Goodman. Edward Portman was 20 when the reorganization of the family estate had taken place in 1954. Advised by his father and Goodman, he signed everything he was told to: 'I didn't need more than a certain amount to live on and couldn't have the rest. Eventually I had my nasty suspicions about Lord Goodman'.[11] Once the writ was issued, Lord Portman's accountants, Littlejohn Frazer, investigated further and discovered, according to the *Independent* story, that there was evidence that 40 per cent of everything taken had been lent or given to leading figures in the Labour Party. Lord Portman estimated that the amount that went missing over the period would be worth around £10 million today. A family member told the *Independent* that 'they found the most desperately incriminating things. There were lists of people to whom money had been given or loaned, and many senior Labour figures.'[12]

When the allegations against Goodman were first made in January 1999 there was little response from his friends. A couple of letters appeared in *The Times* but there was blanket coverage in the broadsheet and even some tabloid press which assumed that the substance of the allegations was true. Joe Haines, writing in the *Spectator* on 23 January, summed up the tone of the coverage: 'At first, I didn't believe it. Not of Arnold . . . And then, I thought, "Why not Arnold?"' *Private Eye* could barely contain its glee and in the 5 February edition ran the following item:

Lord Badman
   An Apology

In common with all other newspapers over the past 30 years, we may have given the impression that the late Lord Goodman was in some way a saintly figure who had devoted his life to service of the nation and to philanthropic acts too numerous to mention. We may further have given the impression that he was a man of the utmost probity, totally scrupulous in all his business dealings, who had rightly won the admiration of all with whom he came in contact for his profound sense of honour, duty and rectitude.

We now recognise that there was not a jot, tittle, scintilla or vestige of truth in any of the above farrago of falsehoods. We accept unreservedly that Lord Badman was nothing more than a thief, swindler, crook and conman whose sharp practice with his clients' funds was matched only by his inordinate gluttony.

We would like to apologise to our readers for any distress that our misrepresentation of Lord Badman may inadvertently have given rise to. We have made a substantial donation to ourselves in full recompense for writing this apology.

© All newspapers

Goodman's old firm decided against issuing a statement at this point, perhaps judging that this would merely fuel the speculation about his reputation. There matters rested until June 1999. This book was in the final stages of completion and the balance of the evidence was stacked heavily towards the Lord Badman picture painted by *Private Eye*, when Goodman's partners in Goodman Derrick changed their minds and decided to issue a statement to the author. They categorically deny that there was any wrongdoing by the late Lord Goodman, stating that:

> There is no truth in the recent allegations that Lord Goodman stole money from Lord Portman or any member of his family or the Portman Trusts. It is also untrue that Lord Goodman used Portman money to give to the Labour Party or to buy influence with them.[13]

They take particular exception to the idea that Lord Portman's papers contained a list of Labour politicians with the amounts that each had received. The writ asked for a statement of account. A Goodman Derrick partner produced one for all transactions handled by the practice on behalf of Lord Portman for 40 years. Goodman was not the best record-keeper in the world and carried many things around in his head, but they could fully account for every item:

> The preparation of that account required a review of hundreds of files and thousands of ledger entries, many recording minor personal expenditure by Lord Portman. Notwithstanding the long period the account was required to cover, and the very large number of transactions it involved, it was duly prepared and delivered. All funds were accounted for and it was accepted that the account satisfied the directions of the court in respect of the obligation of the firm to produce an account.[14]

When the relationship between Goodman and the Portman family had started there was no need for a written agreement and Goodman, who was also very close to Edward Portman's mother, was given a free hand to manage the family's affairs. This he did with great success. Lord Portman was fully aware of the role Goodman played, and indeed he and his children had looked on him as a father-figure: his children continue to honour the name of Goodman, who was, in a phrase used by his old firm, 'not only a solicitor but also paterfamilias'.[15] Lord Portman's statement that 'we never seemed to have any money' might well be because he spent it and because the estate was resettled on his son Christopher in the same way that it had been resettled on him. The writ arrived during the final phase of Goodman's illness and he died while it was being dealt with, and therefore his partners handled the negotiations with Lord Portman's lawyers, Lewis Silkin and Co:

> After the death of Lord Goodman, who was the only person who would have been able to give evidence about events which had occurred during the preceding forty years, Goodman Derrick decided, for commercial reasons, to settle litigation with Lord Portman. The terms of the settlement remain confidential.[16]

The 'commercial reasons' must have comprised a combination of things. Goodman Derrick had been closely associated with Goodman until the last 15 years of his life. After that time the practice gradually began to develop a more independent existence and in the five years before his death he had had less and less to do with it. Nevertheless, his death was bound to have a negative impact. If the case had dragged on it would have been misrepresented in the press and

Goodman Derrick would have lost many more clients than Goodman's death alone might have accounted for. Moreover, there was the cost of the litigation itself, in which the main witness would not have been able to testify. Goodman Derrick might have been able to transcend Goodman's death, but they might not have survived his death and a long and high-profile court case about his conduct of a major account. The remaining partners decided on a quick settlement so that they could concentrate on ensuring the firm's continued success.

The writ against Goodman Derrick was dropped and Lord Portman settled for a payment of £500,000. This was considerably less than the cash amount he alleged had been taken and massively less than the value of the money at today's prices. The real question must be, if Lord Portman had been defrauded for such a huge sum of money and he could prove it, why did he settle for so little? A close friend of Goodman over many years, David Astor, is sure that when the papers are revealed Goodman's name will be cleared: 'I have been given enough confidential information about Lord Portman's allegations from reliable sources to say that these allegations and the way they have been publicly presented have given a false impression. That impression will be effectively demolished in due course. I can say no more than this but I can assure you that is the case.'[17] In other words the files will show that all Lord Portman's money could be accounted for.

With the publication of these refutations and the death, in May 1999, of Lord Portman, the balance of the argument swung back decisively in Goodman's favour. One of the key problems for the practice was that the case would have come down to Lord Portman's word against Goodman's. By the time it reached court Goodman would have been incapable of testifying and in the event would have been dead. If the files show what Goodman Derrick and David Astor say they show, then Lord Portman must have judged that perjury was not a price worth paying for a larger settlement. If they do not make the case for the defence, then presumably Lord Portman would not have settled so quickly and for so little. The balance of the evidence suggests that Lord Portman's allegations were without foundation.

However, Lord Portman's writ laid bare the controversy surrounding Goodman's reputation that *Private Eye* and others had kept alive since the 1960s and provoked a considerable debate about his reputation when the story became public.

In 1993 the assault on his reputation represented by the writs was accompanied by physical deterioration. On a sea journey in 1980 he had knocked his ankle and subsequently developed phlebitis. He was warned that, given his size, if he ever stopped walking he could lose his leg. He seems to have become more physically active for a while and tried not to sit for long periods. As walking became more difficult he sometimes used a wheelchair to get around. Lord's cricket ground and the Savoy Grill presented problems. At the former he was eventually winched into the members' pavilion. At the latter the side doors were opened for him so that he could go straight in. He began to work entirely from home instead of visiting the office every day. His voice became weaker and he sometimes slept through as much as he watched of the plays or concerts he continued to attend with Clarissa. Each weekend he went to his house in Oxford. In the winter of 1991 he had an especially bad bout of bronchitis and was brought back from Oxford to hospital in London. He was ill enough to be off his feet for six months, and by the time he had recovered he could no longer walk.

On Sunday 22 August 1993 Goodman received the long line of guests who attended his eightieth birthday party at Lincoln's Inn. As he welcomed 400 friends and clients, it would have been natural for him to have pondered the life that he had led. It had been a highly compartmentalized life. One might argue that the debits in the professional department, poor record-keeping and an occasional sloppiness as a lawyer, can be balanced by credits in the deeds compartment, especially in relation to private acts of kindness, personal generosity, humour and friendship. In the end did Goodman do more good than harm? Do the minor irregularities of his business life outweigh his other contributions? Perhaps if he had acted with a little more humility and a little less pomposity then the answer would be an unequivocal yes. But the way in which he served the public, his anger and haughtiness when challenged to explain some of his decisions, the defensiveness that became almost a way of life in his last years, the hypocrisy with which he claimed to have always advised clients against taking libel actions when he often did the opposite, all these weigh heavily in the deficit column. As do, in the end, his bully-boy tactics towards the press.

Goodman was frequently the *consigliere* of the powerful in politics and business. His job was to protect them and the closer to the top he got, and the more known he became, the more he could be evoked as a threat. His record would then do the rest. But just as often, the threat or the invocation of the great man would have no effect at all. Maybe it is the cowardice of journalists rather than the power of Goodman that is at issue? There were times when actual writs were issued and substantive articles suppressed because of the possibility of offence or damage. In some cases the claims of damage by Goodman's clients were legitimate, but in others they were utterly bogus. There is a natural tendency for journalists to give stories equal value and to condemn the suppression of these stories with equal vigour. But not all the writs or threats of writs were challenges to democracy and free speech and the reality must be a balance between the power of the press and the defence of citizens – the powerful and the not so powerful – from unfair attack. Journalists were sometimes cowards, the stories were sometimes wrong and Goodman was acting as a counterweight against the press.

For many of his fellow-members of the Great and the Good, whom he welcomed at Lincoln's Inn on his eightieth birthday, he was and will always remain the wise old man of the Age of Harold Wilson, the problem-solver, the fixer and the benevolent godfather who sat at the point where the worlds of politics, the media and the arts meet the law, libel and deal-making. He sat there through the collectivist age, settling strikes, saving galleries, advising Prime Ministers: in love with power and desperate to be a cog in the mechanism of running the country. Call Arnold was all you had to do. He saved Lord Boothby's reputation and tried to save Jeremy Thorpe. He fixed a deal with Ian Smith, fought a losing battle against the closed shop in Fleet Street and capped his career with wise words in the ear of Charles Windsor, Sarah Ferguson and Diana Spencer as they contemplated their failed marriages. Through all these years of public service he frequently worked for nothing and deployed his formidable network in the service of others. Did he, that August day, see himself as the Blessed Arnold? If he did, should we? Whether we can accept this vision of the man at face value really depends on whether or not we believe in altruism: do people do things purely for the goodness of the act?

There is a story that on one occasion money was needed for a good cause. Goodman picked up *Who's Who*, the book he choose for his 'Desert Island' read, and with a glint in his eye said, 'Right, who can we squeeze?' Like a child he loved to be able to show people how clever he was. But he was much more than just mischievous.

He was also a brilliant negotiator and settler of disputes; and the particular quality that he brought to these roles was his ability to see the point at which two sides could find common ground. He made himself the key to the solution by the structure of the negotiation. There was no question of who would get the credit: it was he. In other cases he loved being in a position to use his access creatively. During the passage of the 1968 Race Relations Act, Geoffrey Bindman, who was advising the Race Relations Board, noticed that the Bill did not prevent segregation – separate but equal treatment – which was occurring in some places, for example the workplace. Bindman contacted Goodman, who in turn contacted Dennis Lloyd and the relevant amendment was inserted in the Act. As Bindman remembers, it was not, on Goodman's part, a burning belief in the cause but the 'challenge to fix something, it didn't matter if it was good, bad or indifferent'.[18] It was a party trick for Bertha, nurtured across three decades, into a unique contribution to the corporatist age.

If he did not see his life as having been blessed, what might have troubled him most? The spark that Goodman lacked, and he seems to have been painfully aware of this lack, was creativity. He was at pains to deny it and once maintained that he could have a greater impact in the arts than as a Lord Justice of Appeal. He also admitted:

> You can stimulate artistic activity, which I rate more important than serving the legal system . . . I would rather have been anything than a solicitor . . . But I have never had any pretensions to be an artist. You have to have a God-given talent which, alas, I have not got. When I gave up the violin there was a sigh of relief among the neighbours; my painting at school was the most derided in the school's history. My interest in the arts has always been as a spectator. But the spectator's role is itself most important. The spectator provides the audience, buys the tickets and furnishes the applause. It is a role which is basic to the continuance of the arts and the survival of the artist.[19]

He loved creative people, whether in the arts, in social situations, like the brilliant conversationalist Ann Fleming, or in politics, like Jennie Lee, because he did not have that spark within him. There were a number of significant motivating forces in his relentless social climb, but there was also a sense of disappointment and of frustration. One can almost see Goodman's endless energy, his great productive contribution, as a form of sublimation of his unrealizable creative urges. Not all arts administrators are by definition failed artists; but Goodman's constant desire for more social recognition, which was to become increasingly evident after he left the Arts Council in 1972, was for him a compensation for not being more like his brother or the creative people he constantly dealt with and was entertained by. It was compensation for a central lack of creativity in his own make-up. Yet, he must have thought to himself, to be the lawyer of the arts and politics, if one has to be a lawyer, was not a life choice to be despised.

It is not clear if he always had a plan. We do not know if ambition sat in his various flats as a companion in the many lonely nights after considerable dinners and long days on the phone. But ambition was there. As he encountered people with power he became besotted with it and as he became known as someone with such access, so others were attracted to him because of what they saw as *his* power. With fame came acceptance and courtship. He made a certain amount of money, but not much and most of it was gone by the end. He received a certain number of honours, including his early peerage and a later Companion of Honour, though never the Order of Merit. To what use did he put all these? In many cases he used his position to help ordinary people from all sorts of backgrounds either directly or through his charitable work. But what he liked most was to be there for the socially well connected.

He took pleasure in taking the predominantly gentile British Establishment and making it his client: titled people, important people, needed him for virtually every day of his life between 1964 and 1990. It was like a drug of which he needed his daily fix. It was an addiction to social recognition, it was snobbery as a lifestyle, almost a philosophy:

> I will not be persuaded to support any proposition on the basis of total ignorance about its truth. But if the messenger is someone I admire, and in whom I have faith, I will listen to his message . . . But although I have done my best to appear inhuman some human attributes remain to me. One of them is to like certain people, and on that account to be disposed to be persuaded by them.[20]

That a man should take the arguments of his friends more seriously than the arguments of his enemies makes a great deal of sense, but Goodman goes on:

A Man? No, Lord God

> Today in this country, you can find people without a single 'O' level applying to be Archbishop of Canterbury, Prime Minister or Governor of the Bank of England. This is a serious backwards step.[21]

Snobbery in private life choices is a minor vice which hurts no one but other snobs who are snubbed. Snobbery in the decision-making processes of public bodies led to some very bad decisions. Was Goodman laughing quietly to himself at the way the world that Bertha had strived for him to join beat a path to his door each day with their problems and their dirty washing, even as he watched them honouring his eightieth year? His role in their lives was based on a kind of altruism which was also, for him, a dependency. This addiction did not take kindly to hindrances. Whenever he bent the rules he thought he could always get away with it because of who he was. It should be stated that though he expressed extreme resentment at the routine investigations of the public bodies that he chaired, and though there were many criticisms of his method in these various reports, no wrongdoing was ever suggested until after he was dead. In most of these ventures there was no wrongdoing, but there was incompetence and bad decision-making – decisions made too quickly and systems for audit not properly implemented, because he had no self-control over what he took on and would rather do five things badly than one thing well. For some – the *Private Eye* team, some of the victims of his more successful property deals and others who saw the darker and vindictive side of Goodman – he was one of the rogues that mixed in the world that big government, regulation and corporatism produced in the 1960s and 1970s: the Establishment's hatchet man for keeping unwanted attacks on the élite from soiling the newspapers. One person who crossed his path and whom he took against left the country and only felt safe to come back after Goodman was dead. Another believed that his parents were swindled by Goodman and his clients in a huge property deal. We should not be surprised that someone who operated at this level in British public life should have made enemies. What is interesting is the consistent element of malice in these stories. Goodman, when crossed, had the ability to seek and destroy.

Goodman's life was, in the end, a lonely one and a sobering lesson from an era in which men believed that they could successfully forge their identities in terms of their public selves alone. Goodman sacrificed everything to the social and professional climb and finally it left him with very little of real value. The nature of the 'power fix' was the need for its constant replenishment. When the phone stopped ringing, the point went out of his life.

On leaving the birthday party, Isaiah Berlin commented acidly that Arnold must have known at least half of the guests. In fact, if one looks at the guest list, he probably knew most of them. Shortly before his party he had been made an honorary QC and the *Observer* had serialized his memoirs. The ritual of Establishment farewells was almost complete, its hollowness echoed loudly.

As his illness got worse the two housekeepers, Mrs Hargraves, who ran the London flat, and Mrs Sullivan, who came down from Oxford, could no longer cope and were both given notice by his loyal secretary, Miss Miller. He was cared for first in the London Clinic and then in the Cromwell Hospital. Allowed home in the spring of 1994, he again became ill and was moved to a nursing home in Highgate. Miss Miller organized a rota for visitors, who included his old friends like Sue Hammerson and people he had helped over the years, like his first cousin Amanda Content. The money raised by Max Rayne and Clarissa Avon, as a travel fund, on his eightieth birthday, plus discreet help from other friends, paid the nursing and hospital bills. During his final illness many of his friends rallied round to help take care of him. Clarissa was often there. As Kenneth Rose put it: 'Throughout . . . the last distressing years of his life, it was Clarissa who selflessly, even heroically gave him the comfort that his home would otherwise have lacked.'[22] Goodman died on 12 May 1995. He was 81.

His memorial service was held at the Liberal Jewish Synagogue on 19 June 1995 in St John's Wood, close to his beloved Lord's. There was no play that day. St John's Wood Road was busy. The occupants of chauffeur-driven cars, business people, lawyers, politicians and a few journalists gathered. 'Together, the great, the good and the grateful, gave thanks for the life of the late Lord Goodman CH.'[23]

Lord Annan noted that when Goodman died a newspaper carried, under his photograph, a caption which read: 'Britain's most distinguished citizen outside government.' The Minister, Rabbi David Goldberg, recalled Goodman's 'kindness and gentleness, his dedication, his wisdom and discretion, his loyalty to friends, his ever-ready helpfulness to young and old, and his devotion to the cause of the unfortunate'. Sir Evelyn Rothschild spoke of the Sunday-evening dinners, when Goodman enjoyed 'good company, good conversation and a considerable amount of gossip'. Janet Suzman read Psalm 90 and Lord Rayne the Prophetical Lesson (1 Kings 3:5–14). Josephine Barstow from the ENO performed Mimi's Farewell from *La Bohème* and then joined Rebecca Caine, John Hudson and Andrew Greenan for the Quartet from Act One of *Fidelio*, Goodman's favourite opera. Berlin approached Annan at the end and asked: was he able to book Annan for his own memorial service? Goodman would have enjoyed the joke.

Notes

Chapter 1 Five Miles Across North London

1 *Private Eye*, 19 May 1972
2 Geoffrey Alderman, *Modern British Jewry*, Clarendon Press, Oxford, 1992
3 Peter Hudson interview
4 Arnold Goodman, *Tell Them I'm on My Way. Memoirs*, Chapman Publishers, London, 1993, p.2. Hereafter referred to as Goodman, *Memoirs*.
5 ibid., p.2
6 Mendel Kaplan, *Jewish Roots in the South African Economy*, C. Struik, Cape Town, 1986, p.312
7 Naim Attallah, *Singular Encounters*, Quartet Books, London, 1990, p.270 and Goodman, *Memoirs*, p.3
8 Attallah, p.269
9 Goodman, *Memoirs*, p.7
10 Shirley Goodman interview
11 Charles Redstone interview
12 Margaret Reiss interview
13 Goodman, *Memoirs*, p.1
14 ibid., p.34
15 David Selbourne, *Not An Englishman*, Sinclair-Stevenson, London, 1993, p.22
16 Goodman, *Memoirs*, p.3
17 Attallah, p.269
18 ibid., p.270
19 Goodman, *Memoirs*, p.2 and Rev. William Dowling interview
20 Goodman, *Memoirs*, p.5
21 Selbourne, p.17
22 Dowling interview
23 Goodman, *Memoirs*, p.10
24 Jim Gower interview
25 Goodman, *Memoirs*, p.12
26 Reiss interview
27 Goodman, *Memoirs*, p.24
28 Gower interview
29 Goodman, *Memoirs*, pp.24–5
30 John A. Franks, letter to *Solicitors Journal*, 1 September 1995
31 Goodman, *Memoirs*, pp.41–3
32 ibid., p.42
33 *Guardian*, 21 August 1993
34 *The Times*, 18 August 1983
35 *News of the World*, 28 April 1972
36 Goodman, *Memoirs*, p.23
37 ibid., p.26
38 Abe Kramer interview
39 Downing College, Cambridge, Archive, Tutorial File for Abraham Goodman, Jolowitz to the Senior Tutor, 29 July 1935
40 *New Statesman and Nation*, 18 March 1939, p.440

Notes

Chapter 2 From Widmerpool to Goodman Derrick

1 Goodman, *Memoirs*, p.47
2 Downing College, Cambridge, Archive: Goodman to Whalley-Tooker, 28 September 1938
3 Jim Gower interview
4 Sir Mortimer Wheeler, *Still Digging*, Michael Joseph, London, 1955
5 PRO: WO 166/2715, War diary of 42nd Light Anti-Aircraft Regiment 1939–41
6 Gower interview
7 PRO: WO 166/2715
8 Naim Attallah, *Singular Encounters*, Quartet Books, London, 1990, p.271
9 Anne Kisch interview
10 Kisch interview
11 Gower interview
12 In this connection there is a record (WO 70/25) of thefts occurring from the office of 42nd Anti-Aircraft Battalion in 1939, probably Gunner Particle.
13 PRO: WO 166/2795 48th Anti-Aircraft Battery
14 Frank Johnson, 'The Man Behind Lord Goodman', *Now*, 21 September 1979
15 Goodman, *Memoirs*, p.55
16 ibid., pp.57–8
17 ibid., p.61
18 Richard Mordant interview
19 Insight Profile, *Sunday Times*, 26 February 1967 and Frank Coven to Brivati, 26 April 1999
20 Frank Coven interview
21 Goodman, *Memoirs*, p.63
22 ibid., p.65
23 ibid., p.66
24 Charles Redstone interview
25 In his *Memoirs* Goodman has this lecturing beginning just after the Second World War, but the Downing College records show that the lectures were delivered in 1956 and replaced those of Ashton-Cross and not Dr Oliver. As there is no record of earlier references being supplied by Downing it is unlikely that the 'special lectureship' in the immediate post-war years existed.
26 Goodman, *Memoirs*, pp.69–71
27 ibid., pp.70–71
28 ibid., p.69
29 As soon as practical Hill asked Goodman if he could join the new practice and this he did two months after Goodman Derrick had been formed.
30 Goodman, *Memoirs*, p.69
31 Elliott Bernerd interview
32 Goodman, *Memoirs*, p.68
33 Ronald Hill letter to Iris Freeman
34 Jeffrey Maunsell interview
35 Christopher Booker interview and Frank Johnson, 'The Man Behind Lord Goodman', *Now*, 21 September 1979
36 Edward Heath interview
37 Ben Pimlott, *Harold Wilson*, HarperCollins, London, 1992, pp.185–6
38 Anthony Howard interview
39 *George Wigg by Lord Wigg*, Michael Joseph, London 1972, p.1
40 Ruth Dudley Edwards, *Victor Gollancz*, Victor Gollancz, London, 1987, p.128
41 Goodman, *Memoirs*, p.91 and Ruth Dudley Edwards, p.129
42 Goodman, *Memoirs*, p.93
43 Ronald Hill letter to Iris Freeman

Chapter 3 The Venetian Blind: the 1957 *Spectator* Libel Trial

1 Goodman to Beyfus at first meeting, quoted by John Baker at Institute of Historical Research Witness Seminar, The *Spectator* Libel Trial of 1957, 25 November 1998
2 Goodman's alleged words to Carter Ruck, quoted by John Baker at Institute of Historical Research Witness Seminar, 25 November 1998. When these words were put to Goodman

in the court he denied having used them, though he did not challenge the sense of what he was asking Carter Ruck for. Baker to Brivati, 30 April 1999

3 Richard Crossman, *The Backbench Diaries of Richard Crossman* (ed. Janet Morgan), Hamish Hamilton and Jonathan Cape, London, 1981, pp.573–4
4 David Hooper, *Public Scandal, Odium and Contempt: an Investigation of Recent Libel Cases*, London, 1986, p.104
5 Crossman, p.574
6 Hooper, p.115
7 Crossman, pp.574–5
8 Jenny Nicholson, 'Death in Venice', *Spectator*, 1 March 1957
9 Jennie Lee, *My Life with Nye*, London, 1980
10 Goodman, *Memoirs*, p.164
11 ibid.
12 ibid., p.165
13 ibid., pp.163–5
14 Christopher Booker interview and Booker to Brivati, 26 April 1999
15 *Sunday Telegraph*, 22 August 1993
16 Crossman Papers, Modern Records Centre, MSS 154/3/SPL/25
17 ibid.
18 Crossman Papers, MSS 154/3/SPL/8
19 Crossman Papers, MSS 154/3/SPL/9
20 Crossman Papers, MSS 154/3/SPL/23
21 Crossman Papers, MSS 154/3/SPL/24
22 Crossman Papers, MSS 154/3/SPL/25
23 Crossman Papers, MSS 154/3/SPL/13/14
24 Crossman Papers, MSS 154/3/SPL/30
25 Crossman Papers, MSS 154/3/SPL/36
26 Crossman Papers, MSS 154/3/SPL/37
27 Crossman Papers, MSS 154/3/SPL/18
28 Hooper, p.109
29 Crossman, *The Backbench Diaries*, p.629
30 Quoted in Hooper, p.110
31 Crossman, p.630
32 ibid., pp.630–31, Hooper, pp.111–12 and Goodman, *Memoirs*, p.166
33 Michael Foot, *Aneurin Bevan II 1945–1960*, MacGibbon & Kee, London, 1973
34 Anthony Howard interview
35 Goodman, *Memoirs*, p.163
36 Auberon Waugh at Institute of Historical Research Witness Seminar, 25 November 1998

Chapter 4 The Inside Track

1 Quotations from Goodman in this section from David Selbourne, *Not An Englishman*, pp.38–42
2 Anthony Crosland, *The Future of Socialism*, Jonathan Cape, London, 1956
3 Lord Goodman, *Not for the Record*, André Deutsch, London, 1972, p.17
4 David Selbourne interview
5 Noel Annan in Goodman, *Not for the Record*, pp.11–12
6 Goodman, *Memoirs*, pp.185–6
7 Quoted in George Wigg, *George Wigg by Lord Wigg*, Michael Joseph, London, 1972, p.237
8 ibid., p.236
9 Goodman, *Memoirs*, p.187
10 John Cole, *As It Seemed To Me*, Weidenfeld & Nicolson, London, 1995, p.30
11 Goodman, *Memoirs*, p.186
12 ibid., p.102
13 ibid., p.206
14 Pimlott, *Harold Wilson*, HarperCollins, London, 1992, p.265
15 Goodman, *Memoirs*, p.206
16 Abe Kramer interview
17 Wigg, p.263

Notes

18 Goodman, *Memoirs*, pp.194–5
19 Christine Keeler, *Scandal*, Xanadu, London, 1989, p.148
20 Wigg, p.263 and Pimlott, pp.286–7
21 Wigg, p.264 and Pimlott, p.287
22 Goodman, *Memoirs*, p.195
23 Wigg, p.267
24 Version 'A' of 'An appreciation of the Keeler case by George Wigg, 29 March 1963'; papers shown to the author by Lord Gilmour
25 Version 'B' of 'An appreciation of the Keeler case by George Wigg, 29 March 1963'; papers shown to the author by Lord Gilmour
26 Philip Ziegler, *Harold Wilson*, Weidenfeld and Nicolson, London, 1993, pp.145–6
27 Pimlott, p.297
28 Goodman Derrick to the *Spectator*, 9 July 1963; papers shown to the author by Lord Gilmour
29 Oswald Hickson, Collier and Co. to Goodman Derrick and Co., 24 March 1966; papers shown to the author by Lord Gilmour
30 Peter Carter Ruck to Ian Gilmour, 29 February 1968; papers shown to the author by Lord Gilmour
31 Goodman, *Memoirs*, p.214
32 John Pearson *The Profession of Violence*, HarperCollins, London, 1995, p.193
33 Pearson, p.194
34 *The Times*, 2 August 1964
35 See Robert Rhodes James, *Bob Boothby*, Hodder & Stoughton, London, 1991, pp.416–18 in contrast to Pearson, p.196 and *The Secret History : Lords of the Underworld*, 3BM Productions, 1997, to which Pearson acted as a consultant.
36 Pearson, *The Profession of Violence*, p.194
37 ibid., p.198
38 Francis Wheen, *Tom Driberg: His Life and Indiscretions*, Pan, London, 1990, p.350
39 ibid., p.352
40 Rhodes James, p.421
41 Pimlott, p.315
42 ibid., p.314
43 Ziegler, p.158
44 Pimlott, p.316, quoting Alf Richman, a Wilson aide
45 Goodman, *Memoirs*, p.247
46 Pimlott, p.316, Ziegler, p.158
47 Anthony Howard interview

Chapter 5 A Very English Sexuality

1 Frank Coven interview
2 Selbourne, *Not An Englishman*, p.22
3 ibid., p.167
4 Sue Hammerson interview
5 Patricia Hollis, *Jennie Lee*, OUP, Oxford, 1997, pp.260–61
6 ibid., p.364
7 Mark Amory (ed.), *The Letters of Ann Fleming*, Collins Harvill, London, 1985, p.354
8 Ann Fleming to Evelyn Waugh, 15 November 1964, *The Letters of Ann Fleming*, p.360
9 Fleming to Waugh, 18 March 1966, *The Letters of Ann Fleming*, p.377
10 Fleming to Joan Rayner, 26 October 1967, *The Letters of Ann Fleming*, p.387
11 Selbourne, p.173
12 ibid., p.167
13 Private information
14 Selbourne, pp.160–79
15 ibid., p.175
16 *Sunday Telegraph*, 14 May 1995
17 Selbourne, p.1. All quotations in this section not otherwise referenced come from Selbourne, pp.1–15
18 These two war stories are in Goodman, *Memoirs*, pp.191–2.

19 ibid., p.445
20 Selbourne, p.40
21 ibid., pp.220–22

Chapter 6 From Mr X to Lord G

1 Richard Crossman, *The Diaries of a Cabinet Minister. Volume One. Minister of Housing, 1964–66*, Book Club Associates, London, 1975, 2 November 1964, p.40
2 Goodman, *Memoirs*, pp.190–91
3 Peter Hennessy, *Whitehall*, Fontana, London, 1989, p.438, quoting Anthony Sampson, *Anatomy of Britain Today*, Hodder & Stoughton, London, 1965, pp.287–8
4 Goodman, *Memoirs*, p.191
5 ibid., p.191
6 Crossman, *Diaries*, 18 November 1964
7 ibid., 22 October 1964, p.26
8 ibid., 5 November 1964, p.48
9 ibid., 26 October 1964, p.30
10 ibid., 2 December 1964, p.78
11 Goodman, *Memoirs*, p.191
12 Naim Attallah, *Singular Encounters*, Quartet Books, London, 1990, p.275
13 Elliott Bernerd interview
14 Jeffrey Maunsell interview
15 Edward Walker Arnott interview
16 Susanna Walton, *William Walton: Behind the Façade*, Oxford University Press, 1988
17 Goodman, *Memoirs*, p.294
18 ibid. p.192
19 PRO: ED 221/68, Letter from Cottesloe to H. F. Rossetti (DES), 22 April 1965
20 PRO: ED 221/68, Letter from Jennie Lee to James Callaghan, 6 May 1965
21 PRO: ED 221/68 internal DES report, undated
22 PRO: ED 221/68, Rossetti, 10 June 1965
23 Leonard Hoffmann interview
24 PRO: ED 221/68, Goodman to George Wigg, by hand, 13 August 1965
25 Ben Pimlott, *Harold Wilson*, HarperCollins, London, 1992, p.514
26 Philip Ziegler, *Harold Wilson*, Weidenfeld and Nicolson, London, 1993, p.201
27 Patricia Hollis, *Jennie Lee*, OUP, Oxford, 1997, p.298
28 ibid., p.306
29 Brian McArthur, *The Open University Opens*, Routledge & Kegan Paul, London, 1974
30 White Paper, *A University of the Air*, Cmnd 2922 HMSO, London, 1966
31 Walter Perry, *The Open University*, Open University Press, Milton Keynes, 1976, p.227
32 Goodman, *Memoirs*, p.414
33 Richard Seifert interview

Chapter 7 The Chair of Quangoland

1 Goodman, *Memoirs*, p.294
2 Peter Hennessy, *Whitehall*, Fontana, London, 1989, p.686
3 William Cooper, 'The Committee Men and the Technician', *Twentieth Century*, October 1957, quoted in Anthony Sampson, *Anatomy of Britain Today*, Hodder & Stoughton, London, 1965, pp.287–8
4 John S. Harris, *Government Patronage of the Arts in Great Britain*, The University of Chicago Press, Chicago, 1970, pp.1–18 and F. F. Ridley, 'Tradition, Change and Crisis in Great Britain', in Milton C. Cummings and Richard S. Katz, *The Patron State, Government and the Arts in Europe, North America and Japan*, OUP, Oxford, 1987, pp.225–53
5 For a discussion of this theme, see Brian Brivati and Harriet Jones (eds.) *What Difference Did the War Make?*, Leicester University Press, London, 1992
6 White Paper, *A Policy for the Arts: The First Steps*, Cmnd 2601. HMSO, London, 1965
7 *Birmingham Post*, 1 April 1965
8 *Spectator*, 9 April 1965
9 Goodman to Booker, 8 April 1965. The letter is in marked contrast to the account offered by

Goodman in his *Memoirs* in which he says he strongly disapproved of the article, Goodman, *Memoirs*, p.266.

10 Goodman, *Memoirs*, p.267
11 From Noel Annan's Gala Tribute to Goodman, 21 December 1986, quoted in Patricia Hollis, *Jennie Lee*, OUP, Oxford, 1997, p.261
12 Hollis, p.262
13 Goodman, *Memoirs*, p.271
14 ibid., p.270
15 ibid., p.268
16 Hugh Willatt interview
17 Goodman, *Memoirs*, p.269
18 Arts Council: Minutes, 31 March 1965
19 ibid.
20 Goodman, *Memoirs*, p.271
21 Arts Council: Minutes, 28 July 1965
22 Anthony Field interview
23 Arts Council: Minutes, 26 January 1966
24 ibid. Further discussion that day ranged from the approval of grants and guarantees from £100 for a soprano for singing lessons with Dame Eva Turner to £25,000 to the Ballet Trust Ltd. The latter amount was itself supplementary to a grant previously agreed of £42,000 in respect of Ballet Rambert.
25 Hollis, p.364
26 *Evening Standard*, 25 June 1970
27 Speech in House of Lords, 26 February 1969
28 Field interview and Andrew Sinclair, *Arts and Cultures: The History of the 50 Years of the Arts Council of Great Britain*, Sinclair-Stevenson, London, 1985, p.147
29 Charles Osborne, *Giving It Away*, Secker & Warburg , London, 1986, p.265

Chapter 8 The Catfish Murders
1 Quoted in Andrew Sinclair, *Arts and Cultures: The History of the 50 Years of the Arts Council of Great Britain*, Sinclair-Stevenson, London, 1985, p.149
2 Goodman, *Not for the Record*, p.134
3 Arts Council: Minutes, 24 April 1968
4 ibid., 29 May 1968
5 ibid., 31 July 1968
6 Goodman, *Memoirs*, p.354
7 Anthony Field interview
8 Goodman, *Memoirs*, p.355
9 Field interview and Goodman, *Memoirs*, p.356
10 Speech in the House of Lords, 26 February 1969
11 Donald Thomas, *A Long Time Burning. The History of Literary Censorship in England*, Routledge and Kegan Paul, London, 1962
12 Bernard Levin, *The Pendulum Years. Britain and the Sixties*, Pan, London, 1977, p.280
13 Roy Jenkins, *A Life at the Centre*, Macmillan, London, 1991, p.180
14 Goodman, *Not for the Record*, André Deutsch, London, 1972, p.117
15 Goodman, *Memoirs*, p.366
16 Thomas, p.309
17 Goodman, *Not for the Record*, p.119
18 Thomas, p.310
19 Goodman, *Not for the Record*, pp.119–20
20 Goodman, *Memoirs*, p.367
21 Arts Council: Minutes, 25 June 1969
22 ibid.
23 ibid. and Goodman, *Memoirs*, p.367
24 Goodman, *Memoirs*, pp.367–8
25 ibid., p.368
26 Sinclair, p.143

27 Goodman, *Not for the Record*, p.138
28 Sinclair, p.156
29 Arts Council: Minutes, 24 April 1968. Rather than force a vote when another request was received, Goodman neatly sidestepped the issue. In May 1968 Dr C. R. B. Joyce, Head of Pharmacology at London Hospital Medical College, requested a grant for research on the effect of drugs on the creative process. Goodman ruled the application inadmissible but said he would advise the doctor on finding funding from other sources.
30 David Selbourne, *Not An Englishman*, Sinclair-Stevenson, London, 1993, p.218
31 Frank Johnson, 'The Man Behind Lord Goodman', *Now*, 21 September 1979
32 Selbourne, p.219
33 *Private Eye*, 18 April 1975
34 Selbourne, p.219
35 Arts Council Minutes: 29 September 1971
36 ibid., *The Times*, 29 September 1971 and Goodman, *Memoirs*, pp.372–3
37 Goodman, *Memoirs*, p.374
38 Arts Council Minutes: 29 September 1971, Goodman, *Memoirs*, p.374, Sinclair, pp.160–61

Chapter 9 Operatic Deficits

 1 Arts Council Minutes: 26 April 1967
 2 Goodman in the *Evening Standard*, 2 April 1970
 3 Andrew Sinclair, *Arts and Cultures: The History of the 50 Years of the Arts Council of Great Britain*, Sinclair-Stevenson, London, 1985, p.159
 4 Goodman, *Not for the Record*, pp.161–2
 5 ibid., p.128
 6 Quoted in Sinclair, p.159
 7 Goodman, *Not for the Record*, p.142
 8 Speech in the House of Lords, 26 February 1969
 9 Anthony Field interview
10 Goodman, *Not for the Record*, p.142
11 ibid., p.142
12 Hugh Willatt interview
13 Goodman, *Memoirs*, pp.272–3
14 Arts Council Minutes: 26 June 1968
15 Goodman, *Memoirs*, p.273 and Willatt interview
16 Noel Annan interview with Iris Freeman
17 Willatt interview
18 Lina Emery interview
19 Goodman, *Memoirs*, p.302
20 Willatt interview
21 Lord Harewood interview
22 Willatt interview
23 Goodman, *Memoirs*, p.281
24 Field interview
25 Goodman, *Memoirs*, p.282
26 ibid., p.281
27 Field interview
28 Goodman, *Memoirs*, p.283
29 ibid., p.283
30 The Estimates Committee (Sub-Committee B), *Minutes of Evidence*, 23 April 1968, Session 1967–68, 'The Arts Council of Great Britain', HMSO, London, 1968, p.482
31 Goodman, *Not for the Record*, pp.126–7
32 Goodman, *Memoirs*, p.336
33 Stephen Fay, *Power Play. The Life and Times of Peter Hall*, Hodder & Stoughton, London, 1995, pp.132–33
34 Fay, p.133
35 Fay, pp.133–4
36 Goodman, *Memoirs*, p.337

Notes

37 ibid., pp.337–8
38 Kathleen Tynan, *Life of Kenneth Tynan*, Weidenfeld and Nicolson, London, 1987, pp.240–51 and Fay, p.206
39 Goodman, *Memoirs*, p.340
40 Kenneth Tynan's diary for 12 April 1972, quoted in Kathleen Tynan, p.251
41 Kathleen Tynan, p.240
42 Goodman, *Not for the Record*, p.127
43 Goodman, *Memoirs*, p.261
44 Goodman, *Not for the Record*, p.127
45 ibid.
46 Philip Ziegler, *Harold Wilson*, Weidenfeld and Nicolson, London, 1993, p.358
47 Marcia Falkender, *Downing Street in Perspective*, Weidenfeld and Nicolson, London, 1983, pp.24–6
48 Ziegler, p.360
49 ibid., p.367
50 ibid., p.366
51 Ben Pimlott, *Harold Wilson*, HarperCollins, London, 1992, p.708
52 *Private Eye*, 23 February 1977
53 Ziegler, p.358
54 ibid., p.369

Chapter 10 Hot Dogs and Diaries

1 All quotations in this section from Goodman, *Memoirs*, pp.73–5
2 Elaine Windrich, *Britain and the Politics of Rhodesian Independence*, Croom Helm, London, 1978, p.138
3 *Private Eye*, 19 November 1971
4 Kenneth Younger, *Rhodesia and Independence*, Eyre and Spottiswoode, London, 1967, p.123
5 Ian Smith, *The Great Betrayal*, Blake, London, 1997, p.141
6 Lady Aitken interview
7 Harold Wilson, *A Personal Record. The Labour Government, 1964–1970*, Little Brown and Company, London, 1971, p.565
8 *Daily Mail*, 26 November 1971
9 Goodman, *Memoirs*, p.219
10 Leighton Davis interview
11 Wilson, p.566
12 Smith, p.141
13 Goodman, *Memoirs*, p.220
14 Wilson, p.566
15 *Daily Mail*, 26 November 1971
16 ibid.
17 Goodman, *Memoirs*, p.220
18 ibid., p.223
19 Miles Hudson, *Triumph or Tragedy? Rhodesia to Zimbabwe*, Hamish Hamilton, London, 1981, p.93
20 *Daily Telegraph*, 30 June 1971
21 *The Times*, 8 July 1971
22 *Evening Standard*, 6 July 1971
23 *Daily Mail*, 8 July 1971
24 Goodman, *Memoirs*, p.228
25 *Daily Telegraph*, 30 July 1971
26 *Daily Mail*, 8 September 1971
27 Geoffrey Bindman interview
28 D. R. Thorpe, *Alec Douglas-Home*, Sinclair-Stevenson, London, 1996, p.423
29 ibid., p.424
30 ibid, p.425
31 Hudson, p.99
32 Speech in House of Lords, 1 December 1971

33 *Private Eye*, 17 December 1971
34 Naim Attallah, *Singular Encounters*, Quartet Books, London, 1990, p.273
35 *Private Eye*, 3 December 1971
36 Goodman, *Memoirs*, p.226
37 David L. Ellis, 'Collective Ministerial Responsibility and Collective Solidarity', quoting Lord Salisbury and then Ivor Jennings, in Geoffrey Marshall (ed.), *Ministerial Responsibility*, OUP, Oxford, 1989, p.46
38 David L. Ellis, 'Collective Ministerial Responsibility and Collective Solidarity', quoting Sir John Hunt the Cabinet Secretary, in Geoffrey Marshall (ed.), *Ministerial Responsibility*, OUP, Oxford, 1989, p.49
39 Graham C. Greene interview
40 Tam Dalyell, *Dick Crossman, A Portrait*, Weidenfeld and Nicolson, London, 1989, p.232
41 Mervyn Jones, *Michael Foot*, Victor Gollancz, London, 1994, p.386
42 Peter Hennessy, *Whitehall*, Fontana, London, 1989, p.254
43 Hennessy, p.254, quoting Joe Haines, *The Politics of Power*, Jonathan Cape, London, 1977, p.96, caption to picture 6
44 Anthony Howard in introduction to Richard Crossman, *The Crossman Diaries*, Book Club Associates, London, 1979, p.19
45 Hugo Young, *The Crossman Affair*, Hamish Hamilton, Jonathan Cape, *Sunday Times*, London, 1976, pp.13–16
46 Jones, p.387
47 Young, p.16
48 Goodman, *Memoirs*, p.192
49 Jones, p.385
50 Young, pp.20–21
51 Anthony Howard, *Crossman*, Jonathan Cape, London, 1990, p.6
52 Young, p.23
53 ibid., pp.21–2
54 Goodman, *Memoirs*, p.193
55 Young, p.28
56 ibid., p.41
57 ibid., pp.42–6
58 ibid., p.41
59 Greene interview
60 Young, p.70
61 Goodman, *Memoirs*, p.193 and Young, pp.164–5
62 Goodman, *Memoirs*, p.193
63 Young, pp.94–5

Chapter 11 The Fear of Arnold

1 Goodman, *Memoirs*, p.375
2 ibid., p.379
3 See Richard Cockett, *David Astor and the Observer*, André Deutsch, London, 1991
4 Goodman, *Memoirs*, p.380
5 ibid., p.393
6 ibid., p.394
7 Donald Trelford interview
8 Caroline Moorhead, *Sidney Bernstein*, Jonathan Cape, London, 1984, p.186
9 ibid., p.187
10 Trelford interview
11 ibid.
12 Bernard Sendall, *Independent Television in Britain, Volume 1: Origin and Foundation, 1946–62*, Macmillan, Basingstoke, 1982, p.210
13 Bernard Sendall, *Independent Television in Britain, Volume 2: Expansion and Change, 1958–68*, Macmillan, Basingstoke, 1983, pp.134–49
14 Anthony Howard interview
15 Goodman, *Memoirs*, p.389

Notes

16 Cockett, p.270
17 Goodman, *Memoirs*, pp.388–9
18 Trelford interview
19 Cockett, p.271
20 William Shawcross, *Murdoch: The Making of a Media Empire*, Simon and Schuster, New York, 1997, p.73
21 George Munster, *Rupert Murdoch – A Paper Prince*, Penguin Books, Ringwood, Victoria, Australia, 1987, p.178
22 Cockett, p.280
23 Chris Hutchins and Dominic Midgley, *Goldsmith. Money, Women and Power*, Mainstream Publishing, London, 1998, p.102
24 Cockett, p.281
25 ibid.
26 Trelford interview
27 Cockett, p.285
28 Trelford interview
29 Goodman, *Memoirs*, pp.401–2 and Trelford interview
30 Trelford interview, Cockett, p.285
31 Quoted in Cockett, p.286
32 Ian Chapman interview
33 Chapman interview
34 Mervyn Jones, *Michael Foot*, Victor Gollancz, London, 1994, p.370
35 Michael Foot interview
36 Goodman, *Memoirs*, p.404
37 *Daily Mail*, 4 May 1974 and Foot interview
38 Nora Beloff, *Freedom under Foot*, Maurice Temple Smith, London, 1976, p.146
39 House of Lords Debates, Vol. 368, 2 March 1976, cols 903–17
40 Goodman, *Memoirs*, p.408
41 Beloff, pp.100–157
42 House of Commons Debates, Vol. 902, 9 December 1975, col. 270
43 House of Lords Debates, Vol. 368, 2 March 1976, col. 903
44 For the pay-beds dispute, see, for Goodman's side, *Memoirs*, pp.232–41; for Castle's version, Barbara Castle, *The Castle Diaries 1964–76*, PaperMac, London, 1990, pp.730–51 and Barbara Castle, *Fighting All the Way*, Macmillan, London, 1993, pp.484–5.

Chapter 12 The Fall of Jeremy Thorpe
1 Cyril Smith, *Big Cyril*, W. H. Allen, London, 1977, p.205
2 Quoted in Simon Freeman with Barrie Penrose, *Rinkagate*, Bloomsbury, London, 1996, p.81
3 Peter Bessell, *Cover Up*, Simons Publishing, Wilmington, Delaware, 1980, p.128; see also Peter Chippindale and David Leigh, *The Thorpe Committal*, Arrow, London, 1979 and Auberon Waugh, *The Last Word*, Michael Joseph, London, 1980.
4 Bessell, pp.127–8
5 Freeman, p.120 and footnote p.401
6 ibid., p.204
7 ibid.
8 ibid., pp.144–5
9 ibid., p.211
10 ibid., p.214
11 Lewis Chester, Magnus Linklater & David May, *Jeremy Thorpe: A Secret Life*, André Deutsch, London, 1979, p.169
12 Smith, p.189: 'eventually traced him to the office of his solicitor, Lord Goodman, possibly the most influential lawyer in Britain at the time. He had already heard of the news from court.'
13 Bessell, pp.289–90
14 Freeman, p.231
15 Bessell, p.236
16 ibid., p.120
17 Freeman, p.236

18 Barrie Penrose and Roger Courtiour, *The Pencourt File*, Secker & Warburg, London 1978, p.13; see also David Leigh, *The Wilson Plot*, Heinemann, London, 1988
19 Freeman, p.7
20 ibid., p.276
21 Naim Attallah, *Singular Encounters*, Quartet Books, London, 1990, p.285
22 Chester, Linklater & May, p.267
23 ibid., p.268
24 Quotes in Freeman, p.51
25 ibid., p.240
26 Chester, Linklater & May, p.322
27 ibid., p.284
28 Bessell, p.252
29 ibid., p.276
30 *Daily Telegraph*, 22 November 1978
31 Goodman, *Memoirs*, p.125
32 Freeman, p.225
33 Goodman, *Memoirs*, p.126

Chapter 13 The Great and the Goodman

1 *Equipment for the Disabled: Outdoor Transport*, Oxfordshire Area Health Authority, 1982
2 Goodman, *Memoirs*, p.242
3 Oliver Marriott, *The Property Boom*, Hamish Hamilton, London, 1969, revised edition, pp.137–8
4 ibid.
5 Richard Seifert interview
6 Oliver Marriott, *The Property Boom*, Hamish Hamilton, London, 1967, first edition, p.114
7 Housing Corporation, *Annual Report*, 1976, p.27
8 Housing Corporation, *Annual Report*, 1985, p.29
9 Professor Wyndham Albery interview
10 Goodman, *Memoirs*, p.435
11 ibid. and private information
12 Private information
13 Goodman, *Memoirs*, pp.426–7
14 Private information
15 Michael Yudkin to Brian Brivati, 24 April 1999
16 Fionn Morgan interview

Chapter 14 A Man? No, Lord God

1 Anagram of 'Arnold Goodman' by John Sparrow.
2 Joe Haines, Wilson's press secretary, quoted in Chris Hutchins and Dominic Midgely, *Goldsmith*, p.103
3 David Selbourne, *Not An Englishman*, p.40. Selbourne also asked: 'Are you suggesting that Labour politicians in general fail to live up to their principles?' Goodman replied: 'No. Aneurin Bevan and Jennie Lee did not fail to live up to their principles.' Goodman was always loyal to the memory of Nye and Jennie.
4 Naim Attallah, *Singular Encounters*, Quartet Books, London, 1990, p.285
5 Frank Coven interview
6 Fionn Morgan interview
7 Private information
8 Anthony Howard interview
9 *The Times*, 30 January 1993
10 In the High Court of Justice, Chancery Division, in the Matter of Arnold Abraham Goodman and Goodman Derrick, Solicitors, CH1993-P-5032, 29 July 1993
11 *Daily Mail*, 19 January 1999
12 *Independent*, 18 January 1999
13 Statement from Goodman Derrick to Brian Brivati concerning the Lord Portman litigation, 8 June 1999

Notes

14 ibid.
15 ibid.
16 ibid.
17 David Astor to Brian Brivati, 29 April 1999
18 Geoffrey Bindman interview
19 Selbourne, p.191
20 ibid., p.229
21 ibid., p.230
22 *Sunday Telegraph*, 14 May 1995
23 This final sentence is taken from Iris Freeman's notes.

Index

Index

299

Index

Index